"*Annabel Dodd has cogently untangled the wires and switches and technobabble of the telecommunications revolution and explained how the introduction of the word 'digital' into our legislative and regulatory lexicon will affect consumers, companies and society into the next millennium.*"

—Congressman Edward J. Markey, Ranking Member
　　Subcommittee on Telecommunications, Trade and Consumer Protection

"*Your book,* The Essential Guide to Telecommunications, *is one of my favorites. It provides me with a clean explanation of the systems that I must install, operate and maintain. Additionally, it provides me with definitions and essential language to express my telecommunications and IT responsibilities and qualifications to potential civilian employers.*"

—C. Marc Harris
　　Wireless Implementation Engineer, Sprint PCS

"*What a help! Not only was I provided with the basics of telecommunications, I feel that I learned more than others in positions above my own as to how this industry functions and where it has the potential to go. I feel that I am in debt to you due to the information I was able to gain through reading this introductory Bible of the Industry.*"

—Fred Gibbs
　　Bedford, NH

"*Great book—very helpful...I've learned more in 2 weeks of focused reading, than the last 24 months of training in the industry.*"

—Bill Brakemeier
　　Management Consultant and National Sales Trainer

The Essential Guide to Telecommunications

3rd Edition

ISBN 0-13-064907-4

90000

9 790130 649071

Essential Guide Series

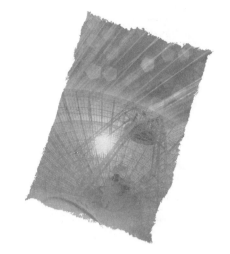

The
Essential
Guide to
Telecommunications

3rd Edition

Annabel Z. Dodd

Prentice Hall PTR, Upper Saddle River, NJ 07458
http://www.phptr.com

Library of Congress Cataloging-in-Publication Date

Dodd, Annabel Z.
    The essential guide to telecommunications / Annabel Z. Dodd. -- 3rd ed.
        p. cm
    Includes index.
    ISBN 0-13-064907-4 (pbk. : alk. paper)
    1. Telecommunication.   I. Title.

    TK5105 .D54 2001
    384--dc21   2001036429

Editorial/Production Supervision: *Patti Guerrieri*
Acquisitions Editor: *Mary Franz*
Editorial Assistant: *Noreen Regina*
Manufacturing Manager: *Maura Zaldivar*
Art Director: *Gail Cocker-Bogusz*
Interior Series Design: *Meg Van Arsdale*
Cover Design: *Bruce Kenselaar*
Cover Design Direction: *Jerry Votta*

© 2002 by Annabel Z. Dodd
Published by Prentice Hall PTR
Prentice-Hall, Inc.
Upper Saddle River, NJ 07458

The publisher offers discounts on this book when ordered in bulk quantities.
For more information, contact
Corporate Sales Department, Prentice Hall PTR, One Lake Street, Upper Saddle River, NJ 07458
Phone: 800-382-3419; FAX: 201-236-7141; E-mail (Internet): corpsales@prenhall.com

Printed in the United States of America

10 9 8 7 6 5 4 3 2 1

ISBN 0-13-064907-4

Pearson Education LTD.
Pearson Education Australia PTY, Limited
Pearson Education Singapore, Pte. Ltd.
Pearson Education North Asia Ltd.
Pearson Education Canada, Ltd.
Pearson Educación de Mexico, S.A. de C.V.
Pearson Education — Japan
Pearson Education Malaysia, Pte. Ltd.
Pearson Education, Upper Saddle River, New Jersey

This book is dedicated to my husband, Bob, who worked with me on every phase of the book. No other person on earth could be so patient and have such keen insights. I also dedicate it to my father, Harry Zalc, known to friends and relatives alike as "Grandpa Harry"; to my three special daughters, Judith Goralnick, Nancy Dodd and Laura Concannon, and their husbands Ross Goralnick and Steve Concannon.

Contents

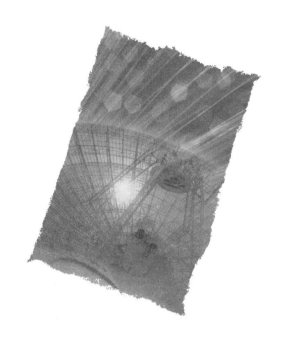

Part 3
Advanced Technologies, The Internet and Wireless

7 Analog, Cable TV and Digital Modems and Set-Top Boxes *291*

8 The Internet *315*

Preface

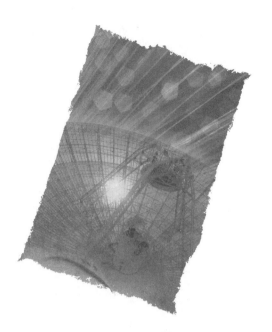

Enormous changes in telecommunications occurred in the two years between the second and third editions of *The Essential Guide to Telecommunications*. The *Essential Guide to Telecommunications* is intended as a road map clarifying technologies, history and trends in telecommunications. Technological innovations in fiber optics and attendant lower costs has led to the construction of vast networks. The book contrasts the glut of these fiber optic networks in long distance routes and some urban areas with their scarcity in developing countries, rural and most suburban regions.

The Essential Guide to Telecommunications explains how technology and regulatory factors impact each other. Deregulation and the presence of competition have resulted in the development of technological innovations. These innovations, particularly those in gigabit Ethernet and optical switching, are examined.

Cellular service has grown tremendously in the last decade. It is a key technology for providing basic voice service in large parts of the world. The book examines technologies used to provide greater capacity for basic voice service in fast growing urban areas, rural communities and tall skyscrapers. It also explains the advanced cellular technologies for transmitting higher speed data and accessing the Internet over wireless networks. It also addresses the concerns about safety. It is not known what impact fears about cancer and driving safety will have on the cellular market.

The Essential Guide to Telecommunications, third edition, reviews telecommunications in Europe, Asia and Latin America, as well as in developing countries, and the wide-reaching impact of wireless technology in these areas. Deregulation of local long distance and international services, as well as industry structure and major carriers, are covered. The structure of the telecommunications industry and steps in deregulation are examined in key areas of the world. The pace of adoption of technologies, such as high-speed Internet access, also is highlighted. The significance of a strong telecommunications infrastructure on the economy and on international trade is widely recognized and has prompted governments' attention worldwide.

The Essential Guide to Telecommunications, third edition, presents profiles of industry segments and vendor types to provide readers an understanding of the industry. The roles of Internet service providers, backbone Internet providers, competitive local exchange carriers, utilities and cable TV companies are explained. The number of network providers and resellers and the fast pace of mergers has created new layers of complexity. In addition, regulatory rulings and the Telecommunications Act of 1996 are examined in light of their impact on consumers, commercial organizations and carriers.

The language and significance of important telecommunications technologies are explored. *The Essential Guide to Telecommunications*, third edition, is not intended to be a deeply technical book. Rather, it is an overview of technologies and an explanation of the structure of the telecommunications industry. Technologies important in competition for local calling, high-capacity communications, third generation wireless services and Internet access are clarified. Intertwined with high-level technical explanations are examples of how the various vendors interconnect their networks. The book explains key technologies and options available for small and large organizations and consumers. It further explores significant trends, applications and the impact of the Internet.

This book is intended for non-technical people working in the field of telecommunications, laymen interested in learning more about the field and people responsible for the administration of telecommunications services for their organizations. They include regulatory staff, salespeople, law firms, research organizations, marketing personnel, human resources professionals, project managers, telecommunications managers and high-level administrators.

The Essential Guide to Telecommunications, third edition, starts out with interpretations of fundamental concepts so that readers will have a basis for understanding more complex, new telecommunications services. It examines the structure of the industry, local competition, regulatory proceedings, the Internet, convergence and wireless services.

Along with explanations of technology are examples of applications and historical highlights. How the industry evolved and how the technology changed is explained. The stories and descriptions that accompany the technical details are key to the book.

Acknowledgments

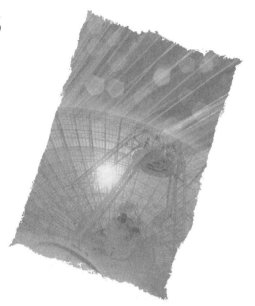

I would like to thank the many people who took the time to speak with me for this book. Staff at the following companies were enormously helpful: Taher Bouzayen at Atlantic-ACM; John Catlin at Agilent Technologies; Pat Peldner at Aquila Broadband Services; Iain Michel at Ariba Inc.; Andrew Pigney and Jack Smith at AT&T Wireless; Rachel Lamont and Richard Lush at Avaya Communications; Peter Chadwick at Avici Systems, Inc.; Donald Blair at Cisco Systems, Inc.; Mike Villa at Dovetail Internet Technologies, LLC; Stephen Fetter at Ektron; Kevin Anderson and Ken Johnson at Everest Connections; Rich Mazurek and Charles Scarborough at Cox Business Services; Cindy McCaffrey at Google, Inc.; E. Glynn Walden at iBiquity Digital Corporation; Eli Silberstein at IDT Wireless, Inc.; Peter Mesnik at iMakeNews.com; Chris O'Brien at Interactive Video Technologies; Kate Strong at Lightbridge, Inc.; Abdul Noury, ViJay Samalam and Barbara Sinclair at Lucent Technologies; Arthur Steinberg at the Massachusetts Institute of Technology; John Redman and Erik Shifflett at Nextel Communications; Greg Mycio at New Paradigm Resources Group; Jim Pullen and Sean Sundstrom at Regent Associates; Steve Chirokas and Eric Peterson at SpeechWorks International; Sam Trotter at Terawave Communications; Lee Knight at Tufts University; and John Armstrong at Yipes Communications.

Thanks also to the following for their time and insights: Joe Berthold, Vice President of Architectures and Standards, and Denny Bilter, Director of Marketing, at Ciena Corporation; Elizabeth Bramson, Manager, Europe, and Guy Zibi, Manager, Africa and the Middle East, Pyramid Research; Joseph Lawrence, Director, International Marketing, Qualcomm; Stephen Chow, Partner, Jerry Cohen, Partner, and Maggie Lange, Associate, at Perkins, Smith & Cohen, LLP; Mike Hluchyj, Founder and Chief Technology Officer at Sonus Networks; Will Biedron, Director of Product Management, Storigen Systems; Dr. Krishna Bala, Chief Technology Officer, Tellium, Inc.; Bob Albee, Director, Telecommunications Engineering, Vanesse Hangen Brustlin, Inc.; and Rajiv Ramaswami, Vice President of Systems Architecture, Xros Division of Nortel Networks.

Experts from the following associations provided information: David Wolcott at the Association for Local Communications Enterprises; Matt Osman and Mike Schwartz at CableLabs; Janice McCoy at the Massachusetts Department of Telecommunications and Energy; Jason D. Alexander at Massachusetts Technology Collaborative; and Steve Trotman of Association of Communications Enterprises. Students who attended the classes I teach at Northeastern University's State-of-the-Art Program helped me more than they can know. They include Kendra Pynn, Wendy Parsons, Claire Stasium and R. Owen Stokes. Many of them brought up issues in class that form the basis of chapters in my book.

Colin Crowell, Congressman Markey's aide for telecommunications, was an inestimable help on updates on regulatory issues and progress toward competition of local telecommunications services. Jennifer F. Brinkley, Associate Corporate Counsel at ITC^DeltaCom, carefully read one of my chapters and offered helpful insights. Walt Tetschner, President of Tern Systems in Acton, Massachusetts, provided background and statistics about cellular and unified messaging services. Fred Goldstein at Arthur D. Little, Inc., provided information on cellular data communications and regulatory issues. The following staff at Fidelity Investments provided helpful insights into telecommunications worldwide: Naved Khan, Kelly Morgan, Paul Mucci, Kevin Schmitz and Mike Wojcik. Thanks to my Acquisitions Editors Mary Franz and Mike Meehan and also to Patti Guerrieri and Lisa Iarkowski for shepherding the book through production.

Thanks also to Peter Barnes; Scott A. Helmers, The Harvard Computing Group, Inc.; Amy Borovoy, Princeton University; Joe McGrath and Rudy Rumohr, Sepracor, Inc.; Ed Geithner and Peter McGowan, m-g marketing; Joel Winett, BMC Software; Jocelyn Young for her insights on China; and Ruth Winett, Winett Associates. I couldn't have written this book without the support and help of all these people.

Most of all, I would like to thank my husband, Bob, for his many hours of research. He took the time to read each chapter multiple times and to offer insightful comments—no easy task. His help was invaluable and filled with common sense and intelligence.

Part 1

Fundamentals

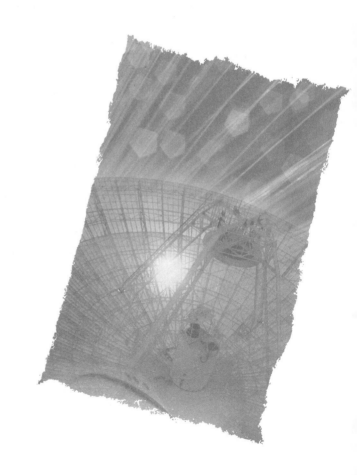

1 Basic Concepts

In this chapter...

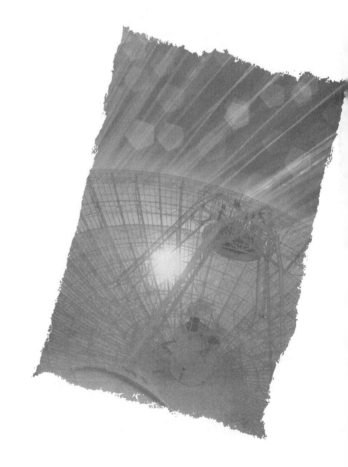

Advanced telecommunications technologies have dramatically changed the way businesses operate, spawning new services and creating an interconnected worldwide community. It's difficult to imagine doing business without the ability to electronically exchange email, PowerPoint®, spreadsheet and PDF documents. The whole pace of innovation and the ability to make informed decisions would be notably slower without this capability. New developments in computer technology have had a major impact on telecommunications. Faster processors have increased the speed and power of routers and made speech recognition viable for applications such as Internet access, access to flight information and directory information.

A grasp of fundamental concepts such as digital, analog, bandwidth, compression, protocols, codes and bits provides a basis for comprehending the myriad concepts used to describe futuristic networks. Understanding cellular services, fiber optics and the Internet all depend on understanding basic terminology.

Protocols are an important ingredient in enabling computers to communicate. A protocol impacts speed, efficiency and the user interface to services. Protocols may be likened to etiquette. Just as etiquette spells out who shakes hands first and how people greet each other, protocols spell out the order in which computers transmit and how long computers should wait before they terminate a transmission. Protocols provide a common way to handle functions such as error detection and error correction. Protocols have an important role in the ease of developing applications. In cellular networks, protocols are used for the important function of defining security standards to make eavesdropping difficult.

Computers from different vendors exchange files, electronic mail and attachments across networks. Architectures and protocol suites make communications between computers and peripherals from different manufacturers possible. Layers within architectures contain protocols that define functions such as routing, error checking and addressing. The architecture or protocol suite is the umbrella under which devices communicate with each other. A protocol suite, Transmission Control Protocol/Internet Protocol (TCP/IP) is the foundation for the Internet.

Computers in homes and offices are connected together by local area networks (LANs), located within a building or in a campus environment. LANs link computers, printers, scanners and shared devices such as modems, videoconferencing units and facsimile machines to each other and to the Internet. LANs are connected to other LANs over metropolitan area networks (MANs) within cities, and wide area networks (WANs) across countries. Large attachments and Internet downloads have added congestion to internal data networks. Network congestion results in delays in transmission of, for example, email and database lookups. High-speed routers, switches, multiplexers and compression lessen congestion.

Multiplexers and compression make networks more efficient. Compression squeezes large amounts of data into smaller "pipes," something like putting data into a corset. Physicians can access x-ray images over networks because improvements in compression make the images small enough to transmit efficiently. Compression has had a major impact on the nature of the Internet, particularly its use in streaming media. Compression in combination with more powerful computers and faster modems is making it possible to hear reasonably good quality music and radio over the Internet. It is changing the way consumers buy and listen to music.

Multiplexing adds efficiency by providing the means for multiple devices to share one transmission path. In the 1960s, T-1 had a significant impact on public network capacity, costs and reliability by allowing 24 communications paths to be carried digitally on one high-speed link. Today, dense wavelength division multiplexing schemes are common with one fiber optic link capable of transmitting 129,024 voice calls at optical carrier (OC) 192 rates of 10 gigabits per second. It is not a surprise, given this capacity, that experts are predicting a glut in backbone carrier networks. *Backbones*, also called the core, carry traffic on high-capacity lines between on and off ramps to networks.

The most common points of congestion in networks are where data enters and leaves the backbone. These on and off ramps, the network edges, are being upgraded. Routers responsible for carrying traffic to carriers' core networks are being developed to keep up with the speed of fiber optic backbone networks. New high-speed routers and wider availability of fiber optic cabling are bringing capacity closer to end-user commercial locations.

ANALOG AND DIGITAL ....

The public telephone network was originally designed for voice telephone calls. When the telephone was invented in 1876, it was used to transmit speech. Because speech is analog, calls were transmitted in an analog form until the late 1960s. While most of the public telephone and cellular networks are digital, there are still many analog services in use, and portions of the telephone network are analog. The majority of telephones that plug into home telephone jacks are analog instruments. Most broadcast TV signals and telephone lines from homes to the nearest telephone company equipment are analog. These analog phone lines are referred to as plain old telephone service (POTS).

As more people use their computers to communicate and calling volume increases, the analog format, designed for lower volumes of voice traffic, is proving inefficient. Digital signals are faster, have more capacity and contain fewer errors than analog waves. High-speed telecommunications signals sent within computers, via fiber optic lines and between most telephone company offices, are digital. With the exception of most broadcast TV and portions of cable TV wiring, analog services are used for slow-speed transmissions and small business customers.

Analog Signals

Analog telecommunications services are slower and more prone to errors than digital service. They also lose strength over shorter distances than digital signals and therefore require more equipment to boost their strength.

Frequency on Analog Services

Analog signals move down telephone lines as electromagnetic waves. The way analog signals travel is expressed in frequency. Frequency refers to the number of times per second that a wave oscillates or swings back and forth in a complete cycle from its starting point to its end point. A complete cycle, as illustrated in Figure 1.1, occurs when a wave starts at a zero point of voltage, goes to the highest positive part of the wave, down to the negative voltage portion and then back to zero. The higher the speed or frequency, the more cycles of a wave are transmitted in a period of time. This speed or frequency is stated in hertz (Hz). For example, a wave that oscillates or swings back and forth 10 times per second has a speed of 10 hertz (Hz) or cycles per second.

The frequencies that analog services use are expressed in abbreviated forms. For example, thousands of cycles per second are expressed as kilohertz (kHz), and millions of cycles per second are expressed as megahertz (MHz). Analog transmissions take place in enclosed media such as coaxial cable, cable TV and on copper wires used for home telephone services. They also are transmitted via "open" media such as microwave, home wireless telephones and cellular phones. Particular services are carried at predefined frequencies. Examples of analog frequencies are:

- kilohertz or kHz = thousands of cycles per second

    Voice is carried in the frequency range of .3 kHz to 3.3 kHz, or 3000 Hz.

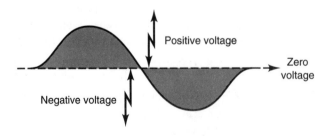

One cycle looks like a "resting" letter S

Figure 1.1
One cycle of an analog wave, 1 hertz (Hz).

- megahertz or MHz = millions of cycles per second
  Analog cable TV signals are carried in the frequency range of 54 MHz to 750 MHz.
- gigahertz or GHz = billions of cycles per second

  Most analog microwave towers operate at between 2 and 12 GHz.

Impairments on Analog Services

Sending an analog telephone signal is analogous to water flowing through a pipe. Rushing water loses force as it travels through a pipe. The further it travels in the pipe, the more force it loses and the weaker it becomes. Similarly, an analog signal weakens as it travels over distances whether it is sent over copper, coaxial cable or through the air as a radio or microwave signal. The signal meets resistance in the media (copper, coaxial cable, air) over which it is sent, which causes the signal to fade or weaken. In voice conversation, the voice might sound softer. In addition to becoming weaker, the analog signal picks up electrical interference, or "noise" on the line. Power lines, lights and electric machinery all inject noise in the form of electrical energy into the analog signal. In voice conversations, noise on analog lines is heard as static.

To overcome resistance and boost the signal, an analog wave is periodically strengthened with a device called an amplifier. In analog services, the amplifier that strengthens the signal cannot tell the difference between the electrical energy present in the form of noise and the actual voice or data. Thus, the noise as well as the signal is amplified. In a voice telephone call, people hear static in the background when this happens. However, they generally still can understand what is being said. When noise on data transmissions is amplified, the noise may cause errors in the transmission.

Digital Signals

The telegraph—the first form of data communications—was invented in 1840 and was used for short text messages. However, it was difficult to use and required special operators. Companies never adopted it for widespread internal operations. It wasn't until the 1960s that the public network started taking advantage of the superiority of digital service. Digital signals have the following advantages over analog:

- Higher speeds
- Clearer video and audio quality
- Fewer errors
- Better reliability

Fewer Errors, Higher Speeds

Instead of waves, digital signals are transmitted in the form of binary bits. The term *binary* means there are two values for transmitted bits: on and off. For data transmitted on copper cabling, on bits are represented by positive voltage and off bits by the absence of voltage. In fiber optic cabling, on bits are represented by light pulses and off bits by the absence of light pulses. On bits are depicted as ones and off bits as zeroes in programming and binary notations.

It is faster to re-create binary ones or zeros than more complex waves. Whereas the highest speed projected for analog modems is 56,000 bits per second when receiving data and 33,600 bits per second when sending data, new routers, which are digital, now run at terabit-per-second speeds. A *terabit* is equal to a thousand gigabits.

Digital signals can be re-created more reliably. Both analog and digital signals are subject to impairments: They decrease in volume over distance, fade and are susceptible to interference, such as noise. However, digital signals can be "repaired" better than analog signals. Figure 1.2 illustrates that when a digital signal loses strength and fades over distance, equipment on the line to regenerate the signal knows that each bit is either a one or a zero and re-creates it. Noise, or static, is discarded. The

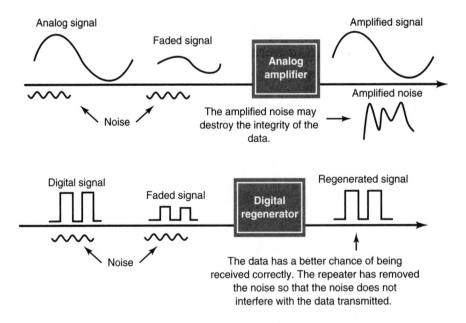

Figure 1.2
Noise amplified on analog lines; eliminated on digital service.

noise is not, as in an analog signal in Figure 1.2, regenerated. In analog transmission, where noise is amplified, receiving equipment may interpret the amplified signal as an information bit rather than as noise. In digital transmissions, where noise is discarded, garbling occurs less frequently; thus, there are fewer errors in the transmission.

Reliability

Digital service is more reliable than analog. Less equipment is required to boost the signal. Analog signals weaken and fade at shorter distances than digital signals. At every point that a signal fades, amplifiers or regenerators are required. Each amplifier is a place for a possible failure. For example, water can leak into a telephone company's manhole or the amplifier itself might fail. Organizations that use digital lines such as T-1 often experience only one or two brief failures in an entire year. High reliability results in lower maintenance costs for the telephone companies.

Terrestrial Digital Radio—Signal Quality vs. Content

Analog radio, which is over 100 years old, is the primary medium over which people receive news and information. Radio is low cost and ubiquitous. Terrestrial radio signals are broadcast from land-based towers. Radio is getting competition from the Internet in the form of streaming music that people listen to on portable MP3 players and Web-based radio stations such as Yahoo! subsidiary Broadcast.com. In an Internet-based article titled "Radio Giant Finally Wakes Up to the Net," published in *The Standard*, 17 November 2000, Laura Rich cites statistics from media research firm Arbitron stating that radio audiences in the United States are down 10% since 1993. The Telecommunications Act of 1996 loosened broadcaster ownership rules of multiple radio stations in the same area. As a result, many stations merged and many people feel there is now too little variety and innovation in programs.

In addition, analog radio tends to be noisy, fades in and out and has uneven reception quality. In an effort to keep up with competition, add new services and improve quality, the major broadcasters and technology companies Lucent, Visteon, and Texas Instruments formed a company called iBiquity to develop digital technology for radio. iBiquity has developed a way for radio broadcasters, using the same spectrum they already use for AM and FM programs, to transmit compact disc digital-quality radio signals along with new services. Reuse of spectrum eliminates the need to acquire new spectrum for digital service. Tests are being conducted to make sure this method, called In-Band On-Channel Digital Audio Broadcasting (IDAB™), does not interfere with analog AM and FM radio. Radios compatible with digital service are expected to initially cost about $100 to $150. The new radios will be capable of play-

DIGITAL SERVICES IN THE BELL SYSTEM

Digital technology was first implemented in the public network in 1962. Digital service, which is faster and has higher capacity than analog service, was implemented as a way to save money on laying cabling. Fewer copper or coaxial lines were needed to carry equal volumes of digital rather than analog traffic. The central office switches at that time were still analog and calls were converted to the digital format to be transmitted on coaxial cable. (Fiber cabling was not introduced until 1977.)

In 1975, Northern Telecom (now Nortel Networks) introduced the first digital telephone switch for routing calls. However, to cut its financial risk, it first introduced the switch as a customer premise rather than as a central office switch. At that time, telephone systems installed on customer premises were highly profitable and it was felt that there was less financial risk in introducing a smaller digital telephone system for end users, rather than a larger, more expensive telephone company central office switch. Digital voice, data and Internet traffic are now carried primarily on fiber optic rather than coaxial cable in the high-traffic portions of public networks.

Significant dates for digital services are:

- 1962: T-1 on two pairs of telephone cable carried 24 voice or data calls in digital format.
- 1975: The first digital telephone system (PBX), the Northern Telecom SL-1, was installed.
- 1976: AT&T's #4 ESS toll office switched calls between central offices.
- 1977: Nortel's central office switch, the DMS 10, was installed in Canada. It was not installed in the U.S. until 1981.
- 1982: AT&T's #5 ESS central office switched calls from central offices to local homes and businesses.

ing both analog and digital programs. The service is awaiting FCC approval and is not expected to be available until about 2003.

A challenge for radio broadcasters is to improve content to compete with new forms of satellite radio and Internet-based programming. In addition to improved signal quality, digital radio will enable broadcasters to offer more services and a larger

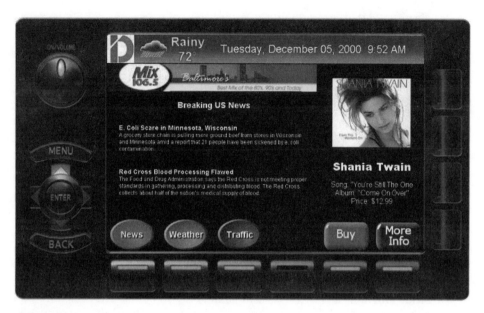

Figure 1.3
A digital radio, courtesy of iBiquity.

variety of content. For example, digital broadcasters can transmit digital images as well as audio. The images will be displayed on screens included with radios to display offerings such as the musician's name, weather, traffic, sports scores and offers for tickets and other purchases (see Figure 1.3).

Because radio is a one-way-only broadcast medium, the radio will need a built-in transmitter linked to a global positioning system (GPS) satellite. The link to GPS satellites will enable a consumer to purchase tickets or any other item. Pushing a button to make a purchase will send the user's identity and purchase choice via the transmitter to a GPS satellite. The radio information on the item selected for purchase will be included automatically and sent when the radio owner pushes the "buy" button on the radio.

Terrestrial Digital Radio Worldwide

Europe and Asia have moved to digital radio using different spectrum than that used for their analog radio. This is the Eureka 147 standard and it is being rolled out now in Europe. Outside of the United States, most countries have only four or five bands for radio so more spectrum was needed to add digital stations. Moreover, many of the government-owned stations such as the BBC in the United Kingdom wanted new spectrum so that stations could have the same band nationwide for their program. People driving in cars do not have to change stations to receive BBC digital radio programs in different parts of England. Japan uses a digital radio technology (ISDB) that is different than any of the preceding. The implementation of a worldwide standard would enable radio manufacturers to ship and produce a single radio that could be used everywhere, decreasing their production and distribution costs.

Satellite Digital Radio—Pay Radio

Digital satellite radio is analogous to cable TV. Listeners pay for programming. Two satellite companies in the United States have launched satellites capable of transmitting digital radio signals. They are XM Satellite Radio Holdings and Sirius Satellite Radio. Each sells 100 channels of specialized programming for $9.95 per month. Customers that purchase satellite radio service need to buy special radios for each service. This contrasts with cable TV in which customers need specialized set-top boxes but keep their televisions. A consumer with a radio compatible with XM cannot use it for Sirius programs and vice versa. In addition to digital clarity, programs work nationwide and there is a minimum of advertising. There are four other satellite radio services worldwide and all of their programs work only on specialized radios. General Motors and Honda have each invested in XM. DaimlerChrysler and Ford have invested in Sirius. These car manufacturers have stated that they will start installing XM and Sirius radios in new cars in 2002 and 2003.

Digital Television—Clarity Does Not Guarantee Sales

High-definition digital television (HDTV) was planned as a means of improving reception and offering new information services such as sports scores. In 1996, the government gave free spectrum to broadcasters for HDTV. In return, broadcasters promised to share revenues with the government derived from services sold in conjunction with HDTV. They also pledged to return the analog spectrum after the transition to HDTV.

Due to the high costs of digital television components, TV station upgrades to digital transmitters and poor availability of digital programming, sales of digital television did not meet expectations. By 2006, networks are required to return spectrum used for analog television to the federal government if 85% of the consumers in each broadcasting area have access to digital broadcasting. The FCC is scheduled to auction the returned spectrum in September 2001 for next-generation cellular service to be used when spectrum is returned in 2006. The prospect of not meeting the 85% goal makes the return of spectrum by 2006 doubtful. This is a problem for wireless providers in the United States because they plan on using spectrum returned by the broadcasters for high-speed third generation (3G) cellular services. However, cellular carriers are unsure if the spectrum in the planned auctions bid will be available to use in a timely fashion. (See Chapter 9 for details on 3G service.) The Senate Commerce Committee is holding hearings to consider changes to these rules that will ensure availability of spectrum for third generation (3G) service.

BAUDS, BITS, BYTES AND CODES—GETTING DOWN TO BASICS ....

Computers communicate with each other using specialized codes made up of bits and bytes. A byte is a character that is made up of seven or eight bits. Computer disc capacity tends to be measured in bytes, but speeds on digital lines are measured in the number of bits transmitted per second.

Overview

Computers can "read" each other's on and off binary bits when these bits are arranged in a standard, predefined series of on and off bits. All English-language IBM and Macintosh personal computers use variations of the same type of codes. The main code, American Standard Code for Information Interchange (ASCII), is used when personal computers communicate over telephone lines. The international version of ACII is known as International Reference Alphabet (IRA). IBM minis and mainframes use a different code, Extended Binary Coded Decimal Interexchange Code, (EBCDIC).

People use the terms bits, baud rate and bytes interchangeably. Their meaning, however, differs significantly. The signaling speed on analog lines is the *baud rate*—the number of times per second a cycle is completed. The baud rate is measured differently than bits per second. *Bits per second* are the actual number of bits sent in a given time from point A to point B. It is also the amount of information or data transmitted on the electrical waves in analog telephone lines.

Baud Rate vs. Bits per Second—Electrical Signal Rates vs. Amount of Information Sent

A *baud* is one analog electrical signal or wave. One cycle of an analog wave equals one baud. A complete cycle starts at zero voltage, goes to the highest voltage and down to the lowest negative voltage and back to zero voltage, the resting S in Figure 1.1. A 1200-baud line means that the analog wave completes 1200 cycles in one second. A 2400-baud line completes 2400 wave cycles in one second. The term *baud rate* refers only to analog electrical signals. It does not indicate the amount of information sent on these waves.

The public switched network runs at 2400 baud. If the public network could carry only 2400 bits in one second, data communications users would be severely hampered in retrieving and sending information over analog lines. To achieve greater capacity, modem manufacturers design modems capable of adding more than one bit on each analog wave or baud. Thus, a 9600 bit per second (bps) modem enables each analog wave to carry 4 bits of data per wave (9600 ÷ 2400 = 4). It is correct to state that the 9600-bps modem runs at 2400 baud. A 28,800-bit per second modem puts 12 bits of data onto each electrical signal or wave. It still uses a 2400-baud line.

Baud rate refers to analog, not digital transmission services. Digital services do not use waves to carry information. Information is carried as on or off electrical signals in the case of copper wires, and on or off light pulses on fiber optic lines. On digital services, 56,000-bit per second lines can carry 56,000 bits in one second. The speed is 56 Kbps, or 56 kilobits per second.

Codes—Adding Meaning to Bits

Codes such as ASCII and EBCDIC enable computers to translate binary off and on bits into information. For example, distant computers can read simple email messages because they are both in ASCII. ASCII (American Standard Code for Information Interchange) is a 7-bit code used by PCs. ASCII code is limited to 128 characters. Extensions to ASCII support 8-bit codes. Most PCs now use extended ASCII. These characters include all of the upper- and lowercase letters of the alphabet, numbers and punctuation such as !, " and : (see Table 1.1).

Table 1.1   *Examples of ASCII Code*

Character	ASCII Representation
!	0100001
A	1000001
m	1101101

Because there are only 128 or 256 characters, ASCII does not include formatting characters such as underlining, tabs and columns. Specialized word processing and spreadsheet programs add their own code to ASCII for formatting and specialized features. Thus, Microsoft® Word® documents, for example, need to be "translated" if they are to be "read" by a WordPerfect® program. Each program uses a different arrangement of bits to format columns, tabs and footers. Sending documents between computers in ASCII enables them to be read by all PCs. However, specialized formatting such as tabs, tables, and columns are not included in email messages.

SENDING ATTACHMENTS WITH EMAIL

Email is the most widely used application on the Internet. To overcome its format limitations that preclude images, tables or spreadsheets, mail protocols make it possible for users to send attachments along with their email messages. The mail protocol, multipurpose Internet mail extensions (MIME), adds special bits to the beginning of the attachment that contain the word processing, spreadsheet or image file. These special bits tell the receiving computer when the attachment begins and ends and the type of encoding used—for example, word processing program, spreadsheet, image and so forth. The receiving computer then opens that particular program and decodes the attachment so the recipient can read the document.

Attachments can be in many formats including Microsoft® Excel® PowerPoint®, and Microsoft® Word®. It also is possible to exchange video, audio and JIF or JPEG image files. (See Chapter 8 for an explanation of email that supports HTML formatting to add color and graphics to email messages.)

A Byte = A Character

Each character of computer-generated code is called a *byte*. The entire 7- or 8-bit character is a byte. A one-page document might have 250 words with an average of five letters per word. This equates to 5×250, or 1250 bytes or characters. It would, however, contain 10,000 bits (8×1250) if each character were made up of 8 bits. To summarize, a byte is a character made up of 7 or 8 bits. A bit is an on or off electrical pulse or light pulse.

BANDWIDTH—MEASURING CAPACITY ....

In telecommunications, bandwidth refers to capacity. Bandwidth is expressed differently in analog and digital transmissions. The carrying capacity of analog media, such as coaxial cable, is referred to as hertz. Hertz is a way of measuring the capacity or frequency of analog services. The bandwidth of an analog service is the difference between the highest and lowest frequency within which the medium carries traffic. For example, in the early 1980s when the government gave spectrum (a range of frequencies) rights to local telephone companies for analog cellular service, it gave it to them in the range of 894 MHz to 869 MHz. It gave them 25 megahertz (894 − 869 = 25) of spectrum. The greater the difference between the highest and lowest frequency, the greater the capacity or bandwidth.

For digital services such as ISDN, T-1 and ATM, speed is stated in bits per second. Simply put, it is the number of bits that can be transmitted in one second. T-1 has a bandwidth of 1.54 million bits per second. Bandwidth or hertz can be expressed in many ways. Some of these include:

- Individual ISDN channels have a bandwidth of 64 thousand bits per second, 64 kilobits per second or 64 Kbps.

- T-1 North American and Japanese circuits have a bandwidth of 1.54 million bits per second, or 1.54 megabits per second (Mbps).

- E-1 European standard circuits have a bandwidth of 2.048 million bits per second, 2.048 megabits per second or 2.048 Mbps.

- Another version of ATM has the capacity for 13.22 billion bits per second, or 13.22 gigabits per second (Gbps).

- One thousand gigabits is called one terabit; 10 terabits per second = 10,000,000,000,000 bits per second.

The letter C for concatenated is sometimes added to high-speed designations used on optical networks. Concatenated means multiple streams from the same source—such as video—travel together so there are no interruptions in the video transmission that might share a multiplexed fiber path with traffic from other sources.

Narrowband vs. Wideband—Slow and Fast

In addition to bits per second and hertz (Hz), speed is sometimes referred to as narrowband, wideband and broadband. Just as more water fits into a wide pipe and moves faster, wideband lines carry more information than narrowband lines, and the term wideband refers to higher speed services than 1.54 megabits. Again, digital speeds are expressed in bits per second and analog speeds are expressed in Hz.

The definition of wideband and narrowband technologies differs within the industry, as can be seen in Table 1.2. Some experts refer to broadband as higher than T-3 speeds.

Table 1.2   Wideband and Narrowband Telecommunication Services

Narrowband	Wideband and Broadband
T-1 at 1.54 Mbps Twenty-four voice or data conversations on fiber optics, infrared, microwave or two pairs of wire.	*Broadcast TV services—* *uses 6 MHz per channel* Newer digital high-definition TV (HDTV) offers enhanced clarity over analog TV.
Analog telephone lines at 3000 Hz Plain old telephone service (POTS) modems enable analog lines to carry data from digital computers.	*Cable TV (CATV) and community antenna television at 700 MHz* Broadcasts local and satellite TV. Also available for data communications and access to the Internet.
BRI ISDN at 144 Kbps Two paths for voice or data, each at 64 Kbps. One path for signals at 16 Kbps.	*ATM—Up to 13.22 Gigabits (Gbps)* A very high-speed service capable of sending voice, video and data.
	SONET—Up to 13.22 Gbps An optical multiplexing interface for high-speed transmission. Used mainly in carrier and telco networks.
	T-3 at 44.7 Mbps, Megabits (equivalent to 28 T-1 circuits) A way of transmitting 672 conversations over fiber optics or digital microwave.

Television and cable TV are carried at broadband speeds. Voice calls, video and data transported within carriers' networks are generally carried at broadband speeds. However, most traffic from telephone company equipment to individual homes and businesses is carried at the slower, narrowband speeds.

COMPRESSION AND MULTIPLEXING ....

Compression and multiplexing are used to improve efficiency on wireless and wire-line networks. Compression shrinks the data and multiplexing combines data from multiple sources onto a single path.

Compression—Manipulating Data for More Capacity

Just as a trash compactor makes trash smaller so that more refuse can be packed into a garbage barrel, compression makes data smaller so that more information can be packed into telephone lines. It is a technique to get more capacity on telephone lines, the Internet, cellular networks and airwaves used for broadcasts. Advances in compression have enormous potential to make dialup, cable modem, DSL and cellular networks adequate for movies, games, music and downloading graphics such as JPEG and PowerPoint images.

Compression Standards = Interoperability

There are many types of compression methods. A device called a codec (short for coder-decoder) encodes text, audio, video or images using a mathematical algorithm. For compression to work, both the sending and receiving ends must use the same compression method. The sending end looks at the data, voice or image. It then compresses it using a mathematical algorithm. The receiving end of the transmission decodes the transmission. For devices from multiple manufacturers to interoperate, compression standards agreed upon for modems, digital television, video teleconferencing and other devices must be used. See the appendix to this chapter for compression standards.

Modems—Using Compression to Get Higher Throughput

When compression is used with text and facsimile, data to be transmitted is made smaller by removing white spaces and redundant images, and by abbreviating the most frequently appearing letters. For example, with facsimile, compression removes white spaces from pictures and only transmits the images. Modems use compression to achieve higher throughput. Throughput is the actual amount of useful data sent on a transmission. When modems equipped with compression transmit text, repeated letters are abbreviated into smaller codes. For example, the letters E, T, O and I appear frequently in text. Compression sends shortened versions of these letters with 3 bits rather than the entire 8 bits for each letter. Thus, a page of text might be sent using 1600 bits rather than 2200 bits. Telecommuters who access and send data to corporate locations often use modems equipped with compression to transmit files more quickly (see Figure 1.4).

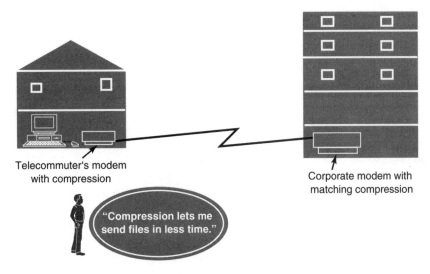

Figure 1.4
Compression in modems.

Compression—Commercially Viable, Full-Motion Videoconferencing

Improvements in the mid-1980s in video compression spawned the commercial viability of full-motion, room-type videoconference systems. Video systems that transmit at 128 Kbps to 768 Kbps are known as full-motion systems. Television is a broadcast-quality service. Compression made it economical to use full-motion video by enabling video to be acceptable on slower, lower cost telephone lines. Older systems required expensive, full T-1 lines for video, the cost of which inhibited sales of room-type video systems. New compression techniques available in the 1980s from companies such as PictureTel and VTEL required only 128 Kbps to 384 Kbps for acceptable picture quality. Thus, videoconferencing became affordable to a wide range of organizations. A new industry boomed.

In video, compression works by transmitting only the changed image, not the same image over and over. For example, in a videoconference, nothing is transmitted after the initial image of a person until that person moves or speaks. Fixed objects such as walls, desks and background are not repeatedly transmitted. Another way video compression works is by not transmitting the entire image. For example, the device performing the compression, the codec, knows that discarding minor changes in the image won't noticeably distort the viewed image.

Compressing and Digitizing Speech

The use of sophisticated compression has enabled audio to be transmitted from the Internet without using high-speed phone lines. Speech, audio and television are all analog in their original form. Before they are transmitted over digital networks, codecs compress them and convert them to digital. Codecs sample speech at different heights (amplitude) along the sound wave and convert them to either a one or a zero. At the receiving end, decoders convert the ones and zeros back to sound waves. With compression, codecs do not have to sample every height on the sound wave to achieve high-quality sound. For example, they skip silence or predict the next sound based on the previous sound. Thus, fewer bits per second are transmitted to represent the speech. Codecs are located in the following digital devices: cellular handsets, telephones, televisions and radios.

Proposed Compression Standard for Digital Radio

iBiquity has proposed a new compression technology, In-Band On-Channel Digital Audio Broadcasting (IDAB™), that uses airwaves within the current AM and FM spectrum to broadcast digital programming. IDAB is based on Perceptual Audio Coder (PAC™). There are many sounds that the ear cannot discern because they are masked by louder sounds. PAC discerns and discards these sounds that the ear cannot hear and that are not necessary to retain the quality of the transmission. This results in transmission with 15 times fewer bits. PAC, Perceptual Audio Coder, was first developed at Bell Labs in the 1930s.

Streaming Media

Streaming media techniques are the major reason the Internet is used to distribute music and multimedia content. It makes on-line music accessible to users without high-speed Internet connections.

Speeding Up Internet Connections

Streaming speeds up transmission of video, images and audio over the Internet. When graphics and text are sent to an Internet user's browser, the text can be viewed as soon as it reaches the PC. The graphics are filled in as they are received. Streaming is different than downloading. When music is streamed, callers listen to the music but cannot store it to listen to it later. Downloading actually stores the music files on a listener's computer hard drive. The Napster court case involved unauthorized downloading of music. The MP3.com case was about unauthorized listening (streaming) of music. (See Chapter 8 for a description of the issues litigated in these cases.)

When text, music or graphics are downloaded, the entire file must be downloaded before it can be viewed or played. With streaming technology, as soon as a URL is clicked, information starts to be viewable by the end user. Streaming is an important feature of browsers. When Web pages with both text and graphical ads are downloaded, the text reaches the end user's computer faster than the graphics. For example, someone reading the online edition of *The Wall Street Journal* can start reading articles while the ads are being received.

MPEG Standards

MPEG standards are used for streaming audio and video. The International Telecommunications Union (ITU) formed the Moving Picture Experts Group (MPEG) in 1991 to develop compression standards for playback of video clips and digital TV. MPEG3 came to be used for streaming audio. MPEG and proprietary streaming media compression schemes are asymmetrical. It takes more processing power to code than to decode an image. Streaming compression algorithms assume that the end user will have less processing power to decode than developers and broadcasters that encode the video and audio.

The two most prevalent streaming media software products are those developed by RealNetworks Inc. and Microsoft Corporation. RealNetworks' RealSystem® and RealPlayer® have a larger market share. Microsoft's product is Windows® Media Player® services. According to *The Wall Street Journal WSJ.com* "Reality Bytes" on January 29, 2001, less than half of computer users had media players capable of playing MP3 files. Statistics in the article from Jupiter Research, Media Metrix indicated that 28% of total home computers had RealPlayer and 22% had Windows Media Player installed by the third quarter of 2000. Both Microsoft and RealNetworks give away their streaming media software for free in the hope that their software will become the *de facto* standard and that developers will purchase server-based products from them.

More powerful personal computers as well as improvements in compression have increased the use of streaming audio and video over the Internet. In December 2000, Microsoft announced new compression software in its products that it claims uses a third of the computer disc space as MP3 and downloads 60% faster. Listen.com's subsidiary TuneTo.com announced in April 2001 a new streaming technology that will cut transmission to 1000 bits of data from 50,000 to 138,000 bits for current streaming methods. Listen.com claims this will make streaming audio viable for slower speed cellular devices.

Speech Recognition—Making the Web and Wireless Services Friendlier

When users call companies they no longer have to press 1 for sales and 2 for service. They can say "sales" or "service." If they know the name of the person they're calling, they can speak the name of the person and the system they've dialed into recognizes the name and transfers them. Internet service provider (ISP) AOL lets people log into and hear their email messages by speaking commands from telephones. Web users no longer need their computers with them to listen to their messages. More powerful, faster computers have given speech recognition software from companies such as Nuance Communications and SpeechWorks International the tools to develop software capable of translating speech into computer commands.

How Speech Recognition Works

Speech recognition works by first detecting and then capturing spoken words (*utterances*). It converts the captured utterances to a digital representation of the words after removing background noises. Capturing the speech and digitally representing it is done by digital signal processors (DSPs), which are high-speed specialized computer chips. The speech recognition software then breaks up the sounds into small chunks, which are easier to define than larger pieces of sound. Next, the software compares various properties of the chunks of sound to large amounts of previously captured data. Based on these comparisons, the speech is assigned probabilities of matching particular phonemes. (*Phonemes* are the most basic sounds such as "b" and "aw.") Finally, the software compares phonemes, matching probabilities with possible user responses from a database. The software puts together possible responses made up of phonemes, vocabulary and grammar in the speech recognition software. Grammar refers to the way the words are strung together.

Faster computer processors are a key factor in improvements in speech recognition. New computers perform the digitization and comparisons in milliseconds. They also take into account gender differences and regional accents. Systems contain different databases of expected responses based on the application. A corporate directory has a different speech database than one for airline scheduling or lost luggage applications. Important speech recognition improvements are:

- *Speaker independence*—Previous systems needed users to "train" the system to recognize words. New systems recognize words from the general population. They are speaker independent.
- *Barge in*—Users who call frequently can interrupt system prompts and say commands or department names as soon as the system answers the phone.

- *Voice authentication*—Voice authentication provides another layer of security for access to secure corporate files. In financial institutions, speech recognition recognizes a particular user's voice. Systems also require passwords on top of voice authentication for access to corporate files.

- *Continuous speech*—Systems can pick out keywords when callers are speaking naturally. If a caller says, "I think I'd like my email," the system picks out the word email from the sentence.

VoiceXML—Linking Speech to Databases

Voice eXtensible Markup Language (VoiceXML) is a markup programming language. A markup language contains tags that tell how code is to be processed. Just as HTML adds tags to format Web pages, VoiceXML is a proposed standard to use tags with audio prompts to describe call flow and dialog in speech recognition applications. The goal of VoiceXML is to create interfaces to Web- and call center–based data for words spoken from cellular phones, landline phones and wireless personal digital assistants. The tags contain fields denoting actions such as if transfer this call <if>. The tags also identify prompts and fields that contain links that transfer calls based on callers' spoken commands.

VoiceXML is interpreted by speech browsers that present speech content to listeners who have requested information. The speech browser is a gateway between the telephone and the Internet or call center. It provides the link between the user and the requested information. It is essentially an integrated voice response unit enabled to interpret speech as well as touch-tone commands. Just as voice response units translate touch-tone to computer commands, speech browsers translate speech and provide access to databases. (See Chapter 2 for integrated voice response systems.)

Having a VoiceXML standard will enable speech browsers from any manufacturer to easily interact with Web servers. Speech access is particularly attractive internationally where many more people have cellular telephones than personal computers for Web access.

Multiplexing—Let's Share

Multiplexing combines traffic from multiple voice or data devices into one stream so that they can share a telecommunications path. Like compression, multiplexing enables companies and carriers to send more information on cellular airwaves and telephone lines. However, unlike compression, multiplexing does not alter the actual data sent. Multiplexing equipment is located in long distance companies, local telephone companies and at end-user premises. It is used with both analog and digital services.

Examples of multiplexing over digital facilities include T-1, fractional T-1, T-3, ISDN and ATM.

The oldest multiplexing techniques were devised by AT&T for use with analog voice services. The goal was to make more efficient use of the most expensive portion of the public telephone network, the outside wires used to connect homes and telephone offices to each other. This analog technique was referred to as *frequency division multiplexing.* Frequency division multiplexing divides the available range of frequencies among multiple users. It enabled multiple voice and later data calls to share paths between central offices. Thus, AT&T did not need to construct a cable connection for each conversation. Rather, multiple conversations could share the same wire between telephone company central offices.

Digital multiplexing schemes also enable multiple channels of voice and data to share one path. Digital multiplexing schemes operate at higher speeds and carry more traffic than analog multiplexing. For example, T-3 carries 672 conversations over one line at a speed of 45 megabits per second (see Figure 1.5). A matching multiplexer is required at both the sending and receiving ends of multiplex equipped communications channels.

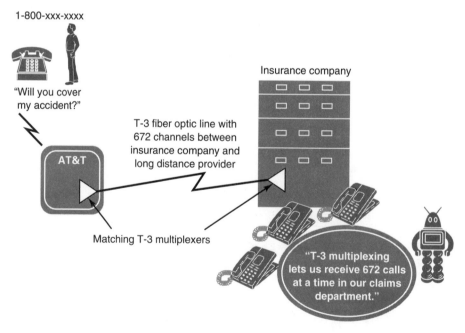

Figure 1.5
Multiplexers for sharing a telephone line.

T-3 is used for very large customers, telephone company and Internet service provider networks. T-1 is the most common form of multiplexing for end-user organizations. T-1 is lower in cost and capacity than T-3. T-1 allows 24 voice and/or data conversations to share one path. T-1 applications include linking organization sites together for voice calls, Internet access and links between end users and telephone companies for discounted rates on telephone calls.

PROTOCOLS AND ARCHITECTURES ....

Protocols are key enablers for all types of communications including Internet access from cellular devices. (See Chapter 9 for cellular service.) New protocols have been developed for lower cost wireless LANs for homes and businesses that provide convenience previously only affordable to large corporations. (See the next section for wireless LANs for homes.)

Protocols—A Common Set of Rules

Protocols enable like devices to communicate with each other by providing a common set of rules. Devices communicate over the Internet using a suite of protocols called TCP/IP. For example, the IP, or Internet protocol portion of TCP/IP, enables portions of messages called datagrams to take different routes through the Internet. The datagrams are assembled into one message at the receiving end of the route. Other protocols, such as Bluetooth, enable wireless communications among devices located within 33 feet of each other.

Examples of protocol functions are:

- Who transmits first?
- Is the other end ready to receive?
- In a network with many devices, how is it decided whose turn it is to send data?
- What is the structure of the addresses of devices such as computers?
- How is it determined if an error has occurred?
- How are errors fixed?
- If no one transmits, how long is the wait before disconnecting?
- If there is an error, does the entire transmission have to be resent or just the portion with the error?

- How is data packaged to be sent—one bit at a time or one block of bits at a time? How many bits are in each block? Should data be put into envelopes called packets?

Protocol structures have implications on speed and efficiency. The following protocols illustrate this point:

- *Secure Sockets Layer (SSL)*—Encrypts communications between a user's browser and the Web site server in electronic transactions so that only the authorized server can read credit card information.

- *Signaling System 7 Protocol (SS7)*—A way for carriers to bill, track and provide enhanced services such as caller ID over their networks. It also enables carriers to manage traffic sent to them from other carriers. The signaling system it supplanted, Signaling System 6 (SS6) did not support enhanced services and used network capacity less efficiently than SS7. (See Chapter 5 for SS7.)

Architectures—A Framework for Multiple Networks to Communicate

The main goal of architectures is to enable dissimilar protocols and computer networks to communicate. Standards bodies and dominant companies such as IBM develop architectures. During the 1970s, the International Standards Organization (ISO) developed an architecture, Open System Interconnection (OSI), to provide the means for devices from multiple vendors to interoperate.

While OSI was not widely implemented because of its complexity, it has had a profound influence on telecommunications and has become a reference model. It laid the foundation for the concept of open communications among multiple manufacturers' devices. The basic concept of OSI is that of layering (see Table 1.3). Groups of functions are broken up into seven layers, which can be changed and developed without having to change any other layer. LANs, public networks and the Internet's TCP/IP suite of protocols are based on concepts for a layered architecture.

The Internet suite of protocols, TCP/IP, corresponds to the functions in Layers 3 and 4 of the OSI model. These functions are addressing, error control and access to the network. The TCP/IP suite of protocols provides a uniform way for diverse devices to communicate with each other from all over the world. It was developed in the 1970s by the U.S. Department of Defense and was provided at no charge to end users in its basic format. Having a readily available, standard protocol is a key ingredient in the spread of the Internet.

Table 1.3   The OSI Layers

Layer Name and Number	Layer Function
Layer 1 physical layer	*Layer 1* is the most basic layer. It defines the electrical interface (RS 232 plugs) that connects modems to computers. Layer 1 defines, for example, which pins are used for sending, which for receiving and which for requests to send on the pins in the connectors. Layer 1 also defines type of media—for example, copper, wireless and fiber optics. SONET, discussed in Chapter 6, is a Layer 1 protocol used to define how information is transmitted on fiber optic networks.
Layer 2 data link layer	Ethernet, used in local area networks (LANs) within corporations and carrier networks, corresponds to *Layer 2* of the OSI model. It provides rules for error correction and access to LANs. Layer 2 devices also have addressing information analogous to the postal system's routing mail all the way to an end user's residence.
Layer 3 network layer	*Layer 3*, also known as the routing layer, is responsible for routing traffic between networks using IP (Internet protocol). It also has error control functions. Layer 3 is analogous to a local post office routing an out-of-town letter by ZIP Code, not looking at the street address. For example, once an email message is received at the distant network, a layer 2 device looks at the device address and delivers it to the correct computer.
Layer 4 transport	*Layer 4* protocols enable networks to differentiate between types of applications. Layer 4 devices route by content. For example, video or voice transmissions over data networks might receive a higher priority or quality of service than email, which can tolerate delay. TCP (Transmission Control Protocol) is a Layer 4 protocol. Filters in routers that check for computer viruses by looking at a message's entire IP address perform a Layer 4 function.
Layer 5 session	*Layer 5* manages the actual dialog of sessions. Encryption that scrambles signals to ensure privacy occurs in Layer 5. Other Layer 5 functions include determining the full- or half-duplex nature of the transmission. For example, can both ends send at the same time (full duplex)? Can transmissions be half duplex, with one-way-at-a-time sending?

Table 1.3   The OSI Layers *(continued)*

Layer Name and Number	Layer Function
Layer 6 presentation	*Layer 6* controls the format or how the information looks on the user's screen.
Layer 7 application	*Layer 7* includes the application itself plus specialized services such as file transfers or print services. Hypertext transfer protocol (HTTP) is a Layer 7 protocol that advanced switches use to transfer Internet users to the server containing the requested content.

In layered architectures or protocol suites, when transmitting, layers communicate with the layer immediately below them. Only Layer 1 actually transmits to the network. On the receiving end, Layer 1 receives the data and sends it to Layer 2, which then reads the Layer 2 protocol before sending the message to the next higher layer and so on to the application layer.

LANS, MANS AND WANS ....

The difference between LANs, MANs and WANs is the distance over which devices can communicate with others. See Table 1.4. As the name implies, a local area network is local in nature. It is owned by one organization and is located in a limited geographic area, usually a single building. In larger organizations, LANs can be linked together within a complex of buildings on a campus. Devices such as computers linked together within a city or metropolitan area are part of a metropolitan area network (MAN). Similarly, devices that are linked together between cities are part of a wide area network (WAN).

Table 1.4   LANs, MANs and WANs—What's the Difference?

Term	Definition
LAN (Local Area Network)	A group of devices, such as computers, printers and scanners, that can communicate with each other within a limited geographic area such as a floor, department or small cluster of buildings.
MAN (Metropolitan Area Network)	A group of data devices, such as LANs, that can communicate with each other within a city or a large campus area covering many city blocks.

Table 1.4 LANs, MANs and WANs—What's the Difference? *(continued)*

Term	Definition
WAN (Wide Area Network)	A group of data devices, usually LANs, that can communicate with each other from multiple cities.
Hub	The intelligent wiring center to which all devices, printers, scanners, PCs and so forth are connected within a segment of a LAN. Hubs enable LANs to be connected to twisted pair cabling instead of coaxial cable. Only one device at a time can transmit via a hub. Hubs provide a point for troubleshooting and relocating devices. Speed is usually 10 Mbps.
Backbone	Wiring running from floor to floor in single buildings and from building to building within campuses. A backbone connects to hubs or switches located in wiring closets on each floor.
Bridge	Bridges usually connect LANs using the same type of protocol together. They have limited intelligence and generally only connect a few LANs together. Bridges were in limited use as of the early 1990s when the price of routers dropped. Layer 2 switches also have replaced bridges.
Layer 2 switch (also called switching hub)	Layer 2 switches are bridges that allow multiple simultaneous transmissions within a single LAN. Total speeds range from 10 Mbps to 100 Mbps (megabits per second). Layer 2 switches provide a dedicated connection during an entire transmission.
Layer 3 switch (also known as routing switch)	Layer 3 switches have the capability to route traffic across the LAN backbone. They are used to connect wiring closets and buildings within a campus. This is typically the LAN backbone.
Router	Routers connect multiple LANs. They are more complex than bridges and can handle a greater number of protocols and LANs. Routers select the best available path over which to send data between LANs. New routers do not look up each packet's address in the CPU's memory. Routing is done in chips on each module or card.
Server	A centrally located computer with common departmental or organizational files, such as personnel records, sales data, price lists, student information and medical records. Servers connect to a hub or a Layer 2 or 3 switch. Access to servers can be restricted to authorized users only.

LANs—Local Area Networks

LANs are used to communicate within a limited area such as a building or campus. Examples of devices within LANs are: shared printers, PCs, alarm devices, factory automation gear, quality control systems, shared databases, factory and retail scanners and security monitors (see Figure 1.6). A discrete LAN is typically located on the same floor or within the same department of an organization.

LANs grew out of the proliferation of PCs. Once people had PCs on their desktops, the next step was to connect these PCs together. LANs first appeared in 1980. The initial impetus for tying PCs together was to share costly peripherals such as high-speed printers. LANs are the building blocks for connecting multiple locations together for the purpose of sending email and sharing databases and applications with remote locations and telecommuters. These email and corporate information files are located in specialized computers called file servers. Access to file servers can be limited by password to only approved users.

The software that runs local networks is called *LAN network operating systems* and is located on servers connected to the LAN. Most operating systems in use today are built on the client-server model. Clients (PCs) request services such as printing and access to databases. Applications such as print and fax servers run access to services (e.g., printers and databases). The network operating system controls access to the LAN where resources such as files, printers and modems are located. Microsoft NT and Novell NetWare are client-server-based LAN network operating systems.

Each device connected to the local area network can communicate with every other device. The connections between devices may be any of the following: twisted pair, coaxial cable, fiber optics or wireless media. For the most part, devices are connected to

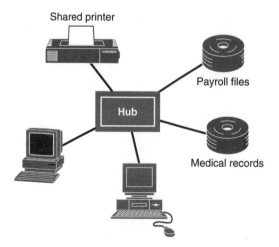

Figure 1.6
A local area network.

a LAN by twisted pair cabling that is similar to but sometimes of a higher quality than that used to tie business telephones together. (Media options are covered in Chapter 2.)

When local area networks became popular in the 1980s, many individual departments purchased their own LANs independent of the central computer operations staff. As the need arose to tie these LANs together for email and file sharing, compatibility between LANs from different manufacturers became a problem. The TCP/IP suite of protocols became a popular choice for overcoming these incompatibilities. Devices called bridges and routers were developed to send data between LANs.

LAN and WAN Devices

New LAN and WAN gear are being developed to handle increases in traffic in carrier and enterprise networks. Lower prices for some of this equipment is making LANs feasible for small businesses and residences.

Server Farms and Multimedia—High-Bandwidth Applications

Original LAN designs lent themselves to "bursty" traffic such as brief email and text messages. Not only are new applications adding traffic to LANs, but the traffic is no longer the short, bursty type with pauses that give other devices a chance to transmit. The fact that the world is more networked is causing huge increases in corporate bandwidth requirements. People are typically sending PowerPoint® attachments with 6 to 16 million bytes between companies. Server farms are centralized locations in corporations' or carriers' networks with groups of servers containing enterprises databases or Web pages. Downloads from server farms are often long, continuous streams of images, audio and video files. In addition, more organizations are connecting applications such as voice mail, call centers and IP-based telephone systems to LANs. (See Chapter 2 for unified messaging, call centers and IP-based telephone systems.)

More Powerful PCs

In addition to applications that require large amounts of data to be transmitted on LANs, more powerful PCs impact LAN requirements. In the 1980s when LANs were first implemented, people had computers with 286 chips on their desks with small amounts of memory and hard disks. In recent years, staffs have Pentium computers with 132 megabytes of memory and gigabyte-sized hard drives. These robust PCs have multimedia capability. This enables them to participate in desktop videoconferences, download large files from the Internet and share large JPEG files. All of this traffic is carried over the LAN.

Hubs

Hubs enable devices on LANs to be linked together by twisted pair copper wire instead of the heavier, thicker coaxial cable typically used in the cable TV industry. When LANs were initially implemented, they were installed using coaxial cable to interconnect devices on the LAN. Coaxial cable is expensive to install and move. It is not unusual in large organizations for entire departments and individuals to move at least once a year. The use of coaxial cabling resulted in a loss of space in dropped ceilings and conduit for the cable.

With a hub, instead of wiring devices to each other, each node or device is wired back to the hub in a star pattern. Using a hub changes the topology of a LAN. The hub creates a star design, or topology. (*Topology* is "the view from above"—in the case of hubs, a star where each device is connected to a central device.) Without a hub, each device in a LAN is wired to another device in a "bus" arrangement. In the bus topology, if one device is taken out of the line or bus, or if there is a break in the line, each device is affected. By employing a hub, a device can be moved or taken out of service if it is defective without affecting other devices on the LAN. A hub is kept in the wiring closet of each floor within a building, as shown in Figure 1.7.

Layer 2 switches are replacing hubs because of hubs' limitations. Only one device at a time can communicate on hub equipped LANs, and speeds are limited to 10 megabits per second. Moreover, hubs are suited to networks with bursty (short in length), messages and LANs now carry more multimedia traffic.

Layer 2 Switches

Layer 2 switches are faster than hubs and provide more bandwidth per device on LANs. Some Layer 2 switches are non-blocking. They have enough capability so that each device can communicate at the same time. For example, a switch capable of forwarding packets at 100 million bits per second would be non-blocking if 10 users were connected to the switch and each needed 10 million packets per second of capacity.

When LANs were first implemented, in addition to assumptions regarding burstiness, it was assumed that applications such as email would not require immediate response. This is not true for newer applications such as unified messaging where users receive voice mail as well as email over the LAN. Delays (latency) are not acceptable when downloading graphics from the World Wide Web or transmitting video and voice on the LAN.

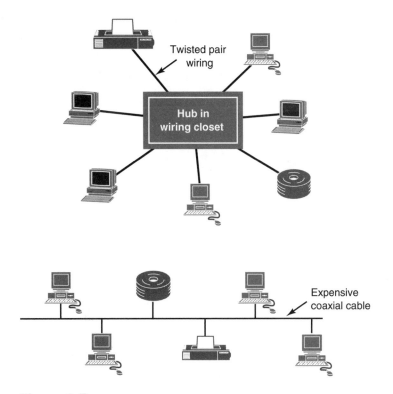

Figure 1.7
Top: LAN with a hub to link devices with twisted pair wiring.
Bottom: LAN without a hub.

Some Layer 2 switches have cut-through capability, which enables them to start sending frames to their destination as soon as they see the address at the beginning of the frame. They don't have to wait to receive the entire frame before they start sending. A frame is an arrangement of bits in a predefined order that includes addressing, error control, user data and bits that mark the end of the frame. Layer 2 switches are located either in work groups where they are connected to a group of ten or so users or in wiring closets serving a few hundred users. The number of nodes connected to a switch depends on the switch's speed and the users' requirements.

Layer 3 Switches—Also Known as Switching Routers

A Layer 3 switch has connections to multiple Layer 2 switches and has routing capability. It generally is located in wiring closets (connecting hundreds of users) or LAN backbones (connecting many wiring closets or buildings together). Some enterprises install Layer 3 switches to replace routers within the LAN or campus. However, they usually keep their router to connect to the Internet and to WANs because routers have more sophisticated WAN protocols and hardware for connections to services such as Frame Relay and T-1. (See Chapter 6 for T-1 and Frame Relay.)

Layer 3 switches are faster and less complex to install than routers. Each port only needs to be programmed with information on the identity of the user connected to the port and what level of priority to assign the port.

Switches support Ethernet, Fast Ethernet and Gigabit Ethernet. Ten-Gigabit Ethernet standards are being developed.

Bridges

Bridges became available in the 1980s as a way to connect a small number of LANs together. Bridges provide one common path over which multiple LANs may be connected together (see Figure 1.8). For example, if an organization has two locations in different cities that need to exchange data, a bridge can be used. Bridges also are used as a way to cut down LAN congestion. The bridge can connect two different departments so that each departmental LAN is not congested with intradepartmental traffic. Bridges most often connect two LANs with like protocols such as an Ethernet LAN to an Ethernet LAN. There are more sophisticated bridges that connect an IBM token ring network to an Ethernet LAN.

Bridges are easy to configure because there are a limited number of choices in configuring them. Each piece of data sent via a bridge takes the same path and is sent to every device on the network. The lack of routing and congestion control puts bridges at Layer 2 in the OSI model. Only the device to which the message is addressed

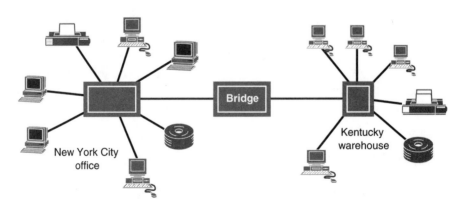

Figure 1.8
A bridge connecting two local area networks.

takes the message off the network. This broadcast feature of bridges can choke the network with too many messages, slowing down the network for everyone. As LANs proliferated and router prices dropped, people turned to routers and then switches rather than bridges.

Routers

Routers connect multiple local area networks. They also connect LANs to the Internet and to wide area networks. These LAN connections are usually between LANs located in distant buildings on a campus or in different buildings in diverse cities. Routers in carriers' networks pick the least congested paths over which to forward packets. To illustrate a user may send two messages from Chicago to Los Angeles. The first message might route via Alaska and the second via Texas. Because of congestion and routing, the second message might arrive before the first one. Routers are more sophisticated and have additional capabilities not available in bridges. A major advantage of routers is their capability to forward differing protocols from varied departmental local area networks. It is important to note that routers do not translate application protocols. A UNIX computer cannot read a Microsoft Windows word processing document. The router merely transports differing LAN protocols in corporate and carrier networks.

Router capabilities include:

- **Flow control**—If the path the data takes is congested, the router can hold the data until capacity is available on the path between the routers.
- **Path optimization**—The sending router selects the best available path by checking routing tables contained within the router.
- **Sequencing**—Routers send data in *packets*, or envelopes. These packets might arrive out of order at the destination router. From information in the packet, the receiving router knows the correct order and arranges the data accordingly.
- **Receipt acknowledgment**—The receiving router sends a message to the router that sent the message acknowledging that the data was received correctly.

Intelligence inherent in routers leads to two major disadvantages: First, routers are complex to install and to maintain. Every router in an organization's network must have up-to-date address tables. Each device on a LAN is called a node and has an address. For example, if a printer or PC is moved from one LAN to another, the router table must be updated or messages will not reach that device. To illustrate the complexity of managing routers, it is common to hear of consultants with full-time contracts for updating router tables for organizations. Second, routers are slower than bridges. The need to look up tables within the router slows down the router's speed. The functions of congestion control, routing, sequencing and receipt acknowledgment make routers network Layer 3 devices.

Home LANs—Sharing Printers and High-Speed Internet Access—A Lack of Technical Support

People with home-based businesses and school-aged children often have multiple computers. Multiple computers per residence is not uncommon. According to International Data Corporation statistics quoted in an article titled "Home Networking," published in *The Boston Globe*, page C2, 12 December 2000, by Hiawatha Bray, 13% of American homes have more than one computer. International Data Corporation predicts that by 2004, 28% of homes will have more than one computer. Many of these consumers have high-speed DSL or cable modem access to the Internet that they wish to use for all their computers. They also share laser or color printers among their computers.

Although often slower and less complex, home networks are created along the same line as corporate networks. Hubs are required to share devices and routers are used to give all PCs access to high-speed telephone lines. The PCs, hub, printers and scanners are connected together wirelessly or by data grade (usually category 5), unshielded twisted pair cabling. (See Chapter 2 for media.) To share a printer, users need an inexpensive hub in which to plug their printer and each of their computers. Each computer connected to the LAN needs an Ethernet card connected to the hub or if the computer is in another room, an RJ-45 data jack connected by unshielded twisted pair cabling to the hub. RJ-45 jacks are similar to jacks that analog phones plug into except that they have four wires (two pair) instead of one pair needed for the phone jack.

To share high-speed DSL or cable modem service, the hub is connected to a router that plugs into the modem. Devices that combine hub and router functions in one "box" are available from vendors such as LinkSys, 3Com, NETGEAR and Xsense (for Macintosh computers). (See Figure 1.9.) In addition to cabling to connect routers and hubs, computer software needs to be added for work on home LANs to operate.

The issue of customer support is a major stumbling block to implementation of home networks. Most carriers that sell high-speed Internet access to consumers do not provide telephone support for routers. Some are concerned that home LANs will generate too much traffic and are considering charging higher fees to customers with more than one computer. Customers get support from router companies, friends and MIS staff where they work.

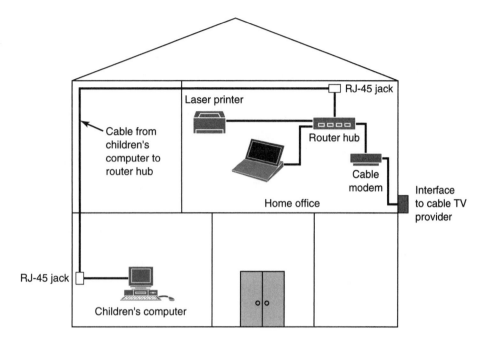

Figure 1.9
Home LANs.

Wireless LANs for Homes and Small Businesses

For customers who don't want the expense and trouble of running unshielded twisted pair cabling to each computer, wireless LANs are an option. With a wireless LAN, laptop computers can be used in any room of the house within range of the wireless antenna. Most systems support devices located about 150 to 200 feet from the transmitter. Moreover, as more devices such as games and appliances are networked, they can be more easily added wirelessly than with cabling. The most prevalent wireless standard is based on 802.11b and is called Wi-Fi. Apple's 802.11b wireless product is called Airport.

Both Macintosh- and Windows-based computers need a radio card added to them. On Windows laptops, the radio card currently uses the PCMCIA slot on the side of the laptop. The PCMCIA slot is not required for new Macintosh laptops because their wireless interface is installed internally. Windows-based laptops are expected to follow suit shortly. In addition, an external base station equipped with a transmitter is plugged into the DSL or cable modem. Each computer communicates wirelessly with the transmitter. Agere Systems (formerly part of Lucent), 3Com, LinkSys and Apple all sell wireless home networks. As with wired home and small office networks, setting up the software is complex in some of these systems.

MANs—Metropolitan Area Networks

Metropolitan area networks, or MANs are connections between local area networks, within a city or over a campus. Campus MANs are spread out over many blocks of a city. Examples of MANs are those of large hospitals and university complexes. For example, a hospital in downtown Boston keeps its x-rays and other records in a nearby section of the city. Instead of trucking records and x-rays between the two sites, the hospital leases high-capacity telephone lines to transmit records and images. The connections between these two sites are metropolitan area network connections. These connections can be leased from a telephone company or constructed by the organization. They can be fiber optic, copper or microwave-based services. They also include the same services mentioned for WANs, such as ISDN and T-1.

WANs—Wide Area Networks

The term WAN refers to connections between locations over long distances via telephone lines. For example, a warehouse in Alabama connected to a sales office in Massachusetts by a T-1 line is a wide area network (WAN) connection. In contrast to a local area network, a WAN is not contained within a limited geographical location. The variety of WAN connections available is complex. Selection of an appropriate WAN service depends on the amount of traffic between locations, quality of service needed, price and compatibility with the organization's computer systems. WAN technologies and WAN vendors are reviewed in Chapters 6. These include ISDN, T-1, T-3, ATM and Frame Relay.

Instead of complex WANs, many organizations now have high-speed connections either to the Internet or to carriers instead of directly to other corporate locations. Carriers manage the security and transmission of their customers' telecommunications in virtual private network (VPN) arrangements. (See Chapter 5 for VPNs.)

Higher Speed Services for LAN Traffic

The following protocols are being used to transmit multimedia, engineering and other high-bandwidth LAN traffic.

- **Fast Ethernet** is a shared protocol. However, it has a speed of 100 megabits—10 times the speed of standard 10-megabit Ethernet, the most prevalent LAN protocol. Standard two-pair wiring is used. New cards are required in each PC attached to the LAN.

- **Gigabit Ethernet** works with existing Ethernet LAN protocols. Because of its high speed, 1000 megabits, Gigabit Ethernet requires either fiber optic cabling or Level 6 unshielded twisted pair. On LANs, servers often have direct Gigabit Ethernet connections because of their high-bandwidth requirements. Gigabit Ethernet is used to connect LAN segments to each other within buildings and campuses.

- Layer 3 switches are faster than routers used in corporations to connect multiple LANs together on campuses and within buildings. They don't have the router requirement of looking up each packet's address in software.

- Fibre Channel protocols are used for gigabit speed, highly reliable short distance access to devices such as disks, graphics equipment, video input/output devices and storage devices that hold massive amounts of data and are often located in server farms. One example of a high-bandwidth application is movie file transfers by movie studios to save time during production. Fewer overhead bits for tasks such as error control and addressing are included in the Fibre Channel Protocol, which uses a device's input/output interface to communicate directly with switches. Enterprise System Connection (ESCON) is another storage-oriented protocol.

- Tag switching, supported by Cisco, is a proprietary protocol based on multiprotocol label switching (MPLS) to increase the speed of connections between LANs. In tag switching, bits representing the address are placed in the router's short-term cache memory. A fixed-length tag is added to each packet. With MPLS, short, fixed-length "labels" tell the router how to route each packet so that the router does not have to examine the entire header of each packet after the first point in the carrier's network. The router merely looks at the tag for routing instructions. This shortens the amount of time required to route packets.

New Devices for Carrier and Internet Service Provider Networks

Manufacturers are developing new high-speed routers for the anticipated continued growth in the amount of data versus voice carried in the public network. They envision a network that will carry a preponderance of data, video and audio rather than voice traffic. Data communications equipment manufacturers such as Cisco Systems and Juniper Networks have high-speed routers that they sell to carriers and Internet service providers. They see their equipment as being primarily designed for data traffic but also fast enough to carry voice and video without any degradation in the quality of the voice or video.

Traditional manufacturers of central office equipment designed to carry voice are developing new equipment to carry data more efficiently. These manufacturers include Siemens AG, Lucent Technologies, LM Ericsson and Nortel Networks. All of these organizations have purchased companies that specialize in equipment that can carry high-speed data services. For example, Lucent purchased Yurie Systems and Ascend Communications. Ascend Communications had previously acquired Cascade, a manufacturer of ATM switches, and Stratus. LM Ericsson bought Torrent Networking Technologies and Cisco Systems purchased Cerent Corporation.

AVAILABILITY VS. RELIABILITY

When carriers purchase telephone company equipment, key criteria for purchases are reliability and availability:

Reliability refers to how often a device breaks. Carriers typically require NEBS Level 3 compliance on equipment they purchase. NEBS stands for Network Equipment Building System. Bellcore, (now Telcordia) the former R&D arm of the Regional Bell Operating Companies, developed NEBS standards. The standards include compliance with thermal, electrical, redundancy and earthquake resistance tests.

Availability refers to how long it takes to repair equipment, or having the equipment in service even though part of it is not working. For example, if ports are inoperable, the other ports should be available to route calls normally handled by the inoperable ports. In the same vein, backup central processing units (CPUs) should be able to automatically take over if the main CPU goes down.

Core routing—Terabit Routers

The term terabit router was coined by Avici Systems in 1997. *Terabit routers* route packets at trillions of bits per second (1,000,000,000,000). Terabit routers generally are geared toward the ISP and carrier market. In planning for and designing their routers, Avici Systems spoke with carriers who stated that they wanted hardware that would be capable of handling the huge amounts of data they expected on the public network from applications such as virtual private networks (VPNs). (See Chapter 5 for VPNs.) They felt that VPNs would be handling a large amount of e-commerce, Extranet and Intranet traffic in the near future. (See Chapter 8 for Extranets and Intranets.)

Avici's terabit routers are computers made on the model of super computers. The switching fabric is made up of up to 560 routers in a single device. If any one of the 560 computers fails, the router still functions and uses the input/output ports associated with the remaining computers. The router uses multiprotocol label switching (MPLS). The smaller headers in MPLS routers enable them to forward packets at high speeds. Avici plans to ship routers at terabit speeds in 2001. One OC-192 equals 10,000 million bits per second of optical carrier (OC) capacity on fiber. 100 OC-192 equals 1 terabit per second. Most new core routers have OC-192 capacity.

Juniper Network core routers are based on Application-Specific Integrated Circuit (ASIC) processors for high performance. ASICs are specialized chips built with the capability of many chips integrated within them. Advances in computers such as memory and connectors have benefited routers that need to check addresses and forward packets at consistently high speeds. For example, the Juniper routers have separate CPUs to select routes and to do the actual forwarding of packets. The routing engine (a CPU) looks up routing tables to select the closest, least congested path through the network. The forwarding engine then puts the packet onto the network.

Other manufacturers of high-speed core routers include Pluris, Nortel Networks and Cisco Systems. Startup Hyperchip in Montreal, Canada has announced that it is developing a router capable of petabit speeds. A petabit equals 1 quadrillion bits per second, or 1000 terabits.

Edge Routers

Edge routers connect enterprises to carriers' networks. They are located at the edge of carrier networks. Edge routers aggregate large numbers of relatively slow circuits from end users at speeds such as T-1 (1.54 megabits) and OC-3 (155 megabits) and send them to core routers at speeds of OC-12 (622 megabits) and OC-48 (2.5 gigabits). See Figure 1.10. Connections between core and edge routers are hierarchical in nature, similar to connections between Layer 2 and Layer 3 switches in LANs.

Edge routers are slower than core routers. They also provide more services because they connect directly to customers as opposed to core routers that transmit to other core routers and to edge routers. When used by ISPs, edge routers furnish services such as filtering, rate limiting and traffic shaping. Filters are used to block traffic to sites such as pornography, Napster and Internet sites of ISP customers who don't want their employees to use the Internet for personal use. With rate limiting, an ISP can equip its router with T-3, 44.5 megabit ports but allow an access speed of 1.54 megabits per customer. An ISP can sell an aggregate speed of more than 44.5 megabits because it assumes that not everyone will use the service to its full capacity. To illustrate, it might sell 36 T-1s, which equals 55.44 megabits (36 × 1.54), 10.9 megabits more than the port's capacity of 44.5 megabits. Edge routers also provide VPN ser-

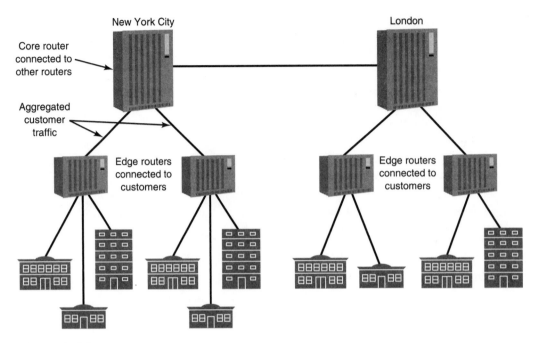

Figure 1.10
Edge and core routers.

vice. VPN networks furnish security and remote access to enterprise customers. (See Chapter 5 for VPNs.)

Vendors that sell edge routers include Juniper Networks, Cisco, Unisphere and Ennovate Networks, Inc.

Table 1.5   Appendix

Compression Standard	Description
MNP 5	Microcom Network Protocol compression protocol developed by Microcom for modems. Provides 2:1 compression.
V.42bis	Data compression protocol for modems. Provides 4:1 compression.
H.320	A family of standards for video adopted by the ITU (International Telecommunications Union). Quality is not as high as proprietary video compression algorithms. Most video codecs employ both proprietary and standard compression algorithms. The proprietary compression is used to transmit to another "like" video unit and the standard algorithm is used when conferencing between differing brands.
H.323	A family of standards for video adopted by the ITU for sending video over packet networks. Microsoft Corporation and Intel Corporation adopted the standard in 1996 for sending voice over packet networks. It is installed on Windows®-based PCs and used to packetize and compress voice when callers with PCs make calls from their computers over the Internet. See Chapter 5.
MPEG3	Moving Picture Experts Group 3 is Layer 3 of MPEG1. It is a compression standard for streaming audio. MPEG3 is the compression algorithm used to download audio files from the Internet. For example, some Internet e-commerce sites allow people with compression software to download samples of music so they can decide if they wish to purchase a particular CD. In addition, people with multimedia computers are playing CDs on their computers or on CD burners and distributing copies to friends without paying royalties.
MPEG2	A Moving Picture Experts Group standard approved in 1993 for coding and decoding video images. MPEG2 uses past images to predict future images and color, and transmits only the changed image. For example, the first in a series of frames is sent in a compressed form. The ensuing frames send only the changes. A frame is a group of bits representing a portion of a picture, text or audio section.

2 Telephone Systems, Peripherals and Cabling

In this chapter...

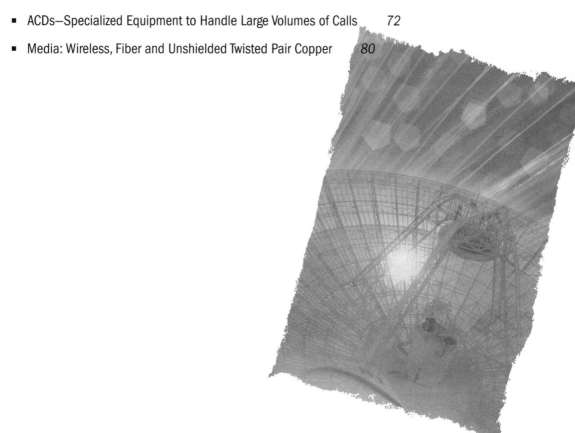

The market for on-site telephone systems such as private branch exchanges (PBXs), key systems and voice mail is highly competitive. Margins are low and growth is slow.

PBXs, Centrex and key systems provide:

- Connections to the public network and to staff at other sites
- The means for on-site personnel to call each other without paying telephone company usage fees

The difference between PBXs and Centrex is in the location and ownership of the equipment that routes calls. Private branch exchanges are located on customers' premises. They are privately owned. Centrex, which stands for central exchange, usually is located at the telephone company and is part of the central exchange, or central office. Customers lease Centrex service from a local telephone company, which owns the switching equipment. Unlike PBXs, the switching equipment is not generally located at customers' premises.

Key systems function much the same as private branch exchanges (PBXs). Key systems generally are smaller than PBXs. They have sophisticated voice mail, call center functionality and support telephones equipped with liquid crystal displays (LCDs) for caller ID and features such as speed dial and redial. Key systems are sold to organizations with fewer than 125 telephones at a site. Systems with 50 to 125 telephones fit into both key system and PBX configurations. The lines of functionality between key systems and PBXs are blurring.

Automatic call distributors (ACDs) route incoming calls to call center agents based on criteria, such as the agent that has been idle the longest. If an agent is not available, the automatic call distributor holds the call in a queue and the caller hears a message such as, "Please hold for our next available agent." ACDs are sold as part of key systems, Centrex and PBXs and as standalone systems for large call centers. ACDs provide sophisticated reports to help companies determine correct staffing levels and number of outside telephone lines.

Telephone systems with voice over IP (VOIP) capabilities, speech recognition and wireless telephones are in various stages of deployment. Organizations are purchasing IP-based telephone systems in limited quantities. However, experts see potential in the future as organizations start replacing existing telephone and key systems with systems with IP capability. These systems have the potential for lowering the cost of new telephone systems and creating easier, lower cost ways to add new functionality and Internet connectivity to call centers.

The desire for mobility is driving wireless LAN and wireless PBX and key system sales. Just as consumers expect to be able to use their cordless home phones from anywhere within their house, so too are corporate employees starting to use phones and laptop computers at training seminars, meetings and corporate cafeterias. Wireless phones are now in use, which operate in any building within a campus. They provide instant two-way access to staff. Moreover, wireless phones equipped with caller ID enable users to screen calls so that they don't miss important calls.

Speech recognition makes cellular and landline-based telephone access to information more convenient. Airline schedules, weather, AOL email and even mundane information such as corporate directories are easier and faster to access. The speech recognition software is becoming more accurate. Speech recognition eliminates cumbersome menus: for example, "Press 1 for a list of departments; press 2 for a corporate directory." With speech recognition, callers merely say the department or employee name they wish to reach.

The American Heritage Dictionary (2nd College Edition) defines a medium as "an intervening substance through which something is transmitted or carried." Telecommunications media are twisted pair copper, commonly used in homes and commercial buildings; coaxial cabling, used in cable TV networks; fiber optics, used for Internet and public network traffic and wireless services. Wireless and fiber optic media have had major impacts on worldwide connectivity. The growth of the Internet and increase in traffic would not have been possible without fiber optics and the electronics, wave division multiplexing (WDM), used to boost fiber optic capacity. The quality and type of media deployed have an impact on capacity, error rates and reliability.

TELEPHONE SYSTEMS— PBXS, CENTREX AND KEY SYSTEMS ....

When the telephone was first invented in 1876, each person's telephone line was wired directly to another individual user. By 1877, a switchboard was installed in Boston so that each telephone could be wired to the central switchboard instead of to every telephone. When an individual wished to call someone, he or she picked up the telephone handset and asked the operator to connect the call to a particular individual. The operator knew all of the town's business. In 1891, Almon Strowger patented a central office switch where operators were not required to complete each call. Strowger's motivation was privacy: He felt that operators were listening in on his telephone conversations.

What Is a PBX?

A PBX is an on-site telephone system that connects organizations to the public switched telephone network. The central office switch is the precursor to on-site private branch exchange (PBX) telephone systems. A central office switch is centrally located and routes calls between users in the public network. PBXs are private and located within an enterprise.

Just as a central office switch eliminates the need to wire each telephone to every other telephone, with a PBX, each telephone is wired to the PBX—not to each telephone in the company. Because the PBX is wired to the central office, each telephone does not need its own line wire to the central office. In essence, with a PBX, each employee does not have to pay for his or her own telephone line to the local telephone company. Nor are there charges for calls between people in the same office.

According to the Telecommunications Industry Association (TIA), PBX shipments in the United States were down 16% in 2000 and are expected to decline 14% in 2001. Various reasons are attributed to these declines. Some customers might be delaying purchases in anticipation of new IP-enabled PBXs (see Convergence and Telephone Systems later in this chapter). In other cases, customers upgrade existing PBXs rather than purchase completely new ones. Many PBXs can be upgraded to add capacity and new features rather than completely replaced.

The two market leaders in PBXs are Avaya Communications (formerly part of Lucent Technologies) and Nortel Networks. Companies with smaller market shares are Siemens, NEC and Mitel Networks. Mitel Networks was sold off from Mitel Corporation in early 2001 to Terry Matthews, one of its founders. Mitel Corporation will be renamed and is keeping the semiconductor operations. Other suppliers include Fujitsu, Ericsson, Intecom and Hitachi. Cisco Systems is investing in IP-based phone systems, voice messaging and speech recognition to position itself for both voice and data sales to enterprises. Alcatel, the largest provider of PBXs in Europe, has established operations to sell systems in the United States.

PBX Trunks

PBXs are connected to telephone company central offices by trunks that carry calls between the PBX and the telephone company. Depending on the volume of calls generated by the staff, eight to ten users can share each trunk. A PBX with 100 users might share 12 trunks. Most companies use T-1 for their trunking. Instead of having 24 separate pairs of wires, the T-1 can carry 24 incoming and/or outgoing calls on two pairs of wire or on fiber optic cable. Fiber optic cables have the ability to carry multiple T-1s.

Demarcation—The Location Where Telcos Wire Trunks

The local telephone company brings telephone lines into buildings and wires them to interfaces. The interface is called a *jack* or a *punch-down block*. Each outside line is

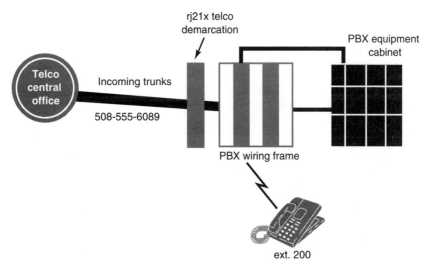

Figure 2.1
A PBX connection to the central office.

punched down (wired) to the connecting block. Jacks that hold one line are called *RJ11c* jacks. The RJ stands for registered jack. These are the jacks found in most homes. The most common interface to which local telephone companies wire multiple outside lines in businesses is the *RJ21x*, which holds 25 lines. The RJ21x jack is a common point from which telephone lines and trunks can be tested. For instance, if there is a question on a repair problem as to where the problem lies, the telephone company can test its trunk to the RJ21x jack and the PBX vendor can test service between the PBX and the interface. The RJ21x jack is the demarcation point between the telephone company line and the inside wiring (see Figure 2.1).

PBX Telephones

Rotary telephones, called *500 sets*, were introduced in 1896. When touch-tone became available in 1963, single-line touch-tone telephones, called *2500 sets*, started being used. (Touch-tone originally was an AT&T brand name for dual tone multi-frequency, or DTMF.) In the 1950s, AT&T started selling electromechanical telephones with up to nine lines on each telephone. A hold button enabled users to put callers on hold to answer multiple calls on the same telephone.

By the 1970s, other manufacturers such as Rolm, initially acquired by IBM, now part of Siemens AG, sold competing PBXs. This was the start of the interconnect industry for customer premise equipment (CPE). On-site telephone systems have become more complex over the years. More features often have been synonymous with more complexity for the end user. Many people in the 1990s were nostalgic for the days when using a phone was as easy as dialing a call and everyone had the same type of "plain vanilla" telephone, and they all worked the same way.

USER-FRIENDLY TECHNOLOGY

The telecommunications industry has made strides in developing affordable, easier-to-use telephones. Features such as conference calling, speed dialing and transfer are available at the touch of a button on the telephone or softkey associated with a liquid crystal display (LCD). LCDs are getting larger and are no longer limited to two-line displays. New ones have eight lines and more displays. Liquid crystal displays have made phones easier to use by:

- Providing context-sensitive prompts such as "Dial the number to which the call will be transferred"
- Including corporate directories so users can dial by name rather than having to know extension numbers
- Displaying the name and/or extension number of the person calling
- Indicating whether calls forwarded to administrative assistants are forwarded because the phone was busy or not answered

Prices of user-friendly phones with feature buttons such as hold, transfer and conference and LCDs have dropped to the point where they are affordable for more employees. This has made it easier for people to use more of the telephone system's features.

Centrex—Telephone Company Supplied Service

The term *Centrex* is derived from the two words "central exchange." In contrast to PBXs, where the switching equipment is located on organizations' sites, Centrex switching equipment is part of the telephone company's central office. Centrex serves only 15% of the total lines in the United States. This statistic was reported in an article titled, "IP Centrex—Are We Ready for It?" published in *Voice 2000,* supplement to Business Communications, page 42, May 2000, by Robert A. Gable. Many local telephone companies are not investing heavily in new Centrex functionality such as IP service. They are concentrating more of their efforts on high-speed data networking and cellular where they see more revenue potential.

The first fully automated Centrex system was installed in 1965 at Prudential Life Insurance Company in Newark, New Jersey. The original motivation for Centrex is much the same as the motivation behind such automated services as voice mail today. Organizations wished to save money on operators, administration and space. Centrex provided four ways of realizing these savings:

- No requirement for on-site switching equipment. The main Centrex switching equipment is in the telephone company's central office.
- Direct-inward dialing to telephone users, saving money on operators to answer calls.
- Direct-outward dialing without having an operator place calls.
- Automatic identification of dialed calls. The telephone company bill identifies the telephone extension from which each outgoing toll call was made.

Where Centrex Is Used

Centrex is used by organizations with buildings spread out across a campus. Centrex provides connections between sites so that enterprises do not need to obtain rights of way for cable connections or purchase wireless infrastructure to connect buildings separated by public streets. Campus-type environments include those for:

- Hospitals
- Cities and towns
- Universities
- Large businesses with many buildings in an area

After divestiture when the local Bell telephone companies were split off from AT&T, local phone companies could no longer sell PBXs and key systems. Therefore, they turned to Centrex as a source of revenue. Regional Bell Operating Companies (RBOCs) such as Ameritech (now part of SBC) and BellSouth broadened their marketing of Centrex to the under-100-line market. Marketing campaigns stressed the reliability, ease of growth and phone company maintenance of Centrex for customers.

Centrex Sales Channels

The Regional Bell Operating Companies did not have the marketing expertise to effectively follow through on the preceding strategy. They therefore turned to sales agents as a channel to sell both Centrex and local toll-calling services. Sales agents generally also sell customer premise equipment such as PBXs, key systems, voice mail, cabling installation and equipment maintenance services. Sales agents receive a monthly fee from the local phone company plus extra commissions for installation of services such as T-1 and data communications lines. In return, the sales agent places all of the end users' repair, installation and change orders with the telephone company. They also sell voice mail and feature-rich telephones as a substitute for Centrex's usually plain vanilla phones.

Competitive local exchange carriers (CLECs) also sell Centrex in areas where they have their own central office switches and fiber optic facilities—generally large cities.

Centrex Telephone Sets

Three choices for Centrex telephone sets are:

- Analog sets, the same type available for homes with or without features built into the telephone
- ISDN and proprietary phones with features provided by the central office
- Proprietary telephones with features provided by on-site key service units

The limitation with off-the-shelf analog telephones is that although they might have feature buttons for speed dial, transfer and conference, each holds only one or two lines. If a user with heavy telephone calling requirements needs two lines, he must pay the monthly fee for two Centrex lines.

Customers can get multiline capability that operate off central office intelligence by purchasing ISDN telephones or Nortel's P phones (the "P" stands for proprietary). Integrated Service Digital Network (ISDN) carries voice and data signals on one pair of wires so phones can handle multiple lines and features. (See Chapter 6 for ISDN.) However, ISDN is not available from all central offices and distance limitations prohibit customers far from the central office from having ISDN. The end result is that Centrex customers also often purchase customer premise equipment (key systems) to power user-friendly telephones. These systems generally include voice mail.

Centrex Connections to Central Offices via T-1

T-1, which can carry 24 lines, often is used to transport Centrex service from the telephone company's office to the customer. (See Chapter 6 for T-1.) The telephone company saves money on outside copper cabling when it supplies Centrex service on T-1 lines rather than on individual copper pairs for each Centrex line. For example, it might use one strand of fiber to carry four T-1s capable of carrying 96 (4 × 24) Centrex lines rather than laying 96 pairs of copper wire to a customer's premise.

Key Systems

Key systems are telephone systems for smaller organizations. While there are some technical differences in the way they handle calls, new key systems have all of the features and most of the functionality of private branch exchanges. Key systems generally serve the under-70-user-per site market.

The major difference between key systems and PBXs is the connection between the central office and the key system. Key systems are loop start and PBXs are ground start. With a ground-start PBX, a trunk is seized or grounded by the PBX or central office before a call is sent between the two locations. With a loop-start key system, if a path is available, the call is sent either to the key system from the central office or to the public network from the key system. The line between the customer location and the central office is not seized by the central office before the call is sent. Analog home phones also are loop start, which is why a person can pick up the handset to make a call and find that someone calling them is already on the phone even though the telephone has not rung.

On a key system, dial tone is derived from the central office. A person making an outside call on a key system does not have to dial an access code such as "9." Pressing an outside line button on a key system telephone signals the central office that the end user wishes to make or receive a telephone call. This is the reason key systems have an outside line button to make or receive outside calls and an intercom button for internal calls.

In PBXs, the PBX provides the dial tone to the user. Users dial an access code, usually "9," to make an outside call. The PBX responds to a lifted handset by sending a dial tone to the end user and then requesting that a trunk to the central office be "grounded" or seized to make a telephone call.

New key systems provide most of the functionality of a PBX. In fact, many larger key systems are "hybrid" systems. They can be installed as either key systems with outside lines, or PBXs with grounded trunk connections to the central office and the requirement to dial an access code such as "9" to make outside calls.

Wireless PBX and Key System Telephones— On-Site Mobility

Anyone who has waited for an important telephone call knows that as soon as you step away from the telephone for a coffee break or to take part in a meeting, the call you have been waiting for arrives. Staff such as nurses, warehouse employees and technicians spend more time away from their desks than at their desks. Wireless telephones enable workers to be reached (and interrupted!) at all times if they take their phones with them and turn them on.

PBX and key system wireless telephones are high profit-margin peripherals. The high costs, about $2000 per telephone, have limited the number of wireless telephones sold. The telephones have the features associated with the PBXs and key telephone systems with which they work. These features include:

- Hold buttons
- Speed dial buttons that enable abbreviated dialing of frequently called numbers
- The same extension number for both the wireless and desk telephone
- LCD screens to show the name of the person calling
- Voice mail message waiting lights

The structure of in-building wireless systems resembles cellular service described in Chapter 9. In-building systems consist of base stations, cards in the telephone system and antennas. However, instead of being connected to a mobile switching office (cellular central office), the base station is connected to the PBX. Base stations and antennas are located on every floor (see Figure 2.2). The base stations are wired to radio controller circuit cards in the telephone system cabinet. Each circuit pack supports two to four base stations. Base stations generally support four antennas. Like cellular systems, base

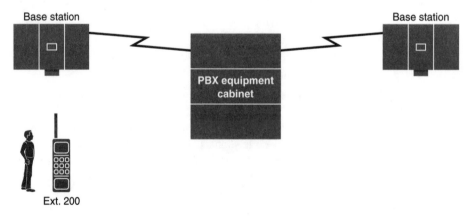

Figure 2.2
In-building wireless telephones.

stations hand off calls to nearby antennas and base stations as workers move around the building. Because in-building base stations cover smaller areas, their coverage areas are referred to as picocells. *Picocell* refers to very small cell sizes.

Outdoor antennas are available for coverage between buildings on a campus. All buildings need to be connected to the same telephone system for this arrangement to work. An engineering study needs to be conducted to determine placement of antennas.

Limited-Range Cordless Phones

Many PBX and key system suppliers provide lower priced "home type" or proprietary 900-megahertz (MHz) wireless phones. Limited-range cordless phones do not work on an in-building cellular structure previously described. The phones only work within range of the antenna in the phone and the phone's base unit. The 900-MHz phones have a range of about 125 to 150 feet, depending on building conditions. There also is an upper limit of about 20 cordless phones supported in the same building.

Proprietary cordless phones have features powered by the phone system to which they are connected. These features, voice mail message lights, multiple call appearances and hold buttons, make the phones easier to use and more functional. In-building wireless phones are used for the following personnel who often use headsets with their phones:

- Console operators, to be able to take calls when they step away from their desk for functions such as making copies
- Warehouse employees
- Retail store personnel who can take calls from anywhere in the store
- Call center agents
- People who work at home

In-Building Wireless Connections to Public Cellular Networks

There are systems on the market in which users can receive cellular calls on their PBX phones. This enables them to use one telephone number for all business calls and check one voice mail system for messages. Unanswered calls to both cellular and PBX phones are answered by the same PBX voice mailbox. The PBX senses when it is out of range for internal PBX calls, which are then sent to the cellular network.

AT&T Wireless and Nextel have offerings that let employees receive four-digit PBX and key system calls on their digital cellular phone. The service works on their

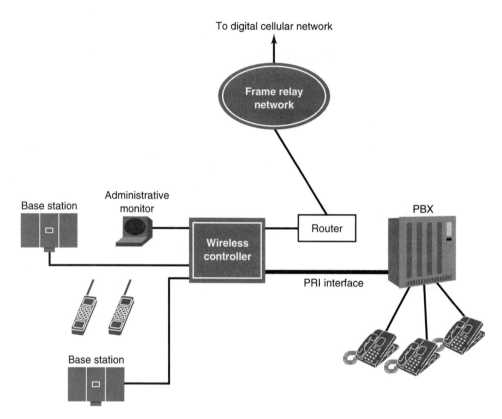

Figure 2.3
In-building Wireless Service

cellular phones in their building (but away from their desk) and, when they are out of their building, in an area with digital AT&T Wireless and Nextel service. The AT&T system uses signaling bits in the TDMA digital control channel to notify the cellular network that the subscriber is part of a particular organization. Calls made within the customer building are routed through the PBX and do not incur cellular air-time fees.

The in-building system is made up of the following devices as depicted in Figure 2.3:

- Picocells located throughout a building contain antennas (transmitter and receiver) and a base station. They are connected to the system controller.

- A controller located adjacent to the PBX. A serial port connects the controller to the PBX by a Primary Rate Interface (PRI) ISDN link. PRI ISDN are digital trunks with 23 voice/data channels and one signaling channel.

(See Chapter 6 for PRI ISDN.) The signaling channel carries information about the cellular user's telephone status and dialing. The controller manages network configuration, controls operation of the picocells and is used for maintenance, billing and provisioning.

- A system administration computer connected to the controller.

- Cellular calls and billing information are routed to the PBX from the on-site controller connected to the network by a Frame Relay data communications link. Frame relay service provides access to carriers' data networks. (See Chapter 6 for Frame Relay service.)

Ericsson, Hughes Network System, Inc., Ascendent Telecommunications and AG Communications manufacture in-building wireless systems that let employees use one number for in-building and cellular digital calls. AT&T Wireless and Nextel sell these products to end users. Siemens is close to offering a product in the United States and Alcatel sells a Global System for Mobile Communications (GSM)-based system in Europe. (See Chapter 9 for a description of GSM cellular service.)

Direct-Inward Dialing—Bypassing the Operator for Incoming Calls

Direct-inward dialing (DID) was a major innovation for handling incoming calls. DID routes incoming calls directly to a PBX or key system telephone without operator intervention. Before the late 1980s, local telephone companies priced DID so high that only large organizations purchased it. Pricing has been lowered considerably, and now small organizations use direct-inward dialing.

Organizations purchase groups of "software" telephone numbers. As Figure 2.4 illustrates, these numbers share trunks. Each number is not assigned a specific trunk. Depending on the traffic requirements at the site, there generally is one trunk per eight to ten DID numbers. The central office looks at the number dialed on the incoming call and identifies it as belonging to a particular organization. The central office then passes the last three or four digits of the dialed number to the organization's key system or PBX. The on-site telephone system reads the digits and passes the call directly to the correct telephone.

Most medium and large companies receive their DID calls over the same T-1 used for their other incoming and outgoing calls. (See Chapter 6 for T-1.) Instead of separate media for each type of service, all services share the same wires, fiber optic cable or fixed wireless service. (See Chapter 4 for fixed wireless service.) For backup purposes, customers may leave a few telephone numbers on individual analog lines or order T-1 from multiple carriers. In the case of a T-1 failure, calls can be routed on the individual analog or the backup T-1 lines.

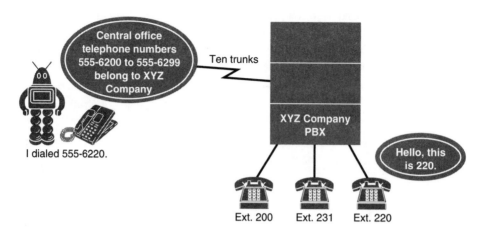

Figure 2.4
Direct-inward dialing from the central office to each telephone in a
building. There are 10 trunks and 100 software numbers.

Convergence and Telephone Systems

Traditional proprietary PBXs and key systems such as Avaya, Nortel and Toshiba systems, carry circuit-switched voice. Circuit-switched networks save a path in the network for the entire duration of a call. Converged phone systems use voice over IP (VOIP) packet technology. Packet-switched networks send traffic in envelopes of bits called packets. Individual packets to the same address can be sent over different routes depending on traffic on a particular route. Because capacity is not saved for the entire length of a transmission, packets of data and voice can share the same LAN infrastructure. Moreover, packets from multiple sources can be sent on the same "path" during very small pauses between messages. However, if traffic is heavy, the voice quality might be degraded if packets are dropped or delayed because of congestion. For telephone systems that share the LAN, two issues are critical: The LAN must have enough capacity and voice needs to be adequately compressed to travel efficiently over the LAN.

Most people with IP-based phone systems have them connected to the public switched network for the majority of their calls. They use their LAN to carry internal calls. They also can use Frame Relay or other connections to carry VOIP between their own sites. Frame Relay service is a way to access carrier networks for traffic between LANs. They also use these links to transfer customer calls between sites. (See Chapter 6 for Frame Relay service.)

IP-Based Telephone Systems

IP-based telephone systems are installed on standard servers such as Windows NT– or Windows 2000–based servers connected to local area networks (LANs). They share the LAN wiring for switching and routing calls. (See Figure 2.5.) Many companies have unveiled telephone systems that work on organizations' LANs using the IP (Internet Protocol). According to Alan Sulkin as cited in the article titled, "IP-PBXs— More Than Technical Hurdles to Overcome," published in *Business Communication Review*, page 80, April 2001, by Richard A. Kuehn, shipments of IP-based PBXs represented 3.5% of total year 2000 sales. While market penetration is still low, potential of the technology and interest in its benefits are high.

Traditional PBX manufacturers such as Avaya, Alcatel, Siemens and Mitel have equipped their key systems and switches with IP capabilities. Data networking vendors Cisco, with its AVVID Product, and 3Com, with its NBX system, also have premises-based IP solutions for voice. The 3Com system mainly is sold to small locations.

Other vendors of IP-based telephone systems are:

- Shoreline Communications
- Fujitsu
- Sphere
- Vertical
- Nortel

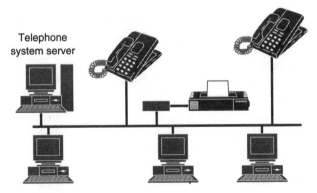

Telephone
system server

Figure 2.5
IP PBX connection to the LAN.

Centrex-Based IP Systems

Telephone companies have announced their intention to offer IP service that customers can use for some employees while retaining their traditional circuit switched Centrex. IP Centrex is available with specialized IP telephones, or *softphones*. Its advantage is that it enables workers to telecommute and to use their phone service when they travel. As long as they can log in remotely to their LAN, their phone service will work if they have a computer or laptop with a microphone. Outside calls to and from Centrex IP would use the public switched network. Gateway devices to convert between circuit switched and IP formats are located at the telephone company offices and are connected to traditional central office switches. It is not currently widely available.

Impetus for IP-Based Phone Systems

The impetus behind IP-based telephone systems is cost savings on hardware, implementation, wiring and the addition of new applications, as well as total cost of ownership. *Total cost of ownership* refers to not only the purchase price but also the cost of a system over its life including maintenance, upgrades and changes. Because IP-based systems operate on standard servers, synergy in staffing may be possible by having the same staff support voice and data networks.

Current PBXs and key systems are based on proprietary protocols and signaling. Adding new applications such as call centers, voice mail and customer service systems to handle Web-originated requests often is costly because of their proprietary nature. An advantage to standards-based products is the development of peripheral products such as "click to talk" service for customer service at Web sites. These enhancements currently require costly links between proprietary PBXs and corporate databases to translate between the unlike platforms. When services work on standards-based platforms, they can interoperate without costly interfaces between them because they use like protocols.

Phones for IP-Based Telephone Systems

IP-based systems support analog phone, multifeatured telephones and softphones. *Softphones* are PC-based phone software that enable users to plug telephone handsets into personal computers. Softphones enable employees to use their PC instead of a phone for telephone calls. Features such as hold buttons, caller ID and message waiting alerts appear on their PC screen. The advantages of softphones are savings on telephone hardware and increased mobility for users. If the software is installed on a laptop, staff can use the softphone anywhere on the corporate network or remotely if remote access is enabled. Because IP systems are in their infancy, not all systems support each of these types of phones.

Each telephone is connected to the organization's local area network. It can share the same telephone cable as the end-user's PC or have its own cable to the wall jack. On some systems, each telephone needs its own power. They can be powered locally or from a power supply in the wiring closet. Most traditional PBX and key system telephones get their power from the telephone system. In a power outage, a two-hour backup of the phone system keeps all of the phones working as well as the telephone system processor.

Voice Quality

Quality of voice on voice over IP (VOIP) systems is improving because of better digital signaling process (DSP) chips and higher capacity LANs with capacity for both voice and data. DSP chips digitize voice and compress it into smaller chunks so that it can be sent on the LAN without disrupting other traffic. Most systems support H.232 and/or Session Initiation Protocol (SIP) VOIP standards. When voice is sent on the LAN, the DSP puts it into packets, which are like envelopes of data. Many of the systems also have ways to give voice priority over data on the LAN to maintain the quality of voice calls.

Barriers to Acceptance

Factors in the slow acceptance of local-area-based phone systems are:

- *Cost*—As is often the case with new technology, initial releases are more expensive than existing technology because of high startup expenses.
- *Reliability*—PBXs and key systems rarely crash. Users are concerned about replicating this reliability on LAN-connected systems. Interestingly, Avaya's small office IP product is based on a proprietary processor board that, according to the article, "More IP-PBX Options," published in *Business Communication Review*, November 2000, page 86, by Alan Sulkin, is more reliable than standards-based servers. Servers are high-capacity computers that store corporate files such as email on LANs.
- *Features*—New systems are just starting to have the features of proprietary PBXs and key systems. To date, many of them don't have the full array of features.
- *Existing installed base of telephone systems*—The average telephone system lasts 10 years. Firms with working telephone systems do not rush to

replace them with new technology. Many telephone systems can be upgraded at a lower cost than buying a total replacement because the upgraded systems reuse certain cards, telephone sets or cabinetry.

IP-based telephone systems have had more initial acceptance by small or startup firms who wish to use their data wiring for both telephone and computer connections. Many of these firms are more open to innovation and don't have legacy proprietary systems. To overcome concerns about reliability of the LANs that support IP-based phone systems, companies sometimes install the system on LANs segregated from their main LAN. If their main LAN crashes, the LAN that supports the telephone system will still operate.

Connecting Telephone Systems to Intracompany IP Networks

Often, customers with private-line, Frame Relay or virtual private network (VPN) connections between their locations use these connections for voice and fax as well as data. (Frame relay and VPN-accessed networks connect locations together via carrier services; see Chapter 6.) If calls are answered in a central location, customer calls are transferred over the voice over Internet protocol (VOIP) links as well. As illustrated in Figure 2.6, the transfers are made by connecting telephone systems to on-site routers. The voice and facsimile traffic use spare capacity in the VPN or private lines. Often, the data connections are upgraded for more capacity to handle voice and fax traffic. The upgrade is less costly than separate T-1s for voice.

At the sending end, the voice is:

- Digitized
- Assembled into packets
- Compressed, or made smaller

At the receiving end, the voice is:

- Put into a format readable by the telephone system
- Reordered into the order in which it was sent
- Decompressed

Voice is converted to IP in gateway devices. Gateways translate protocols so that incompatible devices can communicate with each other. The gateway can be in the telephone system, a separate device or in a router. Gateway functionality in routers is located on cards with digital signal processors in them. For example, Cisco Systems has a voice card that uses Texas Instruments DSPs. The digital signal processor (DSP)

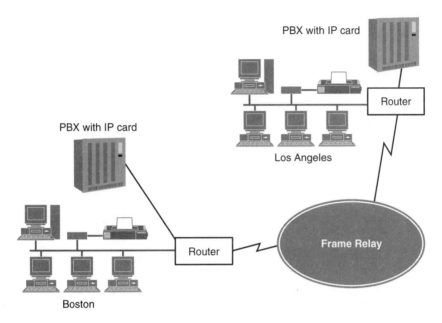

Figure 2.6
PBX connected to an IP network.

compresses the voice from 64,000 bits per second to 8,000 bps. The header adds 4,000 bits per second for a total of 12,000 instead of 64,000 bps.

Certain PBX vendors such as Avaya and Nortel Networks manufacture cards that sit within their telephone systems to convert voice from analog to digitized IP-compatible voice. In this case, the voice can be transmitted from a router not equipped with a voice card. Some gateways have the capability to monitor traffic on IP data lines and route traffic over the public switched network in the event of congestion on the data line.

ADD-ON PERIPHERALS FOR KEY SYSTEMS, PBXS AND CENTREX SYSTEMS ....

Sales of basic on-site telephone systems are extremely competitive and margins are slim. Discounts of up to 40% are common on purchases. Slim margins, the need to raise money and slow growth are among the reasons that Lucent divested itself of Avaya, its PBX and customer premise equipment (CPE) division. Vendors of telephone systems and CPE derive much of their profits in the following areas:

- Maintenance contracts on telephone systems

- Moves, adds and changes of installed-base telephone equipment

- Upgrades to the hardware and software of existing telephone systems

- Feature telephones with built-in speakerphones, feature buttons and liquid crystal displays

- Wireless telephones for PBX and key systems

- Peripheral devices such as voice mail, automatic call distributors and call accounting systems.

Call Accounting—Tracking Calls and Usage

Call accounting systems track each telephone call made by individual users. They provide accountability for call usage. They also indicate the amount of traffic on each telephone line or trunk so that organizations can determine when there are too many or too few outside telephone lines. A large amount of traffic during weekends or nights might indicate hackers are using the system to make free long distance calls. Call accounting systems, also called *station message detail recording* (SMDR) and *call detail recording* (CDR) generally are installed on PCs. The PC is connected through a serial port to the telephone system. An alternative to on-site call accounting systems is the use of service bureaus to collect calling statistics.

Organizations use call accounting reports to:

- Charge time spent on calls back to clients

- Charge calls equitably back to the appropriate internal department

- Determine if hackers are making long distance calls

- Create internal directories

- Make sure agents in credit departments are making the required number of collections calls

Newer call accounting systems are connected to corporate intranets. (*Intranets* use Web technology for internal access to information.) Call accounting systems connected to intranets and LANs enable department managers to download reports in spreadsheet formats if they want to see the calls that their staff made. This obviates the need for telecommunications support staff to print and distribute reports to managers who might have no interest in reviewing them. Call accounting systems also are used to produce corporate directories.

Voice Mail—A Way to Take Messages

Gordon Matthews, the founder of VMX, received the first patent on voice store and forward. VMX's first voice mail system was installed in 1980 at 3M. Octel Communications Corp., founded in 1982 and now part of Avaya Communications, subsequently purchased VMX. Avaya Communications, through its purchase of Octel in 1997, owns the Matthews patent portfolio on basic voice store and forward. All major manufacturers of proprietary and PC-based voice mail systems pay licensing fees to Avaya.

Voice mail systems are changing from plain vanilla to those with unified messaging capability. Unified messaging systems enable users to receive voice mail, email and fax messages from a personal computer or a touch-tone telephone. (See later in this chapter for unified messaging.) TIA (Telecommunications Industry Association) statistics cite year 2000 sales of vanilla voice mail systems at $2.48 billion with a small growth predicted to $2.65 billion in 2001. Because Europe, Asia and Latin America are three to five years behind the United States in voice messaging implementation, many voice mail vendors are having success opening markets overseas. Other strategies they are taking to increase sales are promoting unified messaging and developing systems for cellular and landline-based carriers.

To enhance its premises-based IP telephony offering, Cisco Systems in 2001 purchased Active Voice's unified messaging software that operates on Microsoft Exchange. Active Voice became a privately held company following the sale to Cisco. It retained a product that works on Lotus Notes platforms and is developing a Windows-based product. Figure 2.7 illustrates the way some telephone systems are connected to voice mail systems. Most customers buy voice mail from the same vendor that sells them their telephone system.

Automated Attendants—Machines Instead of Live Operators

Automated attendants are used as adjuncts to company operators. An automated attendant is programmed to answer certain calls to particular telephone lines or departments, for example:

> *"Thank you for calling ABC Company. If you know your party's extension, you may dial it now. For sales, press 1. For customer service, press 2."*

The first automated attendant, manufactured by Dytel, was installed in 1984 to help companies answer calls during peak times. They found, for example, that in slow times such as 8:00 a.m. to 10:00 a.m., operators had too much idle time. However, during the busy hours, operators could not keep up with the call volume. Many orga-

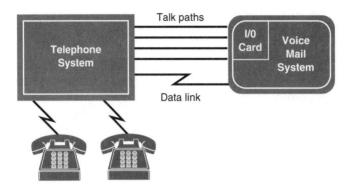

Data Link:

Telephone Number Dialed
Caller ID on internal calls
Messaging Waiting Notification On/Off
No Answer/Busy Notification On Called Party

Figure 2.7
Voice mail connections to a telephone system carry signals
between the voice mail and phone system. In small telephone
systems, the voice mail system may be located within a shelf of the
telephone system.

nizations used automated attendants to answer a special group of telephone numbers
for repeat callers such as vendors, family members and remote employees. Thus, organizations saved money on operators and still answered first-time callers and customers more quickly.

Automated attendants are no longer separate systems. They are software features of voice mail systems. Automated attendant functionality also can be purchased
as a feature of telephone systems, in which the functionality is located on a circuit
packet within the PBX cabinet.

Speech Recognition—Making Automated Attendants More User Friendly

Speech recognition significantly improves automated attendants. It eliminates the
long menus on automated attendants that callers find annoying and cumbersome. (See
Chapter 1 for a discussion of how speech recognition works.) For example, when
someone calls a company with a speech recognition system, instead of hearing,
"Please listen to our menu because our options have recently changed," they might
hear:

> *"Thank you for calling ABCdotcom. Please say the name of the person or depart-
> ment you wish to reach."*

Employees who are traveling or driving don't have to look up telephone extensions—they simply can say the name of the person they want to reach as soon as the system answers. In most automated attendant directories, callers are asked to spell the name of the person they are looking up. With speech recognition systems, callers aren't required to know how to spell names. Speech recognition systems are used in:

- Telephone companies to save on directory assistance salaries
- Internal directories to cut down on the number of employees calling internal operators for extension numbers—this is especially useful in large universities with thousands of students, faculty and staff
- Enterprise organizations such as financial services companies and large companies with many remote salespeople and first-time callers

Organizations that use these systems create a database of names and their associated extensions or, in the case of telcos, telephone numbers. When the speech recognition software recognizes the name spoken, it checks the database for the telephone number. It then either asks the caller if its recognition is correct or transfers the call. When the SpeechWorks International system isn't sure of its recognition, it says, "I think you said Sally Jones; is that correct?" If the system has a high degree of confidence that the name is correct, it repeats the name and transfers the call.

The systems use speech synthesis or prerecorded spoken names for the preceding responses. Speech synthesis translates written names from text to speech. SpeechWorks International, Phonetic Systems and Nuance sell products directly to end users and through partners. Parlance sells systems directly to enterprises and also has a service bureau offering. One of its offerings is one number hospitals can call where they say a physician's name to page him or her. With this system, callers don't have to keep track of numerous pager numbers.

PBX vendors such as Mitel, Siemens, Toshiba and Avaya embed speech recognition in their voice mail products. They license the software from companies such as Nuance and SpeechWorks. Both companies offer speech recognition in many languages. Standalone voice recognition systems not embedded in voice mail are connected to the PBXs by either tie lines or T-1 lines depending on the size of the system. Tie lines are special telephone trunks that support signaling between devices. The speech recognition system sends signals to the phone system telling it the extension to which the call should be transferred. A port connects each caller using the speech recognition system. As soon as the caller is transferred, the port is freed up for the next caller.

Speech recognition is used in the Internet (see Chapter 8), call centers, carrier networks and integrated voice response (IVR) systems. See the following for a description of how these services operate.

Voice Mail Components

The following components make up voice mail systems:

- *Central processing unit (CPU)*—The CPU is responsible for the overall operation of the unit. It executes the application software and operating software that is located in the CPU.

- *Codecs*—These devices convert analog voice to digital signals and digital signals back to analog. Most systems compress voice and take the pauses out of conversations to store voice mail messages on the hard drive more economically.

- *Software*—The software distinguishes one system's features from another system's; for example, the capability to automatically hear the time a message was left rather than having to dial a 7 to hear the time the message was left.

- */O cards*—These printed circuit boards provide the connections between the telephone system and voice mail system. There are usually four ports per board. Each port enables one person to leave or pick up a voice mail message. I/O ports also are used for the receipt and transmission of facsimile messages on systems with voice mail as well as fax mail.

- *Speech recognition cards*—These are specialized cards and software that recognize spoken commands.

- *Other system components*—These include serial ports, scanners, high-speed buses, power supplies and tape and disc drives for system backups.

Unified Messaging—Integration of Voice Mail, Fax Mail and Email

Unified messaging is an optional feature of most new voice mail systems. It provides the capability to retrieve fax, email and voice mail messages from a single device such as a PC (see Figure 2.8). Retrieving messages from PCs gives users the ability to prioritize messages and listen to the most important ones first. It eliminates the need to hear all messages before getting to the critical ones. Systems with only fax and voice mail integration also are considered unified messaging systems. These systems store incoming facsimile messages on the voice mail system's hard drive. When users call in to pick up their messages, the system tells them how many faxes they have. The user can have them printed at their default fax number programmed into the voice mail system or provide the telephone number of a different fax machine. For example, people that travel can receive fax messages at their hotel. In these systems, fax and voice mail notification also can be obtained at the user's computer.

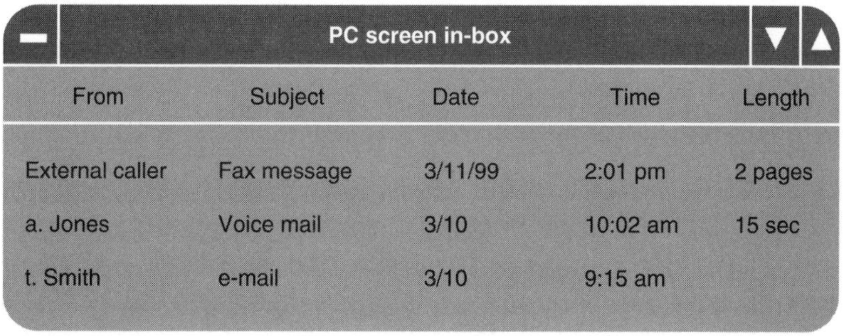

PC screen in-box				
From	Subject	Date	Time	Length
External caller	Fax message	3/11/99	2:01 pm	2 pages
a. Jones	Voice mail	3/10	10:02 am	15 sec
t. Smith	e-mail	3/10	9:15 am	

Figure 2.8
Voice mail, fax mail and email notification from a PC screen.

Unified messaging systems enable users to listen to voice mail and email messages from a touch-tone phone. Speech recognition is available on some systems for retrieval from telephones. On these systems, commands such as delete, rewind and speed up can be spoken and understood. Text-to-speech software converts email to speech for callers and reads their email messages to them. Staffs access messages from the email software on their personal computers. Unified messaging systems need to be compatible with email programs such as Microsoft Exchange, Lotus Notes or HP OpenMail™. Systems typically also support email retrieval from within browsers so remote workers can retrieve all messages from their personal computer. Voice mail messages are heard through the PC's microphone.

> *According to Walt Tetschner, president of Tern Systems, a consultancy in Acton, Massachusetts, 1.8 million of the total 28.2 voice mailboxes shipped in 2000 had unified messaging. Acceptance is held back by the cost of the systems and the organization's perception that it doesn't need these functions.*

In unified messaging, the voice mail and fax messages are stored in the voice mail server that is connected to the LAN and to the on-premise telephone system. Gateway software translates the voice mail and fax messages to Simple Mail Transfer Protocol (SMTP) and multipurpose Internet mail extensions (MIME) so that it is compatible with voice mail and email attachments. See Figure 2.9 for a typical unified messaging connection to the LAN.

When unified messaging systems are connected to LANs, they add voice mail and facsimile traffic to the LAN. To reduce the bandwidth (i.e., capacity) required to transmit voice over LANs, voice mail vendors compress voice to avoid congestion. With compression, the messages require less bandwidth and hard drive space on the local network. Voice mail and facsimile traffic is put into packets before it is transmitted. The packets are similar to envelopes with addressing and error correction in headers plus the messages themselves.

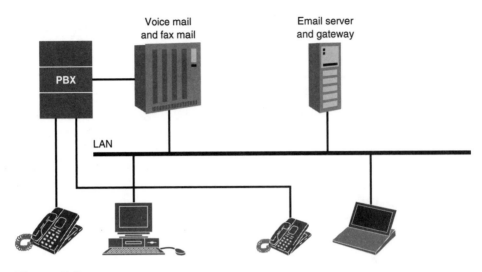

Figure 2.9
LAN connections for unified messaging.

Unified Communications

Unified communications is a term applied to services that go beyond one-device retrieval of faxes, email and voice mail. It also provides integration with short messaging service (short text messages on cellular phones), instant messaging (email chats), "follow me" (one number to reach people wherever they are) and calendaring. Standards are still being developed for unified communications. These services will be available from on-site and service bureaus. (See Chapter 8 for instant messaging and Chapter 9 for short messaging service.)

The vision of unified communications is for people to be reachable (if they so desire) from one phone number and to have the ability to communicate from both wireless and wireline devices.

Voice Mail and Unified Messaging from Service Bureaus and Carriers

In addition to customer-based voice mail, companies such as Comverse Network Systems and its subsidiary Boston Technology, Unisys Corporation, Iperia, Inc., Wildfire, Lucent, Octel and Cisco Systems sell unified messaging and voice mail to telephone companies, cellular carriers, Internet service providers (ISPs) and service bureaus. These companies resell voice mailboxes to the public.

Cellular providers also provide voice mail service. Cellular carriers buy voice mail systems and link them to their cellular mobile-switching office. Cellular-based voice mail is particularly popular in developing countries without cabling infrastructures.

According to Walt Tetschner of Tern Systems, only 1.5 million unified messaging mailboxes were shipped compared to 63.4 million voice messaging mailboxes for cellular service in 2000. Unified messaging as opposed to vanilla voice mail is not being heavily adopted by telephone company customers and is not presently marketed strongly by carriers. Some ISPs offer free email and fax service combinations. Carriers receive revenue for advertising that is played to the owners of the free messaging service. It is not clear if customers will pay for these services if there are monthly fees for them.

Unified Messaging in Mobile Networks

Unified messaging vendors are positioning their offerings to work with advanced cellular networks. They envision customers getting their email, faxes and voice mail from high-speed, data transmission–capable third generation (3G) cellular handsets and laptops with 3G capability. (See Chapter 9 for 3G service.) Service bureaus such as Phone.com and eDial provide, own and manage unified messaging equipment that they connect to cellular carriers' mobile-switching offices. One unified messaging system can support many mobile central offices simultaneously. Signaling system 7 (SS7) links between the voice mail or unified messaging system transmit called-party identification information and other information necessary for billing. Unified messaging systems connected to cellular operators' equipment need to have the following additional capabilities:

- Encryption to scramble data so email messages cannot be intercepted as they are transmitted over the air

- Compatibility with advanced messaging applications such as Lotus Notes and Microsoft Exchange so that people can access their email from computers with these applications

- Ability to convert protocols in wireless devices such as Wireless Application Protocol (WAP) to protocols used in the unified messaging system

- Compatibility with Personal Digital Assistants (PDAs) operating systems such as those used on Palm devices

ACDS—SPECIALIZED EQUIPMENT TO HANDLE LARGE VOLUMES OF CALLS ....

Automatic call distributors (ACDs) are used to manage call traffic and create call center reports. Their most important functions are to save money on call centers' largest expense, agents, and to provide management reports on call volume and agent performance. Departments that use ACDs typically have more calls than people to handle them. Having a machine rather than an operator transfer calls saves about 20 seconds per call. Another saving with ACDs is the consolidation of multiple small groups of agents into fewer large groups as indicated in Figure 2.10.

One large group of agents can handle more calls than the same number of agents scattered throughout small groups. This is analogous to the U.S. Post Office using one long line for postal clerks rather than an individual line for each "agent." With one line for all postal workers, a clerk will free up more quickly from the "pool" and more people will be helped within a given amount of time.

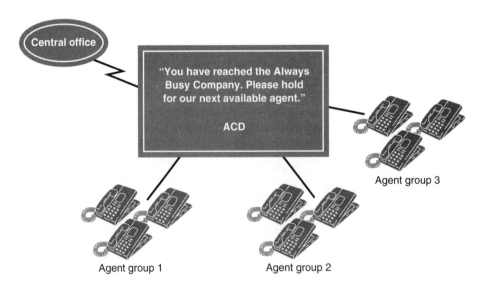

Figure 2.10
An Automatic Call Distributor with three groups of agents. If one group of agents is busy, the ACD can send calls to the second and third groups.

Automatic call distributors (ACDs) perform the following functions:

- Route incoming calls to the agent that has been idle the longest.
- Route incoming calls to the appropriate agent group based on the telephone number dialed or by the customer's telephone number.
- If all agents are busy, either hold the call in a queue, route the call to an alternative group of agents or give the caller the option to leave a voice mail message.
- Enable organizations to locate call centers in any country or part of the world. Cities in India and midwestern parts of the United States are commonly used because of the availability of agents capable of taking phone calls.

Callers to ACDs can recognize when they reach an ACD if they hear a message such as:

> *"All of our agents are busy. Please hold and the next available agent will take your call."*

ACD systems are sold as standalone systems and as add-on software and hardware for PBXs and key systems. The main vendor of standalone systems is Aspect Communications. These systems are aimed at large call centers such as those in the airline and financial services industries. Nortel Networks and Avaya Communications have the largest installed base of PBX-based systems. Most of the larger key systems now offer ACD functionality.

Network-Based ACD Functions

ACD call-routing functionality is available from network service providers as well as with on-site equipment. Network-based services generally are adjuncts to customer premise systems. Network-based call routing enhances functionality without requiring end users to purchase hardware or software for intersite routing. They offer a way to seamlessly route and transfer calls between sites. Network-based services route calls based on:

- Options callers select from a "menu" of selections ("press 1 for sales," etc.)
- Amount of traffic already sent to each location
- Parameters such as time of day or day of the week
- Availability of agents and trunks at each center

Selections from a Menu in Carriers' Networks

The carrier sends the three- or four-dialed number identification service (DNIS) digits associated with menu selections to the on-site ACD identifying the caller's selection. The on-site equipment uses the DNIS digits to route callers to the selected group of agents. For example, DNIS digits 6611 are associated with customer service and DNIS digits 6622 are associated with sales. Network providers generally charge callers a combination of a fixed fee to store menus and a usage fee for every menu selection accessed per month. Toll-free usage charges apply in addition to network routing fees.

LAN/PBX/ACD Connectivity to Enhance Productivity

New ACDs have connections to peripheral devices, the Internet and LANs. They also have links to corporate local area networks for distributing call center reports to managers.

Downloading ACD Statistics to PCs

Reports on real-time status of calls are the lifeblood of an ACD. Downloading ACD statistics is commonly done from PCs connected to local area networks (LANs). Once the information is downloaded, it can be put into a spreadsheet program for manipulation, long-term storage and analysis. Computer- and LAN-to-ACD/PBX connectivity is used to:

- Provide real-time status of incoming and outgoing ACD calls and agents on ACD supervisors' PC screens
- Indicate usage on individual trunks so that managers will know if they have the correct number of lines and that all of the lines are working
- Determine the number of abandoned calls; a high number of abandoned calls is an indication that the call center needs to add staff
- Alert supervisors to unusually high or low call volumes so staffing can be adjusted accordingly

Customer Relationship Management (CRM) for Call Centers

Customer relationship management (CRM) is the ability to offer support to customers over whichever media they use to contact the center. These media include the Internet, telephone and facsimile. According to the MultiMedia Telecommunications Association, as reported in the December 2000 issue of *Business Communications Review*, more than half of all call centers are starting to integrate Web access into their centers.

Call centers need to find ways to:

- Answer callers' questions about products
- Confirm Internet-originated orders and repair reports
- Perform customer service (e.g., returns, credits, exchanges) for Internet inquiries
- Use document sharing to guide customers through Web pages and filling out online forms
- Conduct text-based chats with online customers in real time

Many of the CRM systems provide one integrated queue for email, voice calls and fax messages. Figure 2.11 illustrates this configuration. Specialized software installed on organizations' servers also can recognize email messages by topic and automatically respond to the email. Firewalls screen messages for viruses before they reach LAN-based servers. According to Forrester Research and Giga Information Group, Web self-service generally costs $1 per customer contact. Email contacts range from $3 to $10 and an 800-number telephone contact costs from $10 to $33. Moreover, real-time and historical reports monitor and track calling, response time and, if integrated with back-office systems, revenue per transaction.

Email management in these systems can:

- Route email to a representative trained on the topic in the subject line of the email message
- Create reports based on the number of messages received, by message subject
- Track the number of email messages replied to by each agent

All of the major ACD companies plus Cisco and various software companies offer some type of Web and fax integration.

Connecting specialized packages to ACDs on proprietary PBXs such as those sold by Avaya is costly. Specialized hardware and software is required. The software translates messages between the PBX and the CRM software. These are computer telephony integration (CTI) links described later. In the future, as more customers acquire standards-based, IP telephone systems, the cost of linking specialized CRM solutions to ACDs will be significantly lower.

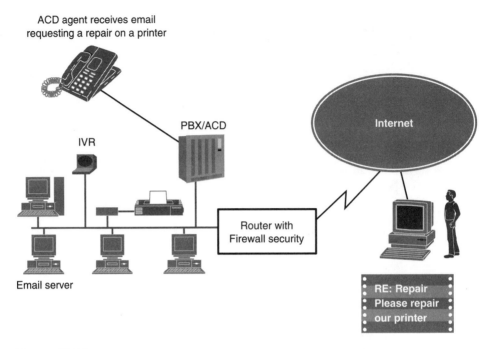

Figure 2.11
Connections between the Internet and call centers.

Integrated Voice Response Units—Using the Telephone as a Computer Terminal

Voice response units respond to DTMF tones (touch-tone) or spoken commands to obtain information from computers. For example, people call their bank or credit card company to find their balance or to learn if a payment has been received. They enter their account number and personal identification number when prompted by an electronic voice. The voice response unit "speaks" back the requested information such as users' bank balances.

Large financial institutions also offer account information retrieval through speech recognition in their integrated voice response (IVR) systems. Companies justify the expense of speech recognition because it means fewer people need to speak with live agents. (The terms *integrated voice response* and *voice response* are used interchangeably.)

Voice response units (see Figure 2.12) enable organizations to provide round-the-clock information to callers without having to pay overtime wages. Manufacturers

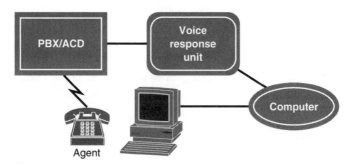

Figure 2.12
A voice response unit connected to an ACD or PBX.

of voice response systems are: Edify, InterVoice-Brite, Phillips through its purchase of Voice Control Systems, Syntellect and Periphonics, which is owned by Nortel Networks. The following are examples of short, simple transactions where voice response technology is used:

- Cable television, to select pay-per-view movies

- Newspapers, to enable subscribers to stop and start papers for vacations and report nondelivery of newspapers

- Mutual fund companies, for trades and account balances

- At airlines (with speech recognition capability) for callers to hear flight information

- Within organizations, so that employees can learn about health and pension benefits

- Universities, for registration and grade reporting

Integrated Voice Response units for voice portals and Web browsing

Speech recognition software installed on integrated voice response (IVR) platforms are used by HeyAnita, Yahoo!, AOL, Tellme, Quack.com (owned by AOL) and BeVocal for voice portals geared toward consumers. *Voice portals* (also known as speech portals) enable people to retrieve information such as weather reports, sports scores and email from Web sites using spoken commands. Some voice portals earn money from advertising played to callers and from cellular carriers who use the service for their own customers.

Informio, Inc. offers a voice portal aimed at business customers. The service lets staff access corporate intranet–located information using audio commands. Informio calls its system a Unified Media Browser™. For example, someone with a wireless Palm pilot can download his or her email by using speech commands. Informio's browsers are located in carrier, large customer and application service provider networks. They translate speech commands to computer commands that they send to servers containing information requested by callers.

Some services such as the AOL voice portal have natural language capability. Natural language systems understand full sentences. For example, AOL says, "Welcome to AOL. What do you want to do today?" AOL uses speech recognition from SpeechWorks International installed on IVR systems. Voice portal IVR systems have connections to computers containing the information callers request. See Figure 2.13. (For more information on speech recognition and VoiceXML, see Chapter 1.)

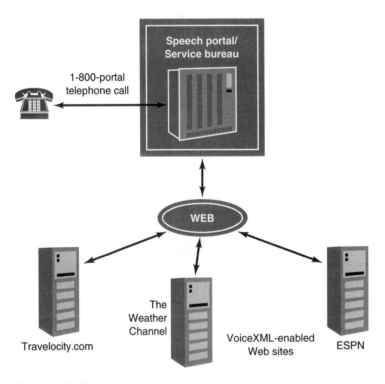

Figure 2.13
Speech portal connected to Web servers. Courtesy of SpeechWorks.

Computer Telephony Integration (CTI)— Routing Callers More Intelligently

Computer telephony integration (CTI), originally available in the late 1980s, is software and hardware that translates signals between telephone systems and computers so that they can coordinate routing calls and account information to agents. For example, the following can be done:

- Route calls to agents based on the caller's telephone number.
- Notify the organization's computers to send the customer's record to the agent handling the call.
- Transfer the customer's record and information on the agent's screen along with calls transferred between representatives.

The motivation for installing these usually expensive systems is to save agent time. Having the account information on the screen, a "screen pop," when the telephone call arrives saves 10 to 20 seconds per call.

The telephone number of the caller can be delivered to an ACD in two different ways:

- Directly from the telephone carrier when the call is received on trunks that capture callers' phone numbers. This functionality is called *automatic number identification* (ANI).
- From voice response systems where callers are asked to enter, for example, their account number.

The computer system matches the telephone number or account number with the caller's records. The computer sends account information to the agent's PC who receives the call. All of the communications between the network and the computer, and the computer and the telephone system are translated by the CTI links. Both the ACD and the computer are connected to the LAN. (See Figure 2.14.) Software in the CTI application is called an *Application Programming Interface* (API). APIs are an interface or "middleware" between unlike devices.

For the most part, because of high costs, only large organizations have implemented CTI applications. Many organizations have purchased computer telephony packages and have not implemented them or have only used them for short periods of time due to the difficulty and expense of implementation.

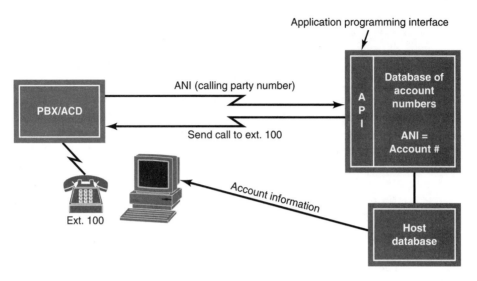

Figure 2.14
Linking ACDs and PBXs to computers.

CRM applications reviewed in the previous section are based on CTI software. They present cookies and IP addresses to computer databases so they can send agents the customer record as well as the message from the Web such as a repair or sales request. (*Cookies* are small text files that sites attach to users' browsers that identify the person's PC.)

MEDIA: WIRELESS, FIBER AND UNSHIELDED TWISTED PAIR COPPER ....

Media (copper, coaxial cable, fiber optics and airwaves) carry voice and data traffic. Characteristics of media have a direct bearing on the speed, accuracy and distance at which traffic can be carried. For example, thin copper lines carry data more slowly than thicker, higher quality copper. Fiber carries vastly more traffic than copper. It is used for high-speed Internet and public switched telephone networks.

Unshielded twisted pair (copper) is the most prevalent medium used to link computers to corporate printers and applications. It also is used to connect telephones to PBXs and key systems. Fiber in enterprise sites is generally used in high-traffic areas such as connections between buildings and floors.

Because it is a nonelectric medium, fiber exhibits superior performance. In contrast to copper, it does not act like an antenna that picks up noise and interference.

New electronics in fiber optic networks are improving fiber's performance. These systems that improve the capacity of fiber are called *wavelength division multiplexing* (WDM) or *dense wavelength division multiplexing* (DWDM).

Wireless is starting to be used to link staff to corporate LANs. LANs connect PCs and devices within buildings for access to email, printers and shared applications. A key attraction of wireless media is the mobility it provides. For example, wireless LANs enable people to use laptops or handheld computers in any location within range of antennas. Prices for wireless LANs are decreasing and interest in using them is increasing. Wireless services including LANs, cellular network and wireless local loops obviate the need to lay expensive cabling. This is particularly important in developing and emerging markets around the world where most of the populations do not have landline telephones.

Wireless as a way to provide local service is called *wireless local loop* (WLL). XO Communications, Sprint and WorldCom sell WLL services. They offer high-speed voice and data connections to commercial buildings in metropolitan areas. Wireless as a medium for local telephone service is discussed in Chapter 4. Cellular service is covered in Chapter 9.

Wireless LANs

Organizations install wireless LANs for the following reasons:

- *The difficulty of pulling wires in existing buildings.* Specialized applications such as engineering and software development often require a second non-Microsoft computer at users' desks. This might require running more cabling.

- *Staff's need to use computers in common areas such as conference rooms, training rooms and cafeterias.*

- *The miniaturization of devices such as laptops and handheld computers that users want to take with them to meetings and training sessions, where there might not be sufficient cabling to accommodate everyone in the area.*

- *Reliance on corporate servers for shared documents (groupware) such as Lotus Notes and intranets* requires that people take their laptops with them to meetings, so they can access corporate data wirelessly.

New wireless LANs work on the Ethernet 802.11b IEEE-specified standard known as Wi-Fi. The agreement by manufacturers to adhere to this standard has resulted in the availability of off-the-shelf, lower cost products. Network interface cards (NICs) that plug into the PCMCIA slot of laptops have dropped from $300 to $150. This is still higher than NICs for wired LANs that typically cost $50. Base stations

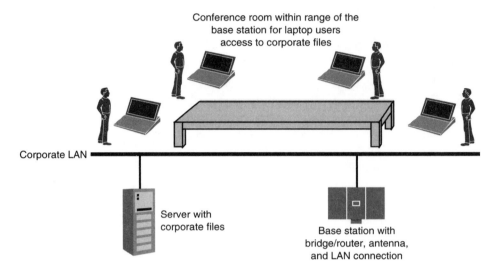

Figure 2.15
Conference room within range of the wireless LAN.

with antennas are integrated with bridges or routers and are wired to the LAN. See Figure 2.15. The bridges and routers provide communications to corporate files and devices on the LAN. Base stations are called access points and cost about $1000. (See Chapter 1 for bridges and routers.) Wireless LAN manufacturers are: Cisco, through its purchase of Aironet, Agere Systems (formerly part of Lucent Technologies), 3Com, Nokia and Ericsson.

In addition to price, security issues hamper Wi-Fi-based LAN sales. In 2001, researchers at the University of California, Intel Corporation and the University of Maryland all reported on security flaws in the 802.11b standard. The flaw is serious and lets people eavesdrop on corporate networks and even get email addresses of legitimate users from which they can forge their own address. Products currently on the market to improve the 802.11b security also are reported to have serious flaws. A special industry task force has already begun circulating draft revisions of new security standards. Products based on new security standards are expected to be available in 2002.

The top speed on 802.11b LANs is 11 million bits per second. This is adequate for most nonmultimedia, engineering and imaging applications. However, speeds can degrade as users get farther away from base stations, and interference from metal in floors or doors can degrade service. New 802.11g and 802.11a standards are expected, which will increase the capacity and speeds of wireless LANs. 802.11g-compatible products are expected by 2002, and 802.11a-compatible products are expected by year-end 2001.

Wireless LAN Connections in Public Places

Wireless LANs based on Wi-Fi are being installed in public places, such as coffee shops (Starbucks), airports and hotels. People who sign up for this service with Internet service providers, such as MobileStar and Wayport, can use their laptop computer to access the Internet and email messages from these locations. The 802.11b wireless LAN installed in the coffee shop or airport is connected to the Internet via a high-speed connection, for instance, a T-1 line. Subscribers need an 802.11b wireless LAN card. They also must sign up for Internet service from an ISP who arranges for connectivity to the Internet from the airport or coffee shop. After it leaves the public place, the data is carried over landline-based networks. The traffic is not transmitted on cellular networks.

Electrical Properties of Copper Cabling

The electrical properties of copper cabling create resistance and interference. Signals weaken the farther they are transmitted on copper wires. The electrical property of copper cabling is the key factor that limits its transmission speeds.

Signals sent over copper wire are, for the most part, direct-current electrical signals. Signals near these wires can introduce interference and noise into the transmission. In particular, copiers, magnetic sources, manufacturing devices and radio stations all can introduce noise. It is not uncommon for office and residential users to complain that they can hear a nearby radio station's programming on their telephone calls. This is the result of interference.

Within homes and businesses, crosstalk is another example of "leaking" electrical transmissions. In homes with two lines, a person speaking on one line often can hear the faint conversation on the other line. Current from one pair of wires has "leaked" into the other wire. One way in which copper cabling is protected from crosstalk and noise introduced from nearby wires is by twisting each copper wire of a two-wire pair. Noise induced into each wire of the twisted pair is canceled at the twist in the wire. Twisted pair copper cabling is used from:

- Telephone sets to PBX common equipment
- Telephone sets to key systems common equipment
- PCs to the wiring closet of a LAN
- Homes to the nearest telephone company equipment

Category 5 Unshielded Twisted Pair—Cat 5

Unshielded twisted pair copper cabling is used to connect individual telephones and PCs to in-building telephone systems and local area networks. Organizations often install category 5 cabling for both voice and data rather than paying technicians to lay one set of cables for data and another set for voice.

Twisted pair cabling and connection components used inside buildings are rated by the Electronics Industry Association/Telecommunications Industry Association (EIA/TIA). In 1992, standards were published for category 5 unshielded twisted pair for data transmitted within buildings at 100 megabits per second (Mbps). Category 5 is the most common twisted pair cabling used within buildings for data. The standard refers to not only the cable but to all of the connections including jacks, plugs and cross connects in wiring closets. Cross connects in wiring closets tie all of a floor or section of a floor's cabling to cabling that runs between floors in the risers. Category 5 is commonly referred to as cat 5. Category 3 unshielded twisted pair is rated as suitable for voice transmission.

Category 6 Unshielded Twisted Pair

Category 6 cabling capable of carrying data at gigabit speed is now available. However, the International Standards Organization/International Electrotechnical Commission (ISO/IEC) has draft specifications for category 6 but has not yet approved the standards. Category 6 cabling requires cables, jacks, and wiring closet connectors to all meet the specifications for category 6 for gigabit speeds. Two problems exist with category 6 cabling: Without standards, customers cannot mix and match cabling from one manufacturer with plugs and RJ-45 jacks [registered jacks for data with connections for eight (four pairs) wires] from other manufacturers. The same applies to wiring closet connectors. The second problem is that customers who plug category 6 cabling into category 5 jacks might not even achieve category 5 performance because of electrical mismatches between the two standards.

Cable currently on the market has the same weight as category 5; however, it is manufactured under more strict guidelines. In essence, it is tested more precisely for characteristics such as near- and far-end crosstalk and jitter. *Jitter* is caused by uneven electrical or mechanical changes. It results in "bumpy" or disruptive transmissions.

Category 6 cable also is referred to as category 5 – level 7 cabling. Standards boards also are considering category 7 standards for even higher performance for twisted pair copper cabling.

Fiber Optic Cabling—High Capacity and High Costs

Fiber optic cabling is immune to electrical interference. Signals are transmitted in the form of off and on light pulses similar to a flashlight. No electricity is present in transmissions over fiber. Thus, signals carried on strands of fiber do not interfere with each other. Therefore, fiber can be run in areas without regard to interference from electrical equipment. Other benefits of fiber are:

- **Security**—Fiber is resistant to taps and does not emit electromagnetic signals; therefore, to tap into fiber strands, the strands have to be physically broken and listening devices spliced into the break. These splices are easily detected.

- **Small size**—Less duct space is required; individual strands of fiber are the diameter of a length of hair. Duct size is particularly significant under city streets where underground conduit is at capacity, filled with old copper cabling.

- **High bandwidth**—Fiber is suitable for new high-speed transmission services such as terabit routers.

- **Low attenuation**—There is less fading or weakening of signals over distances, which means fewer amplifiers are needed to boost the signals.

- **The absence of sparking hazards** in flammable areas results in less danger of fire.

- **Single conductor fiber** weighs nine times less than coaxial cable.

Disadvantages of fiber optic cabling include:

- *Termination, component and connector costs are higher than for copper wiring.* Specialized equipment is required to terminate fiber cables within buildings, test and splice fiber and to convert electrical signals to light pulses and vice versa.

- *More care in handling fiber is needed.* In particular, fiber is not as flexible as twisted pair in bending around corners.

- *When fiber is brought into buildings from telephone companies or to the curb in residential areas, local electrical power is required.* This adds a point of vulnerability in the event of a power outage.

- *Specialized technicians, who might be paid at higher levels, often are required to work with and test fiber cabling.*

According to Corning Incorporated's *Just the Facts* (p. 2, July 1995):

> *The first practical fiber systems were deployed by the telephone industry back in 1977 and consisted of multimode fiber. Single-mode fiber, a more recent development was first installed by MCI in a long-haul system that went into service in 1983.*

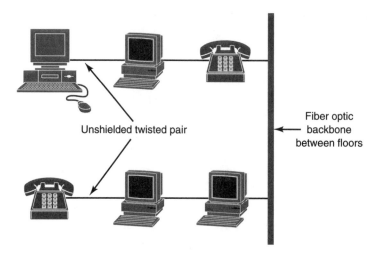

Figure 2.16
Unshielded twisted pair and fiber optic cabling within a building.

Instead of using wide-diameter conduit (pipes) to carry fat lengths of copper or coaxial cabling between buildings or floors, organizations lay thin strands of fiber optic cabling capable of transporting vast amounts of voice and data between buildings or floors within a building.

Individual organizations often use fiber cabling:

- For the riser, between floors within a building portion of their networks (see Figure 2.16.) The extra expense of laying fiber, however, is usually not justified to individual users and devices on LANs.

- In campus environments, for cable runs between buildings.

Many long distance networks are completely fiber. Fiber's greater capacity and higher speeds justifies the added expense. Telephone companies use fiber because they can lay fewer strands of fiber in less space than heavier copper, which requires many more pairs to achieve the same capacity as fiber optic cabling. Moreover, signals can travel farther, in the range of 60 miles, on fiber without the use of amplifiers to strengthen a faded signal. The requirement for fewer amplifiers translates into lower maintenance costs: There are fewer amplifiers to break down.

Other places fiber is used are:

- Between central offices in local telephone company networks
- From local and long distance phone companies to office buildings

- Between central offices and neighborhood wire centers
- In Internet service provider networks
- In the backbone of cellular networks
- Between cellular networks and landline networks
- For undersea cable runs between continents
- In backbone cable TV (CATV) networks (between the cable company headbands and neighborhood coaxial cable wire centers); see Figure 2.17
- In electric utility networks

Fiber optic cabling is made of ultrapure strands of glass. It carries on and off light pulses over the central core of the fiber. The more narrow the core, the faster and farther a light signal can travel without errors and repeaters. The cladding surrounding the core keeps the light contained within the core to prevent the light signal from *dispersing*, that is, spreading and losing strength. Finally, there is a coating, which protects the fiber from environmental hazards such as rain, dust, scratches and snow.

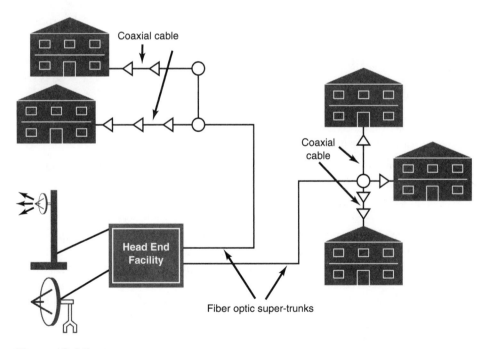

Figure 2.17
Hybrid fiber coaxial (HFC) cabling for cable TV networks.

Single-Mode Fiber—Smaller Is Faster and More Expensive

There are two different types of fiber: single-mode and multimode. Single-mode fiber is smaller, more expensive and supports faster speeds than multimode fiber. Single-mode fiber is the diameter of a strand of hair. Telephone companies, cable companies, ISPs and transoceanic cabling use the more expensive, higher capacity, single-mode fiber optic cabling.

The fact that single-mode fiber carries light pulses faster than multimode fiber can be explained by the geometric rule: A straight line is the shortest distance between two points.

If a person sticks to a straight line over the course of a race, she will get to the end of the race faster than if she zigzagged along the track. Similarly, the small core of the fiber keeps the light signal from bouncing across the diameter of the core of the fiber. Thus, the light signal travels faster than if it had a more "bouncy" ride through the core. Because it travels in a straighter line, the light pulses go farther without attenuation, or weakening. Thus, fewer repeaters are needed to boost the signal. Single-mode fiber can be run for 60 miles without the use of a repeater. In contrast, copper cabling needs to be repeated after approximately 1.5 miles. This is the reason telephone companies use fiber in residential areas with cable runs longer than 2 kilometers, or 1.24 miles.

The main factor in the increased expense of single-mode fiber is the cost of splicing and connecting it to patch panels and other devices. The core is so small that connections and splices need to be done in a more exacting manner than with multimode fiber. If fiber connections on single-mode fiber do not match cores exactly, the light will not be transmitted from one fiber to another. It will leak or disperse out of the core at the splice.

Multimode fiber is used mainly for LAN backbones between buildings on campuses and between floors of buildings.

Dense Wavelength Division Multiplexing (DWDM)

The importance of dense wavelength division multiplexing (DWDM), also called wavelength division multiplexing (WDM), cannot be exaggerated. It is a key technology for providing the capacity to carry traffic associated with applications such as e-commerce, multimedia email, voice over IP (VOIP) and World Wide Web browsing. It is an important part of the infrastructure for voice, high-speed data, streaming video and streaming audio. (See Chapter 1 for an explanation of streaming media.)

DWDM provides the following advantages:

- Higher capacity over fewer strands of fiber

- Lower costs to upgrade networks, because multiplexed speeds up to 10 gigabits per channel can be achieved by changing electronics but reusing old fiber cabling (newer fiber supports higher speeds)

- Space savings in service providers' networks because less amplifying equipment is required

- Lower ongoing maintenance expenses in carriers' networks because less equipment is required

DWDM technology provides long distance networks with immense improvements in capacity. It is a multiplexing technique that enables single strands of fiber to carry multiple channels of voice and data. Early implementations of wavelength division multiplexing (WDM) carried eight channels over a single strand of fiber. By the end of 1998, DWDM multiplexers carried 40 channels at 2.5 gigabits per channel. Capacity is expected to reach 200 channels at 10 gigabits per channel on a single strand of fiber by year-end 2001. This equals 2000 gigabits (billions of bits per second), or 2 terabits per second. These four-fold increases in the number of wavelengths and the speed of each wavelength cost only two and a half times as much as the previous DWDM systems. Thus the cost per unit of bandwidth decreases.

Dense wavelength division multiplexers work like prisms, separating out colors into different beams that are carried on the fiber. WDM divides the light stream into multiple frequencies called colors. Each color or shade is carried at a different frequency. (See Chapter 1 for an explanation of frequencies.) The individual wavelengths also are called *lambdas*.

Wavelength Division Multiplexing (WDM) Components

Connecting fiber to copper lines requires converters called transmitters and receivers to convert electrical signals to light pulses. Transmitters also are called light source transducers. Transmitters in fiber optic systems are either light-emitting diodes (LEDs), or lasers. Lasers are more expensive than LEDs but they provide more power so that the light signals need less amplification, or boosting, over long distance. One laser is required per wavelength. LEDs are commonly used with multimode fiber.

At the receiving end, the light detector transducers (receivers) that change light pulses into electrical signals are either positive intrinsic negatives (PINs) or avalanche photodiodes (APDs). LEDs and PINs are used in applications with lower bandwidth and shorter distance requirements. Once a length of fiber is in place, upgrades in multiplexing technology enable the embedded fiber to carry information at higher speeds.

The multiplexers enable gigabit speeds and multiple applications to share fiber strands.

Amplifiers and Regenerators

Amplifiers and multiplexers are key components of DWDM networks. Amplifiers boost the signals and multiplexers combine light from multiple sources onto a single strand of fiber.

- Optical amplifiers are spaced approximately 60 miles apart from each other. The amplifier boosts the signal, which loses strength as it travels over distances. (In a voice conversation, voice signals sound softer when they lose strength and need to be amplified.) They were first installed in 1990. Prior to that, optical signals first had to be converted back to electrical signals to be regenerated. Without optical amplifiers, both regenerators and multiplexers are required every 30 miles. This results in more expensive equipment in the network and more space needed in network-based equipment huts. Now optical amplifiers only are required every 60 miles.
- Regenerators are placed approximately every 1500 miles. They *multiplex* (combine) and *demultiplex* (separate out) the optical signals. The signals are converted from optical to electrical signals for functions such as electrical clocking, noise removal, and error checking. The multiplexers *concatenate* the signals, a technical term for putting the signals into the correct sequence.

The increased capacity of DWDM is one factor in the bandwidth glut that now exists in carriers' backbone, city-to-city networks. The benefit is that prices on these routes are continuing to decline.

Part 2

Industry Overview

3 The Bell System and Regulatory Affairs

In this chapter...

The regulatory events now occurring in the rest of the world mirror past events in the United States. The following events, which took place in the United States starting in 1984, reflect what is happening across the world as other countries deregulate to promote investments in telecommunications:

- Elimination of artificially high long distance prices that subsidize local rates and make local telephone service available at lower costs to the residents
- Deregulation of the long distance markets, opening them to competition
- Regulations that divest local telephone companies from ownership by long distance companies
- Requirements that incumbent local telephone companies allow competitors to connect to their facilities at reasonable rates in a timely manner

The 1984 divestiture separated AT&T and the local Bell Operating Companies (BOCs) into separate organizations. This was done to ensure that the local telephone companies provided the same quality connections to AT&T's competitors, other interexchange carriers, as it gave AT&T. These connections were necessary to transport calls between long distance networks and local homes and businesses. This separation spurred competition in long distance services.

Seven Regional Bell Operating Companies (RBOCs) were created at the 1984 divestiture. The RBOCs were made up of AT&T's 22 former local Bell Operating Companies. Following passage of the Telecommunications Act of 1996, the seven RBOCs decreased in number to four. Interexchange carrier Qwest purchased U S West and all the others except BellSouth merged. In addition, SBC and Verizon each purchased large independent incumbent telephone companies. Verizon bought the largest independent telephone company, GTE, and SBC bought Southern New England Telecommunications (SNET). SNET is the incumbent telephone company in Connecticut. (Independent phone companies are incumbent telephone companies not previously owned by the Bell system.)

Local competition in telecommunications emerged in the 1980s. Competitive access providers (CAPs) initially provided fiber optic links between customers in major metropolitan areas and interstate long distance providers. The purpose of these links was to connect long distance vendors to local customers without the hefty access fees charged by local telephone companies to long distance carriers. Having fiber optic links in place in major metropolitan areas has enabled CAPs to expand their offerings. They became competitive local exchange carriers (CLECs) and started offering additional services leveraging their investment in fiber optic cabling.

CLECs sell data services, Internet access and local toll calling to business and residential customers, although most of their sales are to business customers in urban areas. Competitive local exchange carriers route calls over a mix of their own fiber optic and wireless facilities as well as over facilities they buy at a discount from local telecommunications companies. They have, in essence, become a combination of local exchange carrier (LEC), interexchange exchange carrier, data communications vendor and Internet access providers.

The Telecommunications Act of 1996 allows telephone carriers, utilities and cable TV companies to sell both local and long distance calling. It also deregulates cable television. Prior to the Act, in most states, interexchange carriers (IEXs) such as AT&T, WorldCom and Sprint were allowed to sell only long distance services, and local telephone companies were restricted to local services. When Congress passed the Telecommunications Act, many legislators thought competition would promote development of new high-speed services. Long distance carriers lobbied for the Act in hopes of expanding sales of local services. Bell telephone companies lobbied for passage of the Act as a way to offer long distance and data services on an interstate basis. In contrast to divestiture, the Telecommunications Act of 1996 did not mandate that the local telephone companies form separate companies to supply connections to the very companies formed to compete with them. This has been a major factor inhibiting competition for local service.

In the years following passage of the Act, the Regional Bell Operating Companies challenged its legality in the courts. The courts denied the validity of these challenges. However, economic conditions and incumbents' delays in processing competitors' requests for services proved more effective in the battle for dominance in local services. Competitors have made the largest inroads by selling service to business customers in large cities. For the most part, the only viable alternative for residential local telephone service is from cable TV providers.

THE BELL SYSTEM PRIOR TO AND AFTER 1984 ....

The telecommunications landscape has changed radically since 1984 when AT&T had a near monopoly on telephone service. In the United States competition for sales of telephone systems started in the 1960s. However, the most dramatic impetus for competition for long distance service occurred in 1984.

Divestiture of the Bell System from AT&T in 1984

Divestiture was designed to open competition for long distance not local service. Before 1984, the Bell system consisted of 22 local Bell telephone companies that were owned by AT&T. *Customers had one point of contact for all of their telecommunications requirements.* AT&T, with its 22 Bell operating companies:

- Sold local, interstate and international long distance
- Manufactured and sold central office switches, customer premises telephone systems, electronics and consumer telephones
- Provided yellow and white page telephone directories

AT&T's control of local central offices hampered competition in long distance. For example, carriers such as MCI (now part of WorldCom) and Sprint that wished to compete against AT&T in New York City needed connections provided by the AT&T subsidiary, New York Telephone Company, to complete calls to New York residents.

Interexchange long distance companies, such as Sprint, owned network facilities between Boston and New York City on which it carried calls. It had no lines to individual homes and businesses. Local Bell telephone company lines and central office facilities were required to carry calls from an individual subscriber to Sprint's long distance facilities. Calls could not reach the interexchange carriers' networks without connections to local telco's central offices. The local telephone companies at this time (prior to 1984) were owned by the very organization, AT&T, with which the new carriers competed. Access to AT&T's local telephone companies by competitive carriers such as Sprint is illustrated in Figure 3.1.

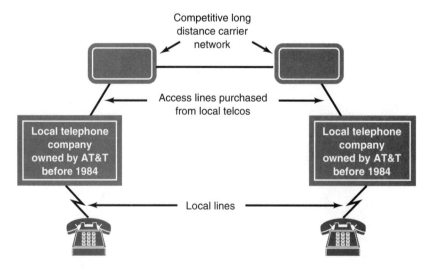

Figure 3.1
Interconnection for local access.

By 1974, so many complaints had been filed by long distance competitors with the Justice Department about AT&T's lack of cooperation in supplying connections to local phone companies that the Justice Department filed an antitrust suit against AT&T. In 1984 the suit was resolved. The Justice Department divested AT&T of its 22 local phone companies. The resolution of the Justice Department case against AT&T is known as the Modified Final Judgment, or divestiture. Ownership of the 22 local phone companies was transferred from AT&T to seven Regional Bell Operating Companies (RBOCs). The seven RBOCs at that time were: (The indented companies are the former 22 Bell telephone companies.)

- Ameritech
  - Michigan Bell Telephone Company
  - Ohio Bell Telephone Company
  - Indiana Bell Telephone Company
  - Illinois Bell Telephone Company
  - Wisconsin Bell Telephone Company
- Bell Atlantic
  - New Jersey Bell Telephone Company
  - Bell Telephone Company of Pennsylvania
  - Diamond State Telephone Company
  - Chesapeake and Potomac State Telephone Company of Virginia
  - Potomac State Telephone Company of Maryland
  - Potomac State Telephone Company of West Virginia
  - Potomac State Telephone Company of Washington, D.C.
- BellSouth
  - Southern Bell Telephone Company
  - South Central Bell Telephone Company
- NYNEX
  - New England Telephone Company
  - New York Telephone Company
- Pacific Telesis
  - Pacific Bell Telephone Company
  - Nevada Bell Telephone Company
- Southwestern Bell Communications (SBC Communications)
  - Southwestern Bell Telephone Company
- U S West
  - Mountain Bell Telephone Company
  - Northwestern Bell Telephone Company
  - Pacific Northwest Bell Telephone Company

The seven Regional Bell Operating Companies (RBOCs) retained the Bell logo and the right to sell local and toll calling within local areas. They also retained the lucrative white and yellow page directory markets. However, they were denied the right to manufacture equipment. A centralized organization, Bellcore, owned jointly by the RBOCs, was formed. This centralized organization had two functions: It was a central point for National Security and Emergency Preparedness, and it was a technical resource for the local telephone companies. As part of its technical resource services, it administered the North American Numbering Plan (e.g., it coordinated allocation of area codes); (Bellcore has since been renamed Telcordia Technologies, Inc. and in 1997 was purchased by Fortune 500 company Science Applications International Corporation, or SAIC.)

AT&T retained the right to manufacture and sell telephone and central office systems and to sell interstate and international long distance. AT&T kept Western Electric for manufacturing and Bell Labs as its research arm. In 1996, AT&T spun off Lucent Technologies and NCR. Lucent kept Bell Labs and Western Electric and the central office, networking and customer premise equipment (CPE) divisions. NCR retained the computer systems and services business. In September 2000, Lucent spun off its customer premises business to newly formed Avaya Inc.

From 1984 to 1996, the Bell companies sold basic services such as local and intra-state long distance services. On March 7, 1988, U.S. District Court Judge Harold Greene lifted some line of business restrictions against the Bells. He allowed them to offer enhanced services, which employ computer processing to act on subscriber-transmitted information. Examples of enhanced services are voice mail, audiotext ("Press 1 to hear about skiing conditions," etc.) and electronic mail services. In exchange, the Bell System opened up more than 100 network features to competitors so that competitors could offer network-based voice mail in conjunction with Bell features. These features include call forwarding on busy and no answer to competitive vendors' voice mail.

Regional Bell Operating Companies (RBOCs) after 1996

The Telecommunications Act of 1996 opened Bell territories to competition from long distance vendors, cable companies, local access providers and utility companies. In anticipation of the requirement for capital to expand into markets opened by the Telecommunications Act of 1996 and to compete in their own territories more effectively all of the RBOCs except BellSouth were involved in mergers. SBC purchased Pacific Telesis and Ameritech. Bell Atlantic bought NYNEX and GTE. In 2000, Qwest Communications, a long distance carrier, completed a merger with U S West. It sold its long distance business in the U S West territory to TOUCHAMERICA Inc., a

LATAs Defined

In 1984, in conjunction with divestiture, the Justice Department created local access and transport areas (LATAs). LATAs define the contiguous geographic areas in which local Bell telephone companies are allowed to sell local and long distance services. Calls between the 197 LATAs are carried by interexchange carriers and competitive local exchange carriers (CLECs). Local exchange carriers were allowed to carry calls within LATAs. States with small populations such as Maine, Alaska and Wyoming are made up of one LATA. Thus, Qwest (formerly U S West), the Bell company serving Wyoming, is allowed to provide long distance to all sites within Wyoming. California has eleven LATAs and New York State has eight.

Local toll calling is long distance within a LATA. The concept of a local Bell being allowed to transport toll calls within a local area is confusing. For example, there are three LATAs in the Qwest (formerly U S West) territory of Nebraska. Qwest is allowed to carry calls within the Omaha 402 area code. Some of these are local toll calls. However, calls within Nebraska between the 402 and 308 area codes must be handed off to interexchange carriers because 308 is in a different LATA than 402.

In states in which RBOCs receive permission from the Federal Communications Commission (FCC) to sell in-region long distance such as New York and Texas, the concept of LATAs has lost its significance. Other carriers are allowed to sell all voice and data services across local and state boundaries.

subsidiary of Montana Power Company because as an RBOC Qwest was not allowed to sell long distance within its territories. Figure 3.2 illustrates the areas encompassed by each RBOC. These mergers decreased the number of RBOCs from seven to four:

- Verizon Communications (formerly Bell Atlantic and NYNEX) also purchased GTE, formerly the largest independent telephone company
- BellSouth
- Southwestern Bell Communications (SBC); [Pacific Bell, Nevada Bell and Ameritech kept their names but are part of SBC, which also owns former independent telephone company Southern New England Telephone Company of Connecticut (SNET)]
- Qwest Communications (formerly U S West)

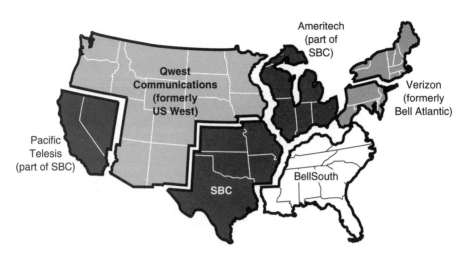

Figure 3.2
Regional Bell Operating Company territories.

Independent Telephone Companies— Mostly in Rural Areas

In addition to the RBOCs, there are close to 1,270 independent telephone companies. Some of these are ALLTEL Corporation, Cincinnati Bell, Inc. (part of Broadwing), Century Telephone Enterprises, Inc. and Sprint Corporation. (Sprint is both an interexchange carrier and an independent telephone company.) Many of the independent telephone companies are in rural areas such as northern Maine and western Massachusetts. According to the telephone company industry association, USTA (United States Telecommunications Association), independent telephone companies supply dial tone to 15% of the telephones in the U.S. but cover half of its geographic area. According to the FCC December 21, 2000 report *Trends in Telephone Service*, in 1999, independent telephone companies had $26,084 million in local revenue. This represented 23.9% of total U.S. revenue from local service.

Independent telephone companies sell all of the same services that RBOCs sell. In addition, following the 1984 divestiture, they were allowed to sell equipment such as telephone systems. This contrasts with the Bell telephone companies, which were not allowed to sell telephone equipment, only voice and data calling services. Independent telephone companies also are allowed to sell out-of-state long distance services from within their territories. Three of the largest independent telephone companies have been purchased. At the time it was purchased, GTE had more access lines in service than Ameritech and U S West:

- GTE by Verizon (GTE changed its name to Verizon)
- Southern New England Telephone Company (SNET) by SBC
- Frontier Telephone of Rochester was purchased by Global Crossing, which sold it to Citizens Communications Company, the largest independent phone company in the U.S.

WHAT IS A *CIC CODE?*

A *CIC code* is a four-digit code used for billing and call routing between local telephone companies. All network service providers route calls from other carriers. They know whom to charge for routing these calls by CIC code assignments. A CIC code, pronounced kick code, is short for carrier identification code. Each carrier is assigned a four-digit CIC code. For example, AT&T's CIC code is 0288, WorldCom's is 0222 and Sprint's is 0333. Users, who dial 101XXXX before they dial a telephone number, have their calls routed on whichever network the CIC code is assigned. For example, someone dialing 1010222 will have his or her call routed on WorldCom's network. WorldCom pays a fee to the carrier, such as Ameritech, that routes the call to it.

Prior to 1998, all carriers had three-digit CIC codes. AT&T had a huge marketing advantage because its CIC code, 288, spelled ATT on the telephone dial pad. It was able to use the slogan "Call 10-ATT" to encourage customers to dial 10288 when making local toll calls. The CIC code format was changed from three-digit to four digits to increase the number of CIC codes from 999 to 9999. WorldCom's CIC code changed from 222 to 0222.

The 101XXXX is referred to as a *carrier access code* (CAC). The CAC code to reach Sprint is 1010333. Consumers use CAC codes for "dial-around" service. People that use "dial around" select long distance providers on a call by call basis rather than by preselecting them.

Transporting Calls Between Carriers

Prior to the 1996 Telecommunications Act, transporting calls from the interexchange portion of the public network to homes and businesses was analogous to taking a trip by airplane: Airplanes transport riders from airport to airport, the interexchange portion of calls. Taxis, limousines and buses transport passengers from airports to their homes and businesses, the local access portion of telephone traffic. Airplanes carry the interexchange, or inter-LATA portion of the call, and taxis and buses provide the local portion of the call. Interexchange carriers (IEXs), like airplanes, pick up and hand off calls at airports to local "transportation," the local telephone company.

The 1984 divestiture ruled that local transportation of calls from IEXs' "airports" belonged to local exchange carriers. In telecommunications parlance, the airport, or interexchange carrier "drop-off" and "pick-up" points, became known as the *point of presence* (POP). It is the location of a carrier's telephone switch that is connected to the local telephone company. Interexchange carriers rent lines and central office connections from their POPs to the local telephone central offices to transport calls to and from their POPs (see Figure 3.3). Interexchange carriers now have connections from their own switches to competitive local exchange carriers (CLECs) as well as to incumbent local Bell telephone companies for local transport.

Carriers have points of presence (POPs) in metropolitan areas. For example, AT&T has two POPs in the Boston area, one in Cambridge and one in Framingham. Every business and residential customer that used AT&T for long distance, prior to the

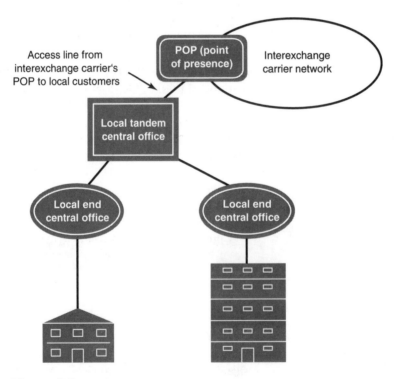

Figure 3.3
Interconnection between carriers.

Telecommunications Act of 1996, had to have "transportation" from their location to the AT&T's POP. The requirement for local access and egress (exit) is a major factor in the development of another type of telecommunications services provider, the competitive access provider (CAP).

LOCAL COMPETITION PRIOR TO THE TELECOMMUNICATIONS ACT OF 1996 ....

Competition for local service has been evolving since the early 1990s. Technological advances in fiber optics and switching equipment as well as regulatory events attracted billions of dollars for new entrants desiring to compete with incumbent telephone companies.

Uneven Competition for Local Telephone Service Throughout the U.S.

Prior to 1996, competitive access providers (CAPs) such as Metropolitan Fiber Systems, now owned by WorldCom and Teleport Communications Group (now part of AT&T), as well as long distance giants AT&T, Sprint and WorldCom, sold local telephone service. CAPs are the precursor of CLECs. CAPs sell fiber optic lines in cities for connections between long distance companies and their customers. However, market penetration of these services was low, 0.7% by December 1995. Local telecommunications was, for the most part, regulated by state public utility commissions. Each state allowed incumbent local telephone companies different levels of monopolistic control of local and intra-LATA toll calling. As state utility commissions opened intra-LATA toll calling, interexchange carriers and competitive access providers (CAPs) heavily promoted ways customers could use their services for local toll calling without the benefit of equal access. Equal access enables customers to select any licensed carrier they wish for local service. A great deal of competitive activity took place in California because of its 25% share of the local calling marketplace. Southern states had little competitive activity.

Competitive Access Providers (CAPs) to Competitive Local Exchange Carriers (CLECs)

The emergence of CAPs in the 1980s and in the early 1990s was the result of technological improvements and high fees that the local telephone companies charged long distance carriers for local access. The cost to transport calls to and from interexchange carriers' networks to their end destinations in local cities was a key factor in the initial development of competitive access. CAPs, such as Metropolitan Fiber System (MFS), Brooks Fiber, Intermedia Communications of Florida, Inc. and Teleport Communications Group (TCG) also were known as alternative access providers and local access providers. CAPs began providing access to long distance at lower prices than the Bell Operating Companies (BOCs).

The cost to carry the local access portion, the "taxi" or "bus" access and egress (exit), was paid by interexchange carriers to local telephone companies and passed on to consumers. Access charges amounted to 5.24¢ per minute of the 32¢ per minute average 1984 cost of long distance. BOCs typically received a third of their revenue from business customers, a third from residential customers and a third from access fees paid by interexchange carriers of which AT&T was the largest. Because of these access fees, AT&T was the Bell telephone companies' largest customer.

In the early 1980s, business customers became aware that access charges added significantly to their long distance costs. Moreover, it took a long time for connections to long distance companies to be installed. In 1983, Merrill Lynch formed Teleport Communications Company to carry its calls from Merrill Lynch's New York City locations to IEXs. It bypassed New York Telephone Company access fees. This was the beginning of the competitive access provider (CAP) industry.

Advances in fiber optics played a key role in the introduction of competitive access. CAPs used fiber optic cabling to transport calls from business customers (initially, primarily financial institutions in large cities) to interexchange carriers' points of presence (POPs). These T-1 digital links enabled customers to eliminate per minute access fees charged by the Bell telephone companies to interexchange carriers and passed to end users. T-1 carries 24 channels of voice and/or data calls on two pairs of copper cable or one pair of fiber cabling. (See Figure 3.4.) The local telephone companies at this time, the early to mid-1980s, transported calls from customer premises on copper cabling. Fiber is more reliable and carries calls with fewer errors.

Impact of Competitive Access Providers (CAPs)

The desire for faster implementation, lower costs and reliable T-1 service led many institutions to select a CAP. This competition motivated the Bell and independent telephone companies to lay fiber more quickly in large cities, directly to customers' buildings. It also pushed the Bells to shorten intervals and lower prices for high-speed digital access to long distance carriers. Thus, the telephone companies made digital T-1 connections over fiber available more quickly and at lower costs than they had planned. Competition from alternative access providers was a factor in the speed of upgrading the Bells' cabling from copper to fiber. Bypass was the main springboard from which the CAPs entered into additional telecommunications services.

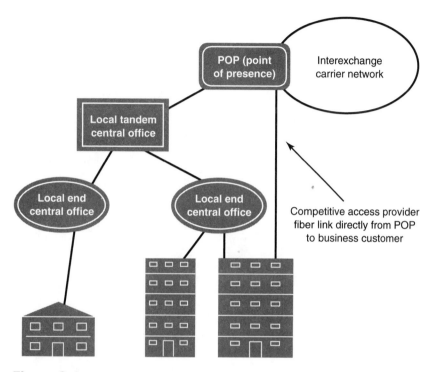

Figure 3.4
Alternative access link to a long distance provider bypassing the local telephone company.

CAPs and CLECs—What Are the Differences?

Competitive access providers became competitive local exchange providers when they branched out from providing bypass and started selling:

- *Connections to the Internet for both end users and Internet service providers* (ISPs)— ISPs resell Internet access to businesses and individuals.

- *Sophisticated data networks within metropolitan areas*—Firms that have, for example, both a warehouse and headquarters in the same metropolitan area might want a high-capacity connection between the two locations to send inventory and/or sales orders between the two sites.

- *Local telephone numbers (dial tone) and local calling services*—Once CLECs had their own fiber in a metropolitan area, the next step was to add switches and begin offering local telephone service.

Competitors' Local Telephone Switches

CLECs initially entered the interexchange business by constructing fiber optic links between major metropolitan areas in the east and west coast corridors. For example, once Los Angeles and San Francisco have fiber within the cities, the next step is to link these two locations for the purpose of selling long distance. The same is true for New York City to Washington, D.C. These fiber optic lines are available for the transmission of voice and data between cities on these high-traffic corridors.

CLEC Central Office Switches Collocated with Bell Switches

On September 17, 1992, the FCC allowed the local Bell telephone companies to open up competition by permitting collocation and virtual collocation. With *collocation*, local competitors install their own central office switch or other equipment in the same building as the local telephone company's switch. This gives competitors access to Bell telephone company lines for egress and/or termination of telephone calls from the competitors' customers. With *virtual collocation*, the incumbent telephone company maintains the CLEC's on-site equipment. The CLEC performs only remote maintenance and administration but the incumbent performs the actual on-site repairs.

The presence of competition made it easier to pass the Telecommunications Act. Local competition was a *fait accompli* in certain places. As the telephone companies lost access lines to competitors, they became eager to enter new markets such as manufacturing and long distance to make up for lost business in local markets. They were willing to compromise on opening their own markets to competition in return for entry into inter-LATA long distance. In large metropolitan areas such as New York City, competition was a reality. This was not the case in the south where competition for local calling was not making headway.

Dial Around—101-XXXX—Competitive Local Toll Service Prior to Local Competition

Before enactment of the Telecommunications Act of 1996, all residential and small business customer calls were routed over the local telephone company's lines for intra-LATA toll calls. To give customers a way to use their services, carriers and resellers conducted media blitzes and mail campaigns promoting their CIC codes. By mid-April of 1994, all but six states allowed intra-LATA toll calling using CIC codes. During the 1990s, long distance resellers and interexchange carriers promoted dial around to mitigate the local telephone companies' lock on local calling. They engaged in heavy promotions of the use of 101-XXXX codes for local toll calling. In particular, AT&T, whose market share had fallen by the first quarter of 1996, according to the FCC, to 54.7% of industry toll revenues of the interstate long distance market following the 1984 divestiture, hoped to gain market share by selling local toll services. Companies such as FiveLine, with a CIC code of 101-0811, and Dial & Save (part of Teleglobe), with 101-0457 advertised dial-around promotions heavily.

Currently, dial-around services are promoted heavily to customers who don't make many long distance calls. AT&T with Lucky Dog, WorldCom with Telecom USA, and Qwest all offer dial-around services.

The Evolving View of the Feasibility of Local Competition

In 1982, when the Justice Department mandated that AT&T divest itself of the local Bell telephone companies, the Justice Department took the stand that interstate, out-of-local-region long distance, was a competitive service, but that local telephone service was a natural monopoly. (See Table 3.1 in the Appendix at the end of this chapter for an overview of regulatory highlights.) This view eroded gradually during the 1990s, when competition gained a foothold in metropolitan areas, but was not generally available in more rural areas.

Technological advances played a role in furthering competition for local calling services. The growing availability of fiber optic cabling and wireless technologies increased the viability of competition in the local loop. Instead of laying miles of individual copper for each customer, competitive telephone carriers supplied a few strands of fiber capable of serving the needs of large corporations. Moreover, improvements in signaling technologies brought down the cost of providing local service by requiring fewer and less sophisticated switches to route calls. Signaling technologies linked central office switches to powerful computers with databases containing customer telephone numbers and telephone service configurations. These innovations have decreased the cost of competing for local telephone service.

The framers of the Telecommunications Act of 1996 wanted to advance innovations and improvements in local calling services by fostering competition. Interexchange carriers had an incentive, in the form of competition, to add innovative telecommunications services. Interexchange carriers were "first on the block" with efficient data services such as Frame Relay, ATM and virtual private data networks. These services were not universally available from local telephone companies. It was envisioned that the growth of competition for local telephone service would make these capabilities and other innovations available from integrated network providers.

FACTORS LEADING TO PASSAGE OF THE TELECOMMUNICATIONS ACT OF 1996...................

The Telecommunications Act of 1996 is the result of many factors. Demand for passage of the Act had been building up in Congress for many years, and Congress had attempted in the early 1990s to pass reform bills. The Republican congressional leadership who took office in 1995 wanted to deregulate cable TV and broadcasting. Through intense lobbying by RBOCs and long distance companies, a compromise was struck. The Act promised to open interexchange competition to Bells after they proved they had opened their networks to competition. The original framers of telecommunications reform hoped that the Telecommunications Act of 1996 would open competitive choices for local services to residential, small businesses and large organizations.

Factors important in pushing passage of the Telecommunications Act of 1996 included:

- A desire in Congress to allow competition for local telecommunications services (the "information super highway") uniformly in all of the states
- A government effort to make access to high-capacity telecommunications services universal and affordable
- Improvements in fiber optic and signaling technologies
- The Bell telephone companies' lobbying efforts for permission to enter interstate long distance and manufacturing
- The interexchange carriers' push for entry into the local calling market
- Viability of wireless services as a substitute for wired local telephone lines
- Increasing demand by customers for telecommunications services to carry data, image, color and video

Regional Bell Companies' Desire to Expand Their Offerings

While the seven (now four) RBOCs wanted to retain their local monopolies as much as possible, they wanted also to expand their range of offerings. They were being hit by competition for their most lucrative customers—big businesses in downtown, metropolitan areas.

Interexchange Carriers', Utility and Cable TV Companies' Desires to Enter New Markets

Demand for voice, Internet access and data services were growing quickly. Bell telephone companies' local and local toll revenues continued to climb. Cable companies, electric utility companies, competitive local exchange carriers, interexchange carriers and resellers all wanted a piece of this lucrative pie. Interexchange carriers were eager to enter new markets as they faced competition from carriers and resellers. Cable TV companies were looking at the telecommunications market as an avenue for growth. They felt they could leverage their existing investment in fiber and coaxial cabling for entry into local and toll calling. Power companies were attracted by the growth potential in telecommunications.

Demand for High-Speed Telecommunications Services

The federal government felt that increasing the amount of competition in the local loop would increase the availability of high-bandwidth services to local businesses and residential customers. In particular, applications such as downloading radio, television and video on demand from the Internet were envisioned, as was the transmission of medical images, such as MRI results. It was felt that competition in the local loop would lead to innovations and the creation of jobs.

Technological Capabilities to Provide High-Speed Services at Low Costs

Technological progress made local competition seem more feasible. Improvements in high-speed computers and fiber optic technologies were bringing down the cost of building telecommunications facilities. This trend started in the 1960s with microwave and continued with T-1, T-3, and wavelength division multiplexing (WDM) fiber optics and wireless local loop technology. It takes less labor and fewer outside cables to transport more data, faster. In addition, the cost and size of switches are decreasing while their power, speed and capabilities are increasing.

The Viability of Wireless Services for Local Exchange Service

In 1993, President Clinton mandated that auctions be held for frequencies within the Personal Communications Services (PCS) airwaves. Frequencies in each metropolitan area would be awarded to the five highest bidders with some awards given to minority and small businesses. This was seen, in addition to adding to the federal coffers, as a way to open up competition to cellular service providers. It was thought that this would drive down the cost of wireless services to the point where people would use their cellular phones for local calling.

The Desire for a Uniform National Policy on Local Competition

Competition for local telephone service proceeded at an uneven rate in the late 1980s to 1990s. Different states' public utility commissions took varying stands toward allowing intra-LATA toll competition and approving rates for competing carriers. The northern states allowed more competition than the southern states. Members of Congress felt that it was important to have a uniform policy and guidelines for implementation of connections between local Bell companies and competitors.

THE TELECOMMUNICATIONS ACT OF 1996 ....

The goal of the framers of the Telecommunications Act of 1996, passed in February of that year, was to promote uniform local telephone competition. A key proviso of the Telecommunications Act of 1996 is that it takes away from each state the capability to approve competition in local telecommunications. It also outlines a procedure for local telephone companies to expand their operations into manufacturing and inter-LATA, in-region and out-of-region, telecommunications. They are not required to form a separate subsidiary to sell out-of-region long distance, electronic publishing and alarm monitoring services.

The Act redefines the responsibilities of the state public utility commissions versus those of the Federal Communications Commission. Essentially, it is up to the states to approve rates for local calling and resale and interconnection of Bell services to competitors based on federal guidelines.

The Telecommunications Act of 1996:

- Permitted RBOCs to sell in-region long distance after completing a 14-point checklist of how they would offer connection into local calling for long distance companies such as AT&T. The 14-point checklist was designed to prove that there were alternative sources for local competitive calling.

- Freed interexchange carriers, CAPs, cable companies, wireless service operators, broadcasters and gas and electric utility companies to sell local telephone services.

- Required local telephone companies to offer resale of and interconnection to local services to the above entities.

- Authorized local telephone companies to sell cable services, television services, equipment and out-of-state long distance from outside their region.

- Raised the limit on the number of TV stations networks could own and phased out cable TV rate regulation.

- Promised carriers reimbursable discounts to schools, health care institutions and libraries in rural areas for access to advanced telecommunications services.
- Allowed RBOCs to manufacture goods through separate subsidiaries after they receive permission to sell in-region long distance services.

Major Features of the Act

The Telecommunications Act of 1996 outlined provisions by which competitors were to be allowed to lease and resell portions of incumbent telephone company networks so they could compete without installing brand new infrastructure in cities and metropolitan areas. Parts of the Act apply also to cable TV providers and broadcasters.

Bell Company Entry into Inter-LATA Services— State-by-State Approval by the FCC

The Bells are not allowed to sell long distance within their regions until the FCC is satisfied that their networks, on a state-by-state basis, are open to competition. Before FCC permission can be granted, each state's public utility commission must approve the Bell Operating Company's application. The FCC with feedback from the Justice Department on a state-by-state basis grants final permission for the Bell companies to sell in-region long distance. Approval is based upon agreements reached with competing carriers and the items on the 14-point checklist. The agreement must be with a facilities-based carrier that uses predominately its own switches and cabling for carrying customers' calls, unless no facilities-based carrier has requested interconnection.

Interconnection—Making Bell Resources Available to Competitors

Incumbent local exchange carriers must supply the following to all state public utilities carriers:

- *Resale*—All telecommunications services it supplies to its retail customers should be available to competitive carriers.

  The wholesale price for resale of call transport and termination of calls must be at cost. No provisions of profit for incumbent LECs are built into this ruling.

  Note that the interconnection, as opposed to resale, of unbundled elements of LEC facilities does include a provision for profits.

- *Number portability*—Telephone number portability is spelled out by the FCC such that customers can keep their telephone number if they change vendors.

- *Dialing parity*—Equal access is the ability of customers to preselect their telephone company for local toll calls. Dialing parity applies as well as to operator services, directory assistance and directory listings and should include no unreasonable dialing delays. Dialing parity eliminates the requirement of dialing a carrier access code, 101-XXXX. Prior to the Telecommunications Act, equal access applied only to out-of-region toll calls carried by interexchange carriers. Equal access requires that competing local exchange carriers connect their central offices to each other. These connections are required so that a customer on vendor A's network can call a customer on vendor B's network. Billing arrangements and agreements also are needed for vendor A to bill vendor B for terminating vendor A's call. Databases in the network must be maintained so that the local telephone company knows that telephone number 555-1234 belongs to vendor A and telephone number 555-6666 belongs to vendor B (see Figure 3.5).

- *Access to rights-of-way, including poles*—Utilities must provide nondiscriminatory rates to cable TV companies and telecommunications carriers other than incumbent local exchange carriers (LECs). If a utility uses its own poles, ducts and rights-of-way to provide telecommunications services, it must charge its own entity the same rate it charges other carriers.

- *Reciprocal compensation*—Telecommunications carriers must establish reciprocal compensation arrangements for the transport and termination of each other's local calls.

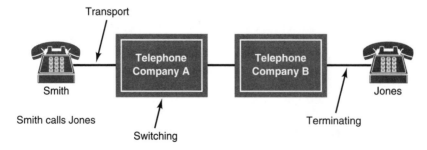

Figure 3.5
Connections between central offices to achieve equal access.

- *Unbundled access*—Incumbent local exchange carriers are required to provide unbundled network elements such that requesting carriers can combine these elements to provide telecommunications services.
- *Collocation*—The incumbent carrier should allow physical collocation of competitive equipment at the incumbent's premise for access to unbundled network features.

The 14-Point Checklist—RBOCs' Requirements Before They Are Allowed to Sell In-Region Long Distance

The 14-point checklist is designed to ensure that the RBOCs open their networks to competition before they are allowed to sell in-region inter-LATA long distance services. All of the following items must be agreed to with competitors on a state-by-state basis before the Bells are granted approval to sell in-region inter-LATA long distance:

1. Interconnection between RBOC networks and competitors
2. Nondiscriminatory access to network elements on an unbundled basis
3. Nondiscriminatory access to Bell-owned poles, ducts and rights-of-way
4. Unbundled local loop transmission from the central office to the customer's premises
5. Unbundled transport from the trunk side of the local switch (*trunks* are telephone lines that run from one central office switch to another central office switch rather than to an end user)
6. Unbundled local switching (routing of calls) separate from transmission services
7. Nondiscriminatory access to 911, E911, directory assistance and operator call completion
8. White pages directory listings for competitors' customers
9. Nondiscriminatory access to telephone numbers by competitors' customers until numbering administration has been given to organizations other than Bell companies
10. Nondiscriminatory access to databases and signaling required for call routing and completion
11. Telephone number portability
12. Nondiscriminatory access to services that allow competitive carriers to supply dialing parity, that is, dial 1 to access customers' Primary Interexchange Carriers Charges (PICC) for local toll and non-toll calling

13. Reciprocal compensation arrangements for Bell and competitive carriers to carry each other's local calls

14. Resale of telecommunications services at cost, without provision of profit for the Bells

Interconnection Agreements—A Timetable

The Act includes a timetable during which the state commissions must rule on interconnection agreements between incumbent local Bell companies and competitors. These agreements are subject to approval by the state public utility commission. Either party in the negotiations may request that the state utility mediate the agreement.

Universal Service Fund—Affordability and Availability

Every interstate carrier, cell phone and paging company must contribute 6.8% of their long distance and international calling revenue to a fund for universal service. State commissions may also create funds for universal service. The universal service fund was originally set at $2.25 billion annually. The FCC reduced it to $1.9 billion under pressure from carriers and some lawmakers. The universal fund program is known as the *E-rate*.

The purpose of the fund is to provide people in rural, insular and high-cost-to-reach areas, as well as poor consumers, access to advanced and interexchange telecommunication services at reasonably comparable rates charged for similar services in urban areas. This provision applies to schools, health care providers and libraries. In 2000, subsidies were extended to Native American reservations where only 70% of the population has telephones versus 97% of the United States population as a whole.

Cream-Skimming and Universal Service— Concentrating on Profitable Markets

CLECs generally concentrate their initial sales efforts in highly populated metropolitan areas. This concept is known as "cream-skimming." Cream is skimmed from lucrative markets such as downtown New York City, where one fiber run has access to thousands of customers in a single skyscraper. There is more potential for profit when an investment in new technology reaches thousands of potential customers in a small area. In a rural area, one fiber run may reach only ten customers.

The desire by the federal government to ensure that telephone service be provided to rural, possibly unprofitable regions is one reason telephone service is regulated. The Bell system has, since the early 1900s, promised to supply universal, affordable, basic "dial tone" in exchange for a monopoly. One consideration in opening up local calling areas to competition is to ensure the continuation of affordable services to poor and rural sections of the country. Telephone providers that only run services to high-profit areas can potentially set their prices lower than Bell Operating Companies, which sell telephone services in locations where operating profits are low and expenses are high.

Prohibitions Against Slamming

The Act expressly forbids any carrier from submitting or changing a subscriber's telephone exchange provider without authorization by the subscriber. State commissions are allowed to enforce these procedures in regard to intrastate services. A carrier that *slams* a customer, that is, makes an unauthorized change, is liable to the previous carrier for all fees paid by the slammed customer. WorldCom in June of 2000 was fined $3.5 million for slamming.

Manufacturing by Bell Operating Companies— Concurrent with Approval for In-Region Long Distance

The Bell companies are allowed to manufacture and sell equipment once they are allowed entry into inter-LATA toll calling. However, they are not allowed to jointly manufacture equipment with a Bell company with whom they are not affiliated. They may, however, collaborate with a manufacturer on the design of equipment prior to their approval to manufacture equipment.

Electronic Publishing by Bell Operating Companies

The RBOCs are allowed into electronic publishing through a separate subsidiary or in a joint venture that is less than 50%-owned by a Bell company. Electronic publishing is defined as providing or disseminating a variety of news, sports and informational material. Basic exchange services cannot be used to disseminate this material. These rules applied until the year 2000.

Broadcast Services—Relaxed Rules

Rules on radio and TV station ownership were relaxed. The Act removes the limit of one radio and one television station an individual organization can own. In addition, it allows one party to own both a broadcast and cable TV system. It also eases the rules on renewal of broadcast licenses.

Cable Services—Deregulation of Rates

The Act allows cable TV rates to be deregulated once effective competition in the serving area exists. Effective competition is defined as the offering of comparable video programming by a local exchange carrier or its affiliate. Premium services were deregulated on March 31, 1999.

Video Programming Services—Opening Cable TV to Competition

Exchange carriers are allowed to offer video programming and are not required to make capacity on their system available to competitors on a nondiscriminatory basis.

Congress hoped that this provision would encourage competition in the cable TV industry. It opened cable companies' *drop wires*, the wire from the pole to a residence, to joint use by cable competitors. New cable companies need only lay new cable down the street. They do not have to provide cable to each building. Competitors are allowed to operate as Open Video Systems (OVSs) without obtaining franchises from each community in which they wish to offer cable TV and cable modem service. Local communities, however, are allowed to charge OVS operators a percentage of their cable revenues.

In addition to the above, the following rules apply to video programming services:

- Cross ownership of more than 10% of cable TV and local exchange carriers is prohibited.
- Local exchange carriers that offer video programming are required to set aside channels for other companies' programming.
- LECs need to obtain FCC certificates to operate.

Broadcasting Obscenity and Violence

Regulations on pornography and indecent material available on the Internet were added as an amendment to the Act. The amendment was called the Communications Decency Act. However, it were found unconstitutional by the Supreme Court on June 12, 1996 because it denied First Amendment, freedom of speech rights. Congress passed subsequent laws, including the Children's Internet Protection Act (CIPA) and the Neighborhood Internet Protection Act (NIPA). It mandated that schools and libraries provide filters on Internet-connected computers to prevent children from accessing obscenities and pornography from the Internet. The Acts prohibited any school not complying with these regulations from receiving funds from the Universal Service Fund, discussed previously. The Supreme Court will review these Acts.

Rural Telephone Companies Exemption from Interconnect and Resale

The interconnection and resale rules intended to promote competition do not apply to rural telephone companies with fewer than 50,000 access lines. Ten percent of the U.S. population is in these territories. Small local exchange carriers with more than 50,000 access lines can apply to their state public utility commission for exemptions to these rules if they feel the rules impose a financial hardship.

POST TELECOMMUNICATIONS ACT OF 1996 DEVELOPMENTS..

Implementation of the Telecommunications Act of 1996 was initially hampered by RBOC legal challenges. Disagreements over pricing, implementation and order placing snafus have further hindered competitors that wished to sell service using incumbents' facilities.

FCC Rulings, Legal Challenges and Progress Toward Deregulation

The Telecommunications Act of 1996 mandated that the very organizations that compete with new entrants, the RBOCs, must also supply connections and services for competitors. The local Bell companies are offered the carrot of entrance into new businesses, out-of-region long distance and manufacturing. Nonetheless, conflicts of interest are inherent in pricing for and arranging for resale and access to Bell resources. It is no surprise that issues of pricing for resale and interconnection were contested in court. (See Table 3.2 in the Appendix at the end of this chapter.)

Enforcement of provisions and details of implementation of the Act were left, for the most part, to the FCC. Its rulings on wholesale rates and its rights to set rates were challenged by the state public utilities, local telephone companies and independent telephone companies. They contended that the 1934 Communications Act granted state utilities the prerogative of setting resale and wholesale discounts in their states. The Supreme Court ruled in January of 1999 that the FCC has jurisdiction on pricing. It also ruled that the Act is constitutional in setting conditions for only the RBOCs but not the independent telephone companies for entry into interregion long distance.

The following are factors that have slowed local competition:

- Legal challenges to the Act
- Interconnection disagreements between incumbents and new local carriers
- Service interruptions when customers change from RBOCs to competitors

Permission for RBOCs to Sell In-Region Long Distance

A new FCC chairman, Michael Powell, took office in January 2001. In the article, "FCC Chairman Signals Change, Plans to Limit U.S. Intervention," published in the *Wall Street Journal*, WSJ.com, January 2001, by Yochi J. Dreazen, concerning allowing ROBCs to offer long distance from within their territories, Mr. Powell stated:

> *"I do not believe that deregulation is like a dessert that you serve after people have fed on their vegetables, as a reward for competition. I believe it's instead a critical ingredient to facilitating competition, not something to be handed out after there are a substantial number of players or competitors in the market."*

This statement can be interpreted to mean that the FCC will be more lenient toward granting approval for Bell entry into long distance. Up until Powell took office, only RBOCs in four states—Kansas, Louisiana, New York State and Texas—had received permission by the Federal Communications Commission (FCC) to sell interstate long distance from within their regions. Verizon received permission in Massachusetts in April 2001 and Connecticut in July 2001. SBC, which already has permission to sell long distance in Kansas, Louisiana and Texas, stated in its 2000 Annual Report that it has filed long distance applications at the state level in Arkansas, California, Indiana and Missouri. It plans to file in 2001 in Indiana, Michigan, Ohio and Wisconsin. Once these approvals are granted, SBC will be able to sell long distance in its entire territory. BellSouth has started the regulatory process of first seeking approval in individual states in North Carolina, Georgia, Florida and South Carolina.

Verizon has a filing before the FCC for permission to sell long distance in Pennsylvania. Pennsylvania state regulators had previously unsuccessfully attempted to have Verizon operate separate retail and wholesale operations. Verizon has stated it plans to file applications in New Hampshire, Rhode Island and Vermont in 2001 and in its entire territory by 2002.

Qwest, in its year 2000 Annual Report, stated that it would file its first request in late summer 2001 and complete all other initial filings by early 2002.

To help them assess Verizon's handling of competitors interconnection orders, state regulatory agencies in New York and Massachusetts hired consulting firm KPMG to conduct an analysis of Verizon's operations support systems (OSS). Other state utility commissions are following suit.

FCC ENFORCEMENT OF ACCESS TO LOCAL NETWORKS AFTER BELLS GAIN IN-REGION LONG DISTANCE

The Telecommunications Act of 1996 granted the FCC post-approval enforcement powers to monitor Bell Operating Company (BOC) adherence to rules providing access to central office and other Bell facilities (unbundled network elements) at fair rates. In their January 19, 2001 approval of SBC's application to provide in-region, inter-LATA services in Kansas and Oklahoma, the FCC made the following statements:

"Section 271 (d)(6)(A) provides for the Commission to receive and review complaints filed by persons concerning alleged failures by a BOC to meet conditions required for long distance approval. Section 271 (d)(6)(A) also specified several enforcement actions that the commission can take on its own motion, including ordering the BOC to correct a deficiency, assessing a forfeiture, and suspending or revoking the BOC's authority to provide long distance service."

The commission further stated that it would monitor SBC's compliance in opening its network by requiring it to provide monthly reports for at least one year for the five-state Southwestern Bell Telephone's region of Arkansas, Kansas, Oklahoma, Missouri and Texas.

The FCC's monitoring of Verizon's compliance with open competition rules after Verizon won the right to sell long distance in New York State resulted in a fine against Verizon. In March 2000, the FCC fined Verizon (then called Bell Atlantic) $13 million for mishandling competitors' orders for access to network elements in New York State. As a result of the fine, Verizon stated that it was delaying its application for permission to sell out-of-region long distance in Massachusetts until it fixed the same order processing system used in Massachusetts. It received permission to sell long distance in Massachusetts in 2001.

Unbundled Network Elements (UNEs)— Competitors Leasing Parts of RBOCs' Networks

There are numerous disagreements between CLECs and incumbent telephone companies regarding rates for interconnection and discounts for resale. State utilities set resale discounts using formulas set by the FCC. These discounts range from the low to high 20%s.

Competitors lease unbundled network elements from incumbents. An *unbundled network element* (UNE) is defined as a facility used to provide telecommunications services. Competitors want fees for these elements to be based on current costs, which are often lower than historical costs. Incumbent phone companies want the costs based on historical costs. The Supreme Court has stated its intention to decide on this issue in 2001. Examples of unbundled network elements include the following:

- *The copper line from the customer to the CLEC equipment collocated at the Bell central office* (see Figure 3.6)—These lines are used for voice and data traffic such as DSL service.

- *T-1, T-3, OC-3 (155 Megabits per second) and higher speed lines between the competitor's Bell collocated equipment and another CLEC site.*

- *Rental of RBOC central office switch ports for provision of local telephone service*—A central office switch port connects to a local loop and routes calls to the public switched telephone network (PSTN).

- *Connections to signaling system 7 (SS7) service for purchases of "smart" features such as caller ID and voice mail.*

- *Fiber optic cabling owned by the incumbent telephone company that has no multiplexing equipment associated with it*—This is called *dark fiber.*

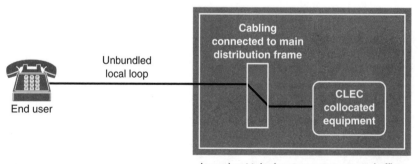

Figure 3.6
A local loop leased as an unbundled network element by a CLEC.

Fines Levied on Incumbents for Failure to Provide Timely Access to Competitors

When customers change local providers from incumbent telephone companies to competitive local exchange carriers, the CLEC submits the change orders to the local telephone company. The CLEC has the responsibility to place the order in the correct format so that the change can be processed correctly. The incumbent telephone company in turn must in a timely and accurate manner process requests it receives from CLECs.

To date the FCC has fined BellSouth, SBC and Verizon for not adhering to these Telecommunications Act of 1996 requirements.

- In May 2000 the Pacific Bell unit of SBC was fined $27.2 million for failing to provide service in a timely fashion to Covad, a DSL provider. SBC appealed the fine. Covad and SBC settled when SBC purchased 6% of Covad.

- In August 2000 the FCC fined GTE (now Verizon) $2.7 million for failing to allow 51 CLECs and Internet Service Providers to place their equipment at central offices without a cage surrounding it. The FCC had previously changed its rules and GTE said they needed more time to get their offices ready to handle competitors' equipment when it was no longer inside cages.

- In November 2000 the FCC fined BellSouth $750,000 for failing to disclose to competitor Covad Communications Group, Inc. data Covad needed about BellSouth costs over a six-month period. BellSouth later agreed to provide the data if Covad would sign a nondisclosure agreement. Nondisclosure agreements about costs are prohibited by the Act.

- Between early 2000 and March 2001, SBC paid a total of $22.3 million in penalties to the FCC for providing inadequate service to competitors in its midwestern Ameritech region.

Reciprocal Payments

The Telecommunications Act of 1996 mandated that carriers compensate each other for carrying each other's local calls. Many local service providers sell telephone service to ISPs that connects users' dial-in Internet calls to the ISPs' Internet access equipment. Calls that CLECs carry to ISPs for the most part originate on incumbent local telephone company's networks. The FCC ruled in February 1999 that calls to the Internet are not usually local. The FCC's 1999 ruling further stated that existing reciprocal contracts should be honored. It directed state commissions to arbitrate disputes over reciprocal payments. However, the U.S. Court of Appeals threw out this ruling in 2000, saying it was unclear.

Prior to new rules promulgated in April 2001, Bell and incumbent independent carriers paid billions of dollars in reciprocal fees for Internet-bound traffic. According to the article, "FCC Is Set to Reduce Fees Paid by Bell to Competitors to Complete Online Calls," published in *The Wall Street Journal*, WSJ.com, 13 April 2001, Verizon spent $1 billion, SBC $0.8 billion and BellSouth $0.3 billion annually on reciprocal payments. On April 19, 2001 the Federal Communications Commission decreased these fees. The lower fees were scheduled to be phased in over a two-year period. In its press release about the change, the FCC stated:

> *The Commission concluded that telecommunications traffic delivered to an ISP is interstate access traffic, specifically "information access," thus not subject to reciprocal compensation.*

The FCC further capped the minutes for which a local carrier can receive payments at not greater than 10% more minutes than it previously received payment for. Various CLECs have warned that decreasing their revenue will lead to an increase in the cost of dial-in Internet access for end users. If the bill-and-keep rules that the FCC is looking at are passed, reciprocal fees will be eliminated altogether. (See the next section for bill-and-keep.)

Local Access Fees—A Shift in Balance Between Local and Long Distance Costs

Interexchange carriers pay access fees to incumbent and competitive local telephone companies for transporting long distance traffic to and from local customers. Access fees were intended to subsidize local service so that telephone companies could keep rates for residential customers affordable. Residential basic telephone service was also subsidized by rates businesses paid for local service and by long distance fees. Rules promulgated by the FCC on May 7, 1997 lowered access fees by $18.5 billion over five years. However, this action shifted costs to residential and business users in the form of higher monthly subscriber line charges (SLCs) described later. It also was a factor in balancing costs between local and long distance service. Lower access fees are one factor in lower long distance rates.

As part of the change in reciprocal fees previously discussed, the FCC released a Notice of Proposed Rulemaking about intercarrier compensation. It announced it is considering eliminating all fees that carriers pay each other for interconnecting their networks and terminating traffic to each other's customers. The FCC called this approach bill-and-keep. With *bill-and-keep*, carriers recoup the costs of originating and terminating traffic from their own customers rather than from other carriers. If these rules are enacted, both access fees and reciprocal payments will be eliminated.

Because they are not considered telecommunications firms, Internet Service Providers (ISPs) have always been exempt from payment of access fees.

Local Number Portability

Local number portability enables subscribers to keep their telephone numbers, at the same location, when they change from one local telephone provider to another.

Creating an Equal Playing Field and Conserving Numbers

Local Bell and independent operating companies assign telephone numbers to local carriers in blocks of 1000. Numbers are assigned from a pool of numbers kept by the incumbent carrier. This is called the *number pooling system of allotting numbers* because pools of 1000 unused numbers are created. Prior to the year 2000, numbers were assigned to carriers in blocks of 10,000. This resulted in wasted numbers because many smaller carriers who did not use up all of their numbers could not share them with other carriers. To further conserve numbers, in 2000 the FCC mandated that phone companies must first use up 60% of their assigned phone numbers before being given new ones. In three years, the percentage will increase to 75%.

Achieving number portability requires costly upgrades to older telephone company switches. For this reason, in 1999 the FCC allowed incumbent carriers to charge customers the fee previously noted for local number portability. However, they only can be charged for five years.

Four Types of Telephone Number Portability

To date, only service provider portability is mandated.

1. *Service provider portability*—An enduser's ability to keep his or her telephone number when changing carriers within the same rate center. The method approved by the FCC to accomplish service provider portability is *local routing number* (LRN). With LRN, every central office switch is assigned a 10-digit number. These switch numbers, or LRNs, reside in network databases. All telephone calls trigger a "dip" into a database to determine to which central office a call should be routed. According to the FCC's December 2000 *Trends in Telephone Service*, as of August 2000, 6.7 million telephone numbers had been ported, mainly from incumbent phone companies to CLECs.

   Wireless number portability must be achieved by November 24, 2002 in the 100 largest metropolitan statistical areas. By that date, customers must be able to change cellular service providers without changing their cellular numbers.

2. *Location portability*—Keeping a telephone number when moving to another rate center.

New Monthly Fees Customers Pay

Customers are confused by fees on their bills unrelated to basic services or minutes of calling. The FCC mandated or approved most of these charges. None of the fees below are taxes. In addition to the charges listed, many states and local municipalities collect taxes on telephone service, as does the federal government.

Subscriber line charges (SLCs), also called FCC line charges—These FCC-mandated fees are charged to business and residential customers to recover a portion of the costs local telephone companies incur for supplying local loops (the telephone line from the telephone company to the customer). The first line a user has incurs a lower fee than additional lines. In 2000 they were $4.35 for a customer's first line and an average of $5.99 for each additional line. SLCs are intended to replace access fees, which are being phased out, that local telcos charge long distance carriers.

Presubscribed interexchange carrier charges (PICCs)—FCC-mandated PICC fees are charged only to business customers. They are used to recover the cost of the lines between long distance and local exchange carriers. They partially replace access fees paid to local carriers to terminate and originate long distance traffic. PICC fees for consumers were rolled into their SLC charges.

Local number portability—All incumbent carriers charge users an FCC-approved fee to recover their cost to upgrade their networks for local number portability previously described.

Universal Service Fund (USF)—A per-line fee some local carriers charge to cover their contribution to the universal service fund mandated by the Telecommunications Act of 1996. See previous description of the Universal Service Fund.

Universal connectivity charge, also called the Universal Service Fund fee—Most long distance carriers charge a fee based on a percentage of customers' long distance charges. They represent the 6.9% of their long distance revenue carriers are mandated to contribute to the Universal Service Fund, a subsidy for rural and low income areas, and educational and health care institutions. People that make no calls are not charged this fee. Many carriers charge more than the 6.9% fee. The FCC is considering instituting limits that carriers can charge for USF charges.

Rate centers are the points within exchanges used to determine toll rates. Location portability is not mandated. It is thought that implementation of location portability will be driven by customer demand. The capability for large businesses to keep their telephone numbers when they move is significant.

3. *Service portability*—Keeping a telephone number when changing from wireline to wireless or voice to data services.

   Service portability is not mandated. Service provider portability would allow users to keep their telephone numbers when they change to wireless providers for their home telephone service.

4. *One number for life portability*—Keeping a telephone number regardless of location or service used.

   This opens up the possibility for out-of-area geographic portability between towns and states as well as between carriers. This is the case with toll-free 800, 888, 866 and 877 calling. These numbers are assigned to customers regardless of their location. No date is set or mandated for one number for life portability.

Running Out of Telephone Numbers

The public switched telephone network in the United States, Canada and many of the Caribbean nations use the North American Numbering Plan (NANP). Telephone numbers consist of a three-digit area code (NPA), a three-digit exchange or central office code (NXX), plus a four-digit line number. Because there is a finite amount of numbers, there is a concern that telephone numbers might be used up in the not-too-distant future. The chairman of the FCC, Michael Powell, has stated that he will review how many numbers are actually being used.

The Industry Numbering Committee (INC), a standing committee of the Carrier Liaison Committee (CLC), is exploring six ways to expand the North American Numbering Plan (NANP)

1. Allow central office codes to begin with a 0 or 1, in addition to 0–9.

2. Increase the length of central office codes from three digits to four digits.

3. Increase the line number length from four digits to five digits.

4. Introduce a National Destination Code (NDC), a single-digit number between 2 and 9, which is placed before the NPA to indicate a specific geographic region within the NANP. In this option, a single digit such as the number 1 might be assigned to Canada and other digits to the United States. Users calling Canada from outside the area would have to first dial the Canadian country code and then the National Destination Code.

This opens all of the area codes to Canada and the United States. Furthermore, the United States could be broken into four quadrants, each assigned its own NDC.

5. Use a four-digit NPA: NXX(X)—where a single digit (0–9) is appended to the area code.

6. Use a four-digit NPA: (N)NXX—where a single digit (2–9) is added to the beginning of the area code

Changing the structure of the North American Numbering Plan will be a larger task to the telecommunications industry than the year 2000 computer compatibility upgrade was to the computer industry. All of the Operational Support Services that identify services by telephone number will have to be changed. This will impact billing, repairs, all network databases and routing. Every switched service has a telephone number. Many non-telecommunications companies identify customers by telephone number. Unlike Social Security numbers, telephone numbers are public unique numbers.

Open Access to Multiple Tenant Buildings

Prior to October 25, 2000, apartment owners could enter into agreements with local carriers giving them exclusive rights to provide telephone service to their multi-tenant buildings. Tenants often lost the right to select whom to use for local telephone service and Internet access. Competitive local exchange carriers felt that they were being excluded from this often-lucrative market. Real estate owners felt that any restrictions by the FCC would violate their constitutional rights in regard to private property.

The FCC made its October open access to buildings ruling in an effort to promote competition. It ruled that:

- Building owners cannot enter into exclusive contracts with telecommunications providers. Any fees charged to CLECs for access to the building must also be charged to incumbent telephone companies. These rules do not apply to residential buildings or pre-existing contracts. The FCC said it might extend these rules to residential multiple dwelling environments at a later date.

- Utilities and local exchange carriers must allow other carriers, including cable operators, access to in-building conduits and rights-of-way used for cabling within multitenant buildings.

- Building owners may not restrict tenants from placing antennas smaller than one meter for fixed wireless service on the tenant's private area.

- The final rule makes the demarcation, the place where a building's inside wiring is connected to a carrier's cabling, more accessible. It required that the local exchange carriers must, at the building owner's request, move the demarcation closer to the building's point of entry. It also required that the local exchange carrier notify within 10 days of a request by the building owner, the location of the demarcation.

IMPACT OF THE TELECOMMUNICATIONS ACT OF 1996 ....

Regulations play a critical role in the rate of innovation, costs and availability of tele-communications technologies. Carriers recognize this and spend enormous amounts of money on lobbying. In the six months prior to passage of the Telecommunications Act, RBOCs gave $2.3 million to congressional campaign funds and the top three long distance carriers donated $2.1 million. A top executive of Verizon stated publicly that his regulatory staff was more important in his business strategy than his marketing staff.

One of the objectives of the Telecommunications Act of 1996 was to open the lucrative, local telephone service market to competition. According to the United States Telephone Association booklet *Phone Facts 1998,* this market was $96 billion in 1997. At that time, the combined market share of all incumbent local telephone companies, including RBOCs and independents, was 97.7%. In the latest period analyzed by the FCC's Industry Analysis Division, December 2000, the incumbent's overall market share was 91.5%. However, according to the June 4, 2001 Barron's Online, "The Bells' Toll" by Jonathon R. Laing, their market share of business customers is 16%. These statistics support the fact that competition is heavier in the more lucrative business market.

The slow growth of local competition is a sharp contrast to AT&T's long distance market share before and after the 1984 divestiture. In 1984, AT&T's share of the long distance market according to the FCC was 90%. Three years later, in 1987, its share was 78.6%. By 1999, AT&T's portion had dropped to 40%. Many factors contribute to the disparity of impact of deregulation on long distance and local telecommunications service. These include the cost and complexity of any one CLECs connecting to a majority of the RBOC's 9825 central offices and other facilities, legal challenges to the Act and delays and high prices from incumbents for leasing unbundled network elements.

The Act spurred new investment in equipment and services for high-speed Internet access telecommunications. According to the Association for Local Telecommunications Services (ALTS) *Annual Report on the State of the Local Telecom Industry, 2001*, 36% ($20 billion) of venture capital spending in the first three quarters of 2000 was for the communications sector. In 1999, that figure was $11.2 billion. The

RBOCs also increased spending dramatically in that period for communications infrastructure. Verizon Communications, in its 2000 Annual Report, stated it spent $3.9 billion for data equipment in 2000 and planned to spend $4.7 billion in 2001. SBC, in its 2000 Annual Report, projected investing $6 billion in 2001 for DSL infrastructure for high-speed Internet access and fiber optic networking.

Unfortunately, these investments have lowered incumbent's 2001 earnings projections. In addition, many new telecommunications providers have gone out of business due to the high cost of building infrastructure, the cost and delays associated with connecting to incumbent facilities and the large number of competitors. It's unclear how these downturns will impact end users. The Telecommunications Act and the resultant increase in competition spurred investment in the telecommunications sector. A major decrease in competition might prove a disincentive for further growth in investments by regional Bell telephone companies. It has already lowered capital investments available to telecommunications entrepreneurs.

Deregulation, technology and competition have major impacts on prices. Cable TV, which was deregulated by the Act, but where because of the high cost of infrastructure, there is very little competition, has seen large price increases. According to the advocacy group Consumers Union, cable television rates have increased 31.9% since passage of the Telecommunications Act of 1996. This is the exact opposite of the trend in long distance prices. Combined factors of improved technology, increased competition and elimination of long distance revenue subsidization of local service has caused the following decreases in average revenue per minute for interstate and international calls. These figures are restated in 1999 dollars as reported by the Federal Communication's Industry Analysis Division:

- 1930 $2.74
- 1984   52¢
- 1999   14¢

A decrease in competition has the potential to cause price increases for high-speed Internet access. This already occurred when Verizon and SBC raised their DSL prices in 2001.

Mergers and acquisitions along with the increased permissions granted Regional Bell Operating Companies to sell long distance is creating a landscape similar to that prior to divestiture when a large company dominated the telecommunications landscape. Verizon is the largest local and cellular telephone company in the United States and SBC is the second largest. Between them they control 61% of the local lines and 65% of the cellular numbers as well as a growing percentage of the long distance market. Judge Harold H. Greene, who presided over the 1984 divestiture, might have been prescient when he made the following statement, which was quoted in *The Wall Street Journal*, 12 February 1996, page B1 article by Leslie Cauley. (The quote was reprinted in the article, "The Failure of Telecom Reform," published in *Telecommunications Online*, September 1996, by D. Linda Garcia.)

> *"I'm a little concerned [whether] there are sufficient safeguards against the kinds of mergers and acquisitions that might give some small group of companies or individuals a stronghold over U.S. telecom markets…I'd hate to see the AT&T monopoly be reconstituted in some form. It would be like I'd wasted the past 18 years."*

APPENDIX ....

Table 3.1   Regulatory Highlights

Landmark Acts and Court Rulings	Summary of Acts and Rulings
The Federal Communications Act of 1934	Congress created the Federal Communications Commission and gave it the authority to regulate interstate telephone, radio and telegraph companies.
The 1956 Consent Decree	The Justice Department allowed AT&T to keep its monopoly but restricted it to common carrier functions. The Consent Decree mandated that any patents developed by Bell Labs, then AT&T, be licensed to all applicants requesting them. This led to microwave technology's availability to MCI and the ability of competitive carriers to build long distance networks.
The 1969 MCI Case	The Federal Communications Commission ruled that MCI, then known as Microwave Communications Inc., could connect its equipment to the public network providing the network was not harmed. This decision opened the CPE market to AT&T rivals such as Rolm and Executone.
The 1982 to 1983 Modified Final Judgment	The Justice Department, in agreement with AT&T and with approval by Judge Harold H. Greene, agreed to a settlement that: • Divested the then 22 Bell Operating Companies (BOCs) from AT&T. • Prohibited BOCs from inter-LATA long distance, sale of CPE and manufacturing. • Mandated that the local exchange companies provide equal access (dial 1) from end users to all interexchange carriers.

Table 3.1   Regulatory Highlights*(continued)*

Landmark Acts and Court Rulings	Summary of Acts and Rulings
The 1984 Divestiture	The terms spelled out in the Modified Final Judgment were implemented on January 1, 1984. The 22 Bell telephone companies were merged into seven Regional Bell Operating Companies (RBOCs). The RBOCs were allowed to sell local and toll calling within the 197 defined local or LATA areas. They also retained the yellow pages. AT&T kept manufacturing, inter-LATA and international toll calling.
The Telecommunications Act of 1996	Decreed that cable TV companies, electric utilities, broadcasters, interexchange carriers and competitive access providers could sell local and local toll calling.
	Allowed local competitors interconnection to and resale of local telephone companies' facilities.
	Set fees for interconnection services at the LECs'* local exchange carriers, costs plus a reasonable profit.
	Set fees for resale at LECs' costs.
	Allowed Bell companies to immediately provide out-of-region long distance.
	Allowed Bell companies to provide inter-LATA toll calling and manufacturing in their regions under FCC approval or by February 1999, whichever is earlier.
	Dictated that FCC approval depends on the incumbent LEC's meeting conditions of a 14-point checklist of opening its regions for competition.
FCC 2001 Deregulation of devices connected to the public switched network	The FCC will no longer set specifications for modems, phones and fax machines connected to the public network. This will be turned over to a private agency. The FCC will continue to set standards for wireless devices.

The term incumbent LEC, or local exchange carrier, refers to the Bell Operating Companies.

Table 3.2   FCC Rulings and Legal Challenges to the Telecommunications Act
of 1996

Date	Decision or Action
June 27, 1996	The FCC spelled out rules on service provider portability. It stated that customers must be able to keep their telephone numbers when they change carriers. It also stated they must be able to keep "smart" features such as call waiting when they change carriers.
August 8, 1996	The FCC set rules for calculating the wholesale fees that BOCs could charge competitors for network elements. It also identified seven pieces of the network that must be leased to rivals. The discounts were in the 17% to 25% range. Access fees to wireless companies were reduced by $1 billion annually.
September 12, 1996	The FCC allowed utilities whose lines cross state boundaries into telecommunications.
October 15, 1996	The U.S. Court of Appeals for the Eighth Circuit stayed (denied) the FCC's jurisdiction in setting interconnection and wholesale pricing at the local level. Stayed the FCC's August 8, 1996 ruling.
October 11, 1996	Justice Clarence Thomas refused to lift the October 15, 1996 stay by the Eighth Court of Appeals. Federal regulators had asked the ruling to be overturned.
November 11, 1996	The FCC appealed Justice Thomas' ruling. The Supreme Court upheld the Eighth Circuit's October 15, 1996 stay on the FCC's ability to set pricing guidelines.
May 7, 1997	The FCC lowered access fees, the fees interexchange carriers charge to transmit and receive calls from the local networks, by $1.7 billion the first year and $18.5 billion over five years. The FCC also raised end-user line charges by $2.75 for each business line and $1.50 for a second home phone line to pay for subsidies for schools and libraries mandated by the Telecommunications Act of 1996.
July 1997	The Eighth Circuit Court of Appeals suspended the FCC's pricing rules.
October 1997	The Eighth Circuit Court of Appeals suspended FCC authority and rules on procedures for interconnection to local networks.

Table 3.2   FCC Rulings and Legal Challenges to the Telecommunications Act
of 1996 *(continued)*

Date	Decision or Action
December 31, 1997	The U.S. District Court excluded October's ban of SBC's and U S West's entry into long distance. After long distance companies, the FCC and the Justice Department appealed, the judge delayed implementation of this ruling.
January 19, 1999	The Supreme Court upheld the constitutionality of the Telecommunications Act of 1996 not to allow the baby Bells into in-region long distance before they open their networks to rivals. U S West, SBC and Bell Atlantic had argued that they were singled out because the Act did not apply to GTE, Frontier and Southern New England Telephone Company.
January 25, 1999	The Supreme Court upheld the FCC's authority to implement the Telecommunications Act of 1996 but directed the Eighth Circuit Court of Appeals to approve the FCC's national pricing plans and allowed exemptions of independent telephone companies to rules of the Act. If a network element is available elsewhere, the Bells should not be required to make it available to competitors (e.g., Internet access, voice mail or high-speed data lines). This effectively reversed the Eighth Circuit Court of Appeals' suspension of FCC jurisdiction of interconnection to local networks.
July 1999 and January 2001	The Eight Circuit Court of Appeals struck down FCC rules for how Bell telephone companies set fees for network elements they rent to CLECs. This ruling would have resulted in higher fees for CLECs. However, the FCC appealed to the Supreme Court, which has stated that it will rule on the issue in 2001. The Court also will rule on whether CLECs can rent packages of services if they request them rather than only individual pieces as now required.
September 1999	The FCC increased the number of unbundled network elements the Bells are required to provide competitors. The most important of these is the right for competitors to share the same Bell lines for voice phone service for DSL Internet access service. (See Chapter 6 for DSL service.)

Table 3.2   FCC Rulings and Legal Challenges to the Telecommunications Act
of 1996 *(continued)*

Date	Decision or Action
January 2001	The U.S. Court of Appeals struck down an FCC rule that absolved SBC from making connections to data services such as DSL to competitors if the incumbent sold these data services through a separate subsidiary. It appears that instead of a separate subsidiary, SBC will be required to sell data service through a separate division that will be required to lease connections to competitors.
February 2001	On his last day of office, William E. Kennard, the outgoing chairman of the FCC ruled that Bells must share local loops for voice and DSL when they are made up of a mix of fiber and copper as well as all copper, as is often the case.

4 Network Service Providers and Local Competition

In this chapter...

The telecommunications industry is made up of hundreds of carriers who sell a mix of leading edge data services as well as mundane items such as voice long distance and white and yellow page directories. Often the same companies sell all of these products.

It used to be possible to neatly classify carriers into the following categories:

- Interexchange long distance carrier
- Local telephone company
- Reseller
- Cable TV provider
- Data communications provider
- Independent local telephone company

This is no longer possible. The Telecommunications Act of 1996 changed the telecommunications landscape. Interexchange carriers (IEXs) now are also competitive local exchange carriers (CLECs). Qwest is now a Regional Bell Operating Company (RBOC) through its purchase of U S West, as well as an IEX. Sprint owns an independent telephone company, sells local service outside of these territories and is the third largest long distance company. RBOCs now sell long distance service from within the states of Connecticut, Massachusetts, New York, Texas, Oklahoma and Kansas and shortly will have permission to sell it in many more states. They also are lobbying lawmakers to pass legislation allowing them to sell data communications services across the entire country without getting permission on a state-by-state basis. Passage of this type of legislation would greatly hamper the competition in the local telecommunications market.

The biggest source of growth for competitors to RBOCs is data communications services. Many of them such as McLeodUSA and Allegiance Telecom purchased new subsidiaries for their expertise in Web and Internet service. In contrast to the growth in data communications, voice long distance revenues are flat and margins are narrow due to steep price declines.

The sector with the least amount of competition is cable TV. New competitors, called overbuilders, are emerging in this area. Overbuilders build cable TV infrastructure in cities and suburban areas that already have an incumbent cable TV supplier. Overbuilders sell cable modem, local phone service and cable TV service. With the emergence of overbuilders and cable TV companies' cable modem offerings, consumers often have more options for high-speed Internet access than small businesses in rural and suburban areas. Due to the high costs of these endeavors and the declining investment in telecommunications, this can take quite some time to come about on a large scale.

Utilities are becoming a major factor in building infrastructure, particularly as overbuilders. They are leveraging their expertise in building and maintaining fiber optic networks for electric distribution to construct fiber networks.

Table 4.1 indicates the tremendous numbers of mergers and acquisitions in telecommunications. WorldCom and AT&T have created tracking stocks for their slow-growing voice divisions. Companies are also spinning off portions of their cellular assets in Initial Private Offerings (IPOs). They hope to raise capital and increase value for their shareholders by both these strategies.

LOCAL COMPETITION ....

There are technical, legal and financial considerations in providing local telephone service. Understanding how calls are passed between competing local carriers and between local carriers, resellers and interexchange carriers is important in comprehending the structure of the industry.

Components of Local Calls

The following should be considered within the context of local calling:

- *Transport*—The line from a home or business to the central office.
- *Switching*—The central office switch directs calls to their destination. It also has links to billing and enhanced feature systems such as voice mail and caller ID.
- *Terminating transport*—The transmission of the call to its end site, or destination.
- *Signaling*—Signals in the network include telephone number dialed, busy signals, ringing and the diagnostic signals generated by carriers for repair and maintenance of the network.

Transport termination and switching functions are illustrated in Figure 4.1.

Other elements of calling include directory assistance, repair reporting, white and yellow pages, 911 and value-added services such as caller ID. It takes large capital investments to install and maintain networks. According to the Association for Local Telecommunications Services (ALTS), CLEC investment in local telecommunications infrastructure was $24.9 billion in 2000. According to ALTS, the Regional Bell Operating Companies invested $33.6 billion during the same period. These capital improvements include central office switches, data equipment and fiber optic cabling. Because

Table 4.1 A Sampling of Mergers and Acquisitions of Carriers
in the Telecommunications Industry (U.S. and Canada)

Purchasing Company	Purchased Entity	Details
Adelphia Communications Corporation	GS Communications Cablevision Systems Cleveland Properties Harron Communications Corporation Century Communications	With purchase of Harron, Adelphia is the sixth largest cable TV company in the U.S. Previously purchased FrontierVision Partners, FPL Group and Verto Communications.
Allegiance Telecom, Inc.	Adgrafix and HarvardNet, Inc.	Companies will be part of CLEC Allegiance's Web hosting and data services unit.
AOL Time Warner (formerly America Online, Inc.)	Time Warner	Largest ISP bought entertainment and cable TV conglomerate Time Warner in 2001, creating the world's largest media company. The FCC imposed three conditions: Cannot restrict customers from other home pages and must open cable Internet access to three other Internet service providers (ISPs); its instant messaging must work with rival multimedia instant messaging systems; must make AOL's DSL available at same price in cable modem–capable areas as elsewhere. Time Warner owned Warner Brothers, HBO and Turner Broadcasting System, which owns CNN, TNT, the Cartoon Network and various sports teams as well as Time Inc. and Warner Trade Publishing.
AT&T	NorthPoint Communications	Announced its purchase of the assets—but not customers—of DSL provider NorthPoint after NorthPoint filed for Chapter 11 bankruptcy.
	Net2Phone	A 32% interest from long distance provider IDT Corporation. Net2Phone sells voice over IP service.
	American Cellular Corporation	Joint venture with Dobson Communications for 398,000 cellular customers in northeast, midwest and southeast.

Table 4.1 A Sampling of Mergers and Acquisitions of Carriers in the Telecommunications Industry (U.S. and Canada) *(continued)*

Chambers Communications Corporation (five properties)	Purchase of five of Chambers' cable TV properties in the northwest.
Honolulu Cellular	Covers Honolulu and Maui. Purchased from BellSouth.
SmarTalk TeleServices, Inc.	SmarTalk is a provider of prepaid telephone calling cards. It was in Chapter 11 when the purchase was announced in 1999.
Vanguard Cellular Systems, Inc.	Vanguard is an independent cellular company headquartered in Greensboro, North Carolina. It covers mid-Pennsylvania, parts of Ohio and West Virginia. Announced in 1998.
IBM Global Network	In 1998, AT&T purchased the global Internet, frame relay and data network from IBM. IBM Global Network covers 850 cities in 59 countries.
Excite At Home	High-speed Internet access and Web portal concern formerly owned by Cox, Cablevision, Comcast and TCI. AT&T acquired 23% when it bought TCI. Cablevision sued to stop AT&T's purchase of Cox and Comcast's shares. In January 2001, Cox and Comcast declared their intention to exchange their ownership in Excite At Home for shares of AT&T.
MediaOne Group, Inc.	MediaOne, the fourth largest cable TV company in the U.S., owned 25% of Time Warner Entertainment, which included its cable business, HBO and Warner Brothers Studio. FCC required that AT&T divest Time Warner Entertainment. It also required AT&T to sell its 8% stake in cable TV ISP Road Runner.

Table 4.1 A Sampling of Mergers and Acquisitions of Carriers in the Telecommunications Industry (U.S. and Canada) *(continued)*

Tele-Communications (TCI)	Approved in 1999. TCI, the largest cable company in the U.S., covers one-third of the U.S. market. Purchase is a way for AT&T to gain access for sale of local Internet access and interactive video service over cable lines. TCI divested itself of its stake in Sprint PCS. AT&T took control of AtHome from TCI. AtHome provides Internet access to the cable industry's customers.
Teleport Communications Group (TCG)	Acquired in 1998 to give AT&T a presence in local telephone service. TCG was the largest competitive local exchange carrier at the time with service in 66 cities. Cable companies TCI, Comcast and Cox Enterprises formerly owned it.
AT&T Canada	Bought out the non-AT&T owners.
McCaw Cellular Communications	Provided AT&T a foothold into wireless services.
BCE	
Teleglobe	Global broadband provider Teleglobe purchased U.S. long distance reseller Excel in 1998. BCE is the largest telephone company in Canada. It owns 80% of Bell Canada and SBC owns 20%. BCE owns the second largest wireless provider in Canada, Bell Mobility, and various media concerns. Purchased in 2000.
CTV	Purchased in 2000. In 2001 BCE combined these properties into Bell
The Globe and Mail	Globemedia, which owns TV, newspapers and Internet portals.
Broadwing, Inc. (formerly Cincinnati Bell)	
IXC Communications, Inc.	IXC is a wholesale carrier with a fiber network. IXC had previously purchased Coastal Telephone Company, which sold telephone service to small and midsize companies. Broadwing operates Cincinnati Bell, an independent telephone company and wireless provider. Purchased in 1999.

Table 4.1 A Sampling of Mergers and Acquisitions of Carriers in the Telecommunications Industry (U.S. and Canada) *(continued)*

	AT&T solutions customer care	Call center service bureau in Florida.
Choice One Communication, Inc.	US Xchange LLC	Rochester, New York–headquartered CLEC purchased US Xchange, a rival serving the midwest. Also offers Web hosting and design, and DSL service. Purchased in 2000.
Cable & Wireless PLC	MCI Internet backbone, wholesale and business customers	Cable & Wireless now carries the third largest amount of Internet traffic. WorldCom carries the most. The European Union required MCI to divest these assets for approval of its merger with WorldCom in 1998.
Call-Net Enterprises, Inc.	Fonorola, Inc.	Fonorola was a long distance rival of Call-Net when it was purchased in 1998. Sprint owns 25% of Canadian based Call-Net, which does business as Sprint Canada.
Charter Communications	Oxygen Media, Go2Net	Paul Allen's venture capital firm Vulcan Ventures made investments in these Web portals.
	Marcus Cable, InterMedia Partners, Helicon Cable Communications, Avalon Cable Television, Falcon Cable, Fanch Communications	With the purchase of these cable companies, Paul Allen, a cofounder of Microsoft, owns the fourth largest cable TV company in the U.S.
Citizens Communications (formerly Citizens Utilities)	Frontier Corporation	Twelfth largest independent telephone company headquartered in Rochester, New York; sold by Global Crossing. Frontier purchase completed in 2001.

Table 4.1 A Sampling of Mergers and Acquisitions of Carriers in the Telecommunications Industry (U.S. and Canada) *(continued)*

	Verizon properties	Various local telephone properties from Verizon in Arizona, California, Illinois, Nebraska and Minnesota that were part of GTE. The Illinois, Nebraska and Minnesota purchases were completed in 2000; Arizona and California are pending.
Comcast Corporation	Lenfest Communications	Lenfest is in mid-Atlantic area. Comcast increased its stake in the Calpers and Jones ventures to 100% from lower stakes. In 2001 Comcast purchased systems in six states from AT&T Broadband for $2.75 billion. Comcast is the fourth largest cable TV provider.
	Calpers cable TV assets	
	Jones Intercable, Inc.	
Cox Communications	Gannett Company's cable TV assets	The purchase of TCA and Media General's cable TV systems gives Cox access to 5 million subscribers. The Gannett purchase in 2000 adds 520,000 subscribers in the midwest. Cox is the fifth largest cable TV provider.
	TCA Cable TV	
	Media General, Inc.	
Deutsche Telekom AG	VoiceStream Wireless Corporation	U.S.'s largest GSM carrier purchased by German incumbent telephone company. The FCC delayed approval until 2001 because of security concerns about foreign government ownership of a telecommunications company.
Exodus Communications	GlobalCenter	Provides Internet services such as Web hosting. Purchased its rival from Global Crossing.
Global Crossing	Cable & Wireless PLC's undersea cable operations	Will enable Global Crossing to install and maintain its own fiber cables.
	IPC	Designs and sells voice trading systems for financial services firms. Voice trading systems enable traders and brokers in different firms to place direct calls to each other. Ixnet, which builds and designs corporate extranets for financial firms, was a subsidiary of IPC. Purchased in 2001.
	Ixnet	

Table 4.1 A Sampling of Mergers and Acquisitions of Carriers in the Telecommunications Industry (U.S. and Canada) *(continued)*

Level 3 Communications, Inc.	GeoNet Communications, Inc.	GeoNet is an ISP to small and medium customers in the Silicon Valley area. It was acquired in 1998.
	RCN Corporation	Owns a 33% common stock interest in RCN, a CLEC and cable TV company. Paul Allen's Vulcan Ventures owns 27%.
	XCOM Technologies	XCOM is a CLEC that sells Internet access to ISPs.
Liberty Media Corporation		AT&T announced that it expects to spin off Liberty Media in August 2001. Liberty Media owns interests in many cable and media companies worldwide. It spun off most of Teligent to IDT in 2001. In 2001 it purchased six cable TV companies from Deutsche Telekom.
McLeodUSA	Intelispan	CLEC McLeodUSA purchased a data services company in 2001: Web security, network monitoring and network design services.
	Splitrock Services, Inc.	Texas-based provider of data networking, Internet access and hosting services.
	CapRock Communications Corporation	Facilities-based Texas CLEC with coverage in six southwestern states. Acquisition of CapRock extends McLeod's coverage to 25 states.
Metromedia Fiber Network, Inc.	SiteSmith	Metromedia Fiber (owned by Metromedia Company) builds fiber optic networks within metropolitan areas. SiteSmith designs, manages and hosts Internet solutions. Purchased in 2000.
Qwest Communications International, Inc.	U S West	Fourth largest long distance carrier purchased the smallest baby Bell in 2000. As a condition of the merger, Qwest sold its long distance arm in the U S West area to Montana Power subsidiary TOUCHAMERICA, Inc.
	LCI International, Inc.	LCI is a reseller of long distance to residential and small business customers. 1997 revenues were $1.64 billion. Provided Qwest LCI's marketing skills and customer base. Acquired in 1998.

Table 4.1   A Sampling of Mergers and Acquisitions of Carriers in the Telecommunications Industry (U.S. and Canada) *(continued)*

	Icon CMT Corporation	Icon is an ISP and Web hosting company. It targets financial, media and pharmaceutical companies.
	EUnet International Ltd.	EUnet, based in Amsterdam, is one of Europe's fastest growing Internet Service Providers. Acquired in 1998.
	Colorado Supernet	Colorado Supernet is an Internet access provider. Acquired in 1998.
	Phoenix Network Systems	Phoenix is a long distance reseller. Acquired in 1998.
U S West Media (Now Qwest)	Continental Cable	Provided a source of cash for Continental Cable to expand its service offerings. New venture called MediaOne. In 1998, U S West split off its cable division into a new company called MediaOne Group, Inc., which was purchased by AT&T.
RCN Corporation	Erols Internet Interport JavaNet UltraNet	RCN purchased these four ISPs in 1998 and rolled them into their Internet access service. Level 3 owns 33% of RCN and Paul Allen's Vulcan Venture owns 27%.
SBC, Inc. (Southwestern Bell Communications)	BellSouth Wireless (Renamed Cingular Wireless)	Cingular Wireless is a joint venture 60% owned by SBC and 40% by BellSouth. This is the second largest cellular company in the USA behind Verizon Wireless.
	Ameritech	A 1999 merger of two RBOCs. Ameritech provides service in five mid-western states.
	The cellular unit of Comcast	This sale was announced in January of 1999. Licenses are in Illinois and Pennsylvania. Comcast is a cable TV company.
	Pacific Telesis Group	A merger of two Regional Bell Operating Companies.

Table 4.1 A Sampling of Mergers and Acquisitions of Carriers in the Telecommunications Industry (U.S. and Canada) *(continued)*

	Southern New England Telecommunications Corporation (SNET)	SNET is the independent telephone company that provides wireless, long distance and 2.3 million local service lines in Connecticut. Completed in 1998.
Science Applications International Corporation, SAIC	Bell Communications Research (Bellcore) Renamed Telcordia Technologies	Announced in September 1996 by all RBOCs, original owners of Bellcore.
Sprint	People's Choice TV Corporation	People's is a wireless cable TV company with licenses in the midwest and west. Service will be used for "last mile" wireless local loop high-speed Internet access and local telephone service.
	American Telecasting, Inc. Wireless Holdings, Inc. Videotron Bay Area, Inc.	Sprint purchased these three companies for their wireless licenses to be used for high-speed Internet access and voice and data services. Service will be deployed using wireless local loop technology.
	Centel Cellular	Became Sprint Cellular in 1993, spun off in 1995 to become an independent company named 360°, which was bought by ALLTEL in 1998.
Telus	BC Telecom (BCT)	Telus was created as the result of a 1999 merger of BC Telecom (incumbent telco in British Columbia). Telus is the second largest telephone company in Canada after BCE. Also bought QuebecTel. Also competes in central and eastern Canada. Verizon owns 27% of Telus.
	Clearnet (renamed Telus Mobility)	The largest wireless provider in Canada.
	Alberta Government Telephones Commission (AGT)	The incumbent telephone company in Alberta. Later purchased the local phone company in Edmonton (ED TEL).

Table 4.1 A Sampling of Mergers and Acquisitions of Carriers
in the Telecommunications Industry (U.S. and Canada) *(continued)*

Verizon Communications (formerly Bell Atlantic)	OnePoint (renamed Verizon Avenue)	Verizon Avenue, purchased in 2000, supplies telecommunications services within multidwelling buildings. For example, it brings DSL equipment into a building's wiring closet.
	Metromedia Fiber Network	In 1999, purchased a 19% stake. Metromedia lays fiber in metropolitan areas. Helps Verizon position itself to sell data networking service outside its regions.
	GTE Corporation	Merged company owns one-third of the access lines in the U.S., 63 million. GTE is the largest independent telco. It has revenue of $100 million in long distance and investments in foreign markets. Also sells cellular service. The FCC required that GTE Internet backbone subsidiary Genuity be divested. It can be bought back in five years if Verizon is approved for long distance in all its states by then.
	Vodafone AirTouch (Joint venture called Verizon Wireless)	Largest cellular company in the U.S. Formed in 2000. Joint venture between Verizon and Vodafone. Consists of Verizon, GTE, PrimeCo and AirTouch wireless assets. Vodafone owns 45% and Verizon owns the rest.
Vodafone Group PLC	AirTouch Communications, Inc.	AirTouch had previously purchased the cellular assets of Pacific Telesis and U S West. Vodafone is the largest cellular company in the world with a presence in 23 countries.
WorldCom Inc.	Digex (part of Intermedia Communications)	WorldCom bought Intermedia but has stated that it only intends to keep Digex, the Web hosting subsidiary of Intermedia. Digex supplies caching (Web content distribution to avoid traffic bottlenecks) and Web services. Sale of Intermedia was required by U.S. government.
	SkyTel Communications	Paging company; part of MCI Group.

Table 4.1 A Sampling of Mergers and Acquisitions of Carriers in the Telecommunications Industry (U.S. and Canada) *(continued)*

CAI Wireless Systems, Inc.	CAI owns 14 wireless cable TV systems, 6 of them in the northeast. Will be used for high-speed wireless local loop telephone service.
MCI	Provides local fiber optic networks as well as interexchange facilities. In 1998, it was WorldCom's fiftieth purchase in four years. MCI previously had purchased Nationwide Cellular, its cellular resale arm, and Western Union Corporation's Advanced Transmission Systems Division. This was the unit building fiber optic networks in cities.
Brooks Fiber Properties	Announced in 1997. Added more local fiber optic networks.
CompuServe Corporation	WorldCom kept CompuServe's 1,200 corporate Internet customers and turned over CompuServe's 3 million residential customers to AOL. AOL, in turn, transferred its Internet access and backbone to WorldCom, which sold it to Cable & Wireless.
MFS	Provided WorldCom with local fiber optic networks and ISP services. MFS had previously purchased UUNET Technologies, a supplier of Internet backbone services.
WilTel, IDB, Metromedia	Enabled WorldCom to become the fourth largest domestic interexchange carrier prior to its purchase of MCI.
ANS Communications, Inc.	Sells Internet access, virtual private networks (VPNs), and security services.
GridNet International	Internet access provider.
XO Communications (formerly Nextlink Communications Inc.)	XO Communications is a competitive local exchange carrier. Concentric is an Internet access provider. It was purchased in 2000. Cellular pioneer Craig McCaw owns a controlling interest in XO.
Concentric Network	

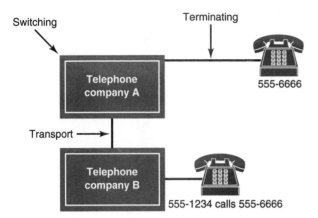

Figure 4.1
Components of local calls, transport, switching
and terminating transport.

of the large numbers of competitive local exchange providers that went out of business, much of this investment was lost.

Strategies for Entering the Local Calling Market—Resale, Wireless, Cable TV and Construction of Facilities

Companies that compete with incumbent local telephone companies either build their own infrastructure or resell incumbents' facilities. Many use a combination of both strategies. However, resale has proved to have slim margins and many remaining providers are concentrating on selling services based on their own facilities.

Resale

The Telecommunications Act of 1996 requires that Bell telephone companies unbundle components of local calling for resale. Competitors can choose to buy, for example, only local loops in some regions and switching and local loops in other regions. They also can pick from an array of services including enhanced services such as caller ID and call forwarding.

Long distance vendors, Internet service providers, carriers and resellers resell local telephone company and CLEC capacity. Resale of local services enables new competitors to avoid the cost of building fiber routes or adding wireless equipment.

Many vendors have a combined strategy that includes both resale and construction of facilities. For example, in high-density areas where there is a potential of many customers, they may construct their fiber and wireless routes. In other, less densely populated locations, they may resell Bell telephone company service.

According to the ASCENT (Association of Communications Enterprises) *2000 Membership Survey and Statistics* filled out by its members and compiled by ASCENT:

- Fifty percent use total service resale of incumbent telephone company facilities as their principal method of offering local exchange services.
- Fifteen percent use a combination of resale and their own fiber optic and wireless facilities.
- Fifteen percent primarily use their own facilities to provide local exchange service.
- Twenty percent do not provide local exchange service.

Competitors buy elements such as transport, switching and terminating services at discounts approved by the local utility commissions under guidelines set by the FCC. Their profits are realized in their markup to end users. Resellers bill end users and handle repair and customer service calls. If a repair problem is on Bell lines, the reseller reports the problem to the Bell company, which either fixes it remotely or dispatches a technician. For example, an end user buying local service on a resale basis from a company such as ITC^DeltaCom might have a BellSouth repairperson come to his or her business to repair the line if the line was resold by ITC^DeltaCom.

Data Services and Internet Access via Resale

Resale of data communications services is a high-growth application. Companies such as DSL.net collocate their equipment in incumbent telephone companies' central offices. They sell data services such as digital subscriber line (DSL), Frame Relay, ATM and SONET. (For specialized data services, see Chapter 6.) The resellers' switches route dialup Internet traffic from Bell lines to interexchange carriers. Their switches often are used to send customers' data traffic to ISPs. ISPs such as Verio sell Web hosting email, Internet services and connections to the Internet.

Some data communications and Internet providers resell services using other companies' switches as well as Bell telephone lines.

Because of the low margins in resale, many carriers are investing in leasing fiber strands and putting their own dense wavelength division multiplexers (DWDM) on the fiber. They also are installing their own switches and routers. However, for many of them, they still need to use incumbent telephone company lines in large parts of their network because they don't have fiber optic cabling to all of their customers' premises.

Wireless Local Loop—WLL for Voice and High-Speed Data

Competitive local exchange carriers such as Sprint, WorldCom, AT&T and XO Communications (formerly Nextlink) use a combination of high-capacity wireless, cable TV lines, fiber optics and resale to enter the local telecommunications market. They find that providing wireless services is less labor-intensive and does not require digging up the street. No carrier at this time relies on wireless as its primary strategy for building local infrastructure. See Figure 4.2 for a diagram local loop using a mix of fiber and fixed wireless.

Some carriers initially implemented fixed wireless as their primary strategy for building local infrastructure. Of these companies, ART (Advanced Radio Telecom Corporation) and WinStar have filed Chapter 11 bankruptcy. Teligent, as of April 2001, had $1.44 billion in long-term debt and only enough cash to see it through the second quar-

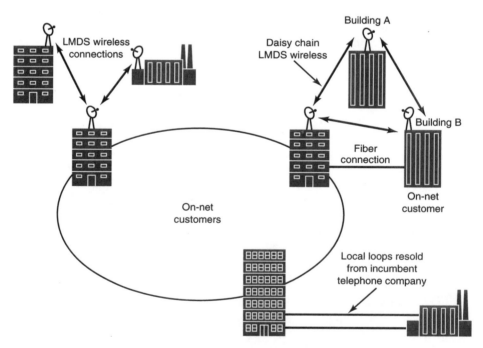

Figure 4.2
Last-Mile Technologies. Diagram courtesy of XO Communications.

ter of 2001. In all of these companies, initial costs to build new infrastructure were high, losses mounted and investors stopped putting money into the companies. Moreover, customer distrust of the technology and early technical glitches hurt sales. Finally, these companies resold incumbent telephone company service as a large part of their strategy while building out their own infrastructure. Because of high wholesale prices incumbents charged for network services resold, this turned out to be a low-profit strategy.

Sales of wireless local loop have been low in developing countries as well as in the United States. The article, "Waiting for Wireless," published in *SmartMoney.com*, 18 April 2001, by Tiernan Ray, cited statistics from Oyster Bay, New York market research firm Allied Business Intelligence that fixed wireless reaches only 100,000 users worldwide. There are, however, expectations that fixed wireless might grow in developing regions because it costs less than laying all new fiber and copper lines. The fact that countries have not standardized on spectrum they will allocate to fixed wireless service means that manufacturers must make different equipment for each frequency band. This, as well as high costs to purchase spectrum in many countries, has kept infrastructure costs high.

Wireless local loop (WLL) services are different than cellular services. Whereas cellular users use their handsets from different locations, wireless local service is a fixed service. It is available between specified points. Antennas placed on customers' roofs send radio signals to vendors' hub-site antennas and receivers. Carriers that use wireless local loop technology run fiber between their central office switches to hubs located on rooftops. Hubs consist of transmitters and receivers cabled to antennas. The antennas located at the hubs beam millimeter-size waves to antennas located on customers' rooftops.

Millimeter wireless technology refers to high-frequency services such as microwave and WLL services. The wavelengths are very small and capable of very fast transmissions. WLLs use gigahertz (GHz) frequencies, billions of waves per second in the 24 to 38 Gigahertz frequencies. (See Chapter 1 for an explanation of frequencies.) Wavelengths at these high frequencies only can travel short distances before they deteriorate. In climates with heavy rain, antennas need to be spaced closer together because heavy rain can destroy small millimeter-sized waves more easily than it damages longer waves in lower frequencies. Most companies that use WLL technology place customer antennas no farther than 1.5 miles from their base station antennas. In rainy areas such as Florida, antennas are spaced as close as .25 miles apart. Heavy rain is more damaging to radio waves than light rain. The heaviness of the rain is more critical than how often it rains. Careful engineering of antennas is required so that rain does not impair service.

In wireless local loop services, antennas must be within the line of sight of each other. No buildings, trees or other objects can obstruct the straight-line path between two antennas.

Local Multipoint Distribution Service (LMDS) and Multipoint Multichannel Distribution Service (MMDS) Fixed Wireless Service

The 28-Gigahertz service is called Local Multipoint Distribution Service (LMDS). The FCC auctioned LMDS frequencies in March 1998 and in 1999. The FCC did not make this spectrum available to the RBOCs. LMDS is known as the wireless version of fiber. It supports high-speed transmissions for voice and data communications. The FCC originally intended this spectrum for cable TV services. XO Communications uses LMDS to reach customers as an alternative to laying fiber or using the incumbent telephone company service. For example, the WLL might cost less than laying fiber for customers who don't need the capacity of fiber. WLL also is deployed for customers as a backup in the event that their fiber is cut. Their voice and data traffic is automatically switched to the wireless service.

Multipoint Multichannel Distribution Service (MMDS) is another wireless service used to provision high-speed local service. It operates at lower frequencies than LMDS and originally was conceived as a way to provide access to cable TV service. Because it uses a lower frequency (2.1–2.7 GHz), MMDS antennas can be farther from each other. Lower frequency signals, because they are based on longer wavelength signals, travel farther before degrading. Because of the longer wavelengths, the speed of MMDS service, 10 megabits per second, is slower than that of Local Multipoint Distribution Service (LMDS), which is 100 megabits per second. Sprint and WorldCom are using MMDS technology for their fixed wireless local loop service. MMDS is less costly to provision than LMDS.

Point-to-Point, Point-to-Multipoint and Daisy Chained Wireless Local Loops

Wireless local loop facilities can be point-to-point or point-to-multipoint. In *point-to-point* wireless, each vendor antenna, the base antenna, can support only one customer antenna. With *point-to-multipoint* wireless technology, each base antenna with electronics maintains communications for multiple customers. Thus, one point—the vendor's hub-site antenna transmitter and receiver—supports multiple customers.

Point-to-multipoint wireless technology was developed by the military for applications such as satellites used for surveillance. The technology is now declassified for commercial applications. Point-to-multipoint wireless services are based on bandwidth-on-demand protocols similar to those used in hybrid fiber cable TV systems. In a point-to-multipoint configuration, customers share the bandwidth. It is available "on demand." The software that manages access to the network is installed on transmitters and receivers connected to antennas. Transmissions are packetized, encrypted and sorted by software on chips. ATM switches at the hub sites transmit customer data over wireless local networks. (See Chapter 6 for ATM service.)

XO Communications sells a daisy chain configuration that provides primary as well as back-up disaster recovery service. In Figure 4.2, building A is connected to XO's fiber by wireless service. Building B is connected to XO's equipment by fiber and to building B by wireless service. If building B's fiber is cut, XO can transmit its traffic through building A's antenna.

High-Capacity Free Space Optics for Fixed Wireless Service • Companies such as Terabeam are developing high-frequency, high-capacity services that use lasers to beam data over short distances. The technology is referred to as *free space optics*, or *fiberless optical service*. Terabeam's service is being developed to support speeds of 1 gigabit. This is a higher speed than traditional [256 kilobits to OC-3 (155 megabits)] fixed wireless service. A one-hub antenna can support multiple antennas from a single originating site. Terabeam's service is not commercially deployed at this time. The high frequencies make it prone to disruption from fog and rain. Lucent Technologies owns 30% of Terabeam.

Construction of Fiber Optic and Cable Routes

Many CLECs, utilities and cable TV companies have fiber optic cabling in metropolitan areas. MCI, before it was part of WorldCom, started a subsidiary in 1994 called MCI Metro to develop fiber networks in major metropolitan areas. When WorldCom bought MFS and Brooks Fiber, it gained the miles of fiber MFS and Brooks had deployed in cities. WorldCom's purchase of MCI gave it this entire fiber infrastructure. These local fiber networks are used to transport calls from local customers to the WorldCom network, as well as for providing local calling and Internet access.

New local carriers often construct their own fiber routes in areas where they have many customers, and initially resell Bell transport in regions where they have fewer customers or have not yet built facilities. Both WorldCom and AT&T resell local telephone company services in areas where they have no fiber or coaxial cable facilities.

Cable TV companies have local networks that consist of both coaxial cable and fiber optic cabling. These networks are known as hybrid fiber coaxial (HFC) systems. Fiber runs from the cable headend or main location to the neighborhood. Coaxial cable is used in neighborhood streets and to individual homes and apartment buildings. (See Figure 2.17 in Chapter 2 for a drawing of an HFC network.) Some cable TV companies directly route fiber to a customer's building. This is generally the case with multi-tenant apartment buildings. Large investments of capital are required to convert one-way cable systems to two-way systems and add switches for telephone and data communications applications. According to the National Cable Television Association

AN EXAMPLE OF A UTILITY AS AN OVERBUILDER

UtiliCorp United, a utility located in Kansas City, Missouri, has a subsidiary, Everest Connections, which is an overbuilder. UtiliCorp's first telecommunications venture was in Australia, where it built fiber networks using in part the incumbent telephone company Telstra's conduit. UtiliCorp is leveraging the telecommunications expertise gained in Australia and its utility resources to start telecommunications ventures in the United States. It also thinks that the telecommunications business looks a lot like the utility business, where companies serve a mass market in every neighborhood and maintain a network. According to UtiliCorp's 2000 Annual Report discussion of Everest,

"Our overall strategy is to enter areas that are underserved by existing broadband providers."

According to Kevin Anderson, President of Everest Connections, "The focus is on last/first mile connections to homes and businesses." Everest sells high-speed Internet access, telephone service and cable TV to customers in 30 municipalities in the Kansas City, Kansas and Missouri areas. Under the Telecommunications Act of 1996, utilities must provide the same access to competitors and, to their own subsidiaries, to telephone poles. Everest has the skills, knows the rules and language of how to obtain these permissions. It also has relationships with construction companies for building hybrid coaxial cable fiber routes.

Everest started selling service in February 2000 and quickly reached 20% penetration in residential neighborhoods. It believes it will reach 30% to 40% penetration quickly. Ninety percent of its customers are taking all three of the services it sells. According to Kevin Anderson, the following is the reaction of customers: "Just give me a local reliable offering that saves me a few dollars and gives me one bill." Business customers are an attractive option for Everest. The investment is the same but monthly revenues are anticipated to be higher than with residential customers. Everest is targeting small businesses in locations such as strip malls. The impact of competition is already being felt in the first city in which Everest started selling service. The incumbent cable TV provider raised prices 5% in all of the neighboring towns but not in the town where Everest provides service.

(NCTA) cable operators sold 1% of their cable TV subscribers, 800,000 customers, telephone service as of year-end 2000. The majority of the service, in 500,000 homes, was sold by AT&T Broadband.

Overbuilders—Cable TV Competitors

For the most part, competitors for local service sell to the business, government, education and health care industries. New cable TV companies are the largest telecommunications segment that target residential customers. Competitors to incumbent cable TV companies are known as *overbuilders*. Overbuilders lay fiber and hybrid co-axial cable fiber systems to which they connect central office switches, television antennas and routers and switches for high-speed Internet access. (See Chapter 5 for details on network architecture.) According to the National Cable Television Association, RCN is the largest overbuilder in the United States. RCN has 335,000 cable TV and 500,000 dialup Internet subscribers in seven markets including New York, Boston and Los Angeles and has raised $6.56 billion in capital. RCN has joint ventures with electric utilities in Boston, Los Angeles and Washington, D.C. for their cable build-outs. In December 2000, RCN announced that it was halting expansion plans due to a cash shortfall.

The overbuilder market is just starting and has not made a serious dent in incumbent cable TV company's monopolies. Overbuilding, building all new infrastructure, requires large capital expenditures of $2500 to $3000 per residence. Because of the cost, widespread competition will develop slowly. Many overbuilders are planning service in suburban areas outside of cities. Overbuilders sell cable TV, telephone service and high-speed cable modem Internet access. They usually offer long distance on a resale basis. For example, they might resell Sprint or WorldCom long distance.

CARRIERS ....

Because of improvements in fiber optic technologies, such as dense wave division multiplexing and the relative ease of building long distance networks alongside railroad tracks and highways, there is a proliferation of high-speed networks in much of the world. The increased competition and capacity has led to lower prices and to the commoditization of bandwidth. Integrated Network Providers who compete with incumbent local telephone companies are building fiber optic and some wireless facilities over which to sell local service in metropolitan areas. (Integrated Network Providers is another term for telecommunication carriers.) Utilities, with their years of experience in constructing fiber optic networks, are actively building telecommunications infrastructure.

Interexchange Carriers—IEXs

Prior to the Telecommunications Act of 1996, interexchange carriers (IEXs) sold long distance services primarily between states and to international locations. These carriers now sell local, international, data services and high-speed Internet access as well as voice long distance. The largest IEXs own most of the switching and transmission equipment over which their interstate traffic is routed. For example, they own fiber optic cabling, microwave towers, multiplexing equipment (to send multiple voice and data conversations over the same fiber cable) and switches that route calls. The distinction between local and long distance service carriers is disappearing. Now that Qwest owns the former RBOC U S West, it is an interexchange carrier only in the territory outside of that region. The four largest interexchange carriers in the United States are:

- AT&T
- WorldCom
- Sprint
- Qwest

Services they sell include:

- Toll-free 800, 877 and 888 services
- Outgoing long distance
- Data communications services
- Web hosting services
- Internet services
- Dedicated private lines

Impact of RBOC Entry into Long Distance

According to the FCC, as restated in 1999 dollars, per-minute long distance prices were .52¢ in 1984. Competition has driven these prices to less than .05¢ for business customers in 2001. Profits for voice services are declining and even more competition from RBOCs who win permission to sell in-region long distance is occurring. Some carriers are getting out of the consumer market for long distance. WorldCom announced plans to spin off its consumer long distance division. They started MCI Group in 2001 as a tracking stock. The group sells long distance to consumers and small businesses as well as dial-up Internet, paging and wholesale long distance. WorldCom's other tracking stock is WorldCom Group. It sells voice, data, international and Internet services to commercial customers.

AT&T and MCI have warned that they might not sell long distance to consumers in states where RBOCs have permission to sell long distance. Sprint already has pulled out of these states. These companies, which need to purchase access lines to connect to local customers, accuse the Bells of pricing these connections prohibitively high. SBC sold long distance to 1.7 million customers and Verizon sold it to 1.4 million customers in Texas and New York by April 2001. Verizon started selling long distance in New York in January 2000 and SBC in early 2000.

A stumbling block for RBOCs in their sales to large business customers is their billing systems. When interexchange carriers and CLECs sell service to customers located in multistate regions, they offer them the option of receiving one bill for all locations. RBOCs still cannot do that. Even when they sell service to customers in different states in their own region, for the most part, customers are flooded with many bills for different services and locations. Although not as profitable as wireless and data sales, carriers often see voice services to commercial and business customers as providing contacts for sales of their more lucrative and faster growing data and Internet services offerings. In addition, high volumes of business calls make up for the lower margins.

Wholesale Carriers—Carrier Sales to Other Carriers

Many carriers sell both to retail and wholesale customers. For example, about 30% of XO's revenue is from other carriers and the rest from retail customers. Some carriers sell primarily to other carriers and Internet service providers (ISPs). These include Level 3 Communications, Williams Communications Group, Broadwing, Inc. and Global Crossing Ltd. Telecommunications companies and ISPs that buy wholesale resell service to consumers and business customers and sometimes to other carriers. Many of these carriers connect to their wholesale customers via carrier hotels. *Carrier hotels* are warehouse-like spaces where telephone companies install their voice and data equipment. Carriers connect to each other's fiber optic lines and equipment at carrier hotels. See Chapter 5 for carrier hotels.

Carriers often both sell to other carriers and buy from other carriers in routes where they don't have fiber. For example, Level 3 stated in its first quarter 2001 results that it leases capacity on other networks for 50% of its customers' traffic in North America and Europe. Level 3 further stated that it intends to migrate 95% of customer traffic to its own fiber by May 2001. To date, AT&T and WorldCom Group have the most complete fiber optic networks.

As carriers build out their own fiber networks, there is concern that there is over-capacity for bandwidth. In the article, "Fed Eases After Telecom Defaults—Coincidence?" published in *Barron's Online*, 4 April 2001, Jennifer Ablan stated that bandwidth prices dropped 50% in 2000 and are expected to be 40% lower in 2001. Falling prices leave carriers with less money to pay for laying fiber and, in particular, for adding electronics such as dense wavelength division multiplexing (DWDM) to their fiber. (The electronics convert copper signals to light pulses and enables the fiber to carry many simultaneous streams of traffic.) Because of the cost of building out their networks, many of these carriers are operating at a loss. At the same time, money from investors is drying up. A new phenomenon resulting from dropping prices and more available capacity is bandwidth trading. Instead of leasing fiber, some carriers are bidding on routes between major cities such as Los Angeles to New York and London to New York.

BANDWIDTH TRADING: THE COMMODITIZATION OF BANDWIDTH ....

Just as commodities such as natural gas, oil and electricity are traded, bandwidth trading in telecommunications is just emerging as a way to buy and sell capacity and hedge the risks of building new routes and buying capacity. For example, a competitive local exchange carrier (CLEC) that sells both long distance and local service can decrease its risk of price spikes by locking in a future price for bandwidth leases. The seller, a carrier, can cut its risk of adding expensive electronics such as wavelength division multiplexing (WDM) to dark fiber by selling future capacity. A future sale locks in a price floor and future revenues. It guarantees the price won't drop below a certain price for the seller and fixes a price ceiling for the buyer. *Bandwidth trading* is the listing, buying and selling of various telecommunications services through participants such as brokers, traders and exchanges. The following factors make bandwidth trading viable:

- *Readily available public lists, or indices, of prices for services*—i.e., DS-3 (45 megabits), OC-3 (155 megabits) routes; for example, Los Angeles to Miami (this is referred to as *price transparency*).

- *Services offered should be essentially the same for all buyers*—Services should be perceived as *commodities*.

- *Widely recognized standards* such as speed, capacity and quality of service (QoS) that can be priced accordingly.

- *Locations with readily available interconnections in which bandwidth can be accessed by multiple carriers*—This creates readily available services and products (liquidity).

- *Multiple buyers and sellers.*

- *Standardized contracts* to shorten negotiation intervals.

- *Guaranteed delivery* with performance guarantees.

In telecommunications, traders buy and sell point-to-point routes at a given speed such as OC-3 between London and New York City. Other products such as dark fiber, conduit for fiber and minutes also are traded. Merchants help manage risk by guaranteeing that prices won't drop beneath a certain level (a floor) or increase above a price (a ceiling). They also guarantee the availability of products in the event of a spike in demand. They offer risk management. Buyers include large enterprises, re-sellers, facilities-based carriers and companies that build networks for other carriers. Sellers are large facilities-based carriers and carriers or resellers with excess capacity.

Bandwidth trading is still in its early stages. It is evolving as a result of growing capacities in long distance networks and commoditization of networks. Technological innovations such as wavelength division multiplexing have added tremendous capacity to telecommunications networks in Europe and the United States. Not only is there more capacity, but services are reliable and there is very little difference to end users and other carriers among the networks. Finally, capital is drying up for expansion of more diverse routes. Thus, when a carrier is faced with the decision of building new routes or leasing them, it often chooses to lease capacity from other carriers to conserve capital. For carriers of existing networks, selling spare capacity lets them fill their "pipes" more fully.

Companies such as Enron Corporation, Dynergy Corporation, Williams Communications Group and Aquila Broadband Services offer different types of brokerage, trading and risk management services. Many of these companies developed skills in the energy business in which brokering, trading and managing risks of building and buying energy is common. Firms that offer brokerage and exchange services don't take title to the routes, fiber or collocation space for which they are the middleman. They operate in a similar fashion to stockbrokers. They receive commissions on routes that are brokered.

Enron and Aquila Broadband Services are traders and merchants. Traders buy the routes they sell or swap routes with carriers or other traders. Examples of routes traded are DS-3 [44 megabits per second (Mbps)], OC-3 (155 Mbps), miles in the United States and STM-1 (155 Mbps) routes internationally. The routes are listed at DS-0 (64 thousand bits per second) monthly per-mile rates. For example, New York to Los Angeles might list at .004¢ per DS-0 mile. Because there are 672 DS-0s in one DS-3, this equals $2.69 per mile (672 × .004). Traders sit at trading desks, their computers, where prices of routes are available. If they see prices of routes they own going up, they hold them and hope to sell them at higher prices. If they think prices are high, they sell routes they don't have and try to buy them later at a lower price. They don't actually take physical possession of most of what they trade.

Merchants—Managing Risk for Carriers

Wholesale telecom merchants do trading and also perform more risk management functions for carriers and large enterprises. They do more actual buying, financing and selling than trading. They offer services to Internet service providers, network build-ers and very large enterprises. The following are types of transactions telecom mer-chants might make:

- Sell a route to a carrier that the merchant doesn't own, at for example, .007¢ per DS-0 mile. Buy the actual physical route for .005¢ per DS-0 mile, making a profit of .02¢ per mile. This guarantees a price to a carrier.

- Some competitive local exchange carriers (CLECs) have contracts for bandwidth at prices that are much higher than those currently available. A merchant will buy the expensive contract that results in high operating costs for the CLEC and sell it back to them at a lower price plus a premi-um (a fee). The merchant will get an agreement from the CLEC to buy routes the following year at a fixed price.

- Sell an option to a carrier that is growing fast to buy bandwidth at a fixed price in the future. This guarantees the carriers' future costs.

Pooling points are being developed as places where, in a short period of time—perhaps a day—interconnections between carriers can be set up. A neutral pooling point is a place where large carriers and local telephone companies terminate and interconnect their circuits. Neutral pooling points are run by third parties rather than by a particular carrier. The company managing the pooling point connects local carriers to large backbone carriers as deals are made. For example, the neutral pooling point operator will make connections between carriers by programming an optical switch such that carrier A's traffic is routed to carrier B. Neutral pooling operators in-clude LighTrade, Equinix and Switch and Data Facilities Company. See Chapter 5 for optical switches.

Williams is using its existing connections in carrier hotels for links with carriers with whom it arranges trades. It calls their carrier hotels *virtual pooling points. Carri-er hotels* are warehouse-type sites where carriers have their routers and multiplexers and exchange traffic with each other and interconnect to local and long distance net-works. Enron uses its own carrier hotels as pooling points and has stated that it also will participate in neutral pooling points.

Exchanges—A Place to Make Trades

Just as the New York Stock Exchange is a place where buyers and sellers come togeth-er to buy and sell stock, exchanges are being developed to exchange excess bandwidth capacity. Exchanges can be electronic or physical sites. Two of these exchanges are Arbinet-thexchange and Band-X. Arbinet-thexchange is an online exchange that lists available routes to, for example, Japan and Brazil, for members of its exchange. Band-

X operates international exchanges where dark fiber, ducts for fiber, minutes of long distance and bandwidth are traded. Popular routes in Europe are between Amsterdam, Frankfurt, London and Paris. Exchanges typically charge about 2.5% for their service. They might require that buyers provide letters of credit. The most popular route in the United States is between New York City and Los Angeles. Some exchanges also offer brokerage services. *Indexes* are lists of prices of trades. Dow Jones and Enron Online have indexes.

Master Trading Agreements— Shortening the Transaction Cycle

Purchasing optical fiber routes from carriers can take six months to a year in a traditional purchase and sale. Master trading agreements are key to shorter negotiating intervals when acquiring bandwidth through trading mechanisms. Master agreements spell out terms in advance for service levels, type of service and liquidated damages. With *liquidated damages*, suppliers agree to pay a penalty if they don't deliver or perform as agreed. Customers with poor credit might be required to prepay for service. According to Pat Peldner, Vice President of Business Development for Aquila Broadband Services,

> *"The development of standard contractual terms and conditions is a vital and necessary effort during the development of a commodity market. The brokers, exchanges and merchants support a contract with strict financial liabilities for non-performance that are similar to agreements that govern the trading of other commodities."*

There are a few standard contracts that businesses use. An industry group, the Competitive Telecommunications Association (CompTel) has formed an *ad hoc* group that is developing a standardized agreement.

LOCAL SERVICE PROVIDERS ....

In addition to incumbent telephone companies, a variety of providers sell local services. These include interexchange carriers, resellers, utilities and agents. A new type of provider, building local exchange carriers, sell services to tenants in office parks and multi-tenant buildings.

AT&T

AT&T has been transformed from "Ma Bell," the telecommunications giant with 330,000 employees in 1995 to a company with 160,000 employees, decreasing long distance revenues, strong cellular sales and massive debt in April 2001.

Background

After AT&T was divested of the local incumbent Bell Operating Companies (BOCs) in 1984, it retained units that sold voice and data communications and switching equipment. Their equipment divisions manufactured and sold gear to carriers as well as general business customers.

Once AT&T started selling local service through bypass and its new subsidiary Teleport, it came to be perceived as a competitor to RBOCs for local and, eventually, long distance service. (See Chapter 3 for bypass.) Thus, for its largest customers of switching equipment, RBOCs, purchasing central office equipment from AT&T could be perceived as buying from competitors. To protect central office sales, AT&T spun off its customer premise and carrier sales and manufacturing units at the end of 1996. The new company was Lucent Technologies. AT&T spun off NCR, its computer systems and services unit early in 1997.

Recent Events

In 2000, AT&T made its wireless unit, AT&T Wireless, a tracking stock to increase its value to shareholders. Tracking stocks may pay dividends and can be traded separately but do not represent ownership in separate companies. AT&T Wireless Group has consistently outperformed the rest of AT&T. It is the third largest cellular provider in the United States and is partly owned by NTT DoCoMo.

AT&T accumulated large amounts of debt by:

- Purchasing cellular assets from Craig McCaw and others
- Purchasing spectrum and building infrastructure for wireless services
- Upgrading its backbone network to OC 192 (10 gigabits) speeds for high-speed data and Internet traffic
- Buying cable TV properties TCI and MediaOne to offer residential Internet access bundled with telephone and cable TV service
- Upgrading its new cable TV assets for phone and high-speed Internet access over the cable TV outside wires—bringing total investment in cable TV to $115 billion by October 2000

In addition, AT&T's earnings were hurt by losses at its cable TV Internet access provider, Excite At Home, lower margins on long distance and competition that cut into its market share. Many analysts felt that AT&T erred by not building more fiber infrastructure in metropolitan areas to beef up sales to businesses. AT&T also alienated business customers with its billing system on which it was difficult to correct billing mistakes. Its fourth quarter 2000 profits fell 51% from the previous period.

Breaking Up AT&T—Again

To attract investors, AT&T announced plans to spin off its wireless division and create tracking stocks for its business, residential and broadband (cable TV) units (see Table 4.2). AT&T felt that there would be more value for shareholders if they had shares in individual companies rather than one large company.

Table 4.2   The AT&T 2001 Planned Break-Up

Name of Unit	Percent of Total Year 2000 AT&T Revenues	Tracking Stock or Independent Company
AT&T Business	42%	Will keep the AT&T brand and stock symbol on the New York Stock Exchange
AT&T Consumer	25%	Tracking stock of AT&T Business (under terms of the contract between the business and consumer units, the consumer unit is required to use the AT&T network for five years for its customer's traffic)
AT&T Wireless	18%	Independent company
AT&T Broadband	15%	Initially a tracking stock; later an independent company

In 2000, AT&T also announced the 2001 planned spin-off of Liberty Media Group, which at the time was a tracking stock. AT&T acquired Liberty Media as part of its acquisition of TCI. Liberty Media chairman is cable TV pioneer John Malone, AT&T's largest shareholder. Liberty Media holds: 49% of Discovery Communications, 21% of USA Networks, 21% of Sprint PCS plus numerous cable holdings in Europe.

To lower its debt, AT&T sold its 10% stake in Japan Telecom and stakes in various cable properties in the United States. It also plans to sell its 30 million shares of Cablevision. It is shedding its 25.5% ownership in Time Warner Entertainment mandated by the FCC as a condition of its merger with MediaOne. Under FCC rulings, no cable company is allowed to own more than 30% of the total cable subscribers in the United States. These steps are expected to lower AT&T's debt from $65 billion in January 2001 to about $32 billion.

Competitive Local Exchange Carriers (Integrated Communications Providers)

According to the Association for Local Telecommunications Services (ALTS) as of third quarter 2000, CLECs serve 8.2% of the nation's 196 million access lines. They are termed competitive local exchange carriers because they compete with independent and Regional Bell Operating Companies. These firms are known as *incumbent telephone companies*. However, when they compete outside of their home territories, which is rare for Regional Bell Operating Companies (RBOCs), they are considered CLECs. CLECs, also known as *integrated communications providers* (ICPs), sell Internet access, data communications services, white and yellow page listings, toll-free (800 and 888) service, long distance and 911 services. CLECs refer to themselves as ICPs when they sell local and data services over their own fiber optic or wireless infrastructure.

The three largest CLECs are WorldCom Group, AT&T and McLeodUSA, headquartered in Rapid City, Iowa. According to Greg Mycio, Director, Broadband Analysis for New Paradigm Resources Group, Inc. (NPRG), WorldCom Group has $15 billion in local sales, AT&T has $14.5 billion and McLeodUSA has $1.4 billion. Between them, AT&T and WorldCom made up 66% of CLEC sales. See Table 4.3 for CLEC revenue by category. WorldCom's purchases of MCI Metro, MFS and Brooks Fiber and AT&T's purchase of Teleport gave them a jump-start on owning fiber infrastructure for local service.

Clark McLeod, who started his career as a junior high school math teacher, founded McLeodUSA. Mr. McLeod first founded long distance company Telecom USA (formerly Teleconnect) in April of 1981. In 1991, two years after Telecom USA was bought by MCI, he started McLeodUSA (at that time, McLeod Telecommunications) with Stephen Gray. With its acquisition of CapRock, McLeodUSA expanded into Texas, Louisiana, Arkansas and Oklahoma. McLeodUSA's local telephone and data services are concentrated in 25 states in the midwest, southwest and Rocky Mountain regions. Interestingly, 25% of McLeodUSA's revenue is derived from the sale of white and yellow page directories to customers in 26 states. It operates an extensive interstate fiber network in its region, and expects to add fiber optic electronics by year-end 2001 to most of the Level 3 fiber for which it has rights.

Some CLECs such as ITC^DeltaCom, headquartered in West Point, Georgia were originally independent local telephone companies. Independent telephone companies were non-AT&T owned incumbent telephone companies, for the most part established prior to the 1984 divestiture. ITC^DeltaCom was established as an independent telephone company, Interstate Telephone Company (ITC), in Alabama in 1986. Through a merger with FiberNet, it owns a 4,600-mile fiber network. It sells wholesale and retail services on the FiberNet facilities as well as on utility companies' fiber networks in the southeastern region of the U.S.

- CLECs sell services via a mix of their own facilities and those they resell or lease from incumbents. According to Credit Suisse First Boston, by the second quarter of 2000, the total CLEC line mix was 36% their own fiber or wireless facilities, 31% total resale and 33% unbundled network elements. With unbundled network elements, the provider owns some of its own equipment, perhaps its switch or DSL-multiplexing equipment and resells a portion of the incumbent network, perhaps the last mile to the customer premise. Total resale means the provider has no equipment connected to the incumbent's network.

- *The Association for Local Telecommunications Services (ALTS) Annual Report on the State of the Local Telecom Industry, 2001* stated that of the 40 public CLECs, only four are profitable. They are Intermedia Communications, NTELOS (formerly known as CFW Communications), Pac-West Telecom and Time Warner Telecom. ALTS used as their sources: WSJ.com, MSNBC.com, New Paradigm Resources Group (NPRG), Morgan Stanley Dean Witter and ALTS.

- CLECs sell mostly to business customers. According to the FCC, by mid-June 2000, 66% of CLEC lines served business, institutional and government lines. In contrast, 79% of incumbent telephone company lines served residential and small business customers.

- The largest area for growth for CLECs is data communications services (e.g., Frame Relay, ATM, Internet access, DSL and Web-related services).

Table 4.3 shows revenue changes by category for CLECs between 1999 and 2000. Long distance is essentially flat and data services grew 101%.

Table 4.3 CLEC Industry Revenue by Service Category

Revenue Category	Revenue (in Millions of $)	
	1999	2000
Switched Local Service[1]	$7,007	$8,685
Long Distance[1]	$2,627	$2,591
Dedicated Access & Private Line	$6,131	$7,358
Data[2]	$10,218	$20,547
Total CLEC Service Revenue	$25,983	$39,181
All Other Revenue[3]	$3,211	$5,361
Total Revenue	$29,194	$44,542

Source: New Paradigm Resources Group, Inc.
Notes:
[1]Includes resale revenues.
[2]Includes all data and data-related services (e.g., Frame Relay, ATM, Internet access).
[3]Includes miscellaneous telecom revenue (e.g., reciprocal compensation) and non-telecom–related revenues (e.g., network development and directory services).

HOMETOWN SOLUTIONS, LLC—THE SMALLEST CLEC

The smallest CLEC in the United States, HomeTown Solutions, LLC, has annual revenues of $25,000 and is located in rural Minnesota. HomeTown Solutions was started in 1998 as a joint effort of the incumbent telephone company, which is Federated Telephone Cooperative (FTC) and electric utility Agralite Electric Cooperative. FTC began operations in 1952 as a cooperative, bringing telephone service to farmers and villages who had no telephone service. FTC today is the incumbent independent telephone company for eight communities with a total population of 2,200 people.

The idea of expansion into another town, nearby Morris outside of the FTC territory, was spurred by businesses and residential customers in Morris having only one choice for service, Qwest (formerly U S West). In addition, some fiber was already installed in Morris. HomeTown installed a remote shelf of the FTC central office in Morris and ran fiber to every business. By the end of 1999 and the beginning of 2000, HomeTown Solutions started offering service to business customers. Fiber will be run to every residence by the fall of 2001. The total population of Morris, including a university, is 5500. HomeTown Solutions is now operating as a CLEC in Morris. It sells local service, long distance, high-speed Internet and dialup Internet as well as cable TV service. It also is an agent for Cellular 2000, a cellular company in the area.

Although small in scope—currently with 18 employees, some of whom work for both FTC and HomeTown Solutions—the HomeTown endeavor illustrates the trend of independent telephone companies expanding service into other areas and working jointly with electric utilities. Certainly, competition in these more rural areas is less intense than in larger metropolitan areas.

Carriers with Their Own Facilities

To avoid the expense of constructing new networks, some new carriers purchase switches and connect them to other carriers' fiber optic networks. The most common way to gain exclusive rights to a set amount of capacity on fiber optic cabling is through a technique called Indefeasible Right of Use (IRU). The owner of the fiber system performs installation and maintenance. The carrier installs the switching equipment and is responsible for customer service, marketing and billing.

With IRU, a carrier purchases the rights to a set number of fiber strands from investors that have built a fiber network. Indefeasible Right of Use is analogous to purchasing a condominium. Where a purchaser of a condominium buys only one or more units in an apartment building and pays a "condo fee" for maintenance, an IRU owner purchases a set amount of fiber capacity on someone else's fiber run. This costs less than hiring crews to lay fiber. It also guarantees a fixed amount of bandwidth.

Resellers and Switchless Resellers

According to ATLANTIC•ACM, a Boston-based consulting firm, in 1999 resellers generated $13.26 billion in long distance revenues. AT&T, MCI Group, ITC^Delta-Com, McLeodUSA, the RBOCs and Sprint sell both directly to end users and to carriers. Resellers buy long distance services from other carriers and resell them at retail prices to end users.

There are three types of resellers:

- **Facilities-based resellers**—Own switches that route calls; lease lines from major carriers over which the calls are routed as well as own some of their own outside cabling.
- **Pure resellers**—Do not own switches; purchase large quantities of switched services that they resell; receive billing tapes from carriers with detail from which they bill customers directly for services.
- **Agents**—Work as independent sales agents for local telephone companies and interexchange carriers. Agents do not issue bills. Customers are billed directly by the telephone company or the IEX.

Resellers buy and resell long distance services, local services, Internet access and data services such as Frame Relay. The services they resell are from national and regional carriers such as RBOCs, Sprint, Qwest Communications, MCI Group and AT&T. Facilities-based resellers own switches in high-volume calling areas that route calls over the fiber cable lines leased from the major carriers. Resellers do not necessarily have switches in all of the locations from which they sell long distance.

Pure resellers purchase and resell services from multiple long distance carriers. The carriers that transport the calls send billing tapes to the reseller. The reseller uses these tapes to generate bills, which it sends to its customers. Resellers have customer service and sales staff to which customers report service problems. The reseller, in turn, coordinates resolution of problems with carriers.

Dial around (10-10xxx), prepaid debit cards and international calling make up a large part of the resale market, as does cellular long distance. Cellular carriers owned by RBOCs that don't have permission to sell in-region long distance rely on resale to transport their customers' long distance traffic.

Another form of reseller is the alternate operator service (AOS) provider company. *AOS companies* supply long distance to privately owned pay phones and telephones in public locations such as airports, hospitals and universities. They buy long distance in bulk from interexchange carriers and resell it at a premium. Calls from these phones are intercepted by alternate operator services equipment. Their highly automated equipment validates credit card numbers and keeps track of calls for billing purposes. They also process debit card calls. The AOS market has been hurt by the proliferation of cellular telephones. People with cell phones do not need to use pay phones. In 2001, BellSouth announced that it is getting out of the pay phone business.

UTILITIES—A NATURAL FIT FOR TELECOMMUNICATIONS

In many ways, utilities operate similarly to incumbent telecommunications companies. They own miles of fiber, and state and national agencies regulate them. Moreover, utilities as well as incumbent telephone companies own telephone poles. Because of this background, they know how to obtain rights to lay fiber and to gain access to each other's conduits and telephone poles. They've had experience in the rules and regulations and know how to go about the tasks of building outside infrastructure.

Utilities are a slow-growth industry. They are faced with deregulation, competition and possible loss of market share. A way some of them hope to expand is by investing in telecommunications. In addition, utility companies have skills in handling billing and customer service issues. The intention is to offer "one-stop shopping" for services such as video-on-demand, Internet access, data services and voice calling.

The following are examples of utilities that are in telecommunications:

- The Montana Power Company started a subsidiary, Telecommunications Resources, Inc., which eventually purchased TOUCHAMERICA and changed its name to TOUCHAMERICA. It has cellular properties, a fiber network in the west and it purchased the long distance assets of Qwest in its 14-state RBOC (formerly U S West) territory. Montana Power plans on taking TOUCHAMERICA public.

- Enron Broadband Services is part of Enron Corporation, a utility headquartered in Houston. Enron Communications has a high-speed interstate fiber optic network. Enron offers bandwidth trading where buyers can bid on fiber optic–based routes to carry traffic. It also sells the routes that carriers bid on through their pooling points. *Pooling points* are places where carriers interconnect their networks to use capacity they have bid on. Enron offers services such as streaming video to ISPs, carriers and corporate customers. Streaming video is a way to carry video to end users more effectively over Internet-type networks by compressing the video so that less network capacity is required. (See Chapter 1 for streaming video.)

- Citizens Communications, formerly Citizens Utilities, sees so much potential in telecommunications that it is selling its electricity, water and natural gas businesses to focus on telecommunications. Citizens Communications Company is headquartered in Stamford, Connecticut. It has 2.5 million access lines in 24 states across the United States. Its subsidiary, Electric Lightwave, Inc., of Vancouver, Washington, operates a broadband fiber optic network in the western United States. Its fiber network consists of two routes from Portland, Oregon to Los Angeles and from the state of Washington to California. It sells both to end users and to carriers.

Other utilities in telecommunications include:

- Pacific Enterprises of Southern California
- Enova Corporation of San Diego
- NStar in the Boston, Massachusetts, area
- UtiliCorp of Kansas and Missouri
- Carolina Power & Light Company of Raleigh, North Carolina

Building Local Exchange Carriers (BLECs)

Building local exchange carriers (Building LECs) build infrastructure inside campus and multidwelling office buildings including hospitals, hotels (there are 3.5 million hotels in the U.S. alone), dormitories, schools and marinas. They essentially are an outsourcing service for all of a tenant's telecommunications needs. Instead of finding providers for all of their voice and data needs, customers are offered one vendor, the Building LEC, for all of their needs. Building local exchange carriers sell:

- High-speed Internet access
- Email
- Web hosting
- Secure remote access to email and corporate files
- "Firewalls" for LAN-connected computers
- Long distance

Building Local Exchange Carriers primarily offer small and medium businesses the convenience of one bill for these services. They connect the in-building cabling, routing and multiplexing equipment to carriers' long distance networks and the Internet.

Initially, most BLECs concentrated on metropolitan areas where they had access to many buildings in each area. Many of them were started by real estate investment trusts (REITs) as a source of revenue. For example, a Building Local Exchange Carrier such as Broadband Office or Advanced Buildings Networks (a division of CLEC Intermedia) signs an agreement with a building owner to offer telecommunications services to its tenants. The building owner receives a monthly commission for each tenant that signs up with the BLEC. Prior to the FCC's ruling that banned exclusive agreements between building owners and carriers, these agreements often barred tenants from using anyone other than the BLEC's long distance or Internet access partner for service. The FCC banned these agreements going forward but allowed pre-existing terms to remain unchanged.

A new breed of building local exchange carrier serves suburban campuses and buildings that might be too far from the central office to qualify for DSL. PhatPipe, based in California, is one example of a BLEC concentrating on suburban areas. In multibuilding office parks, PhatPipe offers to connect the smaller buildings to the main building with wireless service to eliminate laying fiber to these buildings. The main building houses electronics such as routers and T-1 and T-3 access devices. PhatPipe leases T-3 circuits from WorldCom to carry voice and data traffic. PhatPipe puts its Internet access equipment in WorldCom points of presence (POPs) where WorldCom has its switching equipment.

Other Building Equipment Local Exchange Carriers are: Allied Riser, Intellispace and Verizon Avenue (formerly OnePoint Communications). Companies such as Verizon Avenue place DSL multiplexers in building wiring closets and operate the DSL over the building's copper cabling. From the building to the telephone company switch, it sends the data over fiber. Placing the DSL access multiplexer (DSLAM) in the building eliminates the distance limitation between the DSL modem in the customer office and the DSLAM, which is often located in the telephone company central office or remote fiber equipment located between the central office and the customer.

Agents

Agents work on commission for local telephone and interexchange companies. They enter into agreements to sell long distance, local toll calling, data services, cellular service and value-added services such as voice mail, paging and local Centrex services. (See Chapter 2; with Centrex, most of the hardware for business telephone systems is located in the telephone company central office rather than at the customer premise.)

PAY NOW, HOPE TO CALL LATER—PREPAID CARDS

Debit cards represent an area of opportunity for resellers, operator service companies, carriers and agents. Debit cards were introduced in the U.S. in the late 1980s. According to Atlantic▪ACM statistics supplied by the International Prepaid Communications Association, in 2000 prepaid telephone cards generated $3.2 billion in annual sales in the United States.

In 1976, debit cards were first used in Europe, where credit is not a ready option for calling cards. With *debit cards*, people without access to credit or without their own telephone service can purchase telephone calling. Users pay for the card in advance and are allowed a set amount of time or calling units. The cards gained popularity in the U.S. initially as a way for people without telephones or credit to make telephone calls. Prepaid cards are used in landline and cellular networks.

Debit cards are sold directly by carriers, resellers, sales agents, distributors and retail outlets. The debit card industry is a "layered" industry with different segments selling the cards, promoting the cards, handling the administration and billing aspects and actually carrying the calls. For example, many of the local Bell telephone companies merchandise the cards themselves, but outsource the processing of calls to alternate operator service (AOS) providers, which buy bulk long distance from carriers at wholesale prices.

The "prompts" callers hear when they use debit cards (e.g., "Please enter the PIN number on the back of your card") are generated on carrier or prepaid company's integrated voice response (IVR) platforms. Integrated voice response equipment also lets users know how many minutes they have left on their card. According to Sean Sundstrom, Managing Director of the Boston office for UK-headquartered consultancy Regent Associates International, larger companies are leaving the business because of low margins and because of its complexity. Companies acting as consolidators are getting into the business. They sell spare capacity in carriers' networks that they buy for .03¢ to .08¢ per minute.

The biggest players in prepaid cards are AT&T, Sprint, MCI Group and Telefonica. Other companies are IDT, Primus and Teleglobe (part of BCE). Mobile phone card company Red Tango, Inc. sells prepaid service to low-income people in Spain and Latin America, targeting immigrants who wish to call home. It prints all of its own cards with its own logo to build consumer trust and brand awareness. Red Tango sells its cards at a discount to distributors, which sell the cards to retail stores. The Red Tango IVR platforms are located at carrier sites. Figure 4.3 shows how a user's prepaid call is routed.

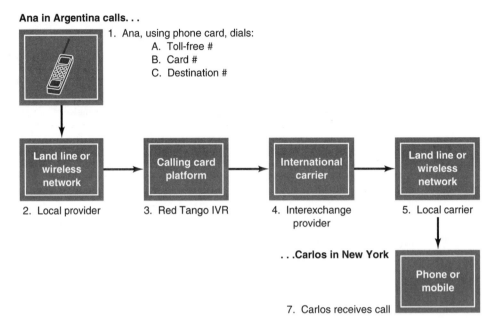

Figure 4.3
Prepaid call flow. Diagram courtesy of Red Tango, Inc.

Many agents sell telephone equipment, inside cabling and other hardware such as videoconferencing systems, as well as long distance, cellular and local calling services.

Typically, customers sign letters of agency with the agent when they agree to purchase telephone calling services. The agent places orders for service with the carrier and/or phone company. The agent also manages the installation and reports repair problems for customers. The customers are billed directly by the phone company or carrier for services sold by agents. The agent receives a monthly commission from the carrier. In the late 1980s, when agents were first in the business of selling local telephone calling, they sold only local toll and value-added services. They subsequently added interexchange calling to their portfolio of services.

Retail outlets also are agents for local telephone and cellular providers. Staples is a case in point. In November 1998, Staples, Inc. and Bell Atlantic (now Verizon) announced that Staples would sell basic telephone lines and enhanced services such as caller ID and voice mail in all of its 229 stores from Maine to Virginia. Staples also is an agent for AT&T Wireless, Verizon Wireless and VoiceStream Wireless Corporation. Previous to this, most telephone service agent programs were aimed at business customers.

SUMMARY ···

By April 2001, 17 CLECs out of a total of approximately 410 in the United States either had ceased operations or filed for Chapter 11 bankruptcy. A majority of the remaining companies are operating at a loss and investors are leery of investing in them. Economic reverberations of business failures were felt beyond telecommunications. According to PriceWaterhouse Coopers, 36% of total first through third quarter investments by venture capitalists were for telecommunications. The article, "Telecom Tightrope," published in *Barron's Online*, 8 January 2001, by Jacqueline Doherty reported that total investment in telecommunications in 2000 was $157.4 billion. Poor performance by telecommunications companies has an impact on banks, stock and bond holders and financial firms that invested in telecommunications.

The industry is in a quandary. It takes enormous investments to build new infrastructure for telecommunications. New cable TV systems capable of supporting high-speed Internet access cost $3000 per customer. Laying fiber, digging up streets and purchasing hardware for voice and data communications also are costly. However, with the proliferation of over 400 local competitors, capital is spread too thin and it's difficult for any one company to have enough resources. Given these problems with developing infrastructure at the local level, there is a concern that innovation will be hampered if there is a lack of competition. Without competition, incumbents have little incentive to invest in capital improvements or improve efficiencies to lower prices for end users. Suppliers have no incentive to develop new products without a diverse group of purchasers. In their first quarter 2001 financial statements, both SBC and Verizon announced cutbacks in capital spending due to poor business conditions. One wonders if declining fortunes of their competitors also is a factor.

In addition to legal issues, there are questions of availability of technical resources at the local level. Metropolitan areas of the country have a higher percentage of advanced central offices than rural and poor areas: Even metropolitan areas have pockets of old equipment. Frequently, poor neighborhoods in major cities have central offices that impair even standard plain old telephone service (POTS). For the most part, competition is already spurring investments in cabling, signaling systems and new switches. The first groups of consumers to gain from these investments are large corporations, hospitals and universities. Gains for middle-class consumers and small-to medium-sized businesses will take longer to achieve.

Regulatory factors also have given an enormous edge to incumbent local telephone companies. There is now a bill before Congress granting RBOCs permission to sell interstate broadband data services without first opening up their networks to local competition. The RBOCs see high-speed data, in addition to cellular, as their most promising opportunity for growth. Passage of a bill such as this would give them an enormous advantage. Finally, the incumbents have an enormous advantage in miles of cabling, thousands of central offices and established business practices they have to rely on. Their challenges are to upgrade their billing and operation systems and sales expertise to serve multilocation customers. Most of the competitors, other than World-Com and AT&T, have new operational and support systems (OSS) with up-to-date billing packages. Their objective is to obtain capital from investors to continue building infrastructure and, in some cases, to conserve cash to continue operating.

5 The Public Network

In this chapter...

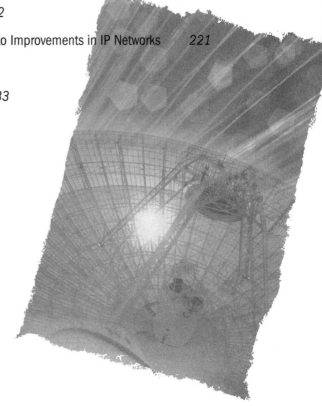

The public switched telephone network (PSTN) is made up of switches, cabling and equipment that simultaneously transmits multiple telephone calls over single pairs of fiber cabling. The extraordinary characteristic of public networks is that carriers from all parts of the world have agreed on ways to transmit calls to each other. Enormous efforts have been made to ensure that systems are reliable and dependable and function as much as possible during power blackouts, hurricanes and national emergencies.

Switching is the primary vehicle for carrying voice, facsimile and dialup modem traffic worldwide. Public network switched services are dialup; users dial a telephone number to create a temporary connection to anyone on the public network. Examples of switched services are home telephone, cellular, dialup Internet access and main business lines. Switched services are used for data as well as voice. Switches connect segments of local area networks (LANs) to each other. Asynchronous transfer mode (ATM) and optical switches in public data and voice networks switch vast quantities of traffic between cities.

Dedicated services, also called private lines, are more specialized than switched lines. Organizations use them to save money when they need to transmit large amounts of data or place hours of voice telephone calls to particular sites. Imagine two tin cans and a string between two locations. This is something like a private line. Organizations have the use of the string 24 hours a day, seven days a week. Users pay a flat monthly fee; there are no per-minute charges for private lines with a fixed configuration.

Dedicated lines are expensive and complex to manage. If a firm only has dedicated lines between a few locations, maintenance might not be a problem. However, once private lines connect many locations, they become cumbersome to manage. Moreover, private lines are costly because carriers can't share the dedicated private lines among many customers. For these reasons, many companies are choosing carrier-managed, value-added virtual private networks (VPNs). Virtual private networks are "virtually" private. They have many of the features of private networks; however, network capacity is shared by many customers. Many customers use VPNs for remote access by employees, branch offices and business partners. The VPN providers offer security services to protect corporate files from viruses and hackers.

Network-based computer intelligence has changed the public network from plain old telephone service (POTS) to one capable of delivering advanced features and generating fat profits. Value-added services such as call forwarding, caller ID and voice mail that depend on signaling systems generate large profits. Services dependent on signaling include advanced features associated with 800 and 900 services such as routing by time of day, integrated services digital network (ISDN) service and the capability to keep the same toll free number when changing carriers.

Signaling is the glue that holds the public switched network together. Routing, billing and transferring calls between carrier networks depend on signaling. Network maintenance information also is carried on signaling systems. The way signals are transported impacts network efficiency, costs, reliability and introduction of new services.

Optical technologies have had a major impact on efficiencies in Internet, long distance and local networks. They have lowered the costs significantly of building high-capacity data and voice networks. Recent developments in optical cross connects are adding potential for more capacity in backbone networks and decreasing the expense of providing redundancy. (All major carriers have backup routes to which they transmit traffic in case the primary path goes down.)

Major efforts in development of new optical technology are bringing the benefits of fiber optics closer to homes and small and medium-sized businesses. Passive optical networking and new digital loop carriers (DLCs) will be particularly significant in parts of the world where new infrastructure is being built in metropolitan areas. Applications such as document sharing, email, Web browsing, distance-based learning and remote access to corporate files are affordable to individuals and small and medium-sized businesses. Small and medium-sized businesses need Internet connections to be able to use these applications. Passive optical networks that make fiber links affordable for these types of customers are important.

Convergence, where a single packet network carries all types of traffic, is still in its infancy. However, as these networks and protocols become more suitable for voice, more networks will be built based on data protocols rather than on switched technologies developed for voice. As data continues to grow as a percentage of total traffic carried, new networks will be built to accommodate it. Existing networks that age will be replaced by new networks built using these technologies. This will be a gradual process.

SWITCHED SERVICES—LOCAL AND LONG DISTANCE CALLING ....

Although revenues for switched services are flat, they still account for large amounts of sales. According to Federal Communications Commission (FCC) statistics, 1999 long distance revenues were $108 billion in the United States. In June 2000, there were 192 million local telephone lines in service in the United States. Cellular switched service generated another $50 billion in revenue. Clearly, switched services are significant. They are necessary for emergency and safety alerts. For example, people reporting a fire don't use email. However, email is definitely a factor in the lack of growth in revenues from switched services.

The public switched telephone network is analogous to a network of major highways originally built by a single organization but added to and expanded by multiple organizations. Traffic enters and exits these highways (backbone networks) from multiple "ramps" built by still more carriers [e.g., the incumbent local telephone companies, cable TV providers and competitive local exchange carriers (CLECs)].

AT&T constructed the "highway" system that is the basis of the public switched network in the United States. Prior to the 1984 divestiture, AT&T set standards via its research arm, Bell Laboratories (now part of Lucent Technologies), such that all central office switches and all lines that carried calls met prescribed standards. As a result of these standards, anyone with a telephone can talk to anyone else. Dialing, ringing, routing and telephone numbering are uniform.

The International Telecommunications Union (ITU) defines switching as "the establishment on demand, of an individual connection from a desired inlet to a desired outlet within a set of inlets and outlets for as long as is required for the transfer of information." The inlets are the lines from customers to telephone company equipment. The outlet is the party called, the connection from the central office switch to the customer. A circuit or connection is established for as long as desired within the network until one party hangs up. Switched calls carry voice, data, video and graphics. They operate on landline and cellular networks.

The mobile or landline central office, which performs the switching function, routes calls based on the telephone number dialed. Carriers and resellers put their own brand names on their switched services. For example, AT&T sells OneRate, and Sprint offers Sprint 500 AnyTime.

Attributes of Real-Time Switching Services

The public switched telephone network (PSTN) provides real-time dial-up connections. Cellular, Internet dial-up and landline voice traffic is routed in real time based on digits dialed.

Addressing—The Ability to Reach Anyone on the Public Network

Telephone calls are routed to destinations based on the number dialed. This is the *addressing* function. Telephones on landline connections send dual tone multi-frequency (DTMF) tones over the network. At the central office, these tones or frequencies are decoded to address signals. In cellular networks, users first dial the number they wish to reach, and then press Send. The telephone number is sent as digital bits within packets to the mobile switching office.

In the North American Numbering Plan (NANP), which covers the United States, Canada and the Caribbean, three-digit area codes are assigned to metropolitan areas. *Exchanges*, the next three digits of a phone number, are assigned to a rate center, and the last four digits, the *line number*, are assigned to a specific business or residential customer. In the rest of the world, each country has country codes, city codes and user numbers. The digits of each vary in length: Country codes and city codes are one to three digits long and numbers assigned to users generally are five to ten digits long. There is no uniform worldwide numbering pattern.

Most residential customers and many small business customers worldwide use dialup access to reach the Internet. If customers change their dialup Internet service provider (ISP) from AOL Time Warner to MSN, they don't need to change their telephone service or modem. They just program their modem to dial into a different ISP. However, if customers change from cable modem to digital subscriber line (DSL) Internet access or vice versa, they need a new modem as well as a new physical line to their provider. DSL and cable modem service are examples of dedicated—as opposed to switched—access.

Pay-as-You-Talk

Charges for switched calls often are based on the length of the call. For example, a 10-minute toll call costs less than a call lasting an hour. Time-of-day rates also can vary. Calls during peak business hours often cost more than at off-peak hours. In this way, carriers hope to even out traffic so that they aren't required to build additional facilities to accommodate peak calling patterns. In most of the world, local as well as toll calls are charged on per minute or package of minutes basis.

Because of the large amount of capacity on network providers' fiber optic networks and in response to competition, some carriers now offer flat-rate calling plans in which customers can make an unlimited number of calls for a set amount of money. Some long distance carriers have plans that charge customers a minimum fee whether or not they make any calls.

Postalized Rates

In the past, calls to distant locations cost more than calls to, for example, nearby states. The cost of long distance service is no longer consistently distance-sensitive. Most carriers have flat 5¢ to 8¢ per minute rate plans. This is known as *postalized pricing.* Just as a first class letter costs the same to mail next door or 2000 miles away, calls often cost the same whether to a friend across the state or to a relative across the country. Once a carrier's high-speed network is in place, it costs the carrier no more to send a call 2000 miles than 400 miles. Capacity is available and carriers want to fill their "pipes."

TEN-DIGIT LOCAL CALLS—OVERLAY AREA CODES AND THE ABSENCE OF A UNIFORM DIALING PLAN

Prior to 1984, one central organization managed dialing plans for the North American numbering plan area (the United States, Canada and the Caribbean). Seven digits, xxx-xxxx were used for local calls, 1-xxx-xxxx for toll calls to the same area code and 1-xxx-xxx-xxxx for toll calls to other area codes. The "1" preceding calls was a toll indicator—it indicated to subscribers that their call would incur toll charges.

After the divestiture of 1984 when the Bell companies were broken off from AT&T into seven companies, a division of Lockheed (now called Neustar, Inc.) managed area code assignments and state utility commissions set dialing plans within FCC parameters. The "1" is no longer consistently used as a toll indicator. In some states, local calls to the same area code require only seven digits and other states require 10 digits (area code plus number). In still others, a "1" is required before the 10 digits even for all local calls.

Much of this confusion can be blamed on what are called *overlay* area codes. States adding new area codes have the choice of adding them as overlays or splits. With *splits*, the geographic area in which the old area code exists is "split." One part of the area keeps its existing code and in the other part are assigned the new area code with all of the expense of changing stationery and marketing communication material. To avoid this hassle, some state public utility commissions use overlays to add new area codes.

With overlays, everyone keeps their existing telephone number and only people getting new service are assigned the new area code. However, the FCC has mandated that with overlays, all local calls must be dialed using 10 digits. This rule was enacted to prevent incumbent telephone companies, which have the greatest number of telephone numbers, from having an advantage. It was felt that without the 10-digit rule, competitors' customers would get more new numbers and would have the burden of using 10-digit numbers more frequently.

To illustrate some of the differences (as of October 2000):

- Virginia: Local calls to another area code require dialing "1" plus 10 digits.
- Colorado: Local calls in area codes 719 and 970 require only 10 digits without the "1."
- Alaska: Local calls still can be made dialing only seven digits.
- Alabama and Mississippi: Local calls between two different area codes can be made using seven digits.

On Demand

Voice and data calls are initiated by picking up the handset or by instructing a modem to dial a call. The service is available "on demand." However, callers might find that on peak traffic days, such as Mother's Day, callers receive a "fast busy" signal. Extreme weather conditions such as blizzards often result in a high number of people working from home and using modems for long stretches of time. This can result in a strain on carriers' network capacity and "fast busies" on call attempts.

Immediate

If capacity is available, service is instantaneous. When someone dials a telephone number, he or she expects the call to be completed immediately. As previously noted, extreme conditions can eliminate the immediate capacity expected by users. Natural disasters, unusual demand and human error all impact availability.

Carriers build in redundant power sources, remote alarm monitoring, backup systems, multiple fiber paths to central offices in case of a fiber cut and hurricane proofing in central offices to ensure continuous telephone service. Customers take for granted immediate telephone service, which carriers take great efforts to provide.

Incoming, Outgoing, and Two-Way

Telephone companies sell trunks that are one-way incoming, one-way outgoing or two-way combination. (Trunks are the connections between commercial organizations' on-site telephone systems and the telephone company's switching equipment.) Incoming-only 800, 877, 866, 855 and 888 toll-free numbers are important marketing tools. Companies spend millions of dollars promoting their toll-free, incoming-only numbers. 900 numbers that callers pay to use are another example of one-way incoming service.

Telemarketing departments use outbound trunks for bill collections and to generate sales. Specialized computers and predictive dialers place calls to potential customers for items such as magazine and newspaper subscriptions. These dialers are programmed to rapidly dial successive calls. The dialers recognize and hang up when they encounter busy signals, ring-no-answers or answering machines. A live agent's time is not used for dialing, busy signals, answering machines and ring-no-answers. When a live person answers calls, the dialer transfers the call to an agent. Agents can thus speak with a higher number of prospects each hour.

Predictive dialers have brought central offices to their knees because of their high volume of calls. For every agent on a call, the predictive dialer ties up central office facilities with busy signals, ring-no-answers and answering machine responses. Some phone companies will add capacity to their switches when they have these types of customers.

The Public Network and National Security

Governments consider telecommunications a necessary service. It's a vital national security and business resource and is regulated accordingly. The Federal Communications Commission (FCC) and the Federal Aviation Administration (FAA) monitor reliability of major carriers' networks but not the Internet. Earthquakes, software glitches and power disturbances have all interrupted telephone service. Consider the software glitch in AT&T central offices on January 15, 1990, which caused a nine-hour outage. Backup, redundancy and power failure are major factors in planning for telecommunications.

Switched Services for Data—Capacity Issues

The public switched telephone network was designed for voice traffic. Voice traffic has different usage patterns than data traffic. For example, voice calls are shorter—an average of three minutes in length. Data calls, on the other hand, tend to be longer. Callers accessing the Internet from homes and businesses often stay online for long stretches at a time.

Use of the public switched network for dialup Internet access, paging and cellular service has resulted in an enormous demand for longer calls, more frequent calls and additional telephone numbers. Incumbent local telephone companies are eager to move data calls off the public network onto digital subscriber lines (DSL) service so they will not need to add capacity to central office switches for Internet access traffic. (DSL service is reviewed in Chapter 6.)

Switching Light—Optical Cross Connects

Optical switches, also called *optical cross connects*, are another example of switching. Network service providers are starting to use optical cross connects to switch streams of light across high-speed backbone networks. They transmit light across long distances, for example, between Denver and New York City. Switching light, also called *photonic switching*, adds enormous capacity to fiber optic networks. Optical cross connects can transmit thousands of light streams simultaneously.

End-to-End Telephone Service

Callers take for granted the ability to reach people on different long distance networks. For instance, WorldCom subscribers assume they can reach AT&T subscribers. This was not always the case. During the early years of the telecommunications industry, 1893 to 1907, people frequently needed two telephones: one phone for people served by The Bell Telephone Company, for example, and another telephone to reach people in a town served by an independent telephone company.

Independent and Bell telephone company networks were not connected to each other at this time. AT&T articulated the strategy of end-to-end telephone service in its 1910 annual report. The public switched telephone network grew out of this concept. The federal government granted AT&T a monopoly on telephone service in return for AT&T's providing end-to-end telephone service.

Circuit Switching—Network Inefficiencies and Convergence

The public switched network uses circuit switching to transmit calls. A circuit is a physical path for the transmission of voice, image or data. The ITU (International Telecommunications Union) defines circuit switching as:

> *"The switching of circuits for the exclusive use of the connection for the duration of a call."*

When a person or a modem dials a call, the network sets up a path between the caller and the dialed party. Importantly, the path is available exclusively for the duration of the call. The path is not shared. Natural pauses in conversation and data transmission cannot be used for other voice or data calls. Capacity is saved in the network for the entire duration of the transmission. When the call is ended, the path is released and becomes available for another phone call. This exclusivity causes wasteful utilization of network capacity.

Newer telecommunications services do not have this limitation. For example, with the Internet Protocol (IP) used in the Internet and in converged networks, transmissions from multiple voice and data sources share the same path. Pauses in one conversation are filled by data from other sources. Network capacity is not saved for the exclusive use of devices when they are idle. This is the basis for convergence, which is covered later in this chapter.

DTMF: Access to Voice Mail and Computers

Touch-tone, or dual tone multifrequency (DTMF), was introduced by AT&T in 1963 to speed call setup in the central office. Prior to 1963, pulse signals (rotary) were used to place calls. A 10-digit call takes approximately 11.3 seconds to dial using rotary pulses. In contrast, a touch-tone, 10-digit DTMF call can be dialed in 1 second. Thus, DTMF or touch-tone calling adds efficiency to the public network because it ties up the central office switches for a shorter period of time than rotary dialing during call set up.

Dual tone multifrequency tones also are used to access voice mail and information in bank accounts. DTMF is used in voice mail and voice response technology in which people send signals to computers via the touch-tone pads of their telephones. Once a telephone connection has been established, the network passes any additional DTMF tones entered to the voice mail or voice response system.

DTMF signals are an example of a standard established by the AT&T Bell system so that all callers in the public switched network in the United States have a consistent format for addressing calls. DTMF tones in other parts of the world vary from American standards.

Store-and-Forward Switching— Nonsimultaneous Sending and Receiving

The storage and transfer of messages such as voice mail, recorded announcements, data and facsimile in a non–real-time fashion is known as *store-and-forward switching*. *Store-and-forward switching* does not require both sender and receiver to be available at the time of transmission. Moreover, the network can hold the message and retry multiple times until the receiving equipment is available. Stored messages can be transferred at off-peak times to minimize network idle time, which also avoids network overload during busy times. For example, political organizations record "get-out-the vote" announcements and send them to lists of voters at preprogrammed times. Pharmacies send "Your prescription is ready" announcements to customers.

Store-and-forward switches also are used in local area networks to connect LANs together. The switch accepts packets on input ports, buffers them briefly and sends them out. When switches buffer packets they hold them briefly to ensure a smooth flow of data. Some LAN switches have cut-through capability. They begin repeating the message as soon as it is received. Cut-through switches are faster than store-and-forward switches.

DEDICATED SERVICES..

Dedicated services, also known as private lines, are similar to having two tin cans and a string between sites. The "string" and "tin cans" are for the exclusive use of the organization that leases them. The "string" portion is the medium over which the voice or data transmission is sent. The medium is generally copper, microwave or fiber optics. The "tin cans" are the devices, such as a telephone, modem or digital modem, that enables sites to transmit data, voice or video between locations.

The advent of the Internet has decreased commercial organizations' use of private lines. Organizations no longer need costly dedicated paths between sites to transmit corporate files and email. Many of them now use the public Internet or intranets which are the use of Internet technologies for the exclusive use of an organization and its employees.

Overview of Dedicated Services

Some organizations have such a high volume of voice, video or data traffic between locations that they opt to use dedicated, private lines to connect sites together. These dedicated, private lines are available for the exclusive use of the customer that leases them from a network service provider. An apparel chain in the Boston area has sufficient data communications traffic between its headquarters, warehouses and stores that it has dedicated links connecting end sites in other cities to headquarters for the purpose of inventory status and updates on store sales. It has a separate set of lines connecting all sites to its centralized voice mail.

The above is an example of an organization's private network. IT is a *wide area network* (WAN) because it runs between cities. *Metropolitan area networks* (MANs) consist of private lines that connect buildings within a city or metropolitan area.

Dedicated links eliminate per-minute toll charges for transmission. Private, dedicated links are priced at flat monthly fees rather than on the amount of voice or data transmitted. They are more reliable, provide faster transmission and are more convenient than switched service.

An important factor in the decision to use dedicated services is the desire for secure transmissions. Some firms believe that public network services such as Frame Relay are too public or open to hacking for applications such as funds transfer.

Because of the high maintenance and monthly telephone company fees associated with dedicated private lines, many companies now use managed data services from network service providers. These services act like private lines but are shared by multiple customers. Because they act like private lines they are called *virtual private networks, (VPNs)*. They are virtually private. In the past, the term VPN referred to managed data and voice networks such as Frame Relay (covered in Chapter 6) and Gigabit Ethernet, in which carriers managed networks for customers. The term VPN (see the later section titled Virtual Private Networks) now refers to carrier managed networks, in which secure remote access to Web pages, company files or email is provided to employees, customers and vendors.

Fixed Monthly Fees

End users pay a fixed monthly fee, such as $400 for a line from New York City to Washington, D.C., rather than pay per-minute fees. The fee is the same whether the line is used two hours per day or 24 hours per day.

Fixed Routes

Dedicated lines are not flexible. Calls only can be sent between the fixed points to which the lines are connected, which might present a problem when organizations wish to add new locations.

Consider room-type videoconferencing equipment. A firm might purchase two video systems, one in New York City and one in California, for conferencing between these two company sites over a dedicated line. As often happens with video systems, the firm might, at some point, wish to hold a conference with a customer or vendor. If the equipment is connected only to the private line running between two fixed points, the flexibility of holding a conference with multiple vendors or customers is lost.

Exclusive Use

Dedicated circuits are not shared. Dedicated, private lines are put into place so that voice or data can be sent exclusively between the points on the private lines. Many organizations own switches [private branch exchanges (PBXs)] with the intelligence to route calls over their own dedicated lines. However, if the dedicated lines are busy when an additional request is made to place a call, the private switch will send the call over the public switched network. This enables firms to pack a high volume of traffic on their dedicated lines, but have the flexibility to route overflow, peak traffic on the public network.

24-Hour-Per-Day Availability

Dedicated services are available around the clock. This is cost-effective for companies that use the dedicated lines for voice, video and email during the day and bulk data transmissions such as transmissions of sales figures after hours. To illustrate, a corporation might use dedicated lines that cost $5000 per month for video and voice calls between two locations during business hours. After hours, they use the line for data communications. The data travels "free" during nonbusiness times.

Voice, Video and Data

Dedicated lines are suitable for transmission of both voice and data. Voice and data can share the same dedicated services or they can use completely different dedicated lines. Firms often lease T-1 lines that have 24 channels to tie locations together. They can use, for example, 12 of the paths for voice and 12 for data or video.

Fixed Capacity

Dedicated services are leased or built with a fixed capacity or bandwidth. For example, circuits are ordered from carriers such as AT&T or WorldCom at specific speeds and numbers of paths, or channels. Most organizations now lease lines with a minimum of 56,000 bits per second (bps) because of the small price difference between 56 kilobits (Kb) and slower lines.

Examples of speeds of dedicated lines are:

- 56,000 bits per second.
- T-1—24 channels, 1.54 megabits per second (Mbps)
- Fractional T-1—2 to 12 paths in increments of 56 or 64 kilobits per path.
- E-1—30 channels, 2.048 Mbps
- T-3—672 channels, 45 megabits per second.
- Fractional T-3—2 to 18 T-1s in increments of 1.54 megabits per second.

(T-1, E-1 and T-3 services are discussed in Chapter 6.)

Analog or Digital

Most end users specify digital private lines because of superior quality, higher speeds and reliability compared to analog private lines. Digital lines also have more capacity and fewer errors. Speeds above 19,200 bits per second are available only in digital formats. Carriers and local telephone companies prefer to lease digital rather than analog lines to customers because they fail less frequently than analog lines and are thus cheaper for vendors to maintain for customers.

Security

Some organizations use private lines to transmit proprietary information or financial data. They feel private lines cannot be as easily tapped into and listened in on as switched lines. Organizations concerned about security may place encryption devices on both ends of dedicated services. The encryption device scrambles the transmission when it leaves the sending location and unscrambles it when it arrives at the receiving location.

Convenience, Functionality and Enhanced Customer Service

For voice calls, end users might want the ease of abbreviated dialing and features that provide one-system functionality between sites. For example, telephone systems connected by private lines might have software installed, enabling users to call each other using four or five digits instead of the 11 digits used on the public switched network. The on-site telephone systems might also allow one set of operators to answer calls for multiple locations, which is a significant cost savings over full-time operators at each location. Some telephone systems offer telephones with displays telling a user the name of the person from another corporate private network location that is calling him or her. Finally, some organizations have one voice mail system shared by all locations and maintained by telecommunications staff at the headquarters.

The availability of private lines between sites improves customer service because it enables staff to transfer calls between sites. Customers are not required to make another call if they wish to speak with someone at a different site.

For data traffic, the speed, capacity and reliability are critical. Analog modem service is unreliable and switched digital ISDN services where an ISDN terminal adapter dials the call is difficult to configure and not available everywhere. If used for any volume, usage charges become prohibitive on ISDN as a switched service for data. (See Chapter 6.)

Network Topologies—The View from the Top

The term topology refers to the geometric shape of the physical connection of the lines in a network, or the "view from the top." The shape of the network, the configuration in which lines are connected to each other, impacts cost, reliability and accessibility. Consider the multipoint configuration in Figure 5.2. The multipoint design is used in polling environments where a computer such as a mainframe polls terminals, one after another, asking if they wish to transmit or receive data. The computer polls the terminals in a predefined order. If one of the links in the multipoint network goes

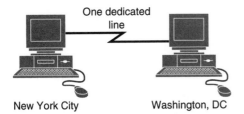

One dedicated line

New York City   Washington, DC

Figure 5.1
Point-to-point private lines; one private line connecting two locations.

down, the entire network is out of service. In the mesh configuration in Figure 5.4, if one link is out of service, traffic can be rerouted over other links.

The following are network configurations:

- **Point-to-point**—One line connecting two locations.
- **Multipoint**—More than one line connecting more than two sites together. In LANs, this is also known as a bus design.
- **Star configuration**—All locations connect to, or "hub into," a central site. PBXs and data switches in LANs are configured in star topologies.
- **Mesh design**—All points on the network, nodes, connect to each other in a flat or nonhierarchical manner. The Internet is made up of mesh networks.

Figures 5.1 through 5.4 illustrate the number of lines used in sample configurations of each topology. Higher numbers of lines result in higher monthly charges.

The star shape in Figure 5.3 is a common private network topology. In the case of a star configuration, all locations are connected to one main location (hub). If the main location goes down, all nodes (locations) on the network are out of service.

A mesh design (see Figure 5.4) costs more, but has more reliability built in than a star arrangement. A mesh configuration results in more paths for information flow. If one link goes down, voice and data can be transmitted via other paths. The customer pays for more links in a mesh configuration, but has higher reliability.

Pricing

Rates for private lines are based on distance and speed. Higher speed, longer distance lines cost more than slower, shorter circuits. For example, a 56,000 bits per second line between New York City and Boston might cost $400 per month. The same speed line from California to Boston might cost $1800. Speed is another factor that affects cost: A T-1 line at 1.544 million bits per second is more expensive than a 56,000-bit per second line. Volume and term discounts are available. A customer with a three-

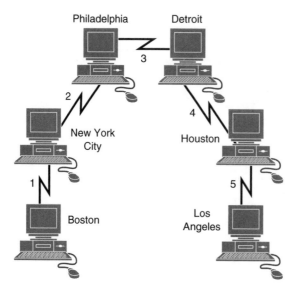

Figure 5.2
Multipoint private lines; five private lines connecting six locations.

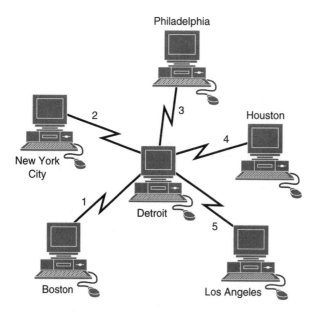

Figure 5.3
Star configuration; five lines connecting six locations. Each point must travel
through the central hub to reach another point.

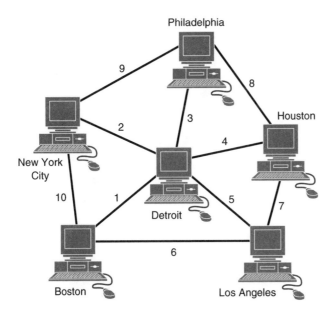

Figure 5.4
Mesh configuration; ten lines connecting six locations via a mesh
configuration provides built-in redundancy but adds costs for additional lines.

year contract for ten lines might pay a lower unit cost than a customer with a month-to-month contract for ten lines.

Pricing for dedicated lines consists of two items (see Figure 5.5):

- **Local channels**—Local channels run from a customer premise to the carrier's equipment. One local channel is required at each end of the private line. A carrier with no fiber installed in the customer's area it will lease the local channel from the incumbent telephone company or another carrier.

- **Interexchange miles**—Interexchange mileage is the portion of the circuit located within a carrier's network. The mileage runs from the access point, where it enters the carrier's network, to the egress point, where it leaves the carrier's switch. These are carriers' points of presence (POPs).

Dedicated private lines are expensive because carriers reserve capacity on them for the sole use of the customer that leases them. Shared networks (virtual private networks) are lower in cost because capacity on all of the routes is shared. In addition, ownership of private networks requires customer expertise for initial design and sizing of dedicated network, ongoing maintenance and redesign for new applications.

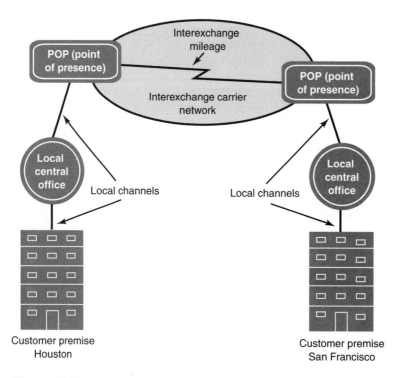

Figure 5.5
Local and interexchange legs of a private line.

Declining Sales of Private Lines

Although, many private lines are still in service, organizations are changing service from private lines to shared services such as Frame Relay and Gigabit Ethernet service in which carriers manage security and reliability between sites. (Frame Relay is a way to access the Internet and LAN-to-LAN service over a shared carrier network. Gigabit Ethernet is faster than Frame Relay for Internet access and LAN-to-LAN traffic. (See Chapter 6 for a description of both services.)

Outsourcing to Manage Private Networks

Companies often hire outside expertise to manage their network services and equipment. Expertise is required for the selection of multiplexers, routers and modems that connect computers to networks, as well as to size the network properly. Ongoing tasks range from maintaining software for adding and deleting PC addresses in routers to determining the cause of failures on private lines and ensuring that capacity keeps up with growth.

One goal of contracting with an outsourcing service is to have one vendor responsible for problem determination regardless of the location of the breakdown. The outsourcing firm determines if the customer premises equipment is faulty or if the fault is in the outside lines. Growth in outsourcing network and on-site networking equipment maintenance is the result of the complexity required to maintain large corporate private networks.

VIRTUAL PRIVATE NETWORKS—CONNECTIVITY FOR REMOTE ACCESS, INTRANETS AND EXTRANETS.................................

A virtual private network (VPN) has all of the features of a private network where dedicated lines tie sites together. However with VPNs, the network connections between sites are shared by multiple organizations. A carrier manages the network. The customer connects dedicated or dialup lines to the carrier's network. The carrier is responsible for connections between customer sites. Many VPNs are based on the Internet Protocol. (See Figure 5.6.) The three most common applications for virtual private networks are:

- Remote access for telecommuters and employees that travel
- Intranet connectivity for branch offices
- Extranet links for business partners

Lower total cost of ownership compared to private networks is a key reason for using VPNs. The total cost of ownership of private networks includes the cost of staff to maintain the lines and equipment used to connect individual users and computers in wide area networks. For these reasons, managed networks as a substitute for administering the implementation, growth and day-to-day maintenance of private networks is growing. Adding capacity to a virtual private network is simpler than adding higher speed dedicated lines and new hardware to each site of a private network. The customer only needs higher speed access lines from its building to the carrier. The carrier is responsible for making sure there is capacity in the network for the customer's applications.

Many organizations have a mix of private lines for routes with the highest amount of voice and data traffic, and switched services and virtual private network (VPNs) services for routes with less voice and data traffic. Frame Relay, discussed in Chapter 6, is another example of a VPN.

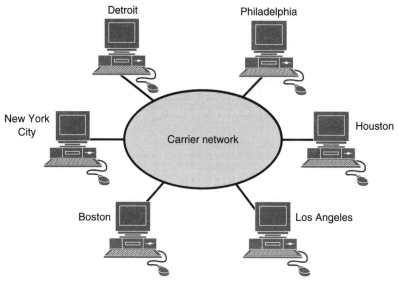

Each location is connected to the network
rather than directly to another location.

Figure 5.6
A virtual private network.

VPNs (Virtual Private Networks) for Electronic Commerce

Extranets are Internet-like connections between organizations and their vendors and customers. Virtual private networks (VPNs) often provide this connectivity. For example, consumers may access their bank to pay bills by phone over a virtual private network. The carrier manages the security, day-to-day reliability and network capacity for the bank. In many cases, the application itself resides at a carrier point of presence (POP).

Customers use VPNs for:

- Inventory updates for business partners
- Tracking delivery of packages
- Electronic commerce (i.e., online shopping)

VPNs for Intranet Service

Intranets use Internet protocols and browsers to provide employees access to corporate information. VPNs based on intranet service provide branch offices with access to corporate files. For example, instead of using private lines to tie branches together, a chain might use a virtual private network. The network might supply security, limiting particular employees access to files based on their profile. Some may only be able to read some documents and other users may have permission to change the file. The VPN provides LAN features to remote offices.

Virtual Private Networks (VPNs) for Remote Access

A robust remote access service enables employees to be productive whether they work from home, a hotel, or their office. According to Cahners In-Stat Group, nearly 5 million employees in the United States telecommute. Organizations frequently supply salespeople and systems engineers with laptop computers for remote access and working off-site. Employees log into their business's computers from the road to access email messages, place orders, check order status and check inventory levels.

Commercial organizations use either remote access servers (RAS) or VPN switches. If they use VPN switches they may also use network-based VPN services from various network providers for additional security. Until recently, most corporations used remote access server (RAS) devices to support dial-in access for employees. A RAS device is a "box" with multiple modem and ISDN ports for dial-in connectivity. However, RAS devices do not support cable and DSL modems. With VPN switch and network solutions, employees' calls are routed into the organization on the same links used for Internet access. VPNs support dial-in and high-speed cable and DSL modem access. Client software is installed on employees' computers to support the VPN service.

As indicated in Figure 5.7, the VPN provider carries remote users' calls over its public network and routes them to an existing T-1 or dedicated line connected to the customer's site. For an additional monthly fee, carriers will manage a customer's on-site router or switch, and security such as a firewall. A *firewall* is software that screens incoming traffic to prevent hackers' access to files.

Organizations that set up virtual private networks for remote access are faced with the following questions:

- How much of our remote access hardware and service should we outsource?
- Should we underwrite high-speed Internet connections for employees?
- Do we need to extend our Help Desk hours to assist employees who access our files after hours?
- Should we use an outside service for our Help Desk functionality?
- What type of support should we provide employees who wish to set up LANs in their homes so that multiple computers can share high-speed Internet access?

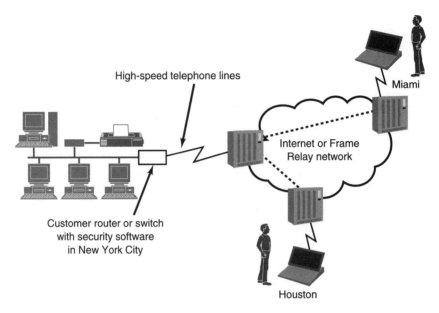

High-speed telephone lines

Miami

Internet or Frame
Relay network

Customer router or switch
with security software
in New York City

Houston

Figure 5.7
Remote access via a Virtual Private Network

Security on Virtual Private Networks

Security in networks is supported by firewalls, which are designed to keep out hackers. They let only designated users have access to networks. Most computer networks with connections to VPNs and the Internet have firewalls. In organizations' networks, firewall software is installed on routers and on remote access switches called VPN Gateways. Organizations that use carriers' firewall protection have on-site firewall protection as well.

Service providers also have firewall protection. Their security service enables them to build profiles of users so that employees can access files from any location. The security software also checks incoming email for viruses.

Tunneling

Tunneling is a way to provide security on VPNs. Because virtual networks are shared services, security is an important issue. Traffic from multiple organizations is carried on the same "pipes" or telephone lines in the public carrier networks. Tunnels surround customer packets with an extra header on each packet to provide security. Encryption, or scrambling of bits, is an important element of tunneling. The encryption makes hacking into a company's data more difficult.

Network-Based Address Filtering

An alternative to tunneling is network-based IP address filtering. With *address filtering*, the software looks at a user's IP address and accepts or rejects it based on the IP address. Address filtering is also commonly used on security software located in organizations' premises. Whether they use tunneling or address filtering, VPNs still use authentication and authorization.

Authentication

Authentication tells the network you are the person you claim to be. For example, a salesperson dialing in from a remote laptop computer claims to be John Smith. The authentication software makes sure that he is in fact John Smith—not someone, for example, from a rival firm.

A popular authentication protocol is Challenge Handshake Authentication Protocol (CHAP). With CHAP, whenever a link is established between a remote network and the virtual private network, the security server challenges the dialup user's computer. The remote user's computer responds with a value calculated by the CHAP software and the user's password. The password itself is not transmitted.

Authorization

Authorization allows organizations to allow or deny a person access to particular databases or services. For example, John Smith may be allowed to view the status of orders from his department. However, he may not see the files showing year-to-date sales figures or technical research. Generally, authorization is done both by the carrier and again at the customer site. The customer's own systems allow or deny particular users access to specific internal servers.

"THE LAST MILE" OR ACCESS NETWORKS ....

The portion of the public network from the central office to the end user's location is the *access network*, or "last mile," as illustrated in Figure 5.8. A major bottleneck of

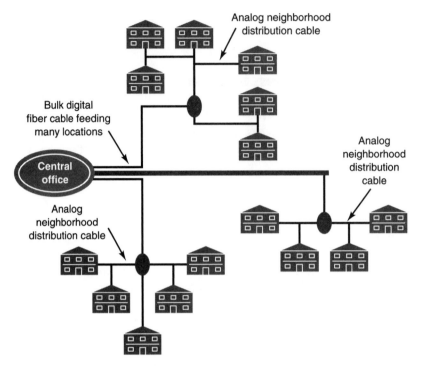

Figure 5.8
The last mile. Bulk cables, often fiber, from the central office into a
neighborhood use digital transmission, while cables to individual homes
often use analog signals. The cable from the telephone pole to the home or
business is called a *drop*.

analog services exists in the cabling to residential and small businesses from the telephone company central office.

Cable modem service is provided over the last mile. Cable modems operate on
hybrid fiber coaxial (HFC) cable infrastructure. (See Figure 2.17 in Chapter 2.) Fiber
runs from the cable company's facility to the neighborhood. Coaxial cable is usually
used to connect each residential customer to the network. Cable modems are a non-
switched, always-on data communications and Internet access service. Cable TV companies are investing huge amounts of money to convert their cabling from one-way
only cable TV service to two-way systems for cable modems and telephone service.

In contrast to the last mile in residential areas in which twisted pair copper is
used, telephone companies and competitive access providers often lay fiber cables capable of transmitting digital services directly to office buildings. The expense of supplying fiber cable to office and apartment buildings with multiple tenants can be

spread across many customers. On the other hand, a fiber cable that terminates at a single household must be paid for from the revenue generated by that one household.

Local telephone providers, cable TV providers and new entrants in local telephone service are faced with the challenge of either upgrading existing cabling or constructing new media capable of sending and receiving growing amounts of video, Internet information, entertainment and multimedia to growing numbers of users. The upgrades and new facilities take the form of added equipment in the central office, fiber optic cabling, wireless transmissions for local telephone service and upgrades to the copper cables themselves.

End and Tandem Central Offices

Central offices switch calls between end users. There are two types of central offices: end and tandem offices in incumbent telephone companies' networks. *Tandem offices* do not have connections to end users. They have trunks to other carriers, other tandem offices and end offices. They provide the connections for central office traffic to other central offices, and central office to interexchange carriers' (IEXs') switches. (See Figure 5.9.) These switches carry high volumes of calls on paths called trunks. The tandem office–to–tandem office portion of Bell networks is their backbone. It also is referred to as the metropolitan network. It carries large amounts of traffic between tandem offices. Without tandem offices, every end office would have to be connected

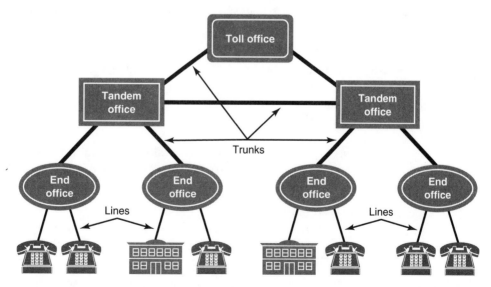

Figure 5.9
Tandem, toll and end offices.

to every other end –office, creating a more complex network with many more trunks to manage.

End central offices connect directly to business, commercial and residential customers as well as to tandem offices. Long distance carriers connect to tandem offices using toll offices. Toll offices are similar in structure to tandem switches. They also are referred to as Class 4 switches. End offices are sometimes referred to as Class 5 switches. The volume of calls between end offices and customers, and between end offices and tandem offices, is lower than on trunks between tandem offices.

Competitive local exchange carriers (CLECs) also have tandem- and end-office functionality in their switches. However, both functions are often installed into one switch because of the smaller size of CLECs. The end office–to-customer portion of networks is the access or last mile portion of the network.

Hardware in central offices includes:

- Line cards with a port for each telephone line (only end offices have line cards because tandem offices have no connections to end users).
- Trunk cards with a port for each trunk connected to a tandem office (i.e., T-3, T-1, E-1 and E-3 ports).
- Cards and software for Centrex service [Centrex service is key system or PBX-like service served from a central office (see Chapter 2)].
- Connections to the Signaling System 7 (SS7) network to support enhanced features such as voice mail and caller ID (see later in this chapter for SS7).
- Administration software with links to carriers' operation and support service (OSS) for billing, maintenance and changes to customer's features.
- Connections for remote central office equipment that serves small communities where the expense of a separate end office is not justified. The remote central office is lower in cost than running large amounts of fiber to the remote town.

Some competitive local exchange carriers are starting to use softswitches for their central office switches. Softswitches work on standard computer platforms rather than the proprietary platforms of traditional switches. See later in this chapter for softswitches.

Non-blocking Switches

Switches in which everyone served by the switch can be on their phone or data device simultaneously are called *non-blocking switches*. Carriers and local telephone companies originally designed their networks with the assumption that, at any given time, not every telephone user will be on a telephone call and that most calls do not tie up the carriers' and local telephone companies' networks for long periods of time. According to *The Business One Irwin Handbook of Telecommunications,* 2nd edition (1991) by James Harry Green, central office switches are equipped such that for every four to six telephone numbers, one path for a telephone call exists. Designing central office switches so that not everyone can make calls at the same time saves money on central office equipment.

Digital Loop Carrier Systems—Fiber Optics and Copper Cabling in the Last Mile

Digital loop carriers (DLCs) are used to economically bring fiber closer to customers. When telephone companies first started using fiber, they used it rather than copper if the distance was longer than 1.5 miles. This is because signals on copper deteriorate and need to be boosted at these distances. Rather than put amplifiers on the line, carriers ran fiber to the neighborhood and terminated it in digital loop carriers. No amplifiers are needed because signals on fiber can travel 64 miles without deteriorating. Fiber also is more reliable and requires less maintenance than copper. With the decreasing cost of electronics for DLC equipment, incumbent telephone companies now use fiber on shorter runs also.

Digital loop carrier systems have multiplexing and demultiplexing functionality. At the central office, traffic is combined into high-speed, up to 155 megabit, streams. The DLC separates out, demultiplexes the traffic and sends it to end users. It also converts the optical pulses to electrical signals and vice versa. The traffic runs on twisted pair cabling from the DLC to end users. Most digital loop carriers support POTS, T-1, E-1 and ISDN. (See Figure 5.10.)

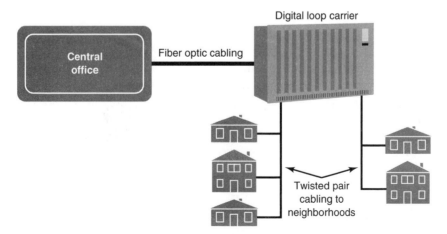

Figure 5.10
Digital loop carriers in the access network.

New DLCs, called *next generation digital loop carrier services*, are also used in cable TV networks. In these applications, they convert the light pulses to electrical signals compatible with coaxial cabling that runs to customers' homes. Next generation DLCs also support digital subscriber line (DSL), high-speed Internet access service.

Carrier Hotels—Interconnecting Carriers and Providing Secure Space for Equipment

Carrier hotels are locations where network service providers locate their switches and routers and connect to each others' networks.

Rather than construct their own buildings to house their switches, carriers lease space in carrier hotels. They place their equipment in cages in the carrier hotel. Locked wire cages surround the equipment and access to the equipment is available only to the carrier that owns the equipment. Leasing space in carrier hotels saves network providers the expense of providing their own:

- Physical security against break-ins
- Access to large amounts of power
- Access to backup power
- Backup generators
- Dual air conditioning systems
- Uninterrupted power supplies
- Fire detection and fire suppression equipment
- Alarming to fire departments and police departments
- Staff to plan and maintain the facilities
- Construction of earthquake-resistant facilities

"Carrier hotels" also are called *collocation* facilities. Carriers in these facilities also lease fiber for connections to other POPs and incumbent local telephone companies. Incumbent local telephone companies and large carriers such as AT&T generally have their own facilities, points-of-presence (POPs) and central offices in which they house their gear. Network service providers use fiber connections between carrier hotels and incumbents' central offices over which they transmit traffic to incumbents.

Carrier Neutral vs. Carrier Run Centers

Carriers such as Sprint, Level 3, Enron and Williams Communications build carrier hotels. Local exchange carriers (LECs) that use these facilities lease bandwidth or dark fiber from the long-haul carriers that operate these facilities. Dark fiber does not have optical gear connected to it. Carriers that lease dark fiber add their own electronics to it. Other carrier hotels are run by third parties such as AboveNet Communications (owned by Metromedia Fiber Networks) and Switch and Data Facilities Company. Carrier-neutral collocation sites worldwide include DigiPlex in Europe, OptiGlobe in Brazil and iAsiaWorks in Hong Kong, Taiwan and Korea. These are carrier-neutral facilities. Carriers that place their switches, wavelength division equipment and routers at these "hotels" can lease capacity or connect to any carrier at the facility.

Adding Internet Services to Collocation Sites

Some carrier hotel providers have expanded their offerings and lease space to many types of providers in addition to Internet service providers and carriers. The providers leasing space sell the following: online music downloading through subscriptions, Web hosting, Internet access, VPNs, outsourcing services for data centers, and out-sourced Web operations (for example, Web hosting, Web design and updating Web pages). Many of these companies are known as managed service providers (MSPs). They manage all facets of Web services for corporate clients and other providers.

OPTICAL NETWORKING.......................................

New passive optical network (PON) technologies lower the cost of deploying fiber optic cabling in cable TV and landline local access networks. They essentially enable one fiber pair from the network provider's facility to the neighborhood to be shared by many customers. They have the added benefits of lowering the maintenance and operating costs of these networks. Changes can be made by computer commands rather than by dispatching a technician. Passive optical networks also have lower space and power requirements than alternative technologies.

Other optical technologies, optical add and drop multiplexers and optical switches are used in high-speed backbone networks. They lower the cost of bringing high-speed service to medium-sized cities and suburban areas. They also lower the cost of providing redundancy in networks.

Most carriers have routes between the following U.S. cities: Manhattan, Washington, D.C., Atlanta, Miami, Dallas, Chicago, Kansas City, Denver, San Francisco, Sacramento and Los Angeles. These routes are like private lines between carriers' points-of-presence (POPs). The majority of routes using dense wavelength division multiplexers (DWDM) are about 2000 kilometers (km) long (1250 miles) and are built along railroad tracks and other rights-of-ways. Smart optical networking devices let carriers drop off smaller amounts of capacity, single wavelengths or lambdas, to local carriers, ISPs or end-user customers in metropolitan or suburban centers. Optical add and drop multiplexers and optical switches (also referred to as optical cross connects) link fiber rings at large hubs. The fiber rings carry traffic between cities. The hubs connect local traffic to the backbone.

The term *lambda* comes from the Greek. It is the eleventh letter of the Greek alphabet. Channels of traffic in fiber networks are known as lambdas. They represent one wavelength or stream of traffic in a strand of fiber.

Passive Optical Networks

Passive optical networks (PONs) are devices located in the access network that enable carriers to dynamically allocate capacity on a single strand or pair of fibers to multiple small and medium-sized customers. Access networks comprise the cabling and infrastructure between the customer and the telephone company. The allocation of bandwidth is done through computer control rather than by dispatching a technician when more bandwidth is requested. PONs increase the capacity, flexibility and efficiency of fiber deployed in the last mile, which can cost $2500 to $3000 per building to provision. In addition, the programmability of passive optical network devices enables carriers to manage complex networks more efficiently. Passive optical networking technologies make it cost effective to provide fiber to small and medium-sized businesses. Just as T-1 multiplexers increased the reliability and efficient deployment of copper, passive optical networks do the same for fiber optic cabling in the last mile.

Passive optical networks are lower in cost than digital loop carriers for serving small and medium size customers. They also connect directly to LANs at speeds of one megabit to 100 megabits. With a data connection served by a PON, a customer does not need a DSU/CSU (digital modem) or a T-1 multiplexer. The service connects directly to a router on the customer's premise.

The PON Standard—Carrier Defined

Full Service Access Network (FSAN) is an organization of 21 carriers that has defined the G.983.1 standard for passive optical networks. Carriers in FSAN include British Telecommunications, BellSouth, France Telecom, KPN-Dutch Telecom and SingTel. The standard is based on asynchronous transfer mode (ATM) technology. *ATM* is a protocol used to aggregate voice and data traffic for transmission across networks. (See Chapter 6.) It is hoped that having a standard will bring down manufacturing costs for PON equipment. PON equipment is sold by companies such as Terawave Communications and Quantum Bridge to network service providers worldwide who are building out fiber networks in metropolitan areas.

PON Technology—Saving Space, Electricity and Costs on Technicians

The equipment consists of a switch that sits at the central office or the cable TV head end called an Optical Line Terminal (OLT). The Optical Line Terminal controls splitters, Optical Network Unit (ONU) and Optical Network Termination (ONT) devices. The Optical Network Termination sits at the customer's premise. See Figure 5.11. The following are an overview of PON devices as defined by FSAN:

- The Optical Line Terminal is located at the central office and has multiple cards, each of which supports up to 32 end users. It has ports for the fiber and backup fiber connected to the splitter. It also interfaces to the network service providers' high-speed backbone network.

- The splitter is like a garden hose with a T splitter that splits the capacity of the fiber among up to 32 end users.

- The Optical Network Unit can be used in cable TV networks or traditional telephone company networks. It converts optical signals to those compatible with coaxial cable and twisted pair. It has interfaces for DSL, cable TV and plain old telephone service (POTS). It brings fiber to the curb or fiber to a neighborhood cabinet.

- The Optical Network Termination, which brings fiber to the building, has cards that connect the fiber to customer premise equipment (CPE). These interfaces include T-1 (24 voice and/or data channels) and E-1 (the European version of T-1 with 30 channels) and LAN ports. Twisted pair copper or fiber connections are supported.

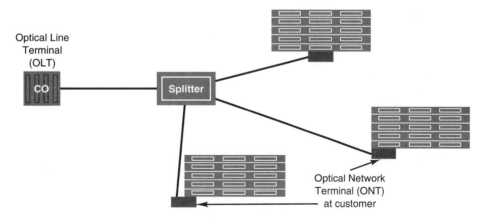

Figure 5.11
Passive optical network components. Drawing courtesy of Terawave

Passive vs. Active PON Devices—Low Electrical and Space Requirements Decrease Costs

The term *passive* in passive optical networks refers to the splitters. The splitters are passive—no electricity is required to operate them. The other devices in PON networks, Optical Line Terminals (OLTs) and Optical Network Terminations (ONTs), are active. They require electricity to operate. The small size of the splitters, about the size of a Personal Digital Assistant (PDA), and the fact that they don't require electricity, lowers the cost of PON service. These are key factors because space in the network is at a premium and electrical costs are soaring.

ASIC High-Speed Processing

Processing speed is critical for Optical Line Terminal (OLT), also called the optical access switch, because it can only communicate with one Optical Network Termination device at a time. Thirty-two devices contend for service from the central office based OLT over fiber links that operate at 155 million bits per second.

Because of this requirement for speed, most PON networks use application-specific integrated circuit (ASIC) chips. An ASIC chip has the whole design of the system burned into the silica on one chip. Because they are "burned" into hardware, they process information faster than field programmable gate array (FPGA) chips. FPGA chips are in software. The up-front design work on ASICs is expensive—it takes 9 to 12 months to develop an ASIC design. However, costs to produce them after the initial design are low.

Passive Optical Network Benefits

- Bandwidth can be dynamically allocated through computer commands; customers can call their provider to increase speed on their data services up to 20 megabits for data and three T-1 or E-1 ports for voice or data without the addition of new customer premise equipment. (Greater capacities will be available in later releases.)

- One strand of fiber is brought to the neighborhood and multiple strands are run from there. This is particularly cost effective in areas that do not have digital loop carrier equipment or where the DLC equipment is at capacity.

- Because of the low cost of the electronics between the carrier-located switch and the customer, redundant routes can be deployed relatively cheaply.

- Maintenance of PON equipment is relatively low because technicians can remotely monitor the system all the way out to the Optical Network Termination at customers' premises.

- PON equipment can be interfaced with DSL service to make low-cost Internet access available where customers are far from the central office.

Passive optical networks are not suitable for large customers because of the limit of three T-1s or E-1s per Optical Network Termination. There is a particular interest in PONs in Asia where much of the infrastructure is being built from scratch. Carriers in Asian countries are interested in bringing fiber to apartments and small businesses with PON electronics, which are lower cost than SONET. (See Chapter 6.) SONET is used for redundancy and to merge voice and data traffic carried over fiber in carriers' networks.

Optical Add and Drop Multiplexers (OADM)

Optical add and drop multiplexers (OADMs) reroute traffic that comes into a carriers' point of presence (POP) from the backbone network. For example, a pair of fibers might carry traffic on 40 different wavelengths. Each wavelength also is called a lambda. Each *wavelength* (*lambda*) is essentially a high-speed path of, for example, 10 gigabits per second (Gbps) of data. A filter in an add and drop multiplexer reroutes a single wavelength in the strand of fiber at, for example, the Detroit POP and "drops" it off, or reroutes it to, Cleveland. (See Figure 5.12.) An add and drop multiplexer ob-

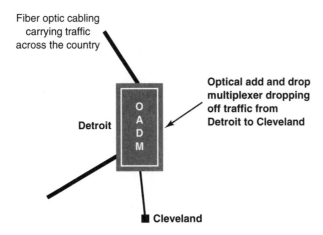

Figure 5.12
An optical add and drop multiplexer

viates the need for more expensive amplifiers in Detroit to convert the signal back to an electronic format before sending the traffic to Cleveland.

Optical Cross Connects (OXC)—Optical Switches

Optical cross connect (OXC) systems, (optical switches) have more capability than optical add and drop multiplexers (OADMs). They are used in POPs with higher traffic than those where OADMs are used. They switch light waves in core, high-speed carrier networks. In the future, they may also be used in the backbone, high-traffic portion of metropolitan networks between central office switches. Optical cross connect (OXC) systems let carriers redirect wavelengths through computer commands without physically unplugging fiber optic cables. A technician at a computer can redirect an individual wavelength from one destination to another on the network using software. Demultiplexers in the optical cross connect separate out the wavelengths to their different routes.

The advantages of optical switches are:

- *Scalability*—Optical switches have ports that run at variable speeds. For example, the Tellium, Inc. switch has a capacity for 512 OC 48 (2.48 gigabits) ports or 128 OC 192 (10 gigabits) ports or a mix of the two up to a total of 1.28 terabits per second. Different parts of the network can be equipped with larger or lower amounts of bandwidth.

- *Reliability*: If one route becomes busy, more capacity can be assigned to it by computer command. This is less prone to error than manually plugging and unplugging cables from a fiber patch panel. It is not uncommon for technicians to mistakenly unplug a route with traffic on it. As networks become larger and more complex with more routes, reconfiguring routing needs to be done by computer control.

- *Less capacity required for service restoration*—SONET rings carry traffic in one direction. If the ring malfunctions, the traffic is carried on the backup ring in the reverse direction. Each 10-gigabit segment needs a 10-gigabit segment for backup. Thus, half of the network capacity generally sits idle. Networks configured using optical switches have a mesh topology. If a route crashes, traffic can be rerouted to any other network location. Thus, each backup route does not have to have the capacity to carry all of the traffic on the main route. See Figure 5.13 for mesh disaster recovery routes.

Optical switches come in two "flavors": all optical, and optical switches with electrical switching.

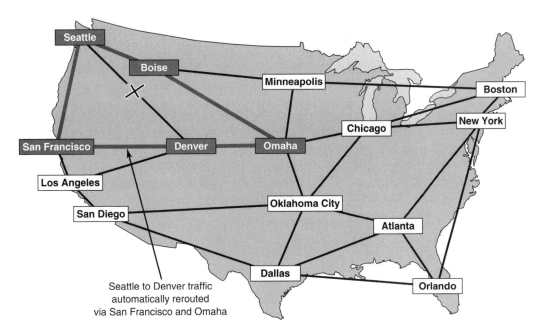

Figure 5.13
Mesh topology. Drawing courtesy of Tellium

Optical Electrical Optical (OEO) Switches

Optical electrical optical (OEO) switches have direct optical interfaces. Fiber optic cables plug directly into them. However, they process traffic electronically. The chips that perform the switching do so electrically. The bits in the electrical signals tell the switch where the traffic should be routed. OEO switches use the same protocols used in the Internet Protocol (IP) such as multi-protocol label switching (MPLS). MPLS looks at the address in the first packet in a stream of data, puts that in hardware on the switch and routes the rest of the stream using the abbreviated address in the hardware. It doesn't have to keep looking up the address. The Resource Reservation Protocol (RSVP) is part of MPLS. It routes packets and circuits based on a user's requested quality of service (QoS).

OOO—All Optical Switches

All optical switches (OOO) have direct fiber connections and they switch wavelengths (lambdas) as light pulses without converting them to electrical signals. The OOO refers to *optical incoming*, *optical switching* (internal) and *optical outgoing*. All optical switches use out-of-band signals to direct light pulses to routes. The traffic itself remains optical and the out-of-band electrical signals generated by routers tell the switch where to send the traffic. The advantage of all optical switches is speed. They are potentially faster than optical electrical optical (OEO) switches because they aren't slowed down by the optical-to-electrical and electrical-back-to-optical conversions. All optical switches use MPLS (previously described), as well as automated switched transport network (ASTN). ASTN is an emerging standard for controlling wavelengths. It provides dynamic class of service assignment and flexible restoration of service. Routers at carriers' points of presence (POPs) send out of band signals to each other for managing the traffic handled by optical switches. The signals are sent separately from the traffic.

Mirrors for Routing Traffic in All Optical Switches • Tiny little mirrors, a few milimeters wide, redirect traffic in OOO optical switches by beaming light to other mirrors. Switches such as those made by Nortel Networks have 1000 mirrors facing another 1000 mirrors in arrays. (See Figure 5.14.) The mirrors route light beams between the two arrays of mirrors. For the switching to operate, two mirrors must face each other at the same time and direct a beam of light to another mirror.

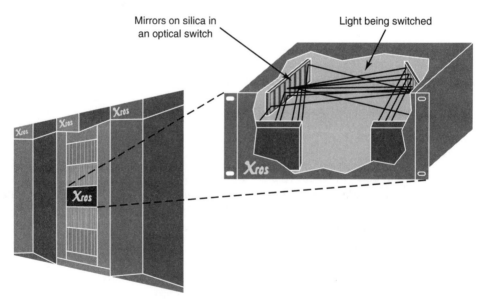

Figure 5.14
Mirrors in optical OOO switches. Drawing courtesy of Xros, part of Nortel Networks

LAYING FIBER IN METROPOLITAN AREAS

In the year 2000, carriers started laying fiber in the 25 largest metropolitan areas in the United States in order to connect them to long haul backbone networks that carry traffic across the country. Routes in cities typically run to incumbent telephone company central offices and carrier hotels, which often are clustered together in the same areas, frequently near AT&T's switches. From there, they have runs to customers, data centers, Internet service providers and application service providers (ASPs).

According to the article "Can They Dig It?" published in *Teledotcom*, 19 March 2001, by Kate Gerwig, right-of-way permits for laying new fiber amount to close to 20% of the cost of building new networks. Difficulties in getting permits can delay projects by a year to 16 months. Cities, with their often-narrow streets, politically powerful neighborhoods, historic districts and public works bureaucracy are more complex than suburban and long haul routes in which to get permits.

According to Bob Albee, Director, Telecommunications Engineering for Vanasse Hangen Brustlin, Inc., a Boston-based structural engineering firm, public works departments feel a responsibility to protect:

- Public investment in road surfaces
- Water mains and gas lines from drilling
- Emergency vehicle access for public safety
- Commerce needs for access by vendors and customers
- Quality of life regarding noise and dirt during construction

In an effort to simplify the process, cities such as Minneapolis and Boston have started joint build processes. With joint builds, a lead fiber supplier is required to canvass all of the registered carriers and ask them if they wish to participate in laying cable. Carriers don't have another opportunity for 5 to 10 years to trench if they turn down the joint build. In Boston, Level 3 canvassed 34 companies and 15 opted to share the costs of the construction. Fiber is being run to 5 central offices with 134 pathways. Another issue is that intersections are sometimes jammed with manholes for water, sewers, surface drains, electricity and telecommunications cables. To promote efficient manhole utilization, some cities require that carriers share manholes. The lead carrier provides security for access for repair and maintenance.

....

LAYING FIBER IN METROPOLITAN AREAS (continued)

Network service providers are looking at creative ways to avoid the worldwide problem of digging up streets. CityNet Telecommunications, Inc. of Silver Springs, Maryland uses miniature robots from Ka-Te System AG of Zurich to run fiber in sewers. Other carriers are attempting to get rights-of-way in subway systems for fiber.

Because of the complexity of the process and the capital crunch, projects to lay fiber in cities are behind schedule. Mr. Albee expects fiber builds to be complete in most of the 25 largest cities by the beginning of 2002. Smaller network developers such as CTC Fiber are building infrastructure in smaller metropolitan and suburban areas. These areas will be completed later than those in the largest cities.

Two hinges attached to the side and top of the mirrors direct the movement of the mirrors. The mirrors move in response to voltage applied between the mirror and the silica substrate to which the mirror is attached.

Some optical switches, such as those made by Agilent (formerly Hewlett Packard) use bubbles off which light is transmitted. The bubbles are generated by technology similar to that used in ink jet printers.

Tunable Lasers

Tunable lasers save manufacturing costs. In dense wavelength division multiplexing (DWMD) a separate laser is used for each color (frequency) of light transmitted. Each color carries a separate channel of traffic. If a DWDM device carries 40 colors of light, 40 lasers are required. With tunable lasers, the same manufacturing process makes lasers for all colors. At the end of the manufacturing process, the laser is "set" to a particular frequency. This saves the manufacturer from having to keep spare lasers for each frequency. Prices of tunable lasers are still high. Many carriers solve the problem of keeping spare lasers by keeping some spare frequencies on their fiber optic networks. If a laser on a particular color fails, they reroute traffic to the spare lambda or color.

NETWORK INTELLIGENCE AND SIGNALING ....

Signals in public networks are used for billing, monitoring, links to advanced features and for carriers to exchange traffic with each other. The public network owes much of its reliability, advanced features and interoperability to signaling.

Overview of Signaling

Signaling is used to process every switched call on the public switched network and the public cellular network. The caller dials a number and hears progress tones such as dial tone, ringing, busy signals or reorder tones. These are all signaling tones carried within the public network. In addition to tones, callers might hear digital messages telling them the number they dialed is not in service or has been changed.

Signaling innovations represent a major improvement in the public network's capabilities. They not only enable carriers to manage their networks more efficiently, but they also provide the means for the introduction of profitable, new services.

Signaling innovations led to:

- Cost reductions and cost stabilization in the price of long distance.

- A platform for new, network-based services such as fax-on-demand, pre-paid calling cards and voice mail.

- Toll-free 800, 877 and 888 number portability between carriers (the ability for an organization to retain its toll-free numbers when changing carriers).

- Local number portability, which allows users to keep their telephone number when they change telephone provider.

- Improved network reliability.

- ISDN Integrated services digital network is a way to carry 2 or 23 voice and data channels over the same cables. The signals are carried in a separate channel on the same cable.

- Lucrative "smart" services such as caller ID, call trace, call return and call waiting.

In addition, signaling is the backbone for interconnection between cellular, global wireless and multiple carriers' networks. The architecture of the signaling network was established by AT&T in conjunction with Bell Labs in the 1970s. Prior to the 1984 divestiture, AT&T owned all of the 22 Bell Operating Companies (BOCs). It had the necessary control of the public network that enabled it to set a standard that was followed across the country and later adopted by the international community.

A new way to carry signals such as ringing, dialing and disconnects was developed by AT&T in the 1970s, resulting in increased efficiency, automation and functionality. The new signaling, known as common channel interoffice signaling, carries signals on a separate data communications network rather than on the same path as a person's voice. Out-of-band signals are faster than in-band signals and use less network time for nonbillable call setup.

A SIGNALING TUTORIAL

Signaling is the process of sending information between two parts of a network to control, route and maintain a telephone call. For example, lifting the handset of a telephone from the receiver sends a signal to the central office, "I want to make a phone call." The central office sends a signal back to the user in the form of a dial tone indicating the network is ready to carry the call.

The three types of signals are:

- *Supervisory signals*—Supervisory signals monitor the busy or idle condition of a telephone. They also are used to request service. They tell the central office when the telephone handset is lifted (off-hook requesting service) or hung-up (on-hook in an idle condition).

- *Alerting signals*—These are bell signals, tones or strobe lights that alert end users that a call has arrived.

- *Addressing signals*—These are touch tones or data pulses that tell the network where to send the call. A computer or person dialing a call sends addressing signals over the network.

Signals can be sent over the same channel as voice or data conversation, or over a separate channel. Prior to 1976, all signals were sent over the same path as voice and data traffic. This is called in-band signaling. In-band signaling resulted in inefficient use of telephone lines. When a call was dialed, the network checked for an available path and tied up an entire path through the network before it sent the call through to the distant end. For example, a call from Miami to Los Angeles tied up a path throughout the network after the digits were dialed, but before the call started.

Prior to the proliferation of voice mail, between 20% and 35% of calls were incomplete due to busy signals, network congestion and ring-no-answers. Therefore, channels that could be used for telephone calls were used to carry in-band signals such as those for incomplete calls, dial tone and ringing. Multiplying this scenario by the millions of calls placed resulted in wasted telephone network facilities.

In addition to tying up telephone facilities, in-band signaling sets up calls more slowly than out-of-band signaling. To illustrate, the time between dialing an 800 call and hearing ring-back tones from the distant end is the call setup part of the call. *Call setup* includes dialing and waiting until the call is actually established. Call setup is slow with in-band signaling. Carriers do not bill for call setup and thus use valuable network capacity for it. Carriers do not receive revenue until the called party answers the phone.

Background

Common channel interoffice signaling, also known as *out-of-band signaling*, is in reality a data communications network laid over carriers' switching networks. It has opened markets for new products and enhancements to carriers' features. Common channel signaling was developed as a way to increase network efficiency by setting up separate channels for signals. It evolved into the basis for intelligent networks. Routing instructions, database information and specialized programs are stored in computers in the carriers' networks and are accessible over out-of-band signaling links.

Beginning in the late 1970s, the public network evolved from purely carrying voice and data calls to a vehicle with intelligence, greater capacity and faster recovery from equipment failure. The impetus to upgrade the network came from AT&T's desire to manage and add capacity to the network more cost-effectively. This upgrade laid the foundation for new services such as enhanced 800 services, prepaid calling cards, roaming in cellular networks, ISDN, call forwarding, three-way calling and call waiting.

Signaling System 7 (SS7)—Lowering Costs and Increasing the Reliability of Public Networks

The Signaling System 7 (SS7) protocol, which is based on common channel signaling, is a factor in lowering barriers to entry into the common carrier market. Routing intelligence is located in lower cost computer-based peripherals rather than in central office switches. For example, powerful parallel processing computers hold massive databases with information such as routing instructions for toll-free and 900 calls. One processor with its database supports multiple central office switches. (See Figure 5.15.) In this case, each central office switch is not required to maintain sophisticated routing information. The expense of the upgrade is shared among many central offices.

The significance of advancements in signaling technology should not be underestimated. When network problems are detected, alerts are sent over the signaling network to centralized network operation centers (NOCs) where technicians see visual indications of alarms on wall-mounted, computerized displays. Moreover, sections of carrier networks can be quickly reconfigured from commands sent by centralized network control centers over signaling channels. Immediately after the 1989 earthquake in California, the network was reconfigured such that no calls were allowed into California. This left paths open for Californians to make calls out of the state to reassure relatives that they were safe.

Adding Features to Carriers' Networks

Specialized servers and central office switches communicate with each other over out-of-band signaling links. For example, databases located in carriers' public networks

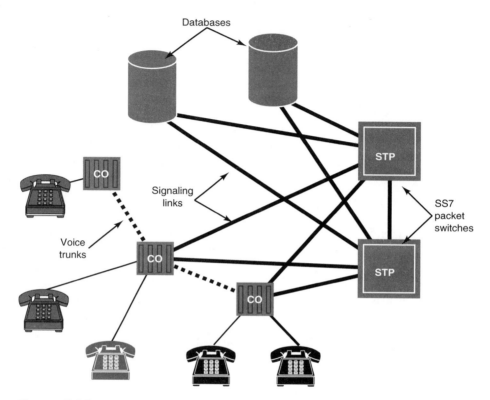

Figure 5.15
Common channel signaling.

are capable of storing the profiles of both the telephone number dialed and the telephone number of the caller for each call. This intelligence enables firms to customize call treatment. For example, from 8:00 a.m. to 5:00 p.m. Eastern Standard Time, 800 calls may be routed to a firm's east coast call center. After 5:00 p.m. Eastern Standard Time, all calls may be routed to California.

Because the databases and specialized processors are on separate computers from the central office switch, the central office and its switch do not have to be upgraded each time new "intelligence" is added to the network. This is a significant factor in allowing faster additions of features to the public network. In addition, multiple central offices access the specialized servers and databases. Thus, adding upgrades through the signaling network provides additional functionality to multiple central offices.

Examples of features available on networks with common channel signaling include:

- Voice-activated dialing for calling cards, car phones and home phone lines supported by speech recognition systems in the network.

- Custom-calling features from local telephone companies such as call forwarding, call conferencing and call waiting.

- Load balancing by call volume (e.g., 50% of the calls sent to California and 50% to the call center in Iowa).

- Calling number and calling name delivery (display of the calling telephone number and name associated with the telephone placing the call).

- Customer links to carrier networks, where customers specify new call destinations for the 800 services into their call centers. For example, calls may be redirected based on unusual traffic patterns.

Cellular networks use SS7 technology for roaming service as well as for the traditional routing and tracking of calls used by landline networks. Every cellular provider has a database called the *home location register* (HLR) where complete information is kept for each subscriber. They also have a *visitor location register* (VLR), which keeps temporary records for callers who are visiting from other areas. When a cellular subscriber roams, each visited system exchanges SS7 messages with the "home" system. The home system also marks its home location register so it knows where to send calls for its customers that are roaming.

As cellular providers upgrade their networks to support higher data rates and more capacity, new signaling services will need to be implemented. For example, general packet radio services (GPRS), which is being planned for higher speed data services, requires GPRS Roaming Exchange. *GPRS Roaming Exchange* standardizes addressing, security and call routing between networks.

Residential, business and cellular voice mail purchased from local telephone companies are examples of services made possible by common channel signaling. Single voice mail systems manufactured by vendors such as Lucent and Comverse Technology support multiple central offices. Following are some of the messages communicated between network-located voice mail and central office switches (see Figure 5.16):

- Initiate stutter dial tone or light message-waiting indicators to tell users they have voice mail messages

- Instruct the voice mail system as to which person should receive specific voice messages (e.g., play Mr. Smith's greeting for this call)

- Turn stutter dial tone and message-waiting indicators off when voice mail messages have been listened to

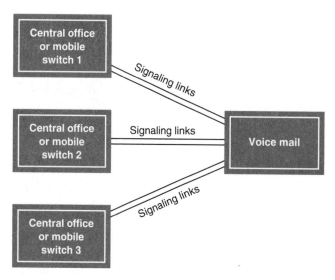

Figure 5.16
Central office links to voice mail.

Common Channel Signaling, Efficiency and Redundancy

SS7 is a separate data network that carries all of the signaling in each carrier's network. The efficiency of common channel signaling is achieved by having one signaling link support multiple voice and data transmissions. The fact that one signaling link supports many trunks (high-speed links between telephone switches) highlights the requirement for reliability. If one signaling link crashes, many trunks are out of service. Redundancy is an important consideration in the design of carriers' signaling networks. (See Figure 5.16 for an illustration of redundant signaling links.)

Signaling System 7—The Glue for Links Between Carriers

A major value of Signaling System 7 (SS7) is its capability to enable all carriers to work in concert with each other. It is a standard protocol approved by the International Telecommunications Union (ITU). Signals are sent between central office, interexchange carriers, international phone companies and to specialized processors and databases. Global billing, toll free and 900 services and international roaming for wireless calls all are dependent on SS7.

Early SS7 Implementations

The Swedish PTT trialed SS7 in 1983. The United Kingdom and France also had early implementations in the early 1980s. MCI (now part of WorldCom) first implemented SS7 in its network in April 1988 in Los Angeles and Philadelphia. According to a May 2, 1988 article in *Network World,* MCI stated that it had halved call setup time on calls over the Philadelphia/Los Angeles route. Freeing up voice paths from signaling enabled carriers to pack more calls on their existing network paths.

The precursor to SS7, Signaling System 6 (SS6), was developed by AT&T in the 1970s for the old Bell system. AT&T took advantage of computer-controlled switching to develop an overlay signaling network. In essence, it created a data communications network that could send more complex messages than the limited in-band tones that notified the network when calls were completed, how they were addressed, and so forth. The first implementation of Signaling System 6 in 1976 by AT&T was automation of calling card validation. SS6 enabled AT&T to eliminate operators for calling card validation.

With common channel interoffice signaling (CCIS), authorization for calling card calls is done automatically by checking the telephone company databases, called *line information databases* (LIDBs). Line information databases contain all valid telephone and calling card numbers. An operator is not required to check a computer database to determine if the calling card number is valid. Instead, the central office sees from the number dialed that the call was made from a calling card. It then initiates a call to the LIDB to determine the validity of the calling card.

AT&T mandated the implementation of Signaling System 6 throughout the entire Bell system in the late 1970s. The faster SS7, a layered protocol with signaling links of 64,000 bps, was specified by AT&T in 1980. SS7 now supports 1.54 megabit per second signaling links. SS7 is used, with variations, on a global basis.

As with many standards, implementation of SS7 differs among countries. For example, the U.S., Canada, Japan and parts of China implemented the American National Standards Institute (ANSI) version of SS7. Europe implemented the European Telecommunications Standards Institute (ETSI) version. Parts of the world also use an International Telecommunications Union (ITU) version of SS7.

Gateways translate these various SS7 protocols so that international carriers can understand each other's signaling. This enables central office switches to communicate, for instance, with Chinese and European SS7 implementations.

SS7 Components

SS7 components include:

- Packet switches, or **signal transfer points** that route signals between databases and central offices
- **Service switching points**, software and ports in central offices that enable switches to query databases
- **Service control points**, specialized databases with billing and customer feature information

See Figure 5.17 for an overview of the following SS7 components. Not all carriers own and operate their SS7 networks. They may, for example, use SS7 networks from companies such as Illuminet. Carriers that use Illuminet have links from their central office to the Illuminet signal transfer points.

Signal Transfer Points (STPs)

Signal transfer points are packet switches that route signals between central offices and specialized databases. Messages are sent between points on the SS7 network in vari-

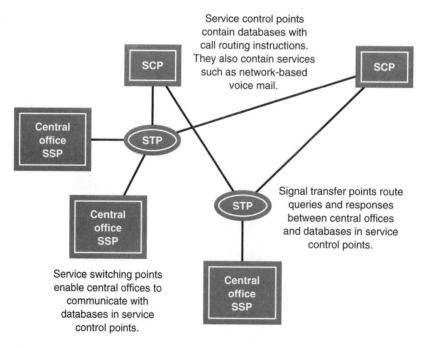

Figure 5.17
SS7 components.

able-length packets with addresses attached. (Think of the packets as envelopes of data containing user information such as the called and calling telephone number, error correction information and sequencing numbers so that the correct packets or envelopes are grouped together in the correct order at the receiving end.) Signal transfer switches read only the address portion of the packets and forward the messages accordingly.

The fact that the signals are sent in a packet format is a significant factor in SS7's efficiency. Packets associated with multiple calls share the same pipe. Packets from transmissions a, b, c, and so forth are broken into small chunks (packets) and sent down over the same 64 or 1540 kilobit SS7 links and reassembled at the destination.

Service Switching Points (SSPs)

Service switching points enable central offices to initiate queries to databases and specialized computers. Service switching points consist of software capable of sending specialized messages to databases and ports connected to the S77 network. For example, when a 900 call is dialed, SSPs set up a special query to a 900 database (the service control point) for information on routing the call.

Service switching points convert the central office query from the central office "machine language" to SS7 language. When signals are received from the signaling network, the service switching points convert the SS7 language to language readable by the central office switch.

Service Control Points (SCPs)

Service control points hold specialized databases with routing instructions for each call based on the calling party and/or the called party. For example, service control points tell the network which carrier to route an 800 call to. Services such as network-based voice mail, fax applications and voice-activated dialing are located on service control points or intelligent peripherals.

CONVERGENCE—TECHNICAL ADVANCES LEADING TO IMPROVEMENTS IN IP NETWORKS ....

The definition of convergence varies throughout the telecommunications industry. For purposes of this chapter, *convergence* is the capability of one public network to carry all types of traffic—voice, data and video—as packets. These networks either use Internet protocol (IP)-based routers or asynchronous transfer mode (ATM) switches, which send information in fixed-sized packets called cells. (See Chapter 6 for ATM.) Internet backbone networks are generally based on IP, a protocol used for routing packets in the Internet and in private networks. Wholesale carriers' networks that carry a mix of voice, data and video tend to be based on ATM- and IP-based routers.

Technical advances are improving the quality of voice and video carried on packet networks. They also are lowering the cost of building high-capacity networks capable of carrying voice along with data over backbone networks. The vast majority of voice traffic is still carried in circuit switched networks. According to the article, "VOIP—Still Only a Drop in the Bucket," published in *Business Communications Review, Voice 2001*, February 2001, page 78, only 1% of traffic in the United States is carried as voice over IP (VOIP).

Packet networks are those that use ATM equipment and IP-based routers. IP is not a connection-oriented protocol. A path is not guaranteed for the entire length of the voice, data or video transmission. If capacity is not available for some of the variable-length packets, they are dropped or retransmitted on another route. This is fine for data such as email, but dropped packets can result in choppy voice or video, called "clipping." Thus, any technology that increases the capacity of networks improves its quality of service and decreases dropped cells or packets resulting from congestion.

The technical advances include:

- Improvements in routers
- Faster digital signal processors (DSPs)
- Dense wavelength division multiplexing (DWDM)
- High-capacity optical switches
- Lower cost, programmable switches, called *softswitches*
- Protocols that improve the quality of voice and video over packet networks

Improvements in Routers

Faster routers enhance the quality of voice and video carried on Internet Protocol networks. In traditional networks, carriers use both routers and asynchronous transfer mode (ATM) switches for their data traffic. ATM switches carry voice, data, video and modem traffic. Routers often take the customer data from the "edge" of the network and send it to ATM switches located in the backbone or core of the network.

The ATM switches provide circuit-like services. They have the capability to establish a path through the network and reserve capacity for high-priority services such as voice and video. They guarantee a particular level of service, referred to as quality of service (QoS).

Older routers keep lists of addresses of devices on the network in tables in the router's memory. When packets are transmitted through the network, each router looks up the destination address in the router's table. These lookups result in delays.

In high-speed terabit routers, addresses are stored in the silicon on cards in the router. They use multi-protocol label switching (MPLS), which speeds up routers.

When ATM switches and routers work together in a network, the ATM switch, if it uses quality of service, must be able to read the quality of service bits in packets sent by routers. This is called mapping bits from the router to the ATM switch.

Routers:

- Directly connect with customers' IP data without converting the data to another format
- Carry voice and video without degrading the quality of either
- Use the ATM portion of the system to read the IP header and know what priority to give it

Some new pure IP networks are eliminating ATM equipment and just using high-speed routers.

Routers in Cellular Networks for IP Backbone Traffic

Many cellular providers are planning to upgrade their backbone networks by installing routers at the edge of their networks. The edge of carriers' networks is the point where traffic from mobile central offices is aggregated before being carried between central offices and to other cellular carriers. The routers will carry cellular voice and mobile data traffic in cellular networks that have been upgraded for high-speed data service.

Digital Signal Processors (DSPs)

Digital signal processors (DSPs) (see Figure 5.18) are special purpose microprocessors on pieces of silicon that execute instructions. These powerful processors are good at performing a small number of repetitive tasks such as compressing voice, packetizing voice and converting analog voice into digital. They also compensate for delay and bit losses in networks. They are used in voice mail, wireless telephone handsets and for handling voice in data networks. DSP vendors include Texas Instruments, Motorola, Lucent Microelectronics and Analog Devices.

Transporting voice over packet networks requires extremely fast processing to replicate the quality in the public switched network. In data communications, email can be delayed a few seconds without a problem. Choppy sound, pieces of conversation received out of sequence, clipped conversations and long silences generally are unacceptable for television and voice. Voice compression done on DSPs has improved voice quality in IP networks.

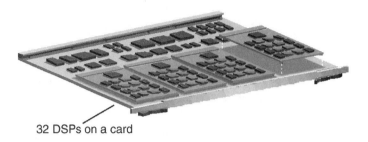

32 DSPs on a card

Figure 5.18
A card with 32 digital signal processors. Drawing courtesy of Cisco Systems

Voice Compression

Voice compression (see Chapter 1) is a key capability of DSPs. Compression uses mathematical algorithms to make voice smaller. Voice is sent through circuit switched networks at 64,000 bits per second. Digital signal processors, using mathematical algorithms, are capable of compressing voice, making it smaller, so that it can be sent intelligibly at lower speeds of from 8,000 to 12,000 bips per second. Thus, the capacity needed to transmit voice over packet networks is lowered. (In packet networks, headers are added to packetized voice, increasing the 8000 bits per second to 12,000 bits per second.)

Digital signal processors have become so fast that they compress voice and video and digitize and packetize it so that voice and video are acceptable over IP networks.

Once the voice or video signal leaves the DSP, delays in the network can impair voice quality. For example, congestion can cause pieces of the voice conversation to be dropped. Slow routers or switches can lead to delays and choppy voice conversations.

Higher Capacity Networks— Optical Technologies

Optical technologies have had a tremendous impact on capacities in the core, backbone sections of long-haul networks. The backbone is the "interstate highway" portion of the network used for routes that carry the highest percentage of traffic. They are starting to have an impact on metropolitan areas as well.

- Dense wavelength division multiplexing (DWDM) is a fiber optic multiplexing technique. New DWDM equipment is capable of carrying 160

DIGITAL SIGNAL PROCESSING IMPACT ON MODEMS, FAX CARDS AND IP

Brough Turner, one of the founders and now Chief Technology Officer at NMS Communications (formerly called Natural Microsystems), has been at NMS since 1980. Brough has seen the impact that DSPs have had on modems, voice mail, fax cards and voice over IP.

In 1980, analog circuitry limited modems to a top speed of 1200 bits per second. Modems converted digital signals to analog and analog signals back to digital using analog circuitry. Once digital signal processors were used, they digitally encoded signals using mathematical algorithms. The digital algorithms were performed consistently and with increasing speeds. Thus, modems increased in speed from 1200 bits per second to 14,400, 19,000, 28,000, 33,600 and eventually 56,000 bits per second.

Digital signal processing systems made by NMS Communications and other vendors digitize speech and convert analog fax signals to digital bits, at real-time speeds in voice mail, speech recognition, videoconferencing, fax modems, and fax cards within voice mail systems. DSPs are installed on chips in routers and switches within the public network. They also are present in wireless handsets, routers and enterprise-based telephone systems. In addition to digitizing signals, they also perform the digital-to-analog conversions.

channels of data over a single pair of fibers. Each channel has a speed of OC-192 (10 gigabits). The single pair thus carries 1.6 terabits (a trillion bits) per second (10 x 160). (See Chapter 2.)

- Optical switches, previously discussed, increase the capacity and routing flexibility of backbone networks by switching thousands of light waves simultaneously.

- Passive optical networking (see above) is bringing the capacity of fiber closer to end-user customers, in the last mile access network.

Softswitches—Programmable Switches

Softswitches are central office switches built on standard computer platforms for sending voice over packet networks. Softswitches are made using standard protocols so that they can easily interface with network-based applications such as unified messaging and billing systems. They also interface with SS7 services for sending traffic to proprietary central office switches. Because softswitch functions are built-in layers, they are low in cost to modify and upgrade. Each layer can be changed without changing the other layers. The following are the three layers of softswitches:

- *Service selection*—Interfaces with databases in the network to determine which carrier to send the call to and which features such as 800-number translation to apply. This layer determines what to do with the call.

- Call control—Sets up and tears down calls and interfaces with tones in the network. This layer interfaces with protocols used in packet networks.

- Transport, signaling and processing calls—Announcements are played, voice is packetized, and calls are transported.

Because they are built on standard platforms, programmable switches cost less than traditional central office switches. Moreover, switches made on these platforms are easier to interface with network-based applications such as unified messaging and network-based systems for call centers when these systems are also based on compatible platforms. Vendors of softswitches include Cisco Systems, Sonus Networks, Telcordia Technologies, and Tellabs. Companies such as Lucent and Nortel sell the largest share of proprietary central office switches in the United States. Siemens and Alcatel have a large international presence. Manufacturers of proprietary switches are in various stages of development for next generation softswitches.

Calls coming into an IP network from the circuit switched network are converted into packets by digital signal processors housed in the programmable switch. The call is then transferred to a router, where it is transmitted through the network in a packet format. In this scenario, the voice travels "free" along with the data.

Softswitches for End Offices vs. Toll Offices— The Core vs. the Edge

Most softswitches currently are installed in long-haul backbone networks rather than as replacements for end-office switches that connect directly to end users. End-offices are part of the last mile, local access network. Last mile networks have the following complexities not found in toll offices:

- Playing announcements such as "All circuits are busy"
- Setting up the call
- Supplying dial tone
- Providing 411 directory and 911 emergency notification services

Edge networks also have more of the following enhanced services to which switches interface:

- Calling card services
- Debit cards
- Voice messaging
- Voice-activated dialing
- Fax services
- International callback
- Three-way calling
- Follow-me calling (calls reaching people wherever they are)

While the vast majority of central office switches installed are proprietary in nature, softswitches with the capability to handle complex features are starting to be deployed mainly by competitive local exchange carriers in local access, or last mile edge networks.

Backbone networks do not have the complex features found in local access networks. Incumbent telephone companies that have been slower to adopt softswitches, have started to issue requests for proposals for softswitches as toll office replacements in their backbone networks. Toll switches do not have connections to end users. They transmit traffic in the backbone portion of incumbent telephone company networks. Telephone companies are purchasing fewer proprietary central office switches. New developments planned for softswitches are the addition of ports compatible with DSL and cable modem service. These will be tested in labs by various manufacturers by year-end 2001.

Softswitches for Internet Access PBX Trunks

Some carriers are starting to use softswitches to offload heavy Internet dialup traffic and PBX trunks from end central offices. Rather than buy a new central office switch when they need more capacity, they purchase a softswitch to handle dialup Internet traffic and PBX trunks. The Internet traffic is sent directly to the Internet via packet networks without tying up circuit switched central office ports.

The Quality of Service Issue for Voice over IP

While quality for voice in packet networks is improving, it still is not as consistent as that in the public switched network. In addition to capacity to ensure quality, protocols used by routers and switches that attach priority to packets carrying voice and video are critical. The following (plus MPLS discussed in the section on optical switches) are key protocols used for sending mixed media messages in packets networks:

- Session Initiation Protocol (SIP) is used between end points for negotiating features of the transmission.
- Realtime Transport Protocol (RTP) is used to identify packet content.
- Differentiated Services (Diffserve) uses bits in packet headers to identify and prioritize traffic.
- H.323 is a suite of protocols for setting up and sending calls over IP networks.

SS7 in Packet Networks

Carriers such as Qwest Communications, Williams Communications and Level 3 are building networks based on the Internet Protocol and ATM rather than on circuit switching. They feel that packet networks are more suitable for the preponderance of data traffic, which is growing at a faster rate than voice traffic. IP-based networks use SS7 signaling information for billing and advanced features.

Gateways translate and deliver SS7 between signaling system networks and IP switches. Gateways also translate signaling messages between the public switched network's central office circuit switches and IP networks. Note that in Figure 5.19,

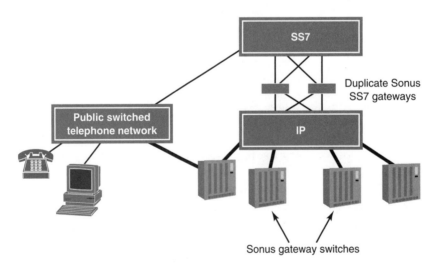

Figure 5.19
SS7 gateway. Diagram courtesy of Sonus Networks

INTERNATIONAL LONG DISTANCE AND REAL-TIME FAX OVER IP

Carriers such as iBasis, Inc. and IDT sell wholesale international voice and real-time fax long distance to domestic and international carriers and Internet service providers. They offer savings on international long distance and real-time fax services. They have switches in worldwide locations such as New York City, Los Angeles, Singapore, China, Korea, Taipei, the Middle East and Latin America.

Carriers that use iBasis route calls to the iBasis switches, or points of presence (POPs). At these POPs, a Cisco System programmable switch aggregates the traffic from multiple carriers and sends it to a Cisco router that acts as a gateway. See Figure 5.20. Some of iBasis's carrier customers are: Telstra, WorldCom, KDD, NTT, Teleglobe, Communications Authority of Thailand and China Unicom. The gateway translates circuit switched traffic to packets. Digital signal processors (DSPs) in the routers packetize and compress the voice and fax traffic. The calls are then routed over backbone Internet facilities rented from carriers such as AT&T, Cable & Wireless and WorldCom Group. At the other end of the call, the gateways reverse the process sending the calls back to the circuit switched network.

iBasis monitors its traffic from a control center in Burlington, Massachusetts. The network management system measures the time it takes packets to travel "round trip," for example, from New York to Singapore and back to New York. If delays (latency) exceed preset parameters, traffic is routed over the public switched network instead of over the Internet backbone. Thus, iBasis eliminates delays (latency) that can impair voice and fax traffic carried over IP. iBasis calls this rerouting Assured Quality Routing.

two signaling gateway systems are pictured. These are mated pairs for redundancy. If one signaling gateway fails, the other one takes over. The links between all systems also are redundant.

EXAMPLES OF CONVERGED NETWORKS ....

Data and voice communications in Internet Protocol packets can be transported over the "public" portion of the Internet used for email and Web surfing. It also can be sent over separate Internet Protocol networks built by carriers. Sending it over carriers'

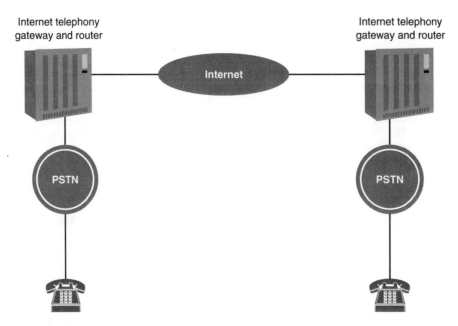

Figure 5.20
Wholesale provision of IP telephony for international calls. Courtesy of iBasis, Inc

own networks provides more assurance of quality for voice. Carriers that build their own IP networks engineer them for certain quality of service standards.

Examples of carriers that will carry converged traffic on upgraded networks include:

- Cable TV companies
- Competitive local exchange carriers (CLECs)
- Traditional long distance suppliers and Internet backbone providers such as AT&T, Sprint Communications, Cable & Wireless and WorldCom
- Long distance providers such as Qwest Communications, Inc., Level 3 Communications, Broadwing and Global Crossing
- Cellular carriers between their switches
- Local Bell operating companies such as Verizon and SBC
- Internet Service Providers
- Utilities entering telecommunications

Many startup competitive local exchange carriers and regional carriers are looking for ways to lower the cost of building networks. Optical networking technologies and softswitches are important enabling technologies.

Free Calls or Low Priced Calls over the Internet

Starting in 1995, users made free voice calls over the Internet from their PCs. (See Figure 5.21.) They did so by installing proprietary software from companies such as VocalTec Communication, Ltd. and sound cards into their personal computers. They also plugged telephones, headsets or microphones into their PCs. The quality of these calls was inferior to that available with standard telephones connected to the public switched network. Moreover, PCs could only be used to call people with compatible software. However, many customers were happy to be able to make free long distance calls. This was particularly popular for international calls and calls between college students and their parents.

Both Net2Phone and Dialpad now offer long distance to consumers from either their own telephone or from PCs. The software to enable consumers to place calls over the Internet is available free from the Net2Phone Web site. Net2Phone has sites all over the world from which people with PCs equipped with its software, a headset or microphone and soundcards can place discount calls back to the United States. Users place local calls to Net2Phone switches, which then route the calls over portions of the Internet backbone that Net2Phone rents from other carriers.

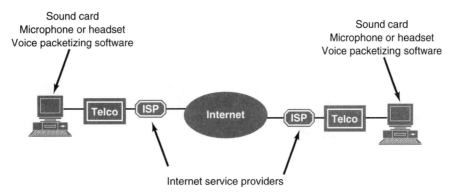

Figure 5.21
PC-to-PC telephone calls.

H.323—A Way to Make Telephone Calls over IP

In July 1996, Intel Corporation announced a free software program that works on Microsoft Windows™ 95 and later operating systems. The software uses the H.323 standard as an agreed-upon way for users to make voice calls from PCs connected to the Internet. Users with H.323-based software from any vendor are able to call any telephone or PC on the public network, as seen in Figure 5.21. H.323 is the International Telecommunications Union-defined standard originally designed for sending video over packet networks. Intel and Microsoft hoped to increase demand for PCs with promotion of an open standard for voice over the Internet Protocol from computers.

Prepaid Calls over the Internet

Carriers including Net2Phone, Dialpad and Delta Three, Inc. sell telephone service that is routed from customers' telephones to the Internet. To use the service, customers dial a toll-free telephone number and their PIN number. The local telephone company then routes the call to the Internet telephony service provider (ITSP) point of presence (POP). The POP contains the Internet Telephony Service Provider's switch, which:

- Packetizes, digitizes and compresses the voice
- Routes the call to the Internet
- At the receiving end, converts the packets back to a form compatible with the circuit switched network (see Figure 5.22)
- Tracks billing information

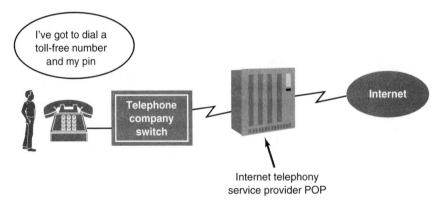

Figure 5.22
Prepaid calls via the Internet.

Many of these providers sell the long distance on a debit card basis. For example, Delta Three sells debit cards to users who can charge the card to any major credit card. The cards are available in increments of $25, $50, $100 and $250. This eliminates credit checks and billing by the Internet telephony provider.

DOCUMENT SHARING AND CLICK TO TALK ....

Document sharing software uses the Internet to enable institutions to share files with employees, customers and vendors. Customer service groups purchase software to enable them to interact more efficiently with customers that contact them via the Internet. It enables them to chat electronically and by telephone with people that surf their Web site.

Document Sharing

Document-sharing systems enable organizations to train end users, sell products and review presentations without the expense of traveling. Document-sharing products are used for:

- Sharing Web pages and forms such as credit applications with customers as they browse the Web
- Sharing documents during meetings
- Distance-based learning, seminars and training

Document-sharing software, also called *collaboration software*, is used to train people at remote locations. At the same time that customers, staff or students are viewing documents on their computers, they also can be speaking on a conference call. For instance, a trainer at headquarters can explain to the organization's salespeople how a new software package that tracks their sales and commissions works. On most of the systems, users can type text messages to the instructor, or chat online.

Collaboration software is used also as a sales tool. Inside salespeople use it to make presentations and hold audio conferences with potential customers. To enter a conference, users log into a uniform resource locator (URL) Internet address. The URL connects the callers to the host's server from which the presentation is sent.

Call centers use document sharing to help customers navigate their Web sites. For example, an inside salesperson can "push" (i.e., transmit) Web pages to customers who are simultaneously speaking with him and browsing the Web. Cisco Systems states 90% of its sales are transacted over the Web. Cisco feels that its ability to help customers navigate its enormously large Web site is a factor. Cisco also states that

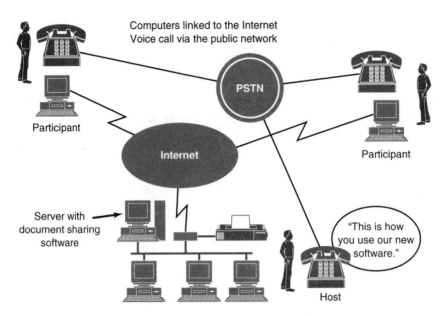

Figure 5.23
Document-sharing connections to the Internet.

customer satisfaction is higher and customers that know how to use the Web site require less customer service. Finally, companies push forms such as mortgage applications for customers to fill out interactively.

Vendors of collaboration software systems include eGain Communications Corporation, Cisco Systems, Lotus and Centra Software. The systems include document-sharing software with Java-based software installed on customers' PC-based servers (see Figure 5.23). Java is used because it has the capability to be downloaded only as needed to users, which are referred to as clients. On systems that work on http-compliant software, a Java collaboration script is downloaded to clients. The Java script repeatedly polls the central site from the client PC to see if information in the form of a Web address [uniform resource locator (URL)] is available. When it finds the address, the Java script pulls the document at the URL to the participant's computer.

Click to Talk—Enhanced E-commerce

The click-to-talk feature lets people speak with live agents while they are browsing. People browsing the Web often have questions they'd like to discuss with call center agents about items they see. Land's End uses Cisco Systems Customer Interaction Suite for this functionality. If a customer "clicks" on voice (rather than chat) when she asks a question, she is prompted for her telephone number. Pretty much instantly after she types in her number, her phone rings and a Land's End agent says, "Hello, this is Land's End Live. I see you're looking at [whichever product]; how can I help you?" The agent knows which page the customer is looking at and can answer questions or push additional pages to the customer. The agent knows the page because the server tracks the customer's browsing through cookies. *Cookies* are small software files that sites send computers browsing their site. It identifies personal computers to the server.

SUMMARY

Entrepreneurs, spurred by perceived opportunities for new networks, developed many of the optical and switching innovations previously discussed. They envisioned that competition would provide opportunities to sell equipment to new carriers. However, in most of Europe and in the United States, competitive network providers underestimated the difficulty of competing with incumbents and the expense of building new infrastructure. Moreover, competitors have been hurt by regulators' failure to uniformly enforce low-priced, timely interconnections to incumbent networks. In addition, new carriers have incurred huge loses and large amounts of debt as a result of the high costs of building out their networks. In the short run, capital investment has dried up for the purchase of new equipment. It's unclear what that impact will be on the continued development of new technologies.

In the short run, incumbent local exchange carriers (ILECs) that have the largest networks are changing their voice switching architecture very slowly. They are conservative and won't adopt a new technology until they see a payback. In particular, they want to make sure their billing, customer care and inventory tracking operation support systems (OSS) built over 25 to 30 years can interoperate with any new switching technologies they install.

Countries in which companies are building new infrastructure are more likely to take advantage of new metropolitan optical technologies—particularly if these technologies, such as passive optical networking, are lower in cost to deploy and maintain. Cellular providers that upgrade to higher speed 2.5G, next generation service, are likely to deploy IP service in their backbone networks. Carriers such as Level 3, Williams, Qwest and Broadwing Inc. that have built new networks since the late 1990s are the ones that, if they have the capital, will continue to deploy packet networks.

Part 3

Advanced Technologies, The Internet and Wireless

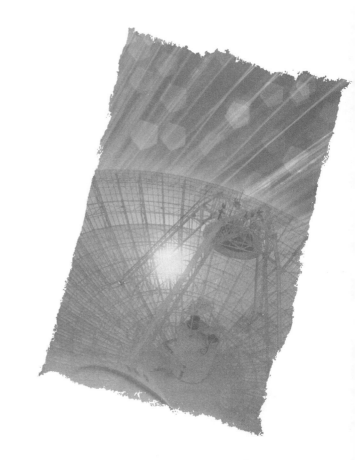

6 Specialized Network Services

In this chapter...

Higher speed computer processors, improvements in optical technologies and investments in telecommunications in the last decade have created new, faster network services. In particular, Gigabit Ethernet shows promise as a vehicle for easily carrying data at millions of bits per second (bps) to the Internet, to data centers and between corporate sites. It has the added benefit of being easy for end users to implement because of its compatibility with most local area networks (LANs).

Frame Relay, while older and slower than Gigabit Ethernet, is used widely for Internet access and as a replacement for private lines between sites. Each of an organization's locations that wishes to use the service has a line to the carrier's Frame Relay network. On-site equipment "packages" LAN data into a format compatible with the Frame Relay network. The carrier is responsible for capacity and network reliability. Incumbent local telephone companies, data communications companies and long distance carriers, as well as competitive local exchange carriers (CLECs) sell Frame Relay service.

Digital subscriber line (DSL) is targeted at residential and small and medium-sized business customers. DSL is a low-cost, high-speed dedicated Internet access service. There are a variety of DSL services. They run at speeds ranging from 128 kilobits per second (Kbps) to 52 megabits per second (Mbps). The DSL industry has been in turmoil. Many of the vendors that provided the infrastructure for DSL have gone out of business. The largest providers of DSL are the local incumbent telephone companies. SBC, the largest DSL provider, had 767,000 lines in service by year-end 2000. SBC has pledged to spend $6 billion for DSL upgrades, and has stated the goal of making DSL available to 80% of their customers by 2004. Regional bell operating companies (RBOCs) have made DSL a cornerstone of their push into data communications and are investing heavily in it.

Although they've been available since the 1960s in carrier networks, T-1 and T-3 services are the key telecommunications technology used by the business community.

- T-1 allows 24 voice or data calls on two pairs of copper, fiber, infrared or microwave. T-1's 1.544 Mbps is the most prevalent speed used in the United States by businesses for Internet access.

- T-3 has the capacity for 672 channels and a speed of 44 megabits per second (Mbps). It is used to carry much of the voice traffic between central offices.

Integrated services digital network (ISDN) is newer than T-1 and T-3. However, it is not nearly as widely used. ISDN comes in two flavors: basic rate (BRI) with two channels for voice or data, and primary rate (PRI) with 23 channels for voice or data. BRI is the second most popular Internet access service in Western Europe and Japan after dialup modems. PRI is used by call centers and commercial organizations mainly for caller ID–type service.

A summary of high-speed, digital network services is listed in Table 6.1.

Table 6.1 An Overview of Specialized Digital Network Services

Network Service	Places Typically Used	How Used
T-1 24 voice or data channels E-1 30 voice or data channels	Commercial organizations	1.54 megabit per second Internet access, connections to long distance and local telephone companies for voice and data, private lines between company sites
	Internet service providers (ISPs)	Connections to the Internet
T-3 672 voice or data channels E-3 480 voice or data channels	Very large organizations	Access to long distance companies, Internet access, high-speed private lines between company sites
	Local exchange carriers (LECs)	Tandem-to- tandem central office traffic
	Large ISPs	Connections to the Internet
BRI ISDN Two voice or data channels and one signaling channel	Residential customers	Telecommuting, Internet access; mostly in Europe and Japan
	Organizations	Desktop videoconferencing, Centrex telephones (see Chapter 2 for Centrex)
PRI ISDN 23 voice/data and one signaling channel in the United States 30 channels voice/data and one signaling channel in Europe	Business and commercial customers	Call centers, videoconferencing, voice and data links to local and long distance providers. PRI ISDN has different speeds in the United States and Europe.
	ISPs	Modem connections to competitive local exchange companies

Table 6.1 An Overview of Specialized Digital Network Services *(continued)*

Network Service	Places Typically Used	How Used
Digital Subscriber Lines DSL 128 kilobits per second (Kbps) to 6 megabits per second (Mbps)	Residential consumers, small and medium- sized businesses	Internet access
	Telecommuters	Remote access to corporate files and email
Frame Relay	Medium to large commercial customers	56 Kbps to 45 megabits access to data networks for LAN-to-LAN communications and Internet access; mostly data but some voice
Gigabit Ethernet	Medium to large commercial customers	1 megabit per second to 1 gigabit (Gb) access to the Internet and LAN-to-LAN connections over fiber, data only; more flexible upgrade and faster access than Frame Relay
	Application service providers (ASPs) and content delivery network providers	1 megabit per second to 1 gigabit links to the Internet and to customers
ATM, Asynchronous Transfer Mode (ATM), 56 Kbps to 2.5 Gigabits per second	Telephone companies	Switches voice, video and data traffic on high-usage network backbone routes over fiber
	Frame Relay networks	Switches traffic in the core of Frame Relay networks
	Large organizations such as major universities	Primarily to transmit voice, video and data across campuses and between LANs
Synchronous optical network (SONET); up to 129,000 channels on fiber optic cable	Carrier networks	Multiplexes voice and data traffic onto fiber optic cables; provides a backup redundant path in the local loop and in carriers' backbone networks

ATM (asynchronous transfer mode) switches carry voice, data, image and video at very high speeds of up to 30 Gigabits per second over fiber optic cabling. ATM is used mainly in Frame Relay networks, cellular networks, carrier networks and to carry DSL traffic to Internet service providers. It originally was envisioned as carrying high-speed data to desktops and for connecting LANs together within a campus environment. However, because of its cost and complexity, it never caught on for these applications. Some very large organizations do use it for specialized applications such as videoconferencing.

SONET (synchronous optical network) is a high-speed optical multiplexing service that works on fiber optic cabling. SONET runs at speeds of up to 13.22 Gigabits. It is used in network service provider networks to carry traffic from multiple customers running at different speeds. For example, SONET networks can accept T-3 traffic from customer A and T-1 traffic from customer B and transport both streams. SONET provides a way for carriers to increase the reliability of their networks. In these applications, SONET bidirectional rings carry traffic on one ring and provide a "protect" ring and multiplexer that automatically takes over if one strand of fiber is cut or if a SONET multiplexer crashes. SONET doesn't have the switching capability found in ATM. It just carries traffic between two points—for example, between one city to another or one central office to another.

T-1—24 VOICE OR DATA PATHS OVER ONE TELEPHONE CIRCUIT ....

The T-1 multiplexing scheme was developed by AT&T in the 1960s as a way to save money on cabling between telephone company switches by enabling one circuit to carry 24 voice or data conversations. (A *circuit* is a path for electrical transmissions between two points.) The technology was not made available directly to end-user locations until 1983.

In the mid-to-late 1980s, large organizations such as universities, financial institutions and Fortune 100 companies used T-1 circuits to tie locations to host computers for applications such as order entry, payroll and inventory. The T-1 often replaced having to physically carry large computer tapes between locations. Once installed, companies found digital T-1 to be light-years ahead of old analog data lines in terms of reliability.

When T-1 first became available, only the very largest organizations could justify paying its (at that time) high rates. Not only were rates high, but the service itself took from six months to a year to install. The lead times became shorter when competitors such as alternate access providers and interexchange carriers (IEXs) such as WorldCom and Sprint offered T-1. A major problem in providing T-1 was that the service, which is digital, often needed to be connected to older, analog telephone switches. This was accomplished through using channel banks between the T-1 line and the central office switch.

Channel Banks—Connecting T-1 to Analog PBXs and Central Offices

Channel banks, as illustrated in Figure 6.1, are the multiplexing devices that connect digital T-1 circuits to analog private branch exchanges (PBXs) and central office switches. The channel bank takes the signals from analog systems such as older analog PBXs and samples each of a possible 24 analog voice or data streams 8000 times each second. It digitizes these voice and data connections and sends them down the digital channel. At the receiving end of the T-1 circuit, the channel bank decodes digital signals back to analog. The methodology used for sampling and coding these signals is pulse code modulation (PCM). Decoders within the channel bank perform coding and decoding functions of converting analog voice to digital, and vice versa. All new PBXs, central office switches and most key systems are digital and channel banks are not required for T-1 connections.

DS-0 and DS-1—64,000 or 56,000 vs. 1,544,000 bps

The speed of a T-1 circuit is 1.54 million bits per second. The letters "DS" stand for digital signal level. DS-0 refers to the 56-Kbps or 64-Kbps speed of each of the 24 individual channels of the T-1 or E-1 circuit. DS-1 refers to the entire 1.54-megabit T-1 line. The terms DS-1 and T-1 are used interchangeably. An entire T-1 or single digital DS-0 line with a speed of 64-Kbps can be purchased. Fractional T-1 service, which is made up of more than one but less than 24 channels of the T-1 circuit, is covered below.

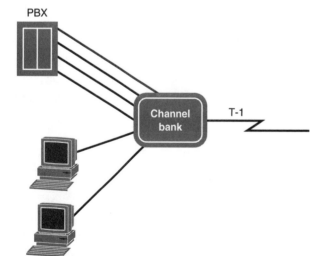

Figure 6.1
Using a channel bank so that a T-1 circuit can be shared for voice and data.

- DS-0 = 64,000 bps
- DS-1 = 1,544,000 bps

Often, organizations want digital connections between their locations, but they don't have enough traffic to warrant paying for a full T-1 line. For example, a T-1 circuit between New York City and Boston costs about $5000 per month. A 56,000-bps DS-0 line might cost only $800 monthly. A publishing organization in Boston with a sales/marketing office in New York has a single 56,000-bps line connecting the two offices. The line is used primarily for transmission of email and sales proposals between the two sites, and the 56-Kbps capacity is sufficient.

Clear Channel Signaling

All DS-0s run at 64,000 bps. However, depending on the signaling available in the telephone company's network, 8000 of the bits might be required for signaling and maintenance functions, leaving only 56 Kbps for user data. Clear channel signaling must be available with the chosen carrier to be able to use the full 64 Kbps for user data. With clear channel signaling, the 8000 bits don't have to be "robbed" for network maintenance. Thus, the full 64,000 bits are available for user data.

The total bandwidth of a T-1 circuit is higher than the sum of all of the channels—24 × 64,000, which equals 1,536,000. The extra 8000 bits (1,544,000 − 1,536,000 = 8000) are used for synchronization, keeping the timing set between frames. A *frame* is a grouping of bits with samples of data from each of the 24 channels. Data from devices connected to the T-1 are sampled, put into frames and sent sequentially on the T-1 line.

Media Used for T-1 Signals

T-1 can be installed on a variety of media, including the following:

- Fiber optics
- Twisted pair
- Coaxial cabling
- Microwave
- Infrared light

In the 1980s, when T-1 was first used by large corporations, the medium it was installed on was mainly twisted pair copper. When T-1 circuits are run over twisted pair, two pairs (four wires) are used. One pair is used for transmitting and one pair for receiving. Telephone companies that used T-1 in its early days (the 1960s and 1970s) used a combination of coaxial cables, twisted pair and microwave media. Microwave works well for hard-to-cable areas such as the Grand Canyon.

As fiber optic cabling became available in the 1980s, its lightweight, high-capacity and low-maintenance characteristics made it a good choice for telephone companies. Local phone companies often bring fiber directly into users' premises when they install T-1 circuits. When fiber is brought into a user's premise, the end user must supply the electricity for the equipment that converts the signals between electrical pulses for internal copper cabling and light pulses for the outside telephone company fiber. If there is no backup power, customers lose their T-1s when they lose power.

European vs. American and Japanese T-1— 24 vs. 30 Channels

The only digital signal speed that is standard throughout the world is the DS-0 speed of 64 kilobits. There are two standard DS-1 speeds: The U.S., Canada and Japan use 1.544 for T-1 with 24 channels, while the rest of the world uses 2.048 with 32 channels—30 channels for user data, one channel for signaling and a channel for framing and remote maintenance (see Table 6.2). People who want to run a T-1 from the U.S. to an office in Europe need rate adaptation equipment so that the carrier in the U.S. can connect the domestic T-1 to the European T-1 line. T-3 speeds also are different in North America, Japan and Europe. DS-0, DS-1 and DS-3 are the most prevalent T carrier speeds. Some people refer to European speeds as E1, E3, and so forth, and Japanese speeds as J-1, J-2 and so forth.

Table 6.2   *Digital Signal Levels*

Level	North America		Japan		Europe	
	User Channels	Speed	User Channels	Speed	User Channels	Speed
DS-0	1	64 Kb	1	64 Kb	1	64 Kb
T-1 (DS-1)	24	1.544 Mb	24	1.544 Mb	30	2.048 Mb
T-2 (DS-2)	96	6.312 Mb	96	6.312 Mb	120	8.448 Mb
T-3 (DS-3)	672	44.7 Mb	480	32.06 Mb	480	34.368 Mb
T-4 (DS-4)	4032	274.17 Mb	5760	400.4 Mb	1920	139.3 Mb

Speeds higher than DS-3 are called *optical carrier* (OC) in North America, and *synchronous transfer mode* (STM) in Europe. See section on SONET later in this chapter.

A Sampling of T-1 Configurations Using T-1 for Combining Voice, Fax, Video and Data

To save costs on wide area networks (WANs), organizations combine voice, fax, video and data over T-1 circuits. The voice lines usually are connected to a PBX and the data is sent to the LAN. An option for these connections is to terminate the T-1 in a drop-and-insert multiplexer. The drop-and-insert multiplexer drops off some channels of the T-1 to data devices. It then "stuffs" bits into the channels it dropped off to the data devices and sends a full T-1, including the "bit-stuffed" channels to the PBX's T-1 multiplexing equipment. See Figure 6.2 for a visual depiction of the drop-and-insert concept.

Digital Cross Connects—Flexible Capacity

Digital cross connect services are commonly used in organizations that have multiple sites they want to connect with private, dedicated lines. T-1 service often is used for dedicated lines for the exclusive, full-time use of organizations. (See Chapter 5.) If a firm needs a full T-1 at headquarters but partial T-1s at its remote sites, one option is to use digital cross connections. With digital cross connects, the network service provider runs a full T-1 from its telephone switch to the organization's headquarters. The carrier divides up 24 channels between the customer's other locations, as shown in Figure 6.3.

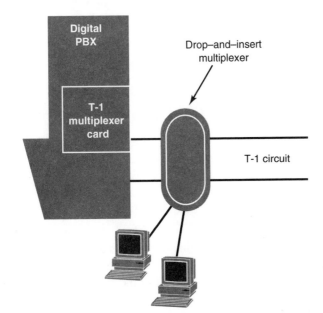

Figure 6.2
A drop-and-insert multiplexer with a digital PBX, so voice, data and video can share a T-1 circuit.

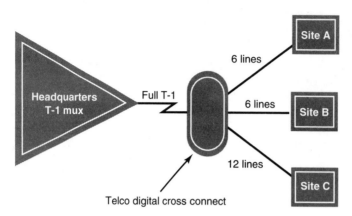

Figure 6.3
Digital cross connect switching used in a four-site
WAN—wide area network. The digital cross connect
enables the headquarters to change the
configuration to, for example, 8 lines to Site A and 10
lines to Site C if traffic patterns change.

Some carriers provide customers the capability to reconfigure their T-1 channels from a terminal or PC at the customer's location. This is useful for applications such as rerouting traffic in the event of a disaster or time-of-day peaks in data communications traffic.

Fractional T-1—When 24 Paths Are Not Required

Customers who require more than 64 Kbps, but less than a full 1.54 megabit T-1, often opt for fractional T-1. Fractional T-1 is sold at speeds of less than full T-1, for example 256, 512 and 768 kilobits per second. Four channels at 256 Kbps (4 × 64 = 256 Kbps) cost less than 1.544 megabits. Some ISPs offer Internet access at fractional T-1 speeds of, for instance, 768,000 bits per second. This is equivalent to 12 DS-0 channels or half of a T-1. This is a lower cost option for small and medium-sized firms than full T-1 access.

Fractional T-1 services are available in increments of two channels starting at 128 Kbps (2 × 64). Customers don't purchase fractional T-1 at higher than eight or twelve DS-0 channels because the price becomes equivalent to the cost of a full T-1. Fractional T-3, E-1 and E-3 service is sold as well.

T-3—The Capacity of 28 T-1 Lines, 672 Channels

A T-3 circuit is equivalent to 28 T-1s, or 672 channels ($28 \times 24 = 672$). The total speed of a T-3 line is 44.736 megabits per second. This speed is higher than 28×1.544 because some bits are needed for overhead (i.e., signaling and maintenance).

Large call centers often require several T-1 circuits at a single location. Rather than install multiple T-1s, companies install T-3 circuits. T-3 services start to cost less than multiple T-1s when customers have between eight to ten T-1s at the same site. Catalog sales, financial institutions, insurance companies and service bureaus that provide call center functions for smaller companies are examples of call centers that might require T-3 capacity.

Fortune 100 companies use T-3 service to carry voice, video and data traffic on private lines connecting their largest sites.

Internet service providers and telephone companies utilize the 672-channel capacity of T-3. Large ISPs use T-3 to connect their switches to the Internet backbone. They also provide T-3 service as a point where customers access their network. For example, customers call into the T-3 network entrance points from individual 56 Kbps to 1.54 T-1 lines. Many telephone carriers and Internet service providers are upgrading from T-3 to optical carrier-level service in their backbone networks.

An Explanation of Time Division Multiplexing and Its Limitations

All T carrier signals (e.g., T-1, E-1, E-3 and T-3) are based on time division multiplexing. Each device that communicates over a T-1 line is assigned a time slot. If there are eight telephones contending for a T-1 circuit, a time slot is saved for each telephone for the duration of the particular telephone call. For example, telephone 1 might be assigned slot A; telephone 2, slot B and so forth. Similarly, if PCs use the T-1, PC 1 is assigned time slot A, PC 2 is assigned time slot B and so forth. If a PC pauses and does not send for a few minutes, the slot is not assigned to another computer. The assigned time slot is transmitted without any bits. This is why time division multiplexing is not an efficient way to use a wide area network. Pauses in data transmission result in idle time slots. In a network with millions of time slots, this can result in many idle time slots and wasted bandwidth (see Figure 6.4). Incumbent local telephone companies' networks around the world use T-3 and E-3 to transmit traffic between tandem central offices.

Newer transmission techniques such as ATM and IP do not assign specific time slots to each device. Rather, only transmitted bits use bandwidth. This results in a more efficient use of transmission capacity. (See the end of this chapter for ATM.)

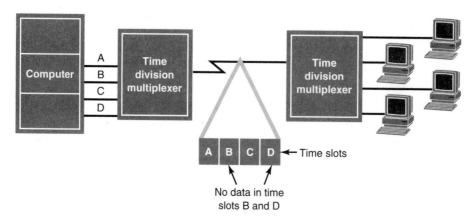

Figure 6.4
Time slots wasted in a time division multiplexing circuit.

ISDN—INTEGRATED SERVICES DIGITAL NETWORK

ISDN is a digital, worldwide public standard for sending voice, video, data or packets over the public switched telephone network (PSTN). It enables customers to transmit voice, data and video with one or two pairs of wires. As previously mentioned, there are two "flavors" of ISDN: basic rate (BRI), and primary rate (PRI), which are defined in Table 6.3.

Both types of ISDN have these important characteristics:

- Digital connectivity to achieve consistent, high-quality voice.
- **Out-of-channel signaling**—Calls are set up quickly; each voice/data channel uses all of the bandwidth for user data. The signaling channel is available for packet service such as alarm monitoring.
- **A switched service**—Users pay long distance or local calling fees for the amount of time they use the line.
- **A standard interface**—Most users with ISDN can communicate with each other. (There are incompatibilities between Europe, North America and Japan.)

ISDN standards were first published in the mid-1980s, but were finalized in the 1990s. Nortel first demonstrated a public network call over ISDN in 1987. ISDN works over existing copper wiring. It does not require fiber as do higher speed ATM and SONET services. However, central offices need ISDN-capable equipment. BRI ISDN was envisioned as an interim service until DSL became available. However,

BERKSHIRE CONNECT—BRINGING LOW COST INTERNET ACCESS TO OUTLYING COMMUNITIES

Because T-1 access prices are distance sensitive, customers far from central offices in rural areas pay higher fees than end users in cities. Until recently, commercial organizations in western Massachusetts paid up to three times as much ($2000 and higher monthly) for T-1 Internet access as customers in the Boston area. Businesses in western Massachusetts felt that the lack of affordable telecommunications services was harmful to business development. The Massachusetts government also recognized this fact.

The state appropriated $1.5 million to remedy this situation. The money was funneled through the Massachusetts Technology Collaborative, which is an economic development organization made up of state, business and educational representatives. The Collaborative developed an aggregation strategy on the assumption that few network providers serve outlying communities because there is not enough demand to warrant the construction of telecommunications facilities for reasonably priced high-speed service.

The Massachusetts Technology Collaborative's first efforts were applied in the western most area of Massachusetts, the Berkshires, the center of which is the town of Pittsfield. The Massachusetts Technology Collaborative helped facilitate the process of bringing high-speed telecommunications services to the Berkshires by sponsoring meetings and hiring a consultant. The plan was to develop a request for proposal for telecommunications service. A group of 30 business people met regularly and the effort became known as Berkshire Connect. The consultant prepared the request for proposal, which was approved and sent to 15 carriers including Verizon, the incumbent local telephone company. Eight carriers responded.

The group selected Global Crossing who had local microwave towers built and linked them to Verizon central offices to supply the T-1 service. The construction is mostly in place and many customers are using the service, which should be complete by the fall of 2001. T-1 prices have dropped to less than $500 monthly. Berkshire Connect used only $500,000 of the $1.5 million for the consultant, RFP printing and miscellaneous expenses. None of the money was used to subsidize the T-1 service. According to Donald Dubendorf, a partner in the Williamstown firm Grinell, Dubendorf & Smith, LLP, the group underestimated demand because previous prices were so high. To date, 50 users representing the nonprofit, public and business sectors have signed contracts with Global Crossing. As hoped, the effort has had a positive impact on the local economy and attracted new businesses to the area.

The Massachusetts Technology Collaborative has sponsored aggregation projects in three additional areas in Massachusetts and one effort also modeled on aggregation is underway in the Monadnock region of New Hampshire.

Table 6.3   Basic Rate and Primary Rate ISDN

ISDN Service	Number and Speed of Channels	Total Speed	Number of Pairs of Wires from Telco to Customer Premise
BRI ISDN	3 total:	144 kilobits per second	1
	2 at 64 kilobits per second		
	1 at 16 kilobits per second for signaling or packetized data		
PRI ISDN	24 total:	1.54 megabits per second;	2
	23 at 64 kilobits per second;		
	1 at 64 kilobits per second for signaling or packetized data		
PRI ISDN – Europe	32 total:	2.05 megabits per second	2
	30 at 64 kilobits		
	2 at 64 kilobits per second for signaling		

BRI ISDN never caught on in the United States. It never reached more than 1% penetration in the United States.

Deployment of BRI ISDN is higher in Europe and Japan than in the United States. France, Germany, Japan and Switzerland are widely acknowledged to have a large base of BRI ISDN customers. In Europe, BRI ISDN is sometimes referred to as ISDN 2 because it has two bearer channels. A user must be within 18,000 feet (3.4 miles) from the central office. According to a Bell employee source, 85% to 95% of telephone lines fit this criterion.

ISDN is a dialup service. To make a connection, the ISDN user dials a phone number. The connection is ended when the caller hangs up.

Telephone companies charge usage fees for ISDN data calls. These fees are either per-minute charges or a combination of usage fees plus flat charges for a set amount of minutes each month. In contrast, cable modems and DSL services have no usage fees. They are available for a flat monthly charge. Moreover, they are "always on." No dialing is required to establish a connection. The usage fees for transmitting data and the lack of availability have greatly hindered acceptance of ISDN. The difficulty of installing it also is a factor—delays of months and customer confusion of how to connect it to computers is common.

Basic Rate Interface ISDN—Two Channels at 64,000 Bit per Second

Basic rate interface (BRI) consists of two bearer channels for customer voice or data at 64 Kbps. In addition, it has one 16-Kbps signaling channel. Figure 6.5 illustrates the characteristics of a BRI ISDN line. It runs over a single pair of twisted wires between the customer and the telephone company.

The most common BRI ISDN applications are:

- Desktop videoconferencing
- Centrex ISDN multiline telephones (see Chapter 2)
- Backup for Frame Relay connections

Videoconferencing Using ISDN

The price of a desktop videoconferencing system is $2500 and lower. Many organizations purchase these systems as a way to try out videoconferencing without having to buy a full-sized unit. Many desktop video systems are connected to two bearer channels of a BRI ISDN line. Two 64-Kbps lines are bonded together for a combined speed of 128,000 bits per second. Often, these video systems are shipped ISDN-ready.

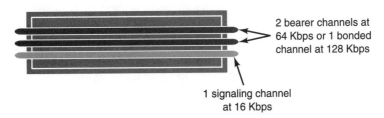

2 bearer channels at 64 Kbps or 1 bonded channel at 128 Kbps

1 signaling channel at 16 Kbps

Figure 6.5
Channels and speed of a BRI line.

The equipment needed to interface with an ISDN line, terminal adapters, is built into the video system.

ISDN for Data—The Need for ISDN at Both Ends

ISDN lines cannot transmit video or data to analog lines. ISDN circuits only are compatible with other ISDN-equipped services. BRI and PRI (ISDN with 24 channels) ISDN can communicate with each other. BRI and PRI users can use ISDN for voice calls to end users that have plain old telephone service (POTS) lines.

BRI Pricing

Pricing for ISDN varies between telephone companies. Installation is in the range of $150 to $300. Monthly fees are anywhere from $10 to $40 more than the charge for an analog line. Most telcos charge business customers extra for each minute of usage. Some plans for residential and business customers include 140 to 300 hours of data transmission plus per-minute fees for usage over the included amount. Others are flat rate, no charge for usage for residential customers.

Primary Rate Interface ISDN—24 Channels

Primary rate interface (PRI) has 24 channels in the United States and Japan and 30 elsewhere in the world. In the United States and Japan, 23 are bearer channels for user data. Each bearer channel has a bandwidth of 64,000 bps. A 64-Kbps twenty-fourth channel is used for signaling. PRI trunks are used on PBXs, Centrex service and data equipment.

PRI lines are similar to T-1 because they both have 24 channels. However, PRI ISDN has out-of-band signaling on the twenty-fourth channel. On T-1 circuits, the signaling is carried within each channel along with user data. The signaling capability enables the delivery of the calling party's telephone number, as described in using a PBX with a PRI line. On data communications, the signaling channel leaves each of the bearer channels "clear" capacity for all 64,000 bits. PRI does not require any bearer channel capacity for signaling such as call setup or tear-down signals.

PRI ISDN is a trunk connection. It is installed on the "trunk" side of a PBX, or into a multiplexer. BRI ISDN is a line-side connection. It connects to the same ports in PBXs as do telephone sets.

PRI ISDN service is used for the following:

- Videoconferencing at speeds generally from 128 Kbps to 384 Kbps

- Backing up LAN-to-LAN connections

- Backing up dedicated, private lines in case the private lines fail

- ISPs for dial-in from BRI ISDN and 56-Kbps modems

- Corporate sites for remote access from 56-Kbps modems and BRI ISDN sites

When PRI is used by ISPs for modem service, CLECs install PRI ISDN from their switch to the Internet service provider modem rack. The CLEC modem rack often is in the same facility, carrier hotel, as the CLEC switch. It also can be located at a remote site. The signaling channel carries the customer telephone number and the type of modem used. This provides billing information and routing information. Moreover, the modems can handle ISDN as well as analog modem traffic.

PBXs with PRI Trunks

PBXs are used with PRI lines for:

- Call centers, to receive the telephone numbers of callers

- Individual telephone users for call screening

- Videoconferencing units that do not require the use of full-time ISDN service

Large call centers use PRI ISDN to receive the telephone number of the person calling. With ISDN, the telephone number is sent at the same time as the call. However, it is sent on the *separate D*, or signaling channel. This is significant because it enables the telephone system, the PBX, to treat the telephone number information differently than the call. When used in a call center, it sends the telephone number to a database that matches the telephone number to the customer account number. It then sends the account number to the agent's terminal that the call is sent to. It saves agents' time by eliminating the need to key in account numbers

Many corporations use PRI ISDN for their direct-inward dialing (DID) traffic. (See Chapter 2 for DID.) The local telephone company sends the caller's name and phone number over the signaling channel. The telephone system captures the information and sends it to the display-equipped ISDN telephone. Figure 6.6 illustrates a PRI line for transporting caller ID. Employees who receive heavy volumes of calls from

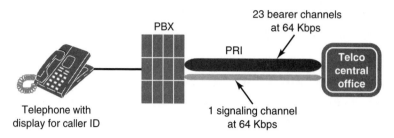

Figure 6.6
A PRI line for carrying caller ID from the telephone company to a PBX.

vendors or who only take calls from certain callers use ISDN to screen calls. Calls not taken are forwarded automatically into voice mail.

Some organizations use ISDN-compatible videoconferencing systems as extensions of a PBX. This is called putting the video "behind" a PBX. In this way, the organization does not have to pay for dedicated BRI lines to its telephone company. Rather, the video equipment shares the PRI along with the voice telephone users. When the video is not in use, all of the PRI channels are available for voice. This capability of sharing the line for voice and data is due to the out-of-band signaling on the twenty-fourth channel. The signaling channel sends an identifier to the network telling the network that the video calls are data calls.

Companies with multiple PRI trunks can use non-facility associated signaling (NFAS) to share the twenty-fourth signaling channel among the PRI trunks. For example, an organization with six PRI trunks might have four of them equipped with 24 channels for voice and data. Two of them would have 23 channels for user data and one for the NFAS channel signaling to support all six PRI trunks.

PRI ISDN also is used on private lines that connect PBXs together. The signaling channel carries voice mail signals that identify mailbox numbers and instructions to turn message-waiting indicators on or off. It enables one voice mail system to be shared between multiple sites.

PRI for Bandwidth-on-Demand—Video and Data Devices Sharing a PRI Line

With PRI, all channels can be dynamically used, on-demand for voice or data. Setup signals carried on the signaling channel notify the public network whether calls should be sent over the public network's data network or its voice network. This is significant because all channels are available on-demand for voice or data. The data channels do not have to be reserved ahead of time strictly for video or data. With T-1, channels must be permanently set aside for data or video. During times when no video or data is sent, the channels are idle and cannot be used for voice traffic.

ISDN multiplexers have what is called "bandwidth-on-demand" for applications such as videoconferencing, which requires multiple bearer channels. For example, many companies want video systems capable of transmitting video at 384 Kbps, six bearer channels. However, the video systems are not used 24 hours a day. With bandwidth-on-demand, when the video system is not in use, the six bearer channels can be used by other data applications. Bandwidth-on-demand provides an economical use of the PRI circuit.

DIGITAL SUBSCRIBER LINE TECHNOLOGY ....

Bellcore first introduced digital subscriber line (DSL) technology in 1989 as a way to transmit video and television signals from telephone companies' central offices to end users over standard copper cable used for voice service. At that time, video-on-demand was perceived as the broadband application that would drive digital subscriber line (DSL) implementation. Asymmetric digital subscriber line (ADSL) service was proposed because of its higher speeds for downloading large video files. The main application for DSL has changed from video-on-demand to Internet access.

DSL is a dedicated, high-speed way to access the Internet or corporate files via a virtual private network (VPN). (See Chapter 5 for VPNs.) It operates over the same copper cabling already installed by the incumbent regional and independent telephone companies. It is an "always on" service in which modems don't dial a telephone number to reach the Internet. There are no usage charges and customers are billed a flat monthly fee regardless of how much time they spend online. It is less costly than T-1 or fractional T-1.

Regional Bell Operating Companies introduced digital subscriber line (DSL) services in the late 1990s as a competitive response to cable modems. There is particular interest in DSL service by RBOCs because it leverages their investment in copper cable in the outside cabling plant. The Bell Operating Companies, network providers such as AT&T, and competitive local exchange carriers such as Covad, Inc. and Internet service providers such as Earthlink sell DSL.

DSL is offered in symmetric and asymmetric versions. Asymmetric DSL, such as ADSL, has different speeds downstream and upstream. Downstream transmissions are from the Internet to the consumer. Upstream transmissions are from the consumer to the Internet. Incumbent telephone companies generally sell asymmetric service to consumers who often download larger files such as music than they send. Versions of DSL services sold to businesses are symmetric. They provide the same speed to the user when they are sending and receiving files. It is felt that businesses send as well as receive large files. For the most part, DSL is sold to small and medium-sized business-es because it is lower in cost than T-1 and does not have the usage fees associated with BRI ISDN. Examples of symmetric DSL services are IDSL, SDSL, HDSL and HDSL2. See Table 6.4.

Table 6.4   *DSL Speeds and Cable Requirements*

Digital Subscriber Line Service	Upstream Data Rate	Downstream Data Rate	Top Distance from Central Office	Voice	Comments
ADSL Asymmetric DSL	176 Kbps* 640 Kbps**	1.54 Kbps 7.1 Mbps	18,000 feet 12,000 feet	Yes	Offered by telephone companies for customers who want speeds higher than DSL lite. Uses one pair of wires.
DSL Lite Splitterless DSL	384 Kbps	1 Mbps	18,000 feet	Yes	Easier installation by telcos. Splitter not required. Operates on one pair of wires.
G.shdsl	192 Kbps 2.3 Mbps 4.62 Mbps	192 Kbps 2.3 Mbps 4.62 Mbps	40,000 feet 6,500 feet 6,500 feet		Single pair of wires speeds up to 2.3 Mb. Two pair speeds up to 4.62 Mbps.
HDSL High-bit-rate DSL	1.54 Mbps	1.54 Mbps	12,000 feet	No	Requires four wires; other DSL services only need two wires.
HDSL2	1.54 Mbps	1.54 Mbps	12,000 feet	No	Same as HDSL except only one pair of wires.

Table 6.4   DSL Speeds and Cable Requirements *(continued)*

Digital Subscriber Line Service	Upstream Data Rate	Downstream Data Rate	Top Distance from Central Office	Voice	Comments
VDSL Very high-bit-rate DSL	640 Kbps 3 Mb	13 Mb 52 Mb	4,500 feet 1,000 feet	Yes	VDSL requires fiber optics on distances higher than these.
SDSL Symmetric DSL	Up to 1.1 Mb	Up to 1.1 Mbps	24,000 feet	No	Requires only one pair of wires. Offered by carriers such as WorldCom and AT&T and Internet service providers.
RADSL Rate-adaptive DSL	128 Kbps 176 Kbps 1 Mb	640 Kbps 1.54 Kbps 2.56 Mbps	21,300 feet 18,000 feet 12,000 feet	Yes	This is a version of ADSL; the speed varies according to condition of the copper. Requires one pair of wires.
IDSL ISDN DSL	128 to 144 Kbps	128 to 144 Kbps	18,000 feet	No	Used when distance to the central office is too far for SDSL. Operates on a single pair of wires.

*Kbps = kilobits per second
**Mbps = million bits per second

   A benefit of DSL technology is its potential to relieve congestion caused by modem traffic on the public network. When DSL traffic hits the central office, it is routed on a data network that is separate from the voice network. Digital subscriber line technology packetizes data traffic and sends it on a parallel data network. Modem traffic, on the other hand, is carried on the public network along with voice traffic. Modems convert digital data to analog so that local and long distance companies cannot distinguish it from voice calling.

Because there are multiple "flavors" of digital subscriber line technology, some people refer to DSL as xDSL. Most DSL services run at different speeds, require dissimilar types of customer interface equipment, are positioned for different types of customers and can run over variable lengths of copper cables. They are listed next; additional information was given in Table 6.4.

- *Asymmetric digital subscriber line (ADSL)* is asymmetric. Incumbent telephone companies sell it mainly to residential customers. Downstream speeds on data that is sent to the customer from the Internet and on upstream data sent away from the customer to the Internet are different. ADSL is also known as full-rate ADSL.

- *Digital subscriber line lite (DSL Lite)*, also known as Universal DSL, is the ITU-based G.lite standard for residential consumers. It is lower in cost to provision because a splitter to separate the data transmission from the voice call is not needed in the central office and at the customer site.

- *Single-Pair High-Speed digital subscriber line (G.shdsl)* offers higher speeds and operates over longer distances than symmetric digital subscriber line service.

- *High-bit-rate digital subscriber line (HDSL)* is symmetric, with the same speed upstream and downstream—1.54 million bits per second. Although the same speed as T-1, it uses different signaling than T-1. It does not have the reliability guarantees associated with T-1.

- *High-bit-rate digital subscriber line 2 (HDSL2)* offers the same speed as HDSL; however, only one pair of wires is required. This is a savings in outside copper required. It is designed as a single-pair replacement for HDSL.

- *Very high-bit-rate digital subscriber line (VDSL)* requires a combination of fiber and copper cabling because of its high speed. It can be used in combination with fiber for fiber-to-the-curb applications where, for example, customers might want broadcast-quality video simultaneously with high-speed Internet access. To date, it is rarely used.

- *Rate-adaptive digital subscriber line (RADSL)* is a variation of ADSL that overcomes varying conditions and lengths of copper cable. RADSL speeds adjust downward to overcome variations in outside cabling. Qwest uses RADSL in the 14-state territory where it operates its local telephone company (formerly U S West) business.

- *Symmetric digital subscriber line (SDSL)* provides the same speed upstream and downstream to the customer. This is the service that is offered by CLECs, mainly to business customers. Speeds of 160 Kbps to 1.1 Mbps depend on distance from central office.

- *Integrated services digital subscriber line (IDSL)* works with the same customer equipment as ISDN. However, this is a dedicated service with a fixed monthly charge without usage fees. IDSL operates as a single 144 kilobit per second pipe. It has no channels for voice.

Competitive Local Exchange Carriers (CLECs) and DSL

DSL was the first product sold by CLECs that promised lower prices and innovative service for Internet access to small and medium-sized businesses as a result of the Telecommunications Act of 1996. They sold symmetric DSL service mainly to business rather than residential customers. Some CLECs known as Data CLECs did not sell directly to end users—they acted as wholesalers and sold through ISPs, other CLECs and long distance carriers. Other Data CLECs sold directly to end users. They leased copper local loops from incumbent telephone companies and installed digital subscriber line access multiplexers (DSLAMs) in their central office. (DSLAMs aggregate traffic from many DSL modems and send it to Internet service providers.) They also provided the DSL modem/routers to small and medium-sized businesses. Retailers that bought DSL wholesale from data CLECs billed end users, provided customer service and Internet services such as email and Web hosting.

However, CLECs were largely unsuccessful. A number of factors contributed to their decline. Many of the Data CLECs claimed they were driven out of the market by the high costs and delays associated with providing service over RBOC facilities. Some of them also cited the fact that capital dried up from sources such as venture capital companies and they were not able to meet expenses. In addition, many of the Internet service providers who resold their DSL service did not pay their bills. For example, by October 2000, of 274,000 DSL lines that Covad installed, ISPs had not paid for 92,000. Many of them had gone bankrupt. Because of the steep competition, DSL service was priced extremely low, making it difficult to achieve profits while building out the infrastructure.

Another problem facing CLECs is that, for the most part, RBOCs are not required to sell space in digital loop carriers (DLCs) to competitors. (Digital loop carriers are also referred to as remote terminals. See later section on digital loop carriers.) To date, only Illinois and New York require incumbents to provide space, where technically feasible, in remote terminals for competitors' DSL access multiplexer cards. The lack of access to DLCs is hampering competitors' ability to overcome long cabling distances between subscribers and central office located DSL multiplexers. The FCC is exploring mandates to require incumbents to allow access by competitors to DLCs. For now, access requirements in remote terminals are up to state regulators as long as they follow FCC guidelines for technical feasibility. Data CLECs were Covad, Rhythms and NorthPoint. NorthPoint and Rhythms are no longer in business and Covad is in bankruptcy. The FCC is studying the issue of CLEC access to incumbent-owned digital loop carriers. RBOCs are concerned that access by competitors will be costly to arrange because of possible space, venting and heat issues in the digital loop carriers.

Because of the poor market conditions and the difficulty of making a profit, many CLECs and other resellers such as ISP Verio have stopped selling DSL. There are small DSL providers still selling service and long distance providers such as AT&T, which purchased NorthPoint's assets, that are still in the market. However, the largest market share, about 80%, belongs to incumbent telephone companies.

Incumbent Telephone Company DSL Offerings

Bell telephone companies' products initially were sold only to residential customers. These were ADSL services that supported only one computer per DSL modem. These offerings only supported dynamic not static IP service. Static IP service is required for customers with their own domain name who want Web hosting from their DSL provider. The dynamic IP service does not support this service because IP addresses are assigned at random rather than to the same device consistently. Customers with their own Web pages and domain names have their Web hosting at a different provider than their DSL provider when their provider does not support static IP service.

RBOCs are now starting to sell symmetric DSL service for small and medium-sized businesses and small office home office (SOHO). The DSL product is part of their strategy of growing their data communications business. They all are investing billions of dollars into new infrastructure for data communications products. While CLEC competition for DSL service is greatly diminished, Frame Relay, VPN and Gigabit Ethernet services from other companies represent viable competition to them.

The RBOCs offer a wholesale DSL product to ISPs that wish to connect their customers via DSL. For example, Qwest (formerly U S West) has signed a contract with MSN. In this arrangement, MSN sells the DSL service to its customers and provides the email and Web hosting. However, the subscriber traffic is routed over Qwest DSL facilities. The RBOCs have formed separate subsidiaries to provide the email and connections to the Internet and customer support for DSL.

DSLAMs—Digital Subscriber Line Access Multiplexers

DSLAMs, or digital subscriber line access multiplexers, are located at network service providers' sites. DSLAMs aggregate traffic from multiple DSL modems and combine it into higher speeds before sending it to the Internet or data networks. (See Figure 6.7.) It sends it out at speeds of T-3, or 44 million bits per second, and ATM

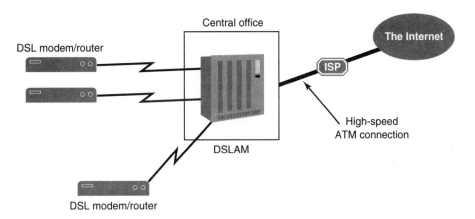

Figure 6.7
Digital subscriber line access multiplexers (DSLAMs) aggregate traffic from multiple customers and send it to the Internet via an ISP.

speeds of OC-3, or 155 million bits per second. DSLAMs are located at central offices, digital loop carriers in neighborhoods (see below) and in the wiring closets of large apartment and office buildings.

Some DSLAMs also perform concatenation. They send data from attached devices in one adjacent stream instead of as individual streams. For example, streams of video may be sent as linked streams rather than being separated by data from other DSL devices. If a DSLAM performs concatenation, its speed is called OC-3C, or concatenated optical carrier level 3.

Customers have dedicated capacity between their DSL modem and the digital subscriber line access multiplexer (DSLAM) but not between the DSLAM and the Internet or the ISP. The connection between the DSLAM and an Internet service provider or is a potential site for network congestion. (See Figure 6.7.) If not enough capacity is available, a customer might experience delays.

Obstacles to Digital Subscriber Line Availability—Cost, Ease of Implementation and Availability

In the article, "My Kingdom for a DSL Line," published in *SmartMoney.com*, 27 March 2001, a Gartner Group study found that as of January 2001, DSL was only available in 35% of the United States. DSL service is available mostly in metropolitan areas of the United States. It also is sold in Western Europe and Asia. However, the largest number of users, over 2 million by May 2001, is in the United States.

Digital Loop Carriers with DSL Equipment to Overcome DSL Distance Limitations

The fact that DSL only works up to 18,000 feet from the central office is a key factor limiting its availability. This is particularly true in countries and areas with less dense populations. Moreover, copper, not a mix of copper and fiber, is required to the nearest DSL access equipment.

When subscribers are located far from the central office, telephone companies often install digital loop carriers (see Chapter 5) closer to customers. Digital loop carriers (DLC) located between the central office and customers, are connected to the central office with fiber cabling. The DLC converts the optical signal to electrical and transmits it to customers over copper cabling. However, DSL requires copper cabling between the DSL modem and the digital subscriber line access multiplexer (DSLAM). Therefore, in order for DSL to operate where digital loop carriers are installed, the DSLAM must be installed in the DLC. SBC, BellSouth and Verizon are investing large sums of money to upgrade DLCs and install DSL-compatible equipment in them. This will increase the availability of DSL in suburban areas where central offices are typically more than 18,000 from many customers. See Figure 6.8 for a DSL connected to central offices via digital loop carrier equipment. Digital loop carriers are also referred to as remote terminals.

A contributing factor to low and uneven availability of DSL services is the fact that loading coils and bridge taps must be removed from copper lines. (Loading coils boost the signal on analog copper telephone wires that are far from the central office. Bridge taps enable the same copper wire from the central office to feed multiple locations.) Telephone companies remove loading coils but not bridge taps because of the cost.

A New Standard for DSL that Works over Longer Distances—G.shdsl

The new (2001) G.shdsl, single-pair high-speed DSL standard works over longer copper local loops than traditional DSL service. It is a standard that supports many different speeds and services. It enables service providers to lower their costs of provisioning DSL by supporting longer distances and a variety of speeds. For example, central office G.shdsl equipment also supports the HDSL2 1.54 million–bit per second service. The service is rate-adaptive. It negotiates the highest speed that the local loop supports during the "handshake," the service setup portion of a data transmission session. It also negotiates the type of service to provision during the handshake. For example, T-1, E-1, ISDN, ATM and IP services all are supported. Most current equipment is suitable for data and video. However, voice transmissions are supported in the standard.

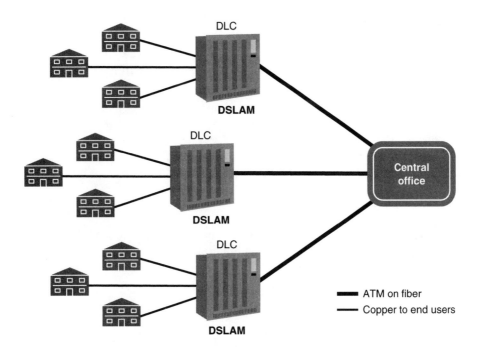

Figure 6.8
DSL service connected to digital loop carriers.

End-User Installation Difficulties

In addition to affordability and availability, ease of installation for end users is a major issue. Telephone companies send out technicians to install the modem. They also have support lines with limited support. However, for the most part, it is up to end users to determine how to program their computer to work with DSL. Small and medium-sized businesses are likely to hire systems integrators if they don't have knowledgeable staff.

A Reputation for Poor Service

By January 2001, class-action suits accusing them of poor service had targeted Verizon, Southwestern Bell and BellSouth. In addition, various Web sites are devoted to stories about delays in installation and network failures. The telephone companies have been accused of overselling and not having resources to support customers. Part of the problem is that records of copper cabling are not always accurate. For example, a telephone company might tell a consumer that DSL is available to their home. However, when the technician goes out to install the service, he or she discovers that bridge taps are installed or that the customer is too far from the telephone company equipment to qualify for service.

Hopefully, as the service matures and as outside cabling plants are upgraded with DSL equipment closer to customers, these problems will be resolved.

DSL Lite—Lower Cost Service

DSL Lite was developed to lower the cost of provisioning DSL service. DSL Lite, also called Universal DSL, works consistently on longer telephone company loops, the distance between the telephone company equipment and the customer's premise. DSL Lite achieves speeds of 1.5 million bits per second downstream and 384 thousand bits per second upstream. These speeds can be reached up to three miles from telephone company equipment.

DSL Lite also is known as *splitterless DSL*. A splitter is not required at the central office or at the customer premise. With full-rate ADSL, a splitter sits between the customer demarcation and the ADSL line. A splitter also is located at the telephone company equipment. The splitter, which is the size of two cigarette packs, separates the low-frequency voice signals from the high-frequency data signals. The fact that a splitter is not required saves the telephone company from having to dispatch a technician for installation.

Another benefit of DSL Lite is that consumers do not have to change their internal wiring. However, filters might be required to be plugged into each telephone jack. Some telephones are not built to standards. In these cases, the telephones might add noise to the telephone cable. The noise interferes with the data transmission. In these cases, filters screen out signals above the 4-kilohertz (KHz) range so interference is eliminated.

DSL—A Technical Explanation

DSL technologies use unused frequencies available in standard telephone wire for data transmission. Voice communications are carried on only 4 kilohertz of the available frequency of copper wires. This leaves the rest of the frequencies on copper cabling available for data communications. The American National Standards Institute (ANSI) and the European Telecommunications Standards Institute (ETSI) standard for ADSL and ADSL Lite is called T1.413. The T1.143 standard endorses discrete multitone modulation (DMT), a line-coding technique, for DSL modems. Modulation varies the frequency of data to be sent over telephone lines so that it is compatible with the provider's network.

DSL modems send data over copper cabling at frequencies above 4000 cycles per second. Discrete Multi-tone modulation (DMT) encodes and compresses data signals into 256 subchannels in increments of 32 kilobits. DMT essentially sends data over 256 discrete frequencies at the same time. It uses different frequencies, or subchannels, for the upstream portion to the network and other subchannels (frequencies) for the downstream transmission away from the carrier's network to the customer.

In addition to line coding and compression, DSL modems have other functions. Three of these functions are:

- Error correction

- Performance monitoring

- Routing

Routing functionality enables multiple personal computers to share one DSL line. All users can be online simultaneously using one DSL connection and a DSL modem with a built-in router. The connection from the modem to the computer is a 10/100base-T Ethernet connection (standards for 10 and 100 megabit per second transmissions over copper wiring).

FRAME RELAY—A SHARED WIDE AREA NETWORK SERVICE..

Frame Relay is a network access method offered by local and long distance telephone companies. First implemented in 1992, *Frame Relay* is a public network offering that enables customers to transmit data between LANs in multiple locations (see Figure 6.9). It also is used to access the Internet. By using Frame Relay, organizations do not have to plan, build and maintain their own duplicate paths to each of their sites. Multiple users share the Frame Relay networks.

While Frame Relay has potential congestion problems, it has the following advantages:

- *The network is managed by a long distance provider, not the end user.* This is critical for companies that want to concentrate on their main business, not on maintaining their networks.

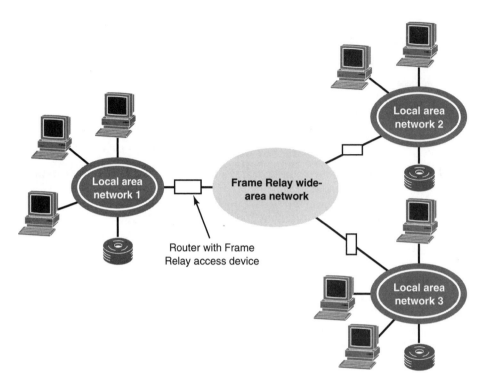

Figure 6.9
A local area network connection to Frame Relay.

- *Less hardware is required at each location than that used for private, dedicated networks.* Fewer modems and multiplexers to connect sites together are needed. Each site need only be connected to the Frame Relay network, not to each location in the network.

- *Capacity on Frame Relay is more flexible than that of private lines.* Many fast-growing small companies, such as high-tech businesses, like the flexibility provided by Frame Relay to add capacity easily.

- *Frame Relay has its own internal backup routes so that customers do not have to provide multiple routes for reaching each location.*

Frame Relay was developed as a replacement for X.25. Frame Relay networks are faster than older X.25 packet networks because they do not perform extensive error checking in the network. X.25 packet networks checked each packet many times as it traveled through the packet network. This slowed down the transmissions. With Frame Relay service, it is up to customers to perform error checking and checks for dropped packets in their own routers. (See Chapter 1 for a description of routers.)

Connections to Frame Relay—Frame Relay Access Devices and Access Line Speeds

The line that connects each customer to the Frame Relay network is called an access line. It provides access from the user equipment to the Frame Relay network. Each site that uses the Frame Relay services leases a circuit, a telephone line, from its equipment to a port on the Frame Relay switch.

Access lines to Frame Relay networks run at various speeds depending on the amount of traffic generated at each site. Sites at different locations in the same organization can be configured with access lines at different speeds. Some Frame Relay vendors also offer dialup (e.g., ISDN) access to their networks for customers with small sites. Dialup connections require modems to dial a telephone number to transmit data. Dedicated connections are "always on." Dialup access services also are used as a backup in case the dedicated access lines to the Frame Relay network fail. Some of the options for access lines are:

- 56 Kbps
- 128 Kbps
- 256 Kbps
- 384 Kbps
- T-1—1.54 megabits
- T-3—44 megabits

Some customers share their T-1 lines for voice and Frame Relay access. For example, 22 channels of the 24 T-1 channels may be terminated on the telephone system for voice traffic. The other two channels are used to carry Frame Relay traffic to the network service provider's Frame Relay port. This saves customers money on leasing access to the Frame Relay network.

Equipment on the customer premise converts the traffic from the local area network packets into frames compatible with the Frame Relay network. This equipment is called a *Frame Relay access device* (FRAD). It is often a card within the router. Each frame has bits called the flag, telling the network when the user data (frame) starts and when it ends. There also are addressing and destination bits in the frame for billing and routing purposes so that the Frame Relay provider knows where to route and bill each frame.

Customers' frames are sent to ports on high-speed switches that carry data from site to site within the carrier's Frame Relay network. The main technology the networks are run on is ATM (asynchronous transfer mode).

Frame Relay for Transmitting Voice

Organizations use Frame Relay to replace private lines for voice traffic between sites. Voice over Frame Relay is improving but is not as good as the voice transmitted on the standard public network.

The technologies used to transmit voice on Frame Relay are voice compression and silence suppression. Silence is suppressed so that pauses between words are used to transmit data and voice from other users. In addition, the voice itself is compressed, or made smaller, so that it does not require as much network capacity. Finally, voice traffic is given a high priority so that delay in voice conversations is minimized. The ATM switches (discussed later) located in core Frame Relay networks are able to prioritize packets containing voice traffic.

If the Frame Relay network becomes highly congested, voice quality can be degraded because packets are dropped or delayed. For this reason, some customer equipment has the ability to monitor traffic levels on the Frame Relay network and send it over the public switched network if there is congestion.

Frame Relay Pricing—Ports, Circuits and Committed Information Rate

Frame Relay service is priced at fixed monthly fees based on the following four elements, plus the cost of the telephone line used to connect each site to the Frame Relay service:

- **The permanent virtual circuit** (PVC) is a logical predefined path or link through a carrier's network. For example, if San Francisco and Tucson sites need to exchange data, the carrier defines a permanent virtual circuit between these two locations. PVCs are priced at fixed monthly fees.

- **The switched virtual circuit** (SVC): Unlike permanent virtual circuits, SVC charges are based on usage. Temporary connections are set up between points on a Frame Relay network. SVCs can be used to carry voice traffic if volumes are low. Thus, users only pay for what they use instead of incurring fixed monthly fees associated with permanent virtual circuits.

- **The Frame Relay port** is the entry point, on a Frame Relay provider's switch, to the Frame Relay network. Multiple permanent virtual circuits can use one port. Ports are available in variable speeds such as T-1, 56 Kbps, 256 Kbps and 512 Kbps.

- **The committed information rate** (CIR) is the minimum guaranteed number of bits-per-second throughput, typically half the capacity of the port the customer is guaranteed to be able to send from each site. Some customers save money by using zero committed information rate. Customers can "burst," sending data at the maximum speed of their Frame Relay port. For example, customers connected to a 1.54 megabit per second port can send data at up to 1.54 megabits per second even if their committed information rate is zero. (This assumes they have a 1.54 megabit per second access line.)

Potential Congestion on Frame Relay

Customers rely on carriers not to oversell capacity on their Frame Relay networks. Once end users have the service, they depend on their carrier's managing capacity, using the best telecommunications switches and providing them with reports on the success of their transmissions. If the carrier's network is oversubscribed, the carrier might drop frames. Organizations with mission-critical data communications or high levels of security requirements often hire the staff and spend the money to manage their own private networks.

Many carriers now offer customers the ability to monitor traffic on Frame Relay networks via connections to the Internet. Customers are able to see traffic levels in terms of packets they are sending and how close to capacity they are. This helps them know if they have ordered the correct speed of permanent virtual circuits between sites, ports into the network and access lines.

Interfacing Between Carriers' Frame Relay Networks

When different public Frame Relay networks send data to each other, they use a standard protocol defined by the Frame Relay Forum called Network-to-Network Interface (NNI). This is useful when customers have locations not served by their Frame Relay network.

GIGABIT ETHERNET—ETHERNET OVER FIBER IN METROPOLITAN AREAS ....

Gigabit Ethernet is a high-speed method for Internet access and data communications. It currently operates at one-megabit per second to one gigabit per second, but manufacturers are developing 10-gigabit products. They use the Ethernet LAN standard, the most prevalent LAN protocol.

Customers use the Gigabit Ethernet for:

- Data links between corporate, hospital and university locations within the same city or metropolitan area
- Connections between Web hosting centers and the hosting centers' customers
- Data connections between corporate sites in different cities
- Internet access (not all Gigabit Ethernet suppliers sell Internet access)
- Links from corporate customers to Application Service Providers (ASPs) or ISPs

Gigabit Ethernet operates over fiber optic cabling deployed in the metropolitan area. Gigabit Ethernet charges vary. Some carriers charge a flat rate based on speed and others charge for the amount of information, for example, per gigabit of data transmitted. Although still not widely available, it is positioned as:

- Lower in cost than T-3 service
- Faster than Frame Relay
- More easily upgraded access speeds than Frame Relay
- Less complex on-site equipment because it uses the same protocol as most LANs [(Frame Relay requires a CSU/DSU, T-1 multiplexing and Frame Relay access device (FRAD)]— Gigabit Ethernet only uses a switch.

Gigabit Ethernet Providers—OLECs

Gigabit Ethernet providers also are called optical local exchange carriers (OLECs). They sell high-speed data communications service over fiber optic cabling to business customers. In addition to the network connection, OLECs provide and manage equipment inside the customer's building that is used to connect customer LANs to outside fiber networks and to the Internet. (See Figure 6.10.)

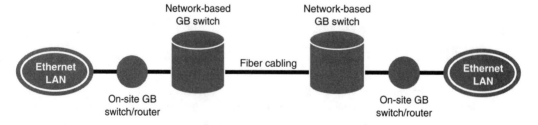

Figure 6.10
Gigabit (GB) Ethernet service over fiber optic cabling with on-site managed router/switches. Figure courtesy of Yipes Communication

Network providers such as Yipes, Cogent Communications and Citynet sell directly to end users. XO Communications sells Gigabit Ethernet in 62 metropolitan areas throughout the United States. XO purchases Gigabit Ethernet switches from Foundry and ONI. Yipes' service operates on switches from Extreme Networks. OLECs place their switches at collocation sites. The *collocation sites* are spaces they rent for their equipment and connections to long-haul networks. Collocation sites are points of presence (POPs).

Gigabit Ethernet Through Partners

Telseon sells service through ISPs and other network service providers. Telseon installs its infrastructure in collocation facilities, or *carrier hotels* (see Chapter 5) that are readily available to its partners which are ISPs, Web hosting firms such as Exodus and other carriers. Qwest sells Gigabit Ethernet that operates over Telseon fiber rings. Broadwing also sells Gigabit Ethernet based on Ethernet third-party fiber rings. The Gigabit Ethernet infrastructure company's partner provides customer service, sales and billing.

Gigabit Ethernet Availability

A major factor in the availability of Gigabit Ethernet is the growing accessibility of dark fiber in metropolitan areas. *Dark fiber* is fiber that does not have electronics such as wavelength division multiplexing (WDM) connected to it. In the Denver area alone, 14 companies are laying fiber. Companies such as MFN (Metromedia Fiber Network), Level 3 and subsidiaries of utilities are actively constructing new fiber routes in cities. Once fiber is widely available, network providers lease it and add their own electronics. Optical Local Exchange carriers (OLECs) trench and provide fiber the last few hundred feet to a building to connect fiber rings in the metropolitan area to particular buildings.

A major challenge for Gigabit Ethernet providers is building up their infrastructure in enough locations so that Fortune 1000 companies with multiple sites are able to use Gigabit Ethernet from one network provider for service to all of their sites. For now, many providers are concentrating their efforts on the top-25 tier-1 metropolitan areas, also called the National Football League (NFL) cities, such as the New York/New Jersey, Los Angeles/Orange County and Seattle areas with populations of over 2 million people.

The Advantages of Using Ethernet

Ethernet is the most common protocol used in LANs. Gigabit Ethernet is based on the 802.3 standard for transmitting 1000 million bits per second (1 billion). Although a standard is not defined for 10-Gigabit Ethernet, new equipment is emerging that operates at 10 gigabits over Ethernet. Because of its speed, Gigabit Ethernet supports transmissions between organizations and access to the Internet.

Because it works on a standard protocol, manufacturing costs for Ethernet products are low compared to, for example, ATM gear. Because these Gigabit Ethernet manufacturers use Ethernet, their costs are lower than carriers that use SONET or ATM in their infrastructure. (ATM and SONET are discussed later.) Manufacturing standardized products in quantity costs less than producing specialized products in lower number. Ethernet-based network interface cards (NICs) are an example of a product based on a standard that has decreased in cost to under $100. Network interface cards are installed in slots of PCs and connect to Ethernet LANs.

Most LANs use Ethernet and are thus already compatible with Gigabit Ethernet. Thus, installation of Ethernet switches at customer locations is not complex and customers aren't faced with expensive upgrades when they implement the service. No CSU/DSU (digital modems) or T-1 multiplexer is required. An on-site switch transmits and receives data directly to and from the outside fiber to a port on the metropolitan area–based Ethernet switch. Using Gigabit Ethernet is essentially like linking customer premise local area networks to local area networks located at carrier facilities in the metropolitan area network (MAN).

Speed Options—Bandwidth on Demand

Gigabit Ethernet is sold at various speeds starting at 1 megabit per second up to 1 Gbps (1000 million bits per second). Most carriers sell it in increments of 1 megabit per second. Some Gigabit Ethernet providers offer fewer options such as 10-megabits, 100-megabits and 1 gigabit per second services.

Customers can purchase 1 megabit per second service to start and later upgrade to, for example, 3 megabits later. It is a lower cost alternative than ATM and T-3 (44.5 megabits per second) services and is faster than T-1, ISDN and DSL, which top out at 1.5 megabits per second. For example, some customers need more capacity than T-1 speeds at 1.54 megabits. They may lease three or four T-1s with a T-1 multiplexer and CSU/DSU for each T-1. With Gigabit Ethernet, they simply increase the speed of their service through software without ordering new hardware or a new line from the telephone company.

With Gigabit Ethernet bandwidth is available on demand: Capacity is flexible and controlled by software—vendors or customers can raise or lower speeds by commands in computers. Customers don't have to change hardware to increase or lower transmission speed.

Gigabit Ethernet Features at Lower Prices

Gigabit Ethernet takes advantage of the wide availability of Ethernet to provide data connectivity over fiber to customers.

- Fiber supports higher speeds more reliably than copper for last-mile applications.

- Services such as those provided by Yipes are meshed—any customer on the Yipes network can request connections to any other site on the Yipes network. The mesh topology is the same as that described above for private line services where all sites are connected to each other.

- Gigabit Ethernet local exchange providers do not require connections to incumbent local exchange carriers (ILECs). Whereas DSL runs over copper cabling owned by incumbent local exchange carriers, Gigabit Ethernet works independently of it. Once an Ethernet carrier has service in an area, new customers can be brought online quickly. Competitive local exchange carriers that provision service over incumbent carriers often experience delays of two to three months.

A Sample Metropolitan Area Gigabit Ethernet Configuration

Gigabit Ethernet switches from vendors such as Extreme Networks, Cisco, ONI Systems and Atrica are located at carrier sites, usually carrier hotels in the local access network. Gigabit Ethernet switches have cards with lasers and photo detectors in them that convert electrical signals to light pulses and vice versa. Some switches also have cards in them with wavelength division multiplexing to send multiple streams of customer data over fiber. The switches are connected to dark fiber installed under city streets without electronics connected to it. A pair of fibers is connected to each 1 gigabit port. The fiber runs in ring configurations throughout the local loop. Spurs run from each ring run to customers' buildings. Many carriers provision spare fiber to each customer in the event that one pair fails.

Carrier-supplied gigabit switches located in customers' buildings are connected to hubs or switches on local area networks LANs. (See Figure 6.11) Most providers offer switches in buildings capable of supporting multiple customers. The vendor-supplied gigabit switch is connected to a switch located in the optical carrier's point-of-presence (POP). For customers that lease Internet access, optical local exchange carriers (OLECs) provide a managed firewall appliance to prevent hackers from accessing

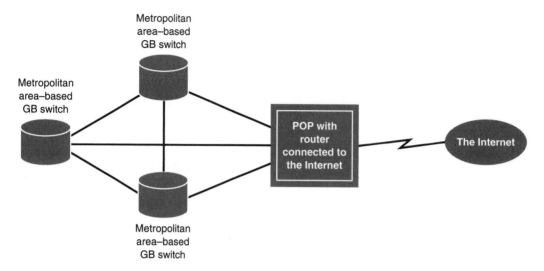

Figure 6.11
Metropolitan area-based Gigabit (GB) Ethernet switches.

customer LANs. (A firewall screens packet addresses and/or applications to block un-authorized users from access to customer data.)

Small POPs where the switches are located are connected to each other and to larger POPs using the Ethernet protocol. Larger POPs are connected via routers to the Internet or to a provider's wide area network (WAN). For example, Yipes uses the Level 3, WorldCom, Genuity and sometimes Qwest IP backbone networks to carry its traffic between metropolitan regions in the cities in which it sells service.

ATM—ASYNCHRONOUS TRANSFER MODE ....

ATM, or asynchronous transfer mode, is a high-speed (up to 30 Gigabits) switching service capable of carrying voice, data, video and multimedia images. ATM is used primarily in Frame Relay networks and in newer carrier networks. The key advantage of ATM is that it enables providers and end users to carry multiple types of traffic without building separate networks for voice, video and data. Currently, many carriers have separate networks for voice, Frame Relay and Internet traffic. They merge the traffic in the core over SONET and dense wavelength division multiplexing (DWDM). (See Figure 6.12.) It was thought that IP routers in converged networks would replace ATM. However, because of ATM's superior quality of service capabilities, this has not happened.

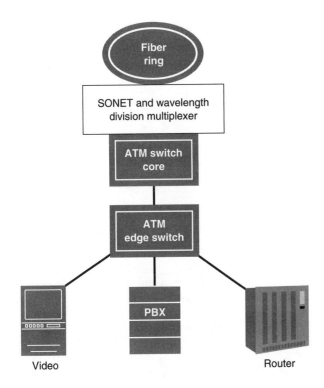

Figure 6.12
ATM for many types of service.

While not widely used by retail customers, large enterprises deploy ATM as a way to send large files such as video between sites. For example, the entertainment industry uses it to ship film clips to other locations for editing. Gigabit Ethernet, where it's available, is a lower cost option than ATM for end users who need to send large files between sites.

The distinguishing point about asynchronous transfer mode (ATM) is that it can prioritize traffic. It assigns qualities of service (QoS) to different types of traffic. ATM carries parallel streams of traffic at different levels of service quality over the same circuit.

Asynchronous transfer mode (ATM) is used by:

- Long distance providers
- Bell telephone companies' data networks
- competitive local exchange carriers
- DSLAM connections to ISPs
- Cable TV networks

- Frame Relay networks
- Fortune 500 companies

ATM's speed is due to three characteristics:

- The cells are fixed in size.
- The cells are switched in hardware in a connection-oriented manner.
- Switching is performed asynchronously.

Fixed-Sized Cells—Less Processing

Asynchronous transfer mode (ATM) packages data into discrete groups called cells. This is analogous to putting the same number of letters into each envelope. Handling fixed-sized cells requires less processing than switching with variable-sized packets. The ATM switch does not have to look for bits telling it when the cell is over. Each cell is 53 bytes long. The switch knows when the cell ends.

Five of the 53 bytes contain header information. This includes bits that identify the type of information contained in the cell (e.g., voice, data or video) so that the cell can be prioritized. Voice and video need constant bit-rate transmission so that there is no interruption in the voice or picture. LAN data typically uses variable bit-rate service. Other header information is used for routing, putting the cells in the correct sequence and error checking. The remaining 48 bytes are the "payload"—user data such as voice, video or sales proposals.

Switching in Hardware—Less Address Lookup

A significant reason why ATM is fast is that the cells are switched in the hardware. This means that an ATM switch does not have to look up each cell's address in software. Rather, an ATM switch sets up a route through the network when it sees the first cell of a transmission. It puts this information into its hardware and sends each cell with the same header routing information down the virtual path previously established. For example, all cells with XXX in the header use route 234. Using the same path for each cell makes ATM a connection-oriented service.

Asynchronous Switching—Improving Network Utilization

With asynchronous switching, every bit of the network capacity is available for every cell. This is different than synchronous multiplexing technologies such as T-1 and T-3.

With T-3 multiplexing, every one of the 672 input transmissions is assigned a time slot. For example, terminal A may be assigned time slot 1 and terminal B assigned time slot 2. If terminal A has nothing to send, the time slot is sent through the network empty. ATM has no synchronous requirements. It statistically multiplexes cells onto the network path based on quality of service information in the header. For example, voice and video need better service, fewer delays and higher aggregate speeds than e-mail messages. With ATM, this is accomplished without wasting network capacity. Every cell is used.

Bursting—Selling More Than the Total Capacity

Because not every device connected to a public network sends data all of the time, Frame Relay and DSL carriers that use ATM have the capability to sell aggregate capacity that is higher than the total available capacity. This is called the capability to oversubscribe. For example, Frame Relay customers may order ports at 64 Kbps. However, they can "burst" to higher speeds, for example, 512 Kbps. Their data is sent in pauses between other customers' data. The same thing happens with digital subscriber line access multiplexers (DSLAMs). DSLAMs that use ATM connections to send DSL data to Internet service providers have a top speed that is lower than the sum of the DSL modems connected to them. (See Figure 6.7 earlier in this chapter.)

Scalability—The Ability to Use ATM for High- and Low-Speed Applications and IP Traffic

ATM can carry traffic of various speeds. It accepts streams from different inputs (e.g., central office switches and routers) and sends them across paths, or virtual circuits established by the ATM switch. This is *scalability*. ATM can be scaled from low-speed (56 kilobit) to high-speeds used for video and multimedia applications. ATM is installed mainly in carrier networks. Many new carriers have built networks capable of transmitting traffic from many sources including ISP Internet traffic, CLEC voice traffic and Gigabit Ethernet traffic. Some ATM switches also carry IP traffic. Some of them have the capability to read IP routing information in packets. The switch puts IP packets into cells and reassembles the cells back into packets at the end of the transmission. This is referred to as *mapping IP onto ATM*.

ATM—Edge and Core Devices

Frame Relay carrier networks use ATM switches extensively for switching multiple customers' traffic at gigabit speeds over their core or backbone facilities. Frame Relay vendors use Frame Relay devices to connect directly to their customers at the edge of the network. The edge of the network is the point where traffic enters and leaves the network. The edge of the network where traffic exits the network is known as the *egress point*. Most carriers now deploy multiplatform switches with both Frame Relay and ATM ports. The switch converts the frames to cells and transports them through the network.

Some carriers are conducting trials of the use of ATM switches as a replacement for tandem central offices. Tandem central offices switch traffic between central offices and do not have connections directly to end users. The use of ATM would increase the speed of circuits between tandem offices, which now use T-3 service. The ATM switches would be able to carry data as well as voice in the backbone of metropolitan area networks.

Elements of an ATM Network

The ITU has defined the elements of an ATM network. The elements are:

- User Network Interface
- Quality of service
- Connections between customer locations

These elements are important because they create a common way to prioritize traffic, send traffic between sites and create connections to ATM networks.

Communicating Between ATM and Frame Relay Services—Frame Relay ATM Interworking

Frame Relay networks use ATM to transmit customer data. This requires Frame Relay to ATM Interworking where frames are converted to ATM cells as they enter the network. The ATM cells are converted back to frames when they are sent to customers Frame Relay access devices (FRADs) at the receiving end. Frame Relay ATM Interworking is possible on multiplatform switches. Manufacturers such as Lucent Technologies, Cisco Systems and Nortel Networks make switches that can accommodate cards for both Frame Relay packets and ATM cells. The carrier's switch internally modifies the frames and cells for the Interworking between Frame Relay and ATM-equipped sites.

User Network Interface (UNI)—The Physical Connection to the ATM Network

The UNI, or user network interface, is the dedicated digital telephone line connection between the customer and the ATM equipment. The dedicated connection to ATM can be implemented at various speeds including:

- T-1
- T-3
- Fractional T-3
- OC-1 (52 megabits per second)
- OC3 (155 megabits per second)
- OC12 (622 megabits per second) and above

ATM service is known as native ATM when customers (often local carriers) contract with wholesale network providers for ATM service. In native ATM where customers lease ATM connections from network service providers, each ATM access line is connected to the carrier's network via the UNI physical telephone line. Figure 6.12 shows ATM over a public ATM network.

Quality of Service Categories—For Different Applications

Quality of service (QoS) parameters include availability, information transfer accuracy, priority and delay. These criteria assume that there is a scarcity of available bandwidth. Customers and carriers have the option of deciding which traffic should be given priority and paying for the priority service. If customers want fewer delays on video and voice communications, they select constant bit-rate quality of service. Level-of-service information is communicated to the network in the ATM cell's 5-byte header.

Carriers that lease ATM services from wholesale carriers pay more for higher levels of constant bit-rate and real-time variable bit-rate services (see bulleted list). Variable bit-rate services are suitable for Internet traffic. This enables service providers to pay for only what they need and use. ISPs that send only data need not pay for constant bit-rate services suited for real-time voice.

- *Constant bit rate* provides the highest priority and lowest delay through a network. Typical applications include videoconferencing, voice, television and video-on-demand.

- *Real-time variable bit-rate* applications are assumed to be able to tolerate small variations in the rate of transmission and small losses of cells. Applications include compressed voice and some types of interactive video.

- *Non–real-time variable bit-rate* applications are bursty, not constant in nature. LAN-to-LAN communications fit into this category. More delay and variation on speeds can be tolerated. Internet service providers use this service for carrying Internet traffic.

- *Available bit-rate services* are intended for applications that can adjust their requirements according to the speed of the available network resources. These applications can tolerate variations in speed and delay. Applications include TCP/IP and Frame Relay router traffic.

- *Unspecified bit-rate services* are for non–time-sensitive applications such as file transfer, email, and message and image retrieval. They take advantage of unused bandwidth and are lower in cost.

Cell Rate Transfers—ATM Speeds

Speeds on ATM services are thought of in terms of cell rate transfer. Cells are sent through the network at specific rates in increments of 64 kilobits per second. For constant bit-rate and variable bit-rate quality of services, the following cell rate transfer parameters are specified:

- *Peak cell rate*—The highest speed cells will be transmitted in increments of 64 kilobits per second.

  - For constant bit-rate service, the peak cell rate is sustained throughout the service.

  - For variable bit-rate service, the peak is the highest rate for an instantaneous "burst" of speed.

- *Sustained cell rate*—For variable bit rates, the sustained cell rate is the length of time the peak cell rate is sustained.

ATM Connections: Permanent Virtual Connections (PVCs)

ATM supports multiple, parallel communications. For example, a videoconference can be transmitted on the same line carrying large file transfers. Thus, even though there is only one physical connection, multiple communications are taking place in parallel. This is a major strength of ATM. Predefined paths between network locations are called PVCs or Permanent Virtual Connections.

The two types of permanent virtual connections are:

- *Virtual path connection (VPC)*—Has many virtual channels running within it. This is analogous to conduit carrying many cables.

- *Virtual Channel Connection (VCC)*—A single channel within the ATM circuit that is defined when the service is put in place.

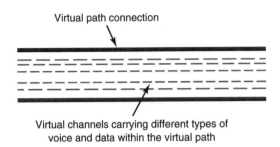

Virtual path connection

Virtual channels carrying different types of
voice and data within the virtual path

Figure 6.13
An ATM virtual path connection
carrying virtual channels.

Each virtual channel can be assigned a different quality of service. Figure 6.13 illustrates the way ATM is used to carry communications at multiple qualities of service.

SONET—SYNCHRONOUS OPTICAL NETWORK ....

Synchronous optical network (SONET) equipment aggregates many types of traffic into uniform streams onto fiber optic cabling. SONET is capable of transporting traffic in redundant rings. Fifty percent of the rings' capacity is set aside for automatic restoral. If one section of the ring is cut, traffic automatically travels on the redundant fiber in the ring. Bellcore, the central research group jointly owned at that time by the RBOCs, introduced SONET in 1984. The ITU has approved standards for OC speeds. The various OC levels and their speeds are shown in Table 6.5.

When it was developed, SONET was envisioned as carrying synchronous traffic such as T-1, E-1, T-3 and E-3 as well as slower rates uniformly on fiber optical equipment. It is not as well suited for data traffic because it carries traffic in "chunks" at 64 kilobits per second up to OC rates. This wastes SONET capacity. Standards committees are exploring altering the SONET standard to make it more compatible with data traffic, in particular, Ethernet packets.

With SONET, operations, provisioning, monitoring and maintenance functions are done uniformly and efficiently. Because restoral is automatic, maintenance is low. The disadvantages of SONET are that it is expensive and inflexible. The entire ring must operate at the same speed and adding capacity to rings takes a long time. Often, a new ring is added when more bandwidth is needed. New multiservice platforms are being developed to address these issues. (See optical cross connects in Chapter 5 and meshed optical technology later in this chapter.)

SONET is a Layer 1 transport service used on fiber optic cabling. Layer 1 functions define interfaces to physical media such as copper and fiber optic cabling. SONET takes data and transports it at high speeds called OC (optical carrier) speeds. In contrast, ATM is a Layer 2 service; it performs switching, addressing and error check-

Table 6.5   Optical Carrier Levels

OC Level	Megabits	Number of 64-Kbps (DS-0) Channels
OC-1	52	672
OC-3	155	2016
OC-9	466	6048
OC-12	622	8064
OC-18†	933	12,096
OC-24	1244	16,128
OC-36	1866	24,192
OC-48	2488	32,256
OC-96	4976	64,512
OC-192	10,000	129,024
OC-256	13,271	172,032
OC-768	39,812	516,096

The number of channels in each optical carrier level is a multiple of the 672 channels in the OC-1 speed. An OC-3 line has 3 × 672 = 2016.

ing. SONET links carry data from ATM switches, IP networks, T-1 and T-3 multiplexers from close to where they enter carrier networks in fiber optic long-haul and metropolitan area networks.

SONET is deployed mainly in long distance and local telco networks.

Synchronous Digital Hierarchy (SDH) and SONET

SONET OC optical carrier level standards were developed to carry U.S., Canadian, Korean, Taiwanese and Hong Kong time division multiplexed 1.54 megabit per second DS-1 (T-1) and 44 megabit per second DS-3 (T-3) streams of voice and data from multiple customers and vendors. They operate at various synchronous transport signals (STSs) levels.

SDH, or synchronous digital hierarchy, essentially is the European version of synchronous optical speeds. SDH signals are carried at Synchronous Transfer Mode (STM) speeds. Europe's time division hierarchy is based on E1 (2-megabit) and E3 (34-megabit) signals. E1 circuits carry 30 channels at 64 kilobits per channel. E3 cir-

Table 6.6   SONET/SDH Capacity

Speed	North American Synchronous Transport Signals (STS) Levels	SONET Channels	European Synchronous Transfer Mode (STM) Levels	Synchronous Digital Hierarchy (SDH) Channels
52 Megabits	OC-1	28 DS-1s or 1 DS3	STM-0	21 E1s
155 Megabits	OC-3	84 DS1s or 3 DS3s	STM-1	63 E1s or 1 E4
622 Megabits	OC-12	336 DS1s or 12 DS3s	STM-4	252 E1s or 4 E4s
2488 Megabits	OC-48	1344 DS1s or 48 DS3s	STM-16	1008 E1s or 16 E4s
9953 Megabits	OC-192	5376 DS1s or 192 DS3s	STM-64	4032 E1s or 64 E4s
39.812 Gigabits	OC-768	21,504 DS1s or 768 DS3s	STM- 256	16,128 E1s or 256 E4s

cuits carry 512 channels at 64 kilobits per channel. Traffic that is carried between cities in Europe or in undersea cables is often referred to as being carried at STM-1 or STM-16 rates.

Table 6.6 illustrates the correlation between the European Synchronous Digital Hierarchy and the North American SONET speeds. SONET is considered a subset of the SDH hierarchy. SONET and SDH speeds almost are compatible with each other. The same SONET equipment can be used for both OC and SDH speeds. Interfaces in the equipment make the signals compatible with each other.

SONET Functions—The Four Layers

SONET has four functions or layers:

- The *photonic* layer converts electrical signals to optical signals and vice versa. If electrical signals from media such as copper are connected to SONET multiplexers, the SONET equipment converts the electrical signals to light signals suitable for fiber optic cabling. At the receiving end of the transmission, it converts optical signals back to electrical signals.

- The *section* layer monitors the condition of the transmission between the SONET equipment and optical amplifiers. (Amplifiers are used to strengthen optical signals that fade over distance.)

- The *line* layer synchronizes and multiplexes multiple streams into one stream or "pipe" of traffic. It also provides monitoring and administration of SONET multiplexers.

- The *path* layer assembles and disassembles voice and data carried on SONET into frames. Frames are arrangements of bits that carry user information as well as bits for monitoring and maintaining the line.

An advantage of SONET is that tributaries or lower bandwidth "pipes" can be fed into SONET multiplexers and carried at high SONET speeds. SONET also can carry ATM traffic, IP traffic and television signals.

CONCATENATION

Concatenation puts streams of data into one "fat" or high-bandwidth contiguous stream. For example, optical carrier 1 (OC-1) speeds of 52 million bits per second, may be used to carry high-speed broadcast video. In this case, OC-1C or concatenated OC-1, carries two OC-1 streams back-to-back or contiguously. They travel through the network in a continuous stream as long as capacity is available. Concatenated speeds are referred to as OC-1C, OC-3C (155 million bits per second) and so forth. Applications for concatenation are high-speed data and broadcast-quality video.

SONET Rings—For Greater Reliability

The higher speeds attainable on fiber make reliability extremely important. When a medium such as copper carries conversation from one telephone subscriber, a copper cut only impacts one customer. The SONET speed, OC-192, can carry 129,000 64-kilobit per second transmissions. If the SONET ring that serves a major hospital, police department or armed forces unit fails, there is an impact on health, safety and possibly national defense. Nearly 5% of the total SONET bandwidth is devoted to network management and maintenance.

To ensure reliability, telephone companies' SONET deployments often use bidirectional ring topology. One set of fiber strands is used for sending and receiving; the other is a spare set, also called the protect ring. If one set of fiber strands is broken, the spare (protect) ring reroutes traffic in the other direction. This is an important advan-

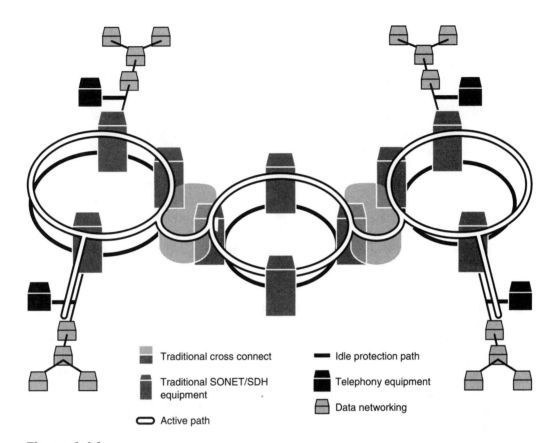

Traditional cross connect   Idle protection path

Traditional SONET/SDH equipment   Telephony equipment

Active path   Data networking

Figure 6.14

A SONET ring in a metropolitan area network where one pair of the fiber is used to transmit and receive data and the other pair is a spare for backup purposes. The backup fiber strands reroute traffic in the opposite direction in the event of a fiber failure. Drawing courtesy of Tellium

tage over fiber that is run in a straight line. If there is a fiber cut on fiber running from one point to another, there is no other route for the traffic to take without the carrier intervening and rerouting calls. Figure 6.14 illustrates this concept. In addition, if one multiplexer on one set of fibers fails, the backup multiplexer on the fiber running in the other direction automatically takes over.

Telephone Company SONET Offerings

Local telephone companies sell fiber-based SONET ring capacity to commercial customers. They offer to interconnect T-1 and (mostly) T-3 services to SONET rings for the extra reliability provided by the SONET ring structure. These services are aimed at call centers that require a high level of both capacity and, more important, reliability. Many call centers, such as airlines, which are in a competitive business, feel they lose large amounts of money in an outage because callers can call another airline if theirs is not available. The financial services industry is another industry that demands a high level of reliability for both voice and data services.

Local telephone companies sell SONET transport for connections between local customers and interexchange carriers. The speeds offered are at OC-3 (155-megabits), OC-12 (622-megabits) and OC-48 (2.5-gigabit) rates. The local telephone companies guarantee 50-millisecond network restoration in the case of a network failure or degradation. They run the SONET rings to multiple interexchange carrier switches and local telephone companies' facilities. In the case of a failure at one central office, service is immediately available from the backup central office. Matching SONET multiplexers are required at the customer premise and at the telephone company office for redundancy.

SONET Connections to Wave Division Multiplexers

Wave division multiplexers increase the capacity of fiber connected to SONET equipment. SONET equipment receives voice and data communications from multiple sources. It converts these streams into optical light and sends them uniformly at high speeds on one pair of fiber. If wave division multiplexing (WDM) is performed, multiple SONET streams can be carried on one fiber. A wave division multiplexer (see Chapter 2) takes SONET streams and sends them out on many different colors of light so that one fiber strand can handle up to 96 times the capacity of a SONET multiplexer.

Manufacturers are finding ways to save carriers' money by combining SONET and wave division multiplexing functions in one piece of equipment. For example, the wave division multiplexer function can be built into a shelf of a SONET device. Nortel Networks includes a card in its SONET equipment for wave division multiplexing. The sending SONET multiplexer couples (connects) light streams to the wave division-multiplexing card. At the receiving end of the fiber, the light is demultiplexed into a single color stream by wave division equipment and sent to the SONET equipment. The SONET equipment demultiplexes the single color stream, disassembles the frames and, if required, converts the optical signal to an electrical signal.

Meshed Optical Technology—Lower Costs, More Suitable for Data than SONET

New gear is being developed called *multiservice switching platforms* which has the capability of SONET plus other functions built into them. For example, the new devices have SONET/SDH, add-and-drop multiplexing, optical switching and dense wavelength division multiplexing capability in one "box." The built-in switching provides SONET gear with the capability of more flexible rerouting of traffic in the event of a fiber cut. For example, rerouted traffic could be split up between two backup routes rather than one route always left spare. It also would make it easier to add capacity just on specific routes rather than on entire rings. Thus, adding bandwidth could be done more quickly.

However, because carriers have invested so much money into existing gear, this change will not happen overnight. Moreover, it may be more cost effective in long-haul long distance networks rather than in metropolitan networks. Metropolitan networks have shorter, less expensive fiber routes with fewer "on" and "off" access points. Therefore, there are fewer savings in being able to reroute traffic using less fiber capacity.

Another consideration on any new equipment purchased by incumbent telephone companies is compatibility with the operations and support systems they use. This system is known as Operations Systems Modifications for the Integration of Network Elements (OSMINE). Large telephone companies have vast operations and support systems. Many of them are automated systems that interface with billing, provisioning and repair systems. A key consideration for them is the capability to interface with these existing systems. This is not such a critical factor for new carriers with more flexible and open operation and support systems.

7 Analog, Cable TV and Digital Modems and Set-Top Boxes

In this chapter...

Cable TV providers are upgrading their networks to offer high-speed Internet access, Voice over IP (VoIP), two-way video, better reliability and improved reception. Some of them are also beginning to sell Internet access service to small- and medium-sized businesses. Their research organization in the United States, CableLabs, is working on standards so that customers can purchase cable modems and set-top boxes from a variety of manufacturers. Cable providers want to take advantage of technology improvements to offer more sophisticated services such as entertainment guides and set-top boxes with email and instant messaging capability. Standards will let them mix and match set-top boxes from a variety of sources. They hope these additional services will increase their revenues.

This chapter takes the mystery out of connecting computers to telephone lines. Anyone sending data, video or images over a telephone line needs a device between the telephone line and the equipment communicating. The vast majority of Internet subscribers worldwide use analog dialup service. Modems convert their computer's digital signals to analog in such a way that the signals are compatible with analog telephone lines. All devices connected to public and private networks need devices for functions such as error correction and timing between computers, multiplexers or local area networks (LANs) and service providers' facilities. Some business and residential subscribers, particularly those in Europe and Japan, access the Internet with basic rate interface (BRI) ISDN service. Because integrated services digital network (ISDN) is digital, modems are not required. However, ISDN requires terminal adapters and network termination type 1 (NT1) devices. Channel services unit/data service units (CSU/DSUs) are used on T-1 and E-1 type digital circuits.

TRANSFERRING DATA FROM COMPUTERS TO TELEPHONE LINES ....

The equipment that makes computer signals compatible with networks for communications is called data circuit-terminating equipment (DCE). Analog and digital telephone lines require different types of DCE devices. These are listed in Table 7.1. Data circuit-terminating equipment (DCE) gear with remote diagnostics can reduce the finger pointing that is often present when maintenance staff try to determine whether repair problems are located in the network, computer, cables or modem. Problem determination, which often involves computer suppliers, network vendors and modem suppliers, is a major dilemma with companies responsible for telecommunications networks. One way technicians pinpoint repair problems is by sending test data bits to the DCE device. If the DCE device receives the data, the assumption is made that the problem is not in the telephone line or DCE.

Data circuit-terminating equipment serves multiple purposes. The functions it provides depends on the network services with which it is used.

Functions of data circuit-terminating equipment (DCE) devices on both analog and digital lines include:

- Ensuring that data flows in an even, synchronous fashion by providing a timing source
- Making sure the proper voltages are present
- Performing error detection and error correction on transmitted and received bits
- Reducing distortion in transmitted signals
- Compressing data so that more information can be transmitted

Functions of DCE devices on digital lines include:

- Ensuring the correct number of 1s and 0s so that errors do not occur
- Shaping the digital signal

Functions of modems on analog lines include:

- Converting digital computer signals to analog when data flows from computers to analog lines
- Converting analog telephone signals to digital signals when signals are received from the network

When technical people talk about data networks, they often use the term DTE to mean the devices and multiplexers used for data communications. DTE stands for data terminal equipment. DTE gear includes laptop computers, personal computers, PBXs, multiplexers and videoconferencing units.

Table 7.1 lists data circuit-terminating devices required to access particular types of network services. Compatible devices need to be at the sending and receiving ends of the communications channel. Standards have been set by the International Telecommunications Union (ITU) such that data communications equipment manufactured by multiple companies can speak to each other.

Table 7.1   DCE Devices as a Function of Telephone Lines

Network Service	DCE Devices
Analog lines (POTS)	Modems
ISDN (integrated services digital network)	NT1s
Other digital services (e.g., T-1 and T-3)	CSU/DSUs, channel service units/data service units
Cellular	Personal Computer Memory Card International Association (PCMCIA) modem with cellular cable
PCS wireless	PCMCIA PCS-ready card
Data over cable TV lines	Cable modems
Cable TV	Set-top boxes

DCE—CONNECTIONS TO TELEPHONE LINES..........

Data circuit-terminating equipment (DCE), also referred to as analog and digital modems, sit between the telephone line and computers or multiplexers. The multiplexers, computers and PBXs, data terminating equipment (DTE) (see Figure 7.1) is connected to the modem. The increase in the computing power of chips and functionality of digital signal processors (DSPs) has resulted in the shrinking size of DCE devices. The following are sample configurations:

- Modems for PCs are either cards located in an internal slot of PCs or external devices that plug into the serial port of the computer. In either case, they are plugged directly into a telephone company jack. Standalone modems need their own power source. Integrated modems do not.

- NT1s and CSUs plug directly into a telephone company T-1 or ISDN two-pair data jack.

- A BRI ISDN NT1 device can be an extension of a PBX or key system. In these configurations, the ISDN adapter plugs into the same type of PBX jack as the telephones. The PBX/key system is then connected to a PRI ISDN trunk.

- Modems and CSU/DSUs can be cards within multiplexers.

- CSU/DSUs also are supplied as cards within PBXs, which have internal T-1 multiplexer cards. A cable from the CSU/DSU card connects the PBX to the telephone company jack.

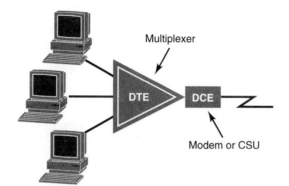

Multiplexer

Modem or CSU

Figure 7.1
Multiplexers as data terminating
devices with a DCE.

MODEMS—ANALOG TELEPHONE LINES FOR TRANSMITTING DATA FROM DIGITAL DEVICES........

Modems convert digital signals received from computers into analog signals and transmit them over analog telephone lines. The process of converting digital signals to analog and modifying them for transmission is called *modulation*. This makes the signals compatible with analog telephone lines. At the receiving end, the modem demodulates the signal or converts it from analog to digital and transmits it to the data terminal equipment (DTE) (e.g., computer or T-1 multiplexer).

When modems were first used, the Bell system, at that time AT&T, set modem standards. (See Table 7.4 at the end of this chapter.) Starting in the 1980s, other modem manufacturers began making higher speed modems. Standards began to be approved by the Consultative Committee on International Telephony and Telegraphy (CCITT), now known as the International Telecommunications Union (ITU). Rather than wait for standards to be set, individual modem makers frequently developed and sold modems based on proprietary standards. This happened with V.90–56-kilobit modems.

Electrical characteristics of analog lines, noise and resistance, inhibit modem speeds. To overcome noise, which adds errors and distortion, modems perform error detection and error correction. Standards have been set for error correction such that modems from different manufacturers can correct errors in conjunction with each other. (See Table 7.5 at the end of this chapter.) Even with error correction, modems do not consistently reach their optimal, stated speed. The higher the stated speed of an analog modem, the lower the percentage of time it actually transmits at that optimal speed. When the modem senses noise on the line, it decreases its speed. For example, a V.34 modem can step back from 33.6 Kbps to 19.2 Kbps. Many modems can increase their speed once line conditions improve.

Modems achieve greater throughput (the amount of data actually transmitted) by using compression. The sending and receiving modem must use the same compression algorithm for the compression to operate. For this reason, manufacturers use agreed-upon compression standards. See Table 7.5 later in this chapter.

Fax Modems

All facsimile machines have internal modems. The modem scans the document to be transmitted into the fax machine as a digital image and changes it into analog signals. When transmitting a fax message, the initial tones heard on the line are the sounds of the sending and receiving fax machines "shaking hands." The "handshake" consists of the sending and receiving modems agreeing on speed, compression and error correction methods. Fax machines connected to analog lines send at the ITU-specified Group 3 standard of 9600 bps.

Fax modems also are a feature of modems purchased either as cards or as standalone units in PCs. Specialized communications software works in conjunction with a modem's fax capability. Documents prepared in word processing and spreadsheet programs can be faxed directly from computers without having to be printed first and then sent from a standalone fax machine. The computer must be turned on to receive faxes.

56-Kbps Modems to Achieve Higher Speeds

56-Kbps (V.90) modem speeds are asymmetric (illustrated in Figure 7.2). "Upstream" from the subscriber to the service provider is slower, (33.6 kilobits) than "downstream" (up to 53 kilobits) from the Internet service provider (ISP) to the subscriber. This is because the subscriber has an analog line to the central office and the Internet service provider has a digital line. The assumption with 56-kilobit modems is that the ISP has digital PRI ISDN service in its remote access server (RAS). (See Figure 7.2.)

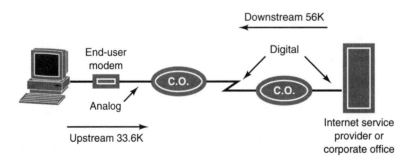

Figure 7.2
56-Kbps modems with faster speeds on the downstream
digital portion of the transmission.

Limitations of 56Kbps Modems— Power and Attainable Speeds

Two problems exist with 56-Kbps modems: power requirements at the local telephone companies and conditions in the analog portion of the public network. To achieve the 56-Kbps speed downstream, certain levels of power must be provided by local telephone companies. If these levels are not present, the modems can only achieve 53-Kbps speeds. Federal Communications Commission (FCC) rules have limited these levels.

Inconsistencies in the local loop—the portion of the telephone path from the end user to the local telephone company—are another variable. Real-world performance does not consistently reach the standard speeds of 33.6 Kbps "upstream" and 53 Kbps "downstream."

V.92—Faster Connections, Data-on-Hold

The International Telecommunication Union (ITU) approved a new standard called V.92 in late 2000 for 56-Kbps modems. V.92 modems have three improvements over V.90 modems. These improvements are only achieved if both the subscriber and the ISP or the telecommuter and the corporation have V.92 modems.

- The upstream transmission is 48,000 bits per second. Improved signaling and compression makes this possible.

- V.92 modems set up calls more quickly because they "remember" information from previous calls to the same location. This translates into less time waiting for the connection to be established.

- The data call can be put on hold for up to 16 minutes when voice calls are received. Customers must have call waiting from their local telephone company for the "on hold" feature to work.

Many customers with V.90 modems will be able to upgrade to V.92 with software downloads rather than having to purchase new modems.

Remote Access Servers (RAS) and Integrated Access Devices (IADs)—Dialup Access to ISPs and Corporations

Instead of leasing individual analog lines for remote access, commercial organizations and ISPs rent 1.54 megabit per second (Mbps) PRI ISDN trunks. PRI trunks route traffic into modem ports on cards in remote access servers (RAS). The ISDN trunks can handle analog modem calls, 53-kilobit digital downstream data and BRI ISDN traffic. The signaling channel on the PRI ISDN line tells the equipment if the signal is from an ISDN device or an analog modem. Because of security concerns, many enterprises are moving away from on-site RAS service. Rather, they are having their remote access traffic screened by carriers for viruses and hackers and then sent into on-site routers. They are also installing switches with built-in security to screen traffic.

New devices, *integrated access devices* (IADs) support many "flavors" of traffic, in addition to dial-in data. These include digital subscriber line (DSL) and voice over IP (VOIP) traffic. The VOIP integrated access devices have cards with protocols that convert voice to data. This features enables carriers to offer voice as well as data over the same lines.

Fax and Modem Servers

Fax/modem servers consolidate outgoing traffic so that each user does not need his or her own modem or fax machine. Instead of giving each user a modem or fax machine, users share modem servers connected to the local area network (LAN). Any user with the appropriate security clearance has access to the pool of modems and fax services. The servers are made up of fax and modem cards located in PC slots. If all the fax ports are busy when someone attempts to send a fax, buffers in the server hold the message until a port is freed up. Figure 7.3 shows this type of setup.

Because of the ease of sending attachments along with email, faxing is decreasing as is the need for fax servers.

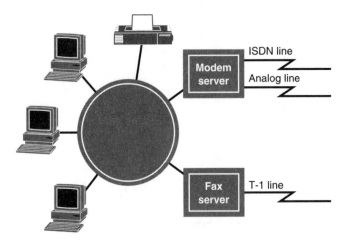

Figure 7.3
Fax and modem servers on a LAN.

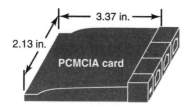

Figure 7.4
A PCMCIA modem card with a telephone line interface.

PCMCIA Modems—Smaller Is Better

PCMCIA stands for Personal Computer Memory Card International Association. PC-MCIA cards are 3.37 inches long by 2.13 inches wide and plug into slots on portable computers such as laptops. They were initially designed as cards with extra memory for laptops. For example, if the hard drive on the laptop was too small, a PCMCIA card was installed to store extra documents or programs. These PCMCIA slots are now commonly used for modems and fax/modems.

PCMCIA cards can be used with:

- Analog POTS lines
- Wireless LAN service
- Cellular services

PCMCIA modems are manufactured in a variety of speeds, including 56 Kbps. When plugged into a standard analog telephone line, they work the same way as standard, full-sized modems. An RJ11 jack for a telephone cord, as shown in Figure 7.4, is attached to the end of the card. Some PCMCIA cards have connections for Ethernet LAN, cellular and ISDN connections as well as landline service. Thus, people can use the same PCMCIA card at their work and home locations and with their cellular phone when they're traveling. People with newer laptop computers have internal modems and Ethernet connections so they don't need the PCMCIA card. They plug the telephone line or Ethernet cable directly into a port of their computer. The small size of PCMCIA modems is made possible by advances in silicon technology such that all of the modem's functionality can be put onto one chip.

NT1S—CONNECTING DEVICES TO AN ISDN LINE....

Devices such as video teleconference units, PCs, PBXs, key systems and multiplexers that are connected to ISDN lines need an NT1 interface to the ISDN line. As reviewed in Chapter 6, ISDN enables voice, data and video to share one telephone circuit. The

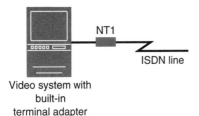

Video system with
built-in
terminal adapter

Figure 7.5
An ISDN line with an NT1 and ISDN-ready videoconferencing system.

network termination type 1 (NT1) corrects the voltage on the signals. It provides the electrical and physical terminations to the carrier's network. In addition, the NT1 provides a point from which line monitoring and maintenance functions can take place. On BRI ISDN services, NT1 devices change the ISDN circuit from two wires that come into the building from the central office to the four wires that are needed by ISDN equipment. (BRI ISDN circuits carry two channels of voice, video or data.)

In the U.S., the FCC requires that the customer be responsible for supplying the NT1. In the rest of the world, telephone carriers supply the NT1.

A terminal adapter (TA) that performs the multiplexing and signaling function on ISDN services is also required. Multiplexing enables one line to be used simultaneously for two voice or data calls. ISDN telephones have built-in terminal adapters. Figure 7.5 illustrates a videoconference system with an internal terminal adapter. Non-ISDN telephones, fax machines, video systems and computers can use ISDN if they are connected to an external terminal adapter or a terminal adapter included in their NT1 device.

CSU/DSUS—CONNECTING DEVICES
TO A DIGITAL LINE ....

Channel service units (CSUs) are required to interface with digital T-1, T-3, fractional T-1 and T-3, switched 56-Kbps and dedicated 56-Kbps lines. T-1 allows 24 voice, data and video transmissions to share one telephone circuit. T-3 circuits carry 672 voice, data and video transmissions (see Chapter 6). They also are used with E-1 and E-3 European service. Often, CSUs are cards within multiplexers and PBXs rather than standalone, external devices.

Although they have different functions, CSU/DSUs are supplied in one integrated piece of equipment. At one time, the DSU and CSU were sold as separate "boxes." Functionally, the CSU sits between the telephone line and data service unit (DSU). The CSU plugs into the telephone jack. The DSU connects to the customer's equipment, such as the T-1 or E-1 multiplexer.

The CSU is similar in function to an NT1. Maintenance and performance tests can be done from it to determine if a repair problem is in the equipment, the CSU/DSU or the telephone line. The CSU also provides clocking and signal reshaping. The clocking function is responsible for sending out bits in an evenly timed fashion. If the clocking is off, the transmission will not work. In this case, the technician might say, "the line is slipping," or "the timing is off." The DSU makes sure the correct positive and negative voltages are present on the signals from the DTE to the CSU.

There are two main types of CSUs: super frame (SF) and extended super frame (ESF). Extended super frame CSUs were developed by AT&T's Bell Labs division in 1985. (Bell Labs is now part of Lucent Technology.) It is superior to SF because T-1 circuits can be monitored while a line is in service. The type of CSU installed on the customer's premise must match the type used in the telephone provider's network. Most network service providers have extended super frame capability.

CABLE MODEMS—USING CABLE TV FACILITIES FOR DATA COMMUNICATIONS ....

Cable modems provide high-speed connections from homes, schools and libraries to the Internet over the same coaxial cable and fiber optic cabling used in cable TV networks. See Table 7.2 for a comparison of download speeds between cable modems, standard modems and one channel of ISDN service.

Cable modems are different than standard modems in how they perform a "handshake." A handshake is an exchange of signals between modems before data is transmitted negotiating parameters such as speeds at which to send. On traditional landline service, modems perform handshakes with the modem with which they are exchanging data. Cable modems, however, "handshake" with modems located at the cable operator site. Complex signaling, use of frequencies and authentication are agreed upon between the two modems.

If consumers purchase cable modems from retailers rather than their cable TV provider, they need to be certain that the modem is compatible with their providers' modem. To that end, the cable industry has set standards for modems. Modem manufacturers can have their modems tested and certified as meeting these standards by CableLabs, the research and development arm of the North and South American cable TV industry.

New cable modem chips are under development that will fit directly into cable TV set-top boxes. Having cable modems that fit into set-top boxes will enable consumers to purchase and install one device instead of two separate devices for Internet access and cable TV. Cable modems will soon be available as cards within PCs.

Cable modems can provide municipalities with connectivity between government buildings. In exchange for granting cable TV franchises to cable companies, city and town governments often are given free access to the cable plant for both Internet access and local area network connectivity. These separate cable segments for municipal buildings in the towns in which they are located are called I-nets, for institutional cable. The local governments are required to pay for the cable modems and new equipment to work with the cable modems at the cable company headend. A *headend* is the point from which programming is transmitted to local customers. The cable TV company agrees to make the cable plant suitable for data communications.

Reverse Channels for Two-Way Data Communications

The creation of "reverse" channels, or two-way capability make cable TV networks suitable for data communications. Most television is currently a one-way broadcast medium. Television signals are transmitted from TV studios, via satellite, to microwave dishes located at cable operators' headend. From the headend, the television signal is transmitted via coaxial cable or a hybrid combination of fiber optic and coaxial cable cabling system.

Reverse channels are created using different frequencies for upstream and downstream transmissions. The upstream channels from the subscriber to the headend uses lower frequencies than the downstream headend-to-subscriber channels. As in 56-Kbps modems, cable TV data communications are asymmetric. Splitting the frequencies into different ranges enables the same coaxial and fiber cables to be used for both sending and receiving signals. A separate cable does not have to be installed for the reverse channel.

Cable Modems

Using cable TV for data communications is analogous to being on an Ethernet LAN. The Ethernet local area networking protocol is a shared protocol. All messages are broadcast onto the cable connecting devices to the LAN. There is no mechanism that ensures that everyone gets a turn to communicate. Local area networks need to be designed carefully without too many heavy users on each network. People using home computers for email and Internet access use the same cable TV facilities as subscribers receiving television signals via cable TV. Figure 7.6 illustrates how cable TV is set up to accommodate email and Internet access.

When home users connect their PCs to the cable TV system for Internet access, they purchase a cable modem from their cable provider. The modem plugs into either

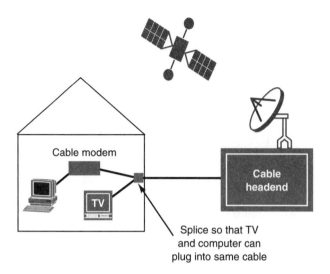

Figure 7.6
A hook-up of cable TV for data communications at a residential location.

an Ethernet card in the PC or Macintosh computers. TCP/IP software is required in the computer. Another cable runs from the cable modem to an outlet that has been spliced into the interface provided by the cable company. Municipal buildings are connected to the cable plant with a combination bridge/modem or router. The bridge/modem or router plugs into the municipal building's LAN with one cord and into the outside cable connection with another cord. In both cases, a TCP/IP address is associated with each cable modem.

Headend and end-user cable modems provide the following functionality:

- Equalization to compensate for signal distortion
- Address filtering so that the modem only accepts messages intended for the correct recipient
- Transmitting and receiving functions
- Automatic power adjustments to compensate for power fluctuations
- Adjustments in amplitude (signal strength or wave height) due to temperature changes
- Modulation of the signal (i.e., analog-to-digital conversions, and vice versa)
- Compensation for delays caused by variable distances from the headend

Factors to keep in mind when using cable TV technology for data communications are:

- Whether used for Internet access by residential customers or as a way to connect municipal buildings, each message is broadcast to every cable modem on the system. Only the modem with the specified address takes the message off the network. This may be a security issue to users considering using these services.

- Every message to another user is transmitted first to the headend first and then to the addressee. With large files, there can be congestion on the network because each file transmitted goes to the headend and then downstream to each user until it is taken off the network by the addressee.

- Bandwidth to each subscriber is shared by customers connected to nodes in neighborhoods. Nodes are located between the headend and subscribers. There are anywhere from 500 to 1200 subscribers per node. Some overbuilders only assign 150 to 200 users per node. Overbuilders are competitors to incumbent cable providers. They include RCN and Everest Communications.

- Each modem requires local power.

- These are "nailed-up" connections where the service is always on. Residential users or people who work at home can leave their computers on all the time and be automatically notified when they have email messages. Dialing into and logging onto the Internet is not required.

- Cable modems are vastly faster than analog modems for downloading documents from the Internet. See Table 7.2.

- A standard for cable modems has been approved by the ITU. It is the V.10 and is known as data over cable system interface specifications (DOCSIS). Suppliers of cable modems are Thomson, Toshiba, 3Com, Samsung, Com21 and Motorola.

Table 7.2   Time to Download a 1.5-megabit PowerPoint™ Presentation

Speed/Type of Service	Time to Download the File
28.8 Kbps modem	6 minutes 56 seconds
56.6 Kbps modem	3 minutes 34 seconds
1 ISDN bearer channel at 64 Kbps	1 minute 34 seconds
Cable modem	8 seconds

Table information provided by AT&T Broadband (formerly MediaOne Express)

- According to Kinetic Strategies, Inc. a Phoenix, Arizona market research firm, as of March 1, 2001, 5.5 million residential users in the United States had cable modem service.

Table 7.3 lists the six largest cable TV providers in the United States and the number of subscribers per cable TV provider. The numbers do not indicate the number of cable modem customers.

Table 7.3 Cable TV Providers in the United States

Cable Company	Number of Subscribers
AT&T Broadband	16 million
Time Warner Cable (part of AOL Time Warner)	12.7 million
Comcast Cable Communications	8.4 million
Charter Communications	6.4 million
Cox Communications	6.2 million
Adelphia Communications	6 million

Source: Company data and National Cable Television Association reports published in the article, "Holding Their Own," in The Standard, *19 March 2001, by Richard Martin.*

Cable Modems for Business and for Remote Access

Cable modem service is primarily targeted to residential customers. Cable TV companies such as Comcast Communications and Cox Communications that have upgraded their infrastructure for cable modem service are starting to leverage that fiber optic and coaxial cable to sell service to business customers. Cox Communications, for example, offers high-speed Internet access to small and medium-sized businesses. They have separate customer service departments to support business customers, promise four-hour repair service and offer higher speed service to business customers. For business customers with over 100 users, Cox will run dedicated fiber from the business to Cox's synchronous optical network (SONET) ring. In contrast to consumer modem service, this service is symmetric in nature. The upstream and downstream portions to and from the Internet have the same speed.

Both Comcast and Cox supply hardware, a switch or router that connects to customers' hubs. The customer-supplied hub connects to each LAN-linked printer and personal computer. The switch or router translates the public Internet Protocol (IP) email addresses received from the Internet to private on-site IP addresses. Router and

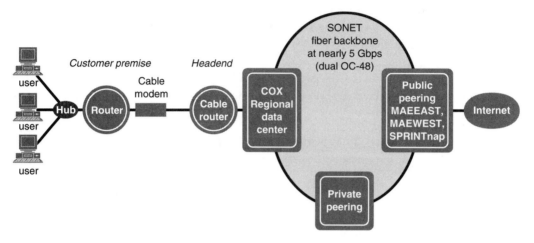

Figure 7.7
VPN service from a cable TV provider. Drawing courtesy of Cox Business Services

hub equipment located at the cable headend supports multiple customers. This equipment is referred to as cable modem termination system (CMTS). Internet traffic is sent to the cable company's' Internet service provider, in the case of Cox and Comcast Excite@home. Carriers such as Sprint, WorldCom and AT&T supply Internet backbone service to cable company's Internet service providers such as Excite@Home and Road Runner. See Figure 7.7.

Static vs. Dynamic IP Addresses

Every Web site has an IP address. When someone types in an address (e.g., www.xyz.com) to reach a company's home pages, the Internet protocol located in a server in the network translates the letters in the address to an IP numeric address. High-speed business offerings are based on static IP, not dynamic IP addresses. A *static IP address*, an address that is the same all the time, is assigned to each Web site. To conserve IP addresses, cable TV and incumbent telephone company DSL providers often sell dynamic IP-based service to residential customers. With dynamic IP address assignments, IP addresses are assigned from a pool of addresses to email messages for users as they are received. This conserves the providers' addresses because not everyone receives messages at the same time.

This has implications on Web hosting, email addressing and file transfer protocol (FTP) service. (FTP service lets companies post files at their Web sites for users to transfer to their own computers. For example, a publishing company might post chapters available for authors to download. This requires static IP addressing.) Without static IP addresses, customers cannot have Web pages or email through their providers with the customers' domain name. With dynamic IP addresses the email is alice-jones@provider.com rather than alice@jonescompany.com, for example.

VPN Service from Cable Companies

Many commercial organizations have employees with cable modem or DSL service who would like to access files remotely. This can be done but security is a major issue. If the organization has virtual private network (VPN) service, remote users can log into their email or other LAN-located files as if they were on-site. In these cases, the corporate headquarters does not need high-speed Internet access from a cable TV provider. However, the teleworker must have "client" software that supports remote access. Companies such as Microsoft supply this.

To prevent hacking into the remote PC, corporate information technology (IT) staff might require that remote users have security appliances that help prevent hackers breaking into the telecommuter's PC. Companies such as McAfee, Network Ice and Symantec supply personal firewalls. The firewall appliance sits between the cable modem and the PC. One cable plugs into the cable modem and the other into the PC.

Cable TV companies such as Comcast Communications and Cox Communications that supply business-class Internet access also supply virtual private network (VPN) hardware for remote access by telecommuters, business partners and small branch offices. Their service includes either a security appliance or switch with VPN software. The equipment, for the most part, is located at the customer site. The VPN functionality includes encryption that scrambles user data as it is sent over the Internet. It may also include security that screens incoming addresses and alerts customers to attacks by other computers. The overhead, extra bits, associated with encryption slow down transmissions.

While the cable TV companies provide the hardware and installation of the VPN hardware and software, in many cases it is up to the customer to provide ongoing management for security.

SET-TOP BOXES ···

Cable TV *set-top boxes* are interfaces between televisions, satellite TV and cable TV networks for access to television and other services. At the most basic level, they are tuners. Cable and satellite TV operators remotely administer filters and traps in set-top boxes to allow subscribers access to basic cable TV or premium channels. The set-top box also has a security function. It scrambles and unscrambles TV signals and also has links to billing systems for information on which channels to allow the subscriber to receive. Credit information is also stored in some set-top boxes.

Digital set-top boxes are available to take advantage of the two-way capability of digital cable TV and satellite TV. These capabilities include:

- *Advanced digital security so that the security is placed on a card in the set-top box that can be installed separately.* If a consumer buys a set-top box from a retailer, the cable TV provider can install the security feature on the card. (Because security is proprietary to each provider, it is not available in retail outlets.)

- *Advanced programming with 30 days worth of programming information.*

- *Embedded modems that will enable televisions to be used as computers for Internet access.* For example, someone watching a football game will be able to view statistics from the Internet in a window of the television. The set-top box will also include infrared links to keyboards and computer mice.

- *Compression so that 6 to 12 compressed digital TV signals can be carried in the same amount of frequency as one analog TV signal.* The set-top box converts digital cable TV or satellite TV into analog signals compatible with analog television. It also can be built directly into digital televisions when the industry agrees on standards compatible with digital cable TV. Some of these extra channels can be used for interactive games for which subscribers will be charged extra on their monthly cable bills.

- *Computer operating systems, software and possibly a hard disc for programming guides and potential new services such as picture-in-picture for viewing statistics while watching sports programs.*

- *An Ethernet plug on the back of the set-top box so that computers or home routers can be connected to the set-top box.* A set-top box can be used to send caller ID to the television screen. For this to work, subscribers must get their telephone service from their cable TV provider.

- *Video on demand so callers do not have to place a separate telephone call to order a premium movie.* The movie can be ordered from the set-top box.

- *Open platform standards so consumers can purchase set-top boxes from a variety of retailers and know they will work with all cable systems.*

Interoperable Set-Top Boxes

The FCC mandated in July 1998 that cable TV set-top boxes be available for retail sale by July 2000. Cable companies received a waiver on this requirement because open cable standards had not been agreed upon. Cable Television Laboratories, Inc. known as CableLabs, is developing standards for set-top boxes with their OpenCable initiative.

Without standards, off-the-shelf gear will not work on all providers' networks. Once standards are agreed upon and equipment is manufactured to the standard, consumers will be able to rent or purchase set-top boxes from retail outlets or cable providers. The FCC has mandated establishment of a standard for security by 2005.

Middleware for Set-Top Boxes

A critical piece of the OpenCable initiative above is the OpenCable Application Platform (OCAP). OCAP will set a standard for middleware. Middleware on set-top boxes enables applications from many different companies to work with set-top box hardware from a variety of manufacturers such as Motorola, Sony, Philips, Nokia and Scientific Atlanta. The middleware translates between the hardware and network protocols and the applications. Applications include electronic commerce, online chatting, digital radio and interactive television program guides. Companies that develop and sell middleware include Canal+, Liberte Technologies, Microsoft, OpenTV and Sun Microsystems.

When the FCC approved the AOL Time Warner merger, they were concerned that AOL would control set-top boxes through its instant messaging product and cable companies owned by Time Warner, the second largest cable company in the United States. Refer to Table 7.3.

Personal Video Recorders (PVRs)

Personal video recorders (also called *digital video recorders*) are set-top boxes that let people record, store and play back television programs. For the most part, they are sold through retail outlets but some cable and satellite TV providers distribute them. The feature that most users find attractive is the ability to fast forward through commercials. In addition, each night the PVR downloads the next day's television listings. Users can select shows and have them recorded through a remote control device. They can be used with satellite TV, cable TV and over-the-air broadcast television.

When they first appeared in 2000, the two main brands were TiVo and ReplayTV. In September 2000, ReplayTV took its hardware product off the market and now sells a software version for cable operators to integrate into their set-top boxes. Microsoft Corporation began offering a product, Ultimate TV, in 2000. Sales of TiVo have been disappointing. The units sell for about $500 which is high compared to analog VCRs and DVD players. Privacy advocates note that these devices send information on customers' viewing habits to the network provider.

If personal video recorders become popular, they will have far-reaching consequences for how companies advertise as more viewers skip commercials. Advertisers may depend more heavily on "product placement" within programs where their products are displayed prominently. For example, lead characters might be prominently displayed drinking a particular brand of soda.

Interactive Program Guides

Set-top boxes often have program guides embedded in them. Interactive program guides are the first screen that viewers see when they turn on their televisions. They are analogous to Internet portals. The largest supplier of interactive program guides is Gemstar-TV Guide. Gemstar has agreements to supply the guides to direct broadcast satellite operators and cable TV companies, as well as television and VCR manufacturers. The on-screen guides make it easier for users to record programs. The founder of Gemstar, Henry Yuen, invented interactive program guide VCR Plus+ to do this. He also made arrangements with newspapers to print numeric codes associated with each program in their guides. Cable TV and direct broadcast satellite companies that use the on-screen guide pay Gemstar 35¢ per subscriber per month in licensing fees.

Interactive program guides could be used as an interface for two-way access to, for example, the Internet. Some providers already use them to link to content providers with whom they have agreements for restaurant, sports scores, entertainment and movie listings. These services are made possible by upgrades to digital cable.

Interactive program guides are used more extensively than personal video recorders and interactive video. Interactive video includes movies on demand as well as two-way consumer information such as entertainment listings. According to Forrester Research, Inc., as of 2000, there were 33.9 million interactive program guides in use compared to 800,000 personal video recorders and 4.9 million users of interactive video subscribers.

Digital Cable TV

It costs cable operators $900 to $1200 per user, including $150 per set-top box to convert their infrastructure from analog to digital service. However, digital cable TV has the following advantages:

- *TV image resolution is improved.* There is less interference from noise to create snow and shadows.
- *Stereo sound in the form of digital radio can be provided.*
- *Less bandwidth is used per television station and movie sent to subscribers.* Providers can put 10 to 12 channels instead of 1 into each 6 megahertz channel of capacity.

- *The extra capacity is a particular benefit for operators that supply Internet access and voice telephony as well as cable TV.*

- *In the future, digital TV could be used for electronic commerce although to date this has not happened.* In Europe, where fewer people than in the United States have computers, expectations for commerce via set-top boxes and digital cable TV have not been met.

- *Operators can download very popular movies in advance to all set-top boxes and only play them for eligible subscribers, thus improving infrastructure peak-rate utilization.* If there is a cable outage, the movies have already been downloaded and the provider still receives revenue for the movies.

Thirteen percent of subscribers were in digital cable territories by the end of 2000. Signals sent over cable infrastructure are converted to digital at cable providers' headends where analog or digital television signals are received from satellites. Encoders convert the signals to digital to be transmitted to end users. Two-way cable modem service can be provided over analog or digital cable service.

Video on Demand vs. Pay Per View

With pay per–view, viewers are offered the opportunity to view a limited number of "premium" movies each week. Users on two-way cable systems can order particular movies from their set-top box without calling their provider. The movies are offered at set, defined times.

Video on demand lets subscribers order from hundreds of movies. They can select the time that the movie will be played. Video on demand requires digital cable TV because of the capacity required to play so many different movies. Video on demand has not been greatly deployed. The major reason for this is the lack of large numbers of available movies. Movie studios and video rental outlets don't want to undercut retail sales. An additional problem is the lack of available infrastructure to carry video on demand.

APPENDIX: MODEM STANDARDS ....

Tables 7.4 and 7.5 list Bell and ITU modem-speed standards. Standards have changed in two ways: Initially, they were set by the Bell system (AT&T). Now the International Telecommunications Union headquartered in Geneva, Switzerland, sets them. Standard modem speeds have increased from 300 bps to 56,000 bps.

Table 7.4   Modem-Speed Standards—From Bell 103 to V.34

Standard	Modem Type	Speed (bps)	Fall-Back Speed	Comments
Bell 103	Dialup	300		
Bell 212	Dialup	1200		
Bell 208A	Leased	4800		
Bell 208B	Dialup	4800		
V.21	Dialup	300	300	Used by Group 3 fax in half duplex mode for negotiation and control.
V.22	Dialup, leased	1200	300	
V.22bis	Dialup	2400	1200	Compatible with V.22.
V.23	Dialup	1200	600	Specifies 75-bps reverse channel.
V.27ter	Dialup	2400 4.8Kbps	2400	Used by Group 3 fax for image transfer.
V.29	Four-wire leased, two-wire leased, dialup	9.6Kbps	4.8Kbps, 7.2Kbps	Used by Group 3 fax for image transfer at 9.6Kbps and 7.2Kbps.
V.32	Two-wire leased, dialup	9.6Kbps	4.8Kbps	With V.42, provides 38.4Kbps throughput.
V.32bis	Two-wire leased, dialup	14.4Kbps	4.8Kbps, 7.2Kbps, 9.6Kbps	Has rapid rate negotiation feature for fast speed changes.
V.32ter	Two-wire leased, dialup	19.2Kbps	18.8Kbps, V.32 V.32 bits	An AT&T specification that is compatible with V.32 and V.32bis.
V.33	Four-wire leased	14.4Kbps	12Kbps	
V.34	Two- and four-wire leased, dialup	33.6Kbps	28.8, 19.2Kbps V.32bis	Initial speed was set at 28.8Kbps, known as V.fast prior to standard being set.

Table 7.4   Modem-Speed Standards—From Bell 103 to V.34 *(continued)*

Standard	Modem Type	Speed (bps)	Fall-Back Speed	Comments
V.90	Dialup	33.6Kbps upstream 56Kbps downstream	V.34	Downstream from network to customer is digital.
V.92	Dialup	48 Kbps upstream 56Kbps downstream	V.34	Same as V.90 with faster upstream, quicker connects and capability to put data call on hold and take a voice call.
V.10	Cable modem standard for North and South America	Upstream frequencies between 5 and 42 MHz; downstream frequencies between 50 and 750 MHz	Actual speed depends on available capacity and traffic levels	DOCSIS, data over cable system interface specifications. DOCSIS 1.0 modems certified and available. DOCSIS 1.1 is being certified in 2001. Availability predicted by 2002. Has improved security, billing and quality of service (QoS) for voice over IP.
DAVIC 1.0-1.4	Cable modem, fixed wireless and set-top box standards for Europe		Sets parameters for fixed rate as well as variable speeds	Standards for Internet access and near video on demand. Adopted by ISO/IEC. Set by Digital Audio Visual Council (DAVIC).

bis = ITU term designating a second-generation standard.
ter = ITU term designating a third-generation standard.
V series standards, except for V.32, are promulgated by ITU.
Fall-back speed is the speed that a modem can drop down to with noisy lines.

Table 7.5 lists various error control standards and techniques available in modems. It also lists compression methods used. Compression removes white spaces and commonly repeated characters to improve throughput (efficiency) on data communicated. The repeated characters are replaced by abbreviated versions of the characters. A text file sent using a 4:1 compression scheme might only need to send 25% as many bits as a noncompressed file.

Table 7.5   Modem Error Control and Compression Standards

Standard/Technique	Description
V.44	A new data compression method used with V.92 modems. It improves V.42 compression 20% to 60% and makes modem downloads faster.
V.42	Specifies both Microcom Networking Protocol (MNP) 2-4 and Link Access Procedure for modems (LAPM) M error correction for full duplex modems. Compatible with V.34, V.22, V.22bis, V.26ter, V.32, V.32bis and the proprietary versions of V.32ter.
V.42bis	A data compression protocol that theoretically allows up to 4:1 file compression.
V.54	A standard for local and remote loop test devices in modems.
LAP M	The preferred error control protocol specified by the V.42 and V.42bis standard for error control in modems.
MNP 1	MNP 1 has been superseded by later versions.
MNP 2-4	Part of the V.42 standard for error control.
MNP 5	A data compression protocol that provides a 2:1 compression ratio.
MNP 10	Optimizes modem performance over adverse line conditions and cellular links.
EC2	Developed by Motorola. Modifies cellular transmission levels to avoid clipping, which is common at high frequencies.
TX-Cel	An error-correcting algorithm that reduces cellular amplitude distortion.
ETC	Enhanced Throughput Cellular (ETC), newer than MNP 10, works with V.42bis, the ITU-specified standard error control that works with V.42bis. Enhances throughput on cellular modems. Owned and licensed by Paradyne (formerly part of AT&T).

8 The Internet

In this chapter...

The Internet is a medium that has fundamentally changed the pace of business processes and the way organizations exchange information with each other. Businesses sell, place orders, receive orders, collaborate, train employees, provide customer service and bid for products over the Internet. Consumers commonly use the Internet to exchange electronic mail with family members, pay bills, conduct online stock transactions, calculate income tax returns, make travel reservations, shop and conduct research. They also spend time on the Internet playing games, listening to music and viewing entertainment.

The Internet is a connection of multiple networks. The networks communicate with each other over a suite of standardized protocols, Transmit Control Protocol/Internet Protocol (TCP/IP), in which data is broken up into "envelopes" called packets. For the most part, network operators use high-speed routers to transmit these packets. Internet traffic is sent at gigabit speeds. The high-speed lines are the backbone of the Internet. They carry the greatest amount of Internet traffic. The Internet backbone transmits requests for information, entertainment, audio and video broadcasts, email and business-to-business transactions. The different carriers that operate Internet backbone exchange traffic with each other at metropolitan area exchanges (MAEs) and network access points (NAPs).

The Web is a vehicle for multimedia presentation of information in the form of music, audio, video and text. The World Wide Web is not separate from the Internet. It is a way to navigate from resource to resource on the Internet by clicking on highlighted text or graphics from within browsers. As long as they use World Wide Web browsers, all PCs are compatible with the Web. Users point and click their way from computer to computer on the Internet. Before the World Wide Web was developed, documents on the Internet were available only as text. There were no pictures, no "buttons" to click on to issue commands and no advertising banners. There was also no color; everything was black and white.

Individuals and organizations connect their locations to the Internet via many types of telecommunications services including T-1, T-3, analog lines, digital subscriber line (DSL) services, integrated services digital network (ISDN) and cable TV facilities. Internet service providers (ISPs) aggregate traffic from many users and send it over high-speed lines to the Internet backbone. ISPs maintain routers and servers at their sites. The servers, powerful PCs that can be accessed by many users, perform various functions. They contain customer email, businesses' e-commerce applications and home pages for consumers as well as specialized content such as sports information and online games. Servers are located at hosting sites as well as ISP data centers. Hosting sites, where Web content such as corporate, ecommerce and entertainment sites are kept, have servers with information from, for example, search companies such as AltaVista and online retailers.

The popularity of the Web has made the creation and implementation of technologies that enable sites to handle spikes in traffic and large amounts of traffic imperative. One of these techniques is caching, which spreads content among servers at the "edge" of the Internet, closer to end users. In addition to lowering traffic at each server, caching lowers the cost of bandwidth. It lowers the amount of distance packets travel to access Web pages.

Innovations also have occurred in search engine techniques and formatting email for marketing. Search engines are an important tool for organizing sources of online information. They have become faster and the results are more accurate. Corporations use them in their own Web pages to help employees, potential customers and trading partners find information on the corporate Web. Email is now used as a way to disseminate spam, marketing announcements and newsletters that look similar to Web pages. These email messages use the same method, Hypertext Markup Language (HTML), as used to apply formatting and insert graphics on Web sites.

Despite the technological improvements in the Internet, Internet companies are struggling to find profits. Scores of businesses that operated Web sites have gone out of business. Moreover, it has been generally agreed that advertising as a primary vehicle for underwriting the Internet is not viable. To date, gambling (which is illegal in most states), auctions, pornography, music and games are popular and often profitable on the Internet. While commercial organizations depend on the Internet for contact with customers and vendors, e-commerce where businesses exchange purchase orders and pay bills directly to one another's order entry and accounting systems are in their infancy.

Because the World Wide Web is new, legal, privacy and security questions are being raised that previously have not been addressed in this context. For example, freedom of speech for adults sometimes conflicts with protecting children from unsuitable online material. Online sharing of music and copyrighted articles may interfere with authors' and musicians' rights to earn royalties. In other instances, Microsoft's control of PC operating systems and browsers and AOL Time Warner's market share in instant messaging (IM) may give both companies unfair advantages on the Internet. All of these issues raise interesting questions about privacy, free enterprise and free speech.

World Wide Web technology is used by commercial organizations to create extranets and intranets. *Extranets* use Web technology to create platforms from which trading partners and customers can communicate. *Intranets* use the technology for internal portals and browser access to corporate data. The adoption of Internet technologies and protocols for internal use by commercial organizations represents a major impact of the Internet. It has led to faster, more convenient access by employees to corporate information.

THE HISTORY OF THE INTERNET ....

The Department of Defense's Advanced Research Projects Agency (DARPA) started the Internet in 1969, in a computer room at the University of California, Los Angeles. It wanted to enable scientists at multiple universities to share research information.

Advanced Research Projects Agency NETwork (ARPANET), the predecessor to the Internet, was created 12 years after Sputnik, during the Cold War. DARPA's original goal was to develop a network secure enough to withstand a nuclear attack.

The first communications switch that routed messages on the ARPANET was developed at Bolt Beranek and Newman (BBN) in Cambridge, Massachusetts. (BBN was bought by GTE. Bell Atlantic acquired GTE, changed its name to Verizon and spun off BBN as Genuity.) ARPANET's network used packet switching developed by Rand Corporation in 1962. Data was broken up into "envelopes" of information that contain addressing, error checking and user data. One advantage of packet switching is that packets from multiple computers can share the same circuit. A separate connection is not needed for each transmission. Moreover, in the case of an attack, if one computer goes down, data can be rerouted to other computers in the packet network. TCP/IP, the protocol still used on the Internet, was developed in 1974 by Vint Cerf and Robert Kahn. It supports a suite of services such as email, file transfer and logging onto remote computers.

In 1984, as more sites were added to ARPANET, the term Internet started to be used. The ARPANET was shut down in 1984, but the Internet was left intact. In 1987, oversight of the Internet was transferred from the Department of Defense to the National Science Foundation.

While still used largely by universities and technical organizations, applications on the Internet expanded from its original defense work. In particular, newsgroups used by computer hobbyists, college faculty and students, were formed around special interests such as cooking, specialized technology and lifestyles. The lifestyles newsgroups included sexual orientation (gay and lesbian), religion and gender issues. Computer-literate people were also using the Internet to log onto computers at distant universities for research and to send electronic mail.

The Internet was completely text prior to 1990. There were no graphics, pictures or color. All tasks were done without the point-and-click assistance of browsers, such as Netscape and Internet Explorer. Rather, people had to learn, for example, UNIX commands. UNIX is a computer operating system developed in 1972 by Bell Labs. UNIX commands include: m for Get Mail, j for Go to the Next Mail Message, d for Delete Mail and u for Undelete Mail. The Internet was not for the timid or for computer neophytes.

The advent of the World Wide Web in 1989 and browsers in 1993 completely changed the Internet. The World Wide Web is a graphics-based vehicle to link users to sources of information. It is based on a method whereby users "click" on graphics or text to be transferred to a site where information can be accessed. In 1993, the Mosaic browser was developed at the University of Illinois as a point-and-click way to access the World Wide Web. This opened up the Internet to users without computer skills. It is no longer necessary to learn arcane commands to open mail, to navigate from site to site for research or to join chat or newsgroups.

In 1995, the National Science Foundation turned the management of the Internet backbone over to commercial organizations. Commercial networks such as Sprint, UU-NET (now part of WorldCom) and Cable & Wireless carry a large portion of the backbone Internet traffic. Backbones are analogous to highways that carry high-speed traffic.

Bulletin Board Systems (BBSs)

Bulletin boards were used independently from the Internet. They allowed people with modems connected to their computers to read information and post information on a PC.

Users throughout the 1980s used modems, personal computers, communications software and telephone lines to dial into information on other computers. Many bulletin boards were used for "chats" and to exchange ideas around specific hobbies. For example, callers would dial in and type ideas or experiences they had with new software or computer equipment. The World Wide Web has largely replaced bulletin boards.

Who Runs the Internet?

The Internet is run informally by a number of organizations. Following is an overview of the key ones:

- The Internet Society (ISOC) is a nonprofit group that promulgates policies and promotes the global connectivity of the Internet. The group is the closest thing to a governing body for the Internet. It was formed in 1992 and is open to anyone who wishes to join.

- The Internet Architecture Board (IAB) is a technical advisory group of the Internet Society. It appoints chairs of the Internet Engineering Task Force (IETF). It provides architectural oversight for the protocols and procedures used by the Internet.

- Internet Corporation for Assigned Names and Numbers (ICANN) is charged with overseeing Internet address allocation and setting rules for domain-name registrations. It oversees the creation of new top-level names. Examples of top-level domain names are .com and .net. ICANN also influences the setting of technical standards. It is a nonprofit organization created in 1998 by the U.S. government to take over from the government-funded Internet Assigned Numbers Authority.

- Internet Engineering Task Force (IETF) is a standards-setting body. The IETF works under the aegis of the Internet Society. It focuses on TCP/IP protocol standards issues. TCP/IP is the protocol used on the Internet.

- VeriSign (formerly called Network Solutions, Inc.) was given the task by the National Science Foundation in January of 1993 to register Internet names, assign addresses and manage the database of names. The registration service was formerly called the InterNIC, or Internet Network Information Center, a registered service mark of the United States Department of Commerce. Veri-Sign purchased Network Solutions in 2000. Although VeriSign manages the master lists of .com, .net and .org, other companies also register them for end users. (Internet names are discussed later in this chapter.)

- IOPS.ORG (Internet Operators' Providers Services) was formed in May of 1997 to address Internet routing robustness—where to send packets based on conditions such as congestion. It was founded by nine of the largest Internet service providers, including AT&T, GTE (now Genuity) and World-Com. The point is to establish standard procedures on routing data between multiple operators' networks.

- The World Wide Web Consortium, also known as W3C, is a group formed to develop common standards for the World Wide Web. It is run jointly by the MIT Laboratory for Computer Science; the National Institute for Research in Computer Science and Automation in France, which is responsible for Europe and Keio University in Japan, which is responsible for Asia. Over 150 organizations are members.

Who Owns the Internet?

No one organization owns the Internet. Rather, the Internet is a worldwide arrangement of interconnected networks. Network service providers, including AT&T, Cable & Wireless, Sprint, Genuity, Verio, Qwest and WorldCom, carry Internet information such as email messages and research conducted on the Internet. These networks are worldwide in scope with backbone networks run by network providers in other countries.

Network providers own the high-speed lines that make up the Internet. Carriers with nationwide networks are called Tier 1 providers. Some Tier 1 providers lease fiber lines from carriers such as AT&T and connect their own switches and routers to the leased lines. The definition of Tier 1 varies by location. It generally means that the carrier has a point of presence in all of the major cities of an area. In the United States, Tier 1 providers have POPs in the 25 largest cities. They transfer data between each other at locations called "peering" sites. At the peering sites, network devices called routers transfer messages between the backbones, high-capacity telephone lines owned by dozens of network service providers.

Peering—A Way to Exchange Data Between Networks

Data carried by different Internet networks needs to exchanged so that sites and users on different networks can send data to each other. In 1995, the National Science Foundation funded four peering, or network access points. They are located in New Jersey; Washington, D.C.; Chicago and San Francisco. These sites are now run by commercial organizations. WorldCom runs MAE® East in Virginia, MAE West in San Jose, California and MAE Central in Dallas, Texas. MAE originally was defined as MERIT-access exchange. (The original exchanges were run by MERIT Access Exchange, which was later purchased by MFS, now a part of WorldCom.) The term is now generally defined as *metropolitan area exchange*. Internet service providers lease ports on WorldCom ATM switches at MAE sites that they connect to their routers. The asynchronous transfer mode (ATM) connections are available at port speeds ranging from 45 megabits (Mb) to 622 Mb with guaranteed or best-effort quality of service (QoS). (See Chapter 6 for ATM service.)

WorldCom has collocation space available for Internet service providers (ISPs) to rent if they wish. WorldCom posts the names of ISPs at the MAE sites and the ISPs make peering agreements to exchange Internet traffic with each other. WorldCom has registered the term MAE. European public exchanges are located in London (London Internet Exchange, or LINX) Amsterdam (AMS-IX) and Frankfurt (MAE-FFT).

In response to concerns about traffic at these peering centers "bogging down" the Internet, network service providers such as Genuity, Sprint and PSINet arranged private peering exchanges. "Meeting places" to exchange data have been set up to avoid possible congestion at the major exchange centers. Pacific Bell has a network access point in San Francisco and Sprint has one called SprintLink in New Jersey. This direct exchange method is seen as a more efficient way to exchange data. Moreover, carriers agree on levels of service, amount of data to be transferred and delay parameters. They feel they can monitor reliability more closely at private peering exchanges.

Content Delivery Networks (CDNs) and Caching—Solving the Problem of Bogged-Down Web Sites

Content delivery networks improve Internet performance by placing Web pages in servers near users, at the edge of the Internet. They replicate data in thousands of servers around the world so that Web pages load faster on people's computers. This is referred to as *caching*. It is analogous to publishing documents and making them available to many "readers" at the same time.

The characteristics of the protocols used in the Internet make content delivery dispersed closer to end users important. If all the requests at busy sites such as Yahoo! went to one server it would result in server "meltdown." In TV networks, which are for the most part one-way, everyone receives programs at the same time. In contrast, the Internet is two-way and servers have the double task of sending and receiving. Servers send an acknowledgment for every request they receive. Moreover, data is not broadcast. It is sent individually to each user.

Distributing content results in fewer servers at content providers' sites and less bandwidth needed at central server sites. Because so much of the content originates in the United States, arranging data closer to end users is important in the rest of the world. Having content closer to client PCs saves bandwidth costs for local access providers, content suppliers and hosting companies. Content delivery networks are based on Layer 4 to Layer 7 protocols that can identify the origin of requests based on IP addresses assigned to access providers including cable modem, dialup and DSL providers.

Content delivery networks (CDNs) are based on two models. One is a service bureau model typified by offerings from Akamai and Digital Island (part of Cable & Wireless). Service bureaus sell to content providers (e.g., CNN, C-SPAN and MSN-BC.COM), organizations with busy sites (e.g., Symantec, Lands End and Barnes & Noble) and portals such as Yahoo! and Excite. Customers pay Akamai and Digital Island by the amount of traffic they handle. CDNs place their servers, usually at no charge, in network provider sites. These sites include cable companies' regional data centers and backbone Internet providers' points of presence (POPs). Akamai operates a worldwide network of 4000 servers located in providers' data centers. Content delivery networks design their networks with enough intelligence to determine, based on the IP address assigned to each user by his ISP, the most effective server from which to direct the traffic.

The other model is the sale of caching servers and switches to network service providers. Inktomi, Nortel (through its purchase of Alteon) and Cisco (through its purchase of ArrowPoint) sell caching hardware and software. Some suppliers call their equipment Web switches. Web switches route traffic based on content requested and are able to balance traffic between multiple servers so that no one server is bogged down and others are idle. Traffic management on these platforms is based on Layer 4 to Layer 7 equipment that analyzes headers and uniform resource locator (URL) requests. A *header* is the preliminary information in packets that contains sender information and routing instructions. Unlike content delivery networks, these companies sell directly to network service providers such as NTT, AT&T, BellSouth and hosting companies. For example, Inktomi supplies a server with special caching software included that is installed in data centers. (A data center is synonymous with a point of presence (POP), where carriers keep their switches or routers.) The server monitors traffic and if it sees a number of requests for a particular Web site it stores that content locally.

Internet Services

Prior to 1995 and the availability of the World Wide Web and browsers, using the Internet and sending email was done without menu-driven software. People who surfed the Internet did so via services such as FTP (File Transfer Protocol) and Telnet. They sent and received electronic mail through a service called Simple Mail Transfer Protocol (SMTP). All of these services relied on users knowing the commands of a computer language.

Researchers used File Transfer Protocol (FTP) to log onto computers at other sites, such as other universities, to retrieve files that were in text form. Graphics, video and voice files were not transmitted over the Internet. Moreover, finding information was a complex task. Researchers were able to search thousands of sites worldwide but commands had to be typed into the computer in an exact format. Dots, spaces and capitalization rules were strict. For example, "dir" let you see the contents of a directory, while "get filename" let you view the file on the computer screen. To simplify the search process, programs such as Archie were created. Archie was meant to simplify FTP use by enabling searches by topic. Gopher, a precursor to Web browsers and introduced in 1991 by the University of Minnesota, was more menu-driven than Archie but was bypassed after 1994 when Mosaic, an early World Wide Web browser, was developed.

Another service available to access information prior to the availability of browsers was Telnet. While File Transfer Protocol is a way to transfer a file, Telnet is an Internet service for creating an interactive session with a computer on a different network. Telnet enables users to log onto computers located on the Internet as if they were local terminals. People used Telnet with arcane commands such as "host name". They had to know the name of the remote computer they wished to log onto. Telnet and FTP are still used; however, access to them is via menu-driven browsers (e.g., Netscape Navigator and Internet Explorer).

THE WORLD WIDE WEB— LINKING AND GRAPHICS ....

The World Wide Web was conceived as a way to make using and navigating the Internet easier. It is not a separate part of the Internet, but a graphical way to use the Internet. The World Wide Web enables users to hear sound and see color, video and graphical representations of information. Moreover, it provides links to information using text and graphic images embedded in documents to "navigate" to other Web sites. These links are in the form of highlighted text and graphics. Users click on them with a mouse to move from one document to another or from one site to another. These two capabilities, linking and graphics, are the strengths of the World Wide Web.

The World Wide Web was created in 1989 by Tim Berners-Lee at CERN, the European Laboratory for Particle Physics. The goal of creating the Web was to merge the techniques of client-server networking and hypertext to make it easy to find information worldwide. The basic concept is that any type of client, the PC, should be able to find information without needing to know a particular computer language or without needing a particular type of terminal. Access is universal.

The name of the protocol used to link sites is Hypertext Transfer Protocol (HTTP). The letters, http, start Web addresses. When a browser sees http, it knows that this is an address for linking to another site.

Hypertext Markup Language (HTML)— Formatting Web Pages

Hypertext Markup Language, or HTML, made available in 1991, is the language that Web page creators use to write Web documents. HTML is the authoring software that controls the "look" of a Web page. Employees who write Web pages for their organizations' home pages use HTML commands. Each hypertext command begins and ends with the <> signs. For example, bolded text is prefaced with <b>. Early users had to know the commands themselves. New HTML word processing software used for creating Web pages has embedded HTML commands.

The fact that there is a standard way to write code for Web pages is significant. It means that corporations can buy software tools and hire outside software companies to develop Web sites for them that operate as an integrated whole.

eXtensible Markup Language (XML)— For E-commerce

eXtensible Markup Language (*XML*) is a Web markup language used to create standard "labels" or fields within Internet pages. Markup languages identify structures within documents. For example, they indicate if the information is part of the header, address field or the footnote. XML has tags within documents specifying the type of information, such as the part number, contained in the field. Using XML, vendors and customers can understand each other's part number even if they have different software packages. The tagged fields are also used for Web searches. For example, if fields are tagged as driving directions or telephone numbers, searches for driving directions or telephone numbers can identify them.

The World Wide Web Consortium (W3C) initially approved XML.1 as a basic standard. In 2001 it approved XML schemas. XML schemas provide more detail than XML.1 for defining fields in documents such as purchase orders (POs) so that they can be exchanged between organizations for purposes such as e-commerce. For example, schemas in purchase orders are defined for ship to, bill to and comment fields. Schemas also will aid in database searches. Industry consortia are meeting to agree on tags for their particular industry. For example, RosettaNet, a nonprofit group made up of 300 members in electronic components, telecommunications and computer systems is setting standards for that industry.

XML and variations of XML are key ingredients of e-commerce. Programs written in XML provide a vehicle for exchanging data and searching for data. For example, once tags for fields such as purchase order numbers, addresses, quantities and prices are agreed on, companies can exchange purchase orders electronically. Alternatively, software that can translate particular suppliers' enterprise resource planning (ERP) into XML schemas can be used to make purchase orders or order tracking between companies with different ERP programs compatible. (ERP software links organizations' back-office functions together. It may link human resource, payroll, accounts payable, accounts receivable and inventory management systems.)

Home Pages

A *home page* is the first page that users see when they visit an organization or individual's Web site, and is a document created with Web-authoring software such as Hypertext Markup Language. All Web pages are linked together with hypertext links. The links are the highlighted pieces of text that represent addresses that transfer surfers to another site or page with the click of a mouse. The addresses are uniform resource locators (URLs).

Improvements in Web Page Designs

When organizations and individuals initially set up home pages on the Internet, they were "brochure-ware." They replicated brochures and marketing communications literature without taking advantage of the multimedia capabilities of the Web. Web page designs have become more varied and suited to the Web's medium. They employ video, audio and streaming music. Web page development using animation and broadcasting have become more streamlined. Software development tools such as Macromedia's Flash™ and Microsoft's Media™ Technologies and Media™ programs have made site development easier. Some of these products have the capability to query and test end users' Internet connections. If they have slow connections, the audio but not the video is played. Likewise, if the user does not have Flash, the design created by Flash is not used. People that view these pages need programs such as QuickTime™ and RealPlayer™ to view and listen to the streaming media content. Web pages also have portable document format (PDF) documents embedded in them so that surfers with any type of computer can view graphics-rich documents as long as they have an Adobe Reader™ installed on their computer.

Dynamic Web Application Servers

Web application servers have software that enables dynamic creation of Web pages based on surfers' queries. The corporate logo and page templates with the elements that are the same for every page are stored on the application server and the information elements are stored in the database. This is different than static Web pages with content and logos or page layouts stored in one server. In static Web sites, the content is part of every page. If there is a change made to the logo, company name or "button" layout, each page on the Web site must be changed.

The appeal of dynamic Web application servers such as Macromedia's Cold Fusion and Microsoft's Web Logic is that they work with databases and operating systems from multiple vendors. They translate between Web servers and customer databases that are in formats such as Oracle and SQL. (See Figure 8.1.) With dynamic Web application servers, surfers ask for information on certain products in a catalog and receive a Web page with the information. The dynamic Web application server stores templates (forms) that the dynamic Web application server populates with information from the database. They send the filled-in template back to the Web server to be viewed by the customer that initiated the request. Dynamic Web application servers can be located on separate servers or on the same computer as the Web server.

Updating Web Pages—Content Management Software

Keeping Web sites current and accurate is a major task. Often, the sites that hypertext links connect users to become defunct or change their addresses. This results in read-

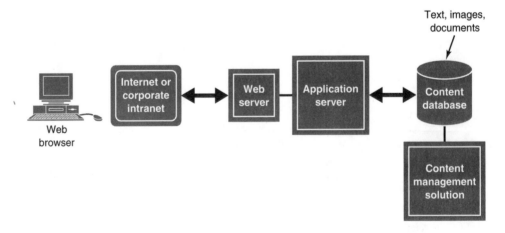

Figure 8.1
Web server, application server, content management software and content database. Figure courtesy of Ektron, Inc.

ers clicking on highlighted text and getting back an error message. Organizations need to post new press releases, financial reports and product updates to keep their sites up-to-date. Without a user-friendly interface, managers need to know how to use HTML software to make changes. This often results in backlogs within the corporate computer departments tasked with keeping Web sites current. Very large companies often hire outside companies to make their changes or purchase expense software that provides a user-friendly browser-type interface to make changes.

New affordable, off-the-shelf packages are now available for smaller and mid-sized companies. They often feature pull-down menus that operate in a similar fashion to word processing programs. Programs like those from Ektron, Inc., geared to small and medium-sized companies, let staff preview and review changes with management before scheduling a time when the change goes "live" on the Web site. In addition, the program stores copies of both the new and old version of Web pages. In essence, the content management software is an authoring tool for Web changes. It runs in conjunction with dynamic Web application servers. Companies such as Broadvision, Eprise, Interwoven, Vignette and Computer Associates sell content management software.

Hosting—Computers Connected to the Internet with Home Pages

A Web server is the computer on which Web page documents are located. The World Wide Web was designed without any centralized facility. Anyone who wishes to may make information available to the Internet community. They can "publish" documents on the Web. The World Wide Web is based on a client-server model. The client is the device—usually a PC that reads information such as Web pages. Clients in the form of set-top boxes and wireless handheld devices also can access the Web. The server is a computer sized to the requirements of the application or documents it is "hosting," as seen in Figure 8.2.

Because of the cost of providing the telephone connections to the Internet and the security to keep hackers out of non-Internet computer files, hosting often is done at an Internet service provider, carrier or hosting company's site. Residential home pages generally are at Internet service provider sites such as AOL, Excite, MSN or at portals such as Yahoo! or Lycos. Examples of companies that provide specialized hosting services are Genuity, Sprint, Verio, Inc. and Exodus Communications, Inc.

Examples of Web pages at host sites are MSNBC broadcasts, online newspapers and various e-commerce sites.

There are various levels of hosting. For example, a customer can supply the hosting company with text, pictures and information, and the host company builds the Web pages on the host's computer. In other cases, the customer designs and creates the Web pages on her own computer. The customer places the computer within a cage at the host's data center. Security, reliability and capacity of telephone connections

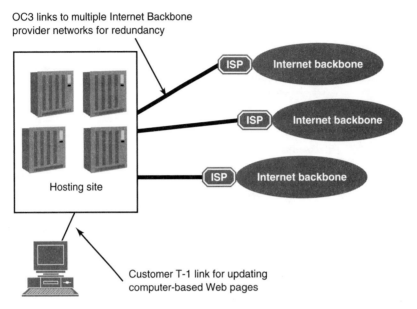

OC3 links to multiple Internet Backbone
provider networks for redundancy

Hosting site

Customer T-1 link for updating
computer-based Web pages

Figure 8.2
Connections between the Internet and hosting companies.

and round-the-clock maintenance and support are reasons that organizations outsource Internet services. Most telephone companies provide hosting as well as Internet backbone service.

Large hosting companies rent high-speed connections such as OC3, 155-mega-
bit links to the Internet from their on-site routers. (Refer to Figure 8.2.) The computers
in the hosting company's data center share these links. Each computer does not need
its own telephone line to the Internet. The hosting company monitors the security so
that hackers do not compromise the data in the Web pages.

Browsers—Moving from Web Site to Web Site

Browsers installed on PCs create graphical interfaces for accessing and navigating the
World Wide Web. Without browsers, users had to be knowledgeable enough to use
computer commands to find sites on the Internet. With browsers, people can go directly to an organization's home page by typing an address or clicking on a bookmark.
Because of their ease of use and proliferation, browser interfaces have become the
preferred method of accessing many types of documents inside organizations on cor-

porate intranets. (See "Intranets—Impact of Web Technology on Internal Operations" later in this chapter.)

The first browser, Mosaic, was created by the National Center for Supercomputing Applications at the University of Illinois and Europe's CERN (the European Laboratory for Particle Physics) research laboratory. Mosaic was created with government funding and was intended to be a standards-based Web browser. However, the University of Illinois did not have the staff to provide user support for the browser and gave the license to Spyglass, Inc. to commercialize. In return, the university expected Spyglass to pay it royalties from sales of Mosaic. However, Jim Clark of Silicon Graphics and people who created the Mosaic browser at the University of Illinois started Netscape Communications. Netscape Navigator eclipsed Mosaic and was a significant step away from government standards and toward commercialization of the Internet.

Netscape's strategy was to set its own *de facto* standard by flooding the market with free copies of Netscape Navigator. Netscape envisioned selling Web page design tools later that would cost from $1500 to $50,000. Netscape Communications also spawned sales of software programs called plug-ins to work with its browser.

Meanwhile, not to be outdone, Microsoft introduced its own browser, Internet Explorer, in 1995. In 1996 Microsoft reached an agreement with AOL whereby AOL agreed to use Microsoft's browser software. Furthermore, in an attempt to control the browser market, Microsoft installed Internet Explorer on all of its new Windows™ PCs. In November 1998, AOL announced its intent to purchase Netscape.

Earlier in 1998, the Justice Department sued Microsoft, accusing it of bundling its browser with Microsoft Windows operating system and thwarting competition in the Web software market from companies such as Apple Computer, Netscape, Intel Corporation and Sun Microsystems. The government's case rested on the fact that Microsoft had a monopoly in operating systems and was using it to stifle competition. One of the government's contentions is that Microsoft used its monopoly in operating systems to persuade AOL to distribute its browser. In return, Microsoft put AOL on its Windows desktop. The courts ruled against Microsoft. They ruled that Microsoft has to separate its operating system business from application sales business. Microsoft appealed the ruling.

In June 2001, a federal appeals court reversed the breakup of Microsoft but agreed with the lower court that Microsoft maintains an illegal monopoly in computer operating systems and illegally squelched competitors. The federal appeals court further concluded that Microsoft should face further hearings as to whether it illegally bundled its Web browser with its operating system. In July 2001, the U.S. Court of Appeals refused to rehear the case, and Microsoft stated that it might appeal to the Supreme Court. Because Microsoft's new Windows XP operating system is integrated with its browser and Internet capabilities, a future ruling finding its bundling illegal, will greatly hamper its current strategy. Microsoft now has over 80% of browser sales in the United States.

Hailstorm—A Notification and E-commerce Vehicle from Microsoft

In 2001, Microsoft announced a new feature for its Windows XP upgraded operating system called HailStorm. HailStorm is a "pop-up" notification that will appear on users' screens notifying them of events such as delayed airline flights, online concert ticket availability and email chat messages. Some HailStorm services, such as online ticketing, may eventually be revenue-producing, fee-based services. HailStorm also will let users forward messages between unlike devices such as wireless handsets and computers. HailStorm is an example of the way bundling an operating system and a browser can give an advantage to Microsoft.

Passport is a central feature of HailStorm, which allows users to log onto multiple Web sites and services using a common password and username. Privacy experts worry about one central company knowing users' buying habits. Microsoft will give users the option of not allowing information about themselves to be released. Microsoft hopes to generate income by licensing the software to developers who will create applications that will work with HailStorm. For example, Web site owners may develop applications linking their sites to consumers using Passport.

EMAIL—COMPUTERS THAT SEND, STORE AND RECEIVE MESSAGES.....................................

Email is a major factor in consumers' motivation to use the Internet. Often consumers purchase computers so that they can send email to children, grandchildren and distant relatives. According to the February 23, 2001 issue of *Messaging Online's Messaging Today*, the number of electronic mailboxes worldwide grew 67% to 891.1 million from 1999 to 2000. The article estimated that 58% of the population in the United States uses email (three quarters of workers and 45% of non-workers). Also, for the first time more mailboxes, 51%, existed outside of the United States than inside. *Messaging Today* attributed this to the growth of wireless mailboxes in Japan. Wireless email accounted for 31.8 million of the 891.1 million mailboxes.

Electronic mail is the computer-based storage and forwarding of text-based messages. Ray Tomlinson, an engineer at BBN in Cambridge, Massachusetts, invented electronic mail in 1972. BBN, then Bolt Beranek and Newman, had built the first Internet network, ARPANET, and users of ARPANET needed a way to communicate with each other. Standard electronic mail used on the Internet is based on Simple Mail Transfer Protocol (SMTP), which is part of the suite of protocols called TCP/IP.

SMTP specifies addressing conventions. For example, the @ sign differentiates between the user's name and his computer. SMTP also specifies how to address mail to multiple locations, ways to copy other people and the fact that ASCII code is used.

Email characters are sent in ASCII, the American Standard Code for Information Interchange code. ASCII code, which translates computer bits into characters, has a limited number of characters. It initially only supported all of the upper- and lower-case letters of the alphabet, numbers and symbols such as *, $, underlining and %. ASCII, however, does not include formatting options such as italics, bolding and columns. If a word processing file is copied and pasted into an email message, it loses its formatting.

Newer email programs bundled with browsers now support Hypertext Markup Language (HTML) formatting. HTML commands enable special formatting such as embedded graphics, colors and unusual fonts to be included in messages. Netscape, Eudora and Internet Explorer email can read HTML commands when they are embedded in email messages. The newest version of AOL browsers, 6.0, also can read the HTML but AOL 5.0 cannot. The advent of HTML-capable email programs has increased the potential of email as a marketing tool.

Email initially was used as a business tool within corporations. Businesses now connect their email servers to the Internet. They use email to check the status of projects, follow up on proposals and check on orders. Email is faster and less intrusive than a telephone call. A telephone call is an interruption, whereas email is stored and can be reviewed when convenient. Users can pick up their email at scheduled times during the day. Unlike voice mail, email provides a hard copy record of communication. As companies where email messages are used against them in trials know, this can be a mixed blessing. Both Chevron and Microsoft have been hurt in trials where email messages were used in evidence against them.

Email has significantly changed the nature of business communications. The following quote from an email message by Toni Profetto, Administration Manager, New Balance Athletic Shoe Company, typifies this change:

I'll talk to you (via e-mail since no one talks anymore) tomorrow.

Email Attachments—To Aid Collaborative Projects

Firms use email services to exchange more than ASCII text messages. Companies exchange spreadsheets, graphics, PowerPoint and word processing documents with consultants, remote employees and business partners. Sending attachments has become the *de facto* way people exchange documents. One standard for sending attachments is multipurpose Internet mail extensions (MIME). The MIME standard can be used for voice, video and graphics programs. MIME enables users to send video, foreign language and audio file attachments.

The MIME standard includes a way to attach bits at the beginning and end of the attachment. These bits tell the receiving computer what type of file is attached and when the attachment ends. For example, the bits may tell the computer, "This is a Microsoft Word for Windows file." The receiving computer then opens the document as a Word file. MIME does not entirely solve the attachment problem. The sending and receiving computers need compatible software platforms and programs for reading attachments. Some early releases of spreadsheet and word processing programs cannot open newer versions of these programs.

Two concerns with attachments are viruses and Internet access speeds. Residential users with dialup connections experience long delays when they receive large multimedia attachments. Moreover, some of these attachments contain viruses. *Viruses* are software programs written to damage computer files. Straight-text email messages cannot "pollute" PCs with viruses. However, a virus included in attachments can harm files when the attachment is opened from within programs. Viruses can wipe out the entire content of a PC's hard drive. As new viruses are discovered, virus protection software is updated and if installed at user sites, can warn people that they have received an attachment with a virus. Some virus protection software blocks the transmission of files containing known viruses.

HTML Email as a Marketing Tool

Email is a fast, inexpensive and effective way to reach customers. According to Cambridge Massachusetts market research firm Forrester Research, it costs $1 to mail a catalog and only 5¢ to send a marketing email message. According to Forrester, about 10% of people respond to marketing email messages and about a quarter of these people make a purchase. These statistics were reported in the article, "You Want Repeat Customers? Try E-Mail," published in *The New York Times Online*, 18 April 2001, by Bernard Stampler. Retailers such as Nordstrom, Lands End, Amazon.com and others regularly send promotional email messages. Palm Computing uses email to notify customers of software upgrades, add-ons and bugs in their operating system. Specialized email providers such as Responsys.com, USA.NET, Inc. and FloNetwork have servers from which they email millions of promotional messages for clients.

A large reason for email's impact is the fact that much of it is sent with Hypertext Markup Language (HTML) commands capable of adding special formatting to email. The email messages have commands embedded in the text files for specialized fonts, Web links, color and placement of images. Thus email contains links to retailers' sites, JPEG pictures, specialized fonts and color backgrounds. Some contain synthesized voice messages that speak their message when recipients click on them. Email messages with images for catalog items and corporate logos contain large amounts of data. When they're sent to residential consumers with dialup Internet connections they download slowly.

Some companies promote their services and stay in touch with contacts through specialized newsletters they send via email. Application service providers (ASPs) such as iMakeNews furnish newsletter templates that customers fill in via the Internet. iMakeNews stores and sends the first page of the newsletters for its clients as email messages. Recipients that wish to read the rest of the newsletter click on a link to iMakeNews' server located at a hosting company. Because early versions of AOL can't read the HTML formatting, iMakeNews is developing software that knows if a recipient has the latest version of AOL's email, so that the newsletter can be formatted accordingly. The use of email for mass mailing is lowering postal revenues.

Instant Messaging—Real-Time Text Chats

Instant messaging (IM) is the ability to exchange messages electronically in near real-time with other people also signed on to the Internet. With instant messaging, a window pops up on people's computers, letting them know who in their chat group is on-line. AOL calls people in the same chat group "buddies." AOL has 80% of the instant messaging market. Instant Messenger software, AOL's product that works independently of its ISP service, has 61 million registered users. Its ISP-based product (ICQ, short for "I seek you"), has 87 million users. AOL acquired ICQ in June 1998 when it purchased rival Israeli instant messaging provider Mirabilis Ltd., the developer of ICQ. AOL's two instant messaging systems are incompatible with each other. The next largest providers of instant messaging software are MSN with its Messenger service, which has 18 million registered users, and Yahoo! Messenger with 10.6 million users.

The large number of people using instant messaging has attracted advertisers. An analyst with investment bank ING Barings LLC estimated that by September 2000, AOL had a backlog of about $100 million in ads for its ICQ instant messaging service. AOL charges advertisers $5 per thousand of times an ad is displayed to users. This information was published in the article, "Pop-Up for Profit for AOL," published in *Washington.com*, 9 January 2001, by Alec Klein. Because teenagers are the largest users of public instant messaging, many of these ads are aimed at young people.

Chat rooms, a feature of instant messaging, often are organized around common interests such as travel and music. People come into and out of the chat room using a name (handle) they select. Users have a split screen, an area for viewing messages and one for typing messages. Chat isn't real-time because participants have an opportunity to type and edit messages before they send them. It's not real-time also in the sense that people see each character as it is typed.

Internet Relay Chat—The Basis for Instant Messaging

Instant messaging based on Internet relay chat (IRC) protocol has been available since the 1980s. Jarkko Oikarinen of Finland designed Internet relay chat in 1988. Internet relay chat (IRC) protocol is based on a client-server model with "channels" defined in the IRC protocol. A *channel* is the path defined to carry messages to chat rooms or "buddy" lists where everyone receives the same message. The IRC protocol defines how a group of clients (end-user computers) all receive the same message from the server to which they're all connected. Chat programs relay a message from single users to a predefined group. This is feasible because IRC is based on TCP/IP, which can deliver packets containing the same message to many computers. Each client that is part of the IRC group of networks downloads special client Internet relay chat software.

Prior to the commercialization of chat by AOL and Yahoo!, chat networks such as EFNet, DALNet and the Undernet were used by thousands of people that logged on through their Internet service provider. Users of IRC typed computer commands such as **/join#Newbies** to join the Newbies chat group. Portal operators such as Excite offered chat as did individual operators. Many of the personal groups were sexual in nature. In the mid-1990s, organizations developed proprietary chat software that was easier to use but did not initially interoperate with each other. Currently, except for AOL, many providers have made their services compatible with each other.

Instant Messaging Interoperability and Future Features

When they approved the AOL Time Warner merger, regulators required that AOL make its instant messaging services compatible with competitors when AOL offers advanced (broadband) services such as videoconferencing in conjunction with instant messaging. With this feature users watching a video, can chat with others also watching the same video. To preserve its lead in instant messaging, AOL has blocked interoperability. In the summer of 1999, MSN and Yahoo! made their messenger services compatible with AOL's service. However, AOL blocked the compatibility by slightly changing its software. To date, AOL has no plans for broadband instant messaging services.

The Internet Engineering Task Force (IETF) has sponsored a working group, Instant Messaging and Presence Protocol (IMPP), to define protocols for interoperable instant messaging and end-user awareness notification. End-user awareness notification lets users know when others in their "channel" are online. All providers of instant messaging (even AOL) have stated that they will support compatibility between products but AOL has stated it will take a long time to work out security and compatibility issues.

Microsoft, who has been gaining IM market share, is embedding Windows Messenger, its instant messaging in its new Windows XP operating system. Prior releases of Windows software included AOL software. Now that AOL and Microsoft compete in instant messaging and as Internet service providers, Microsoft has not yet reached an agreement to include AOL software in its new operating system. It's not known if AOL will continue to use Microsoft's Internet Explorer as the browser that it supplies its customers.

In the future, instant messaging (IM) may be used for revenue-generating applications such as virtual gaming, telephone service and chats on wireless phones. Windows Messenger will support real-time audio, application sharing and videoconferencing. With real-time voice over Internet (VoIP) improvements, instant messaging has the potential to become a vehicle for placing calls over the Internet. For example, AOL's Instant Messenger turns the Buddy List into a speed-dial directory, which could be used to place calls over the Internet. Tom Laemmel, product manager for Microsoft Windows, was quoted in the article, "Microsoft Plans to Add Instant-Messaging to Windows XP as Talks with AOL Falter," published in *The Wall Street Journal WSJ.com*, 5 June 2001, by Rebecca Buckman and Julia Angwin. He characterized Windows Messenger as a:

> *...unified client for doing audio, video conferencing, application sharing... The important thing, really, is it's not just an instant-messaging client, it's a real-time communications client.*

Commercial Applications for Chat—Training and Presentations

Online chat software is often integrated into online collaboration, document-sharing tools for distance learning, training and sales presentations. For example, in online sales presentations the moderator uses PowerPoint to illustrate products or services. At some point in the presentation, the moderator signals that users can submit comments or questions. Users' comments and moderator responses appear in the bottom portion of the computer screen and the PowerPoint demonstration is in the top. (See Chapter 5 for document sharing.) Chat technology also is used for one-to-one customer service and technical support for e-commerce applications.

In addition, companies such as Lotus, Microsoft and Novell include instant messaging in software they sell enterprises. Enterprises that use private instant messaging install servers with the software. The server links to a Lightweight Directory Access Protocol (LDAP)–compatible or Lotus Notes list of email addresses. LDAP is a protocol that defines a standard layout for directories and a standard method of accessing them.

INTERNET SERVICE PROVIDERS, APPLICATION SERVICE PROVIDERS AND PORTALS.......................

Internet service providers (ISPs) sell Internet access, domain registration, email, Web page hosting, Web page design and other Internet services such as security for extranets (discussed later in this chapter). Examples of Internet service providers are Genuity, WorldCom, Sprint, AT&T WorldNet, MindSpring, NetZero, Excite@Home and Road Runner.

ISPs support both dialup and dedicated Internet access. Dialup access is either analog plain old telephone service (POTS) or ISDN digital dialup. ISDN is a digital service that provides two telephone lines for either voice or data plus a signaling link all over one pair of wires. (See Chapter 6.) Examples of dedicated services are cable modems, satellite, DSL, T-1 and T-3 services. Dedicated services enable customers to reach the Internet without dialing a call. They are "always on."

Dialup and Dedicated Internet Access

To reach the Internet, users with dialup service program their modem to dial the local telephone number associated with their ISP. The call is routed to their telephone company's central office, which sends it to the central office connected to their ISP's equipment. Most Internet service providers use competitive local exchange providers (CLECs) for this service. Internet service providers have banks of modems in remote access server (RAS) devices that handle calls handed off from telephone company central offices. The Internet service provider's equipment is often collocated with competitive local exchange carriers' (CLECs) central offices. (See Figure 8.3.) Each CLEC central office is connected to incumbent telephone companies' switches by high-speed T-3, 45 megabits per second (Mbps) trunks. The ISP has links directly to

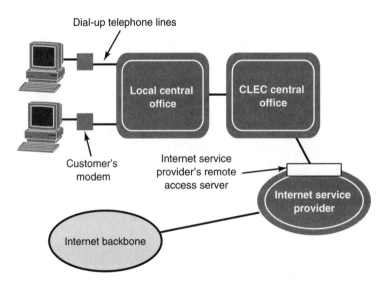

Figure 8.3
A dialup connection to an Internet service provider.

the Internet from the CLEC office or to a regional data center that is connected to the Internet. Some ISPs, such as Genuity, act as wholesalers and provide these connections to other ISPs as well as to end users.

In order to expand the number of points in which they have dial-in service, some Internet service providers partner with each other. An ISP will resell capacity at its site to another ISP that has no equipment in that particular city.

Most medium and large (and even small) businesses find that they need the capacity and convenience of high-speed dedicated access such as T-1, E-1, E-3 and T-3 service or new Gigabit Ethernet service. T-3 is very costly and only used by very large enterprises. All of these services, which range in speed from 1.54 megabits per second to 45 megabits per second are described in Chapter 6. The ISP arranges for a telephone company to run the T-1 line from the customer to the ISP premises.

The ISP data centers have email servers and routers with Internet connections. Large ISPs such as NaviPath, Splitrock (part of McCleodUSA) and Genuity offer business-to-business service such as Web design and Web page hosting in addition to their ISP service. These data centers aggregate customer traffic and send them to Internet backbone providers over high-speed links. Competitive local exchange carriers also operate Internet data centers for commercial organizations and for Internet service providers.

The Demise of Free ISP Service

Many Internet companies offered free ISP service as a way to attract customers to their sites and to build brand recognition. It was anticipated that Web traffic would attract advertising revenue and "click through" fees when users at the free site clicked on a retailer's link. At one time AltaVista, Juno Online Services, NetZero, WorldSpy, Freewwweb and BlueLight.com offered free Internet access. By May 2001, AltaVista had dropped its ISP service and WorldSpy and Freewwweb had declared bankruptcy. BlueLight.com and NetZero are providing only a limited number of hours at no fee and charging for usage above the limit. Ad rates for ISP sites, which have dropped from $50 to $75 per thousand of viewers to $3 to $5, are a major factor in the failure of free ISP service. Because of lowered revenues, Juno and NetZero are combining resources by merging.

The relatively low monthly fees for dialup service for other ISPs have forced them to find other sources of revenue in addition to subscription fees. Main sources of revenue are advertising, commissions on goods bought from ads at the ISP site and transaction fees for services. Juno announced a joint project with researchers at the Space Science Laboratory of the University of California through LaunchCyte LLC. Under the program, Juno's customers' computers will process data for the Seti@homeproject which uses home computers to anaylze research data for medical data when the computers are turned on but the screen saver is active. AOL, which depends on advertising revenues and e-commerce fees, has raised its monthly fee by 9% from $21.95 to $23.95.

Application Service Providers (ASPs)

Application service providers act as service bureaus by renting software to corporations. The types of software they furnish range from voice messaging, database and payroll processing to e-commerce and customer relationship management (CRM) for managing Web and voice-based traffic to call centers. ASPs also provide Internet-based hosting of Web pages and billing type services to network service providers. The application service provider sector is new and revenues are still low. Some of their services overlap with those of hosting companies.

Some of these companies refer to themselves as application infrastructure providers (AIPs). Application infrastructure providers build the data centers and manage the infrastructure in which Internet service providers and application service providers keep their equipment. They also will arrange for network connections at the data centers they manage.

Portals—Content as Well as Internet Access

Portals are the first sites that customers see when they go online. They are the "door" to the Internet. The goal of portals is to earn money on advertising and a percentage on the sale of goods sold at the portal. Portals attempt to attract large numbers of users and keep them there. One way portals attract users is by gearing their content to particular communities of interest. For example, Tripod is targeted at college students and iVillage is directed at women. They offer free email, content, search engines, home pages, instant messaging, calendaring and chat services to attract users. They also offer information such as news, sports statistics and personal finance. Portals purchase content from content suppliers such as SportsLine.com that distribute sports news, commentary scores and statistics as well as audio and video coverage of events. SportsLine.com operates its own site as well as supplying content to AOL and Excite@Home. SportsLine.com has sites in Singapore and London. TicketMaster, 68% of which is owned by USA Networks, supplies syndicated information and online ticketing to portals and other Web sites from its Citysearch operation.

In an effort to enlarge their presence on the Web and attract traffic, broadcasters and companies with existing Internet businesses have bought and merged with portal providers. Large newspapers also have sites on the Internet most of which, with the exception of *The Wall Street Journal*, offer free access to their site. They do charge for copies of archived articles and receive revenue for classified advertising and ads.

More media sites, such as Inside.comand Britannica.com, are starting to charge fees for access to their information. Table 8.1 lists the most popular Web sites.

Table 8.1 Major Internet Web and Portal Sites

Internet Service Providers	Users in Millions, June 2001*	Comments
AOL	30	Owned by AOL Time Warner. Owns Netscape Communications Corp., AOL MovieFone, CompuServe, Digital City, iPlanet E-Commerce Solutions, MapQuest.com, three Internet music firms and Time Warner properties such as *Time Magazine*, Time Warner Cable, Home Box Office, Turner Broadcasting System and Warner Music Group. AOL also operates, with partners, ISP service worldwide in Latin America, Europe and Asia. The 30 million subscribers include CompuServe and international customers.
EarthLink, Inc.	5.0	EarthLink sells dialup and DSL Internet access. Some of its growth is attributable to its purchase of smaller ISPs such as MindSpring and OneMain.com. Sprint owns 29% of EarthLink. It's attempting to provide ISP service over cable TV facilities.
MSN	5.0	Microsoft built up its subscriber base by offering a $400 rebate to computer purchasers who signed up for MSN service. The rebate offer has been discontinued. Also owns Internet travel service CarPoint (Internet car-buying classifieds), Expedia, Hotmail, MSNBC, TransPoint (Internet bill delivery and payment) and WebTV.
Juno Online	4.0	Offers limited number of hours monthly of free ISP service with ad banners or paid service without banners. Also sells Covad-operated DSL service and in a few areas, cable modem access through Time Warner Cable. Merging with NetZero. New company to be called United Online.
NetZero, Inc.	3.5	NetZero provides mostly free email in return for demographic information about users that it sells to marketing firms. It also earns fees from ad revenue on its site. It now offers unlimited ad-free paid service. NetZero is purchasing Juno. The new company will be named United Online, Inc and will have a total of 7 million customers, 1 million of them paying customers.

Table 8.1   Major Internet Web and Portal Sites *(continued)*

Internet Service Providers	Users in Millions, June 2001*	Comments
Excite@ Home	3.0	ISP for cable TV providers Comcast, Cablevision Systems, Cox Cable and AT&T Broadband. Owned by AT&T Broadband.
BlueLight. com	2.8	The partially free Internet service is an adjunct to its online sales business. Online discount retailer owned by Kmart. To jump-start sales, Kmart sells low-priced PCs bundled with BlueLight Internet access software.
Other Popular Sites	**Search Sites Which Generate High Amounts of Traffic**	
Yahoo!	The Yahoo! portal offers free email, chat, search engine, directory, news, online classifieds and shopping service. It also offers portal development service to enterprises through partnerships with software and database companies. Yahoo!, Inc. is independent. It has international operations through partnerships and directly in Latin America, Asia and Europe.	
Terra Lycos S.A.	Terra Lycos owns Tripod, HotBot, WhoWhere directory service, Angelfire.com, Gamesville.com and *Wired News. Terra Lycos is controlled by Spain's incumbent telephone company, Telefonica. Terra Lycos has ISP, instant messaging and e-commerce operations in 41 countries.*	
eBay	eBay has the most trafficked auction sites on the Internet. eBay charges fees to users to list and purchase items. It has chat rooms, bulletin boards and a vehicle for user feedback about buyers and sellers. It also offers auction services to small businesses. It has sites throughout Europe, Australia, New Zealand and Japan.	
About, the Human Internet	About, Inc. operates these 700 Web sites, each of which is managed by experts and focuses on a single topic. It also has Internet classifieds, email newsletters and chat rooms. It generates its revenues from advertising and e-commerce partnerships such as those with e-Bay and BMG Music. It has service in Australia, Canada, India, Ireland and the UK. Magazine publisher Primedia owns About, Inc.	
CNET Networks	Operates informational Web sites CNET.com, Builder.com, Computers.com and comparison shopping service mySimon.com as well as ZDNet Web sites, which have information about technology for consumers.	

Table 8.1   Major Internet Web and Portal Sites *(continued)*

Other Popular Sites	Search Sites Which Generate High Amounts of Traffic
Amazon. com	Amazon.com is the leading online provider of books, videos and music. It also sells computers, electronic items, software, tools and hardware and provides auctions. It operates the Toys "R" Us and Border's Web sites. In addition to the English language site, it has foreign-language sites in France and Japan and distribution facilities in Germany and England.
iWon, Inc.	Web portal offering a sweepstakes to visitors. Users click on site links to enter the sweepstakes. Revenues derived from advertising and e-commerce fees. Its portal offers news, weather, sports and free email.
Walt Disney Internet Group	Formerly Go.com; operates Disney Web sites including Disney Online, Disney's catalog and online retail operation, ESPN.com and ABC.com. It produces and maintains Web sites for the NFL, NBA and NASCAR.
X10.com	X10.com is a retail site that offers hip, easily networked, wireless, remote controlled video and surveillance and PC controlled audio and video devices for homes, small businesses and college students' dorm rooms. It is owned by Hong Kong–based X10 Wireless Technology, Inc.
Flipside	Operates online entertainment and gaming in the United States, France and the UK. Owned by Vivendi Universal publishing, which uses the content on its Vizzavi portal. Flipside is purchasing online gaming company Uproar.
InfoSpace, Inc.	InfoSpace offers syndicated content such as news, weather and sports and searchable databases for yellow pages listings. It also distributes online games and calendars. Its information and services are on over 3200 affiliated sites. Its sites include Dogpile.com and Silicon Investor. It has agreements to provide content for wireless companies Cingular and Verizon.
NBC Internet	Nbci.com offers information and streaming content such as animated shorts as well as free email. Revenues are from site advertising, e-commerce from on-site shopping links and direct marketing services. NBC plans to fold NBC Internet into its main operations because of low earnings.

Internet service provider statistics from the June 8, 2001 The Wall Street Journal WSJ.com "NetZero, Juno to Merge, Creating No. 2 Web-Access Provider in U.S." by Julia Angwin.

SEARCH ENGINES ....

A search engine is a site that searches the Internet based on words that users enter. According to WSJ Market Data Group, Tradeline.com, as reported in *The Wall Street Journal WSJ.com* "Reality Bytes" on January 8, 2001, 72% of consumers find online shopping information through search engines. Some search engines capitalize on this and charge companies a fee for an advantageous placement in search results. Search engines such as GoTo.com rely on paid placements. For example, if someone searches for a retail product, the responses to her query will be listed in descending order depending on the fee paid to the search engine. Yahoo! charges for listings but only in its searches for retail products. Some search engines also get paid every time a user clicks on a link to a sponsor's site. Other search engines such as Northern Lights and Google do not accept paid listings. They do accept advertising but their ranking is based on the results of their searches and is independent of the advertising.

Background

Prior to the advent of the World Wide Web, users, mainly academicians and scientists who searched for information on the Internet, used specialized programs such as Archie, Gopher, Jughead and Veronica. Archie, short for archives, used File Transport Protocol (FTP) to create lists of servers containing files about particular topics. Prior to the availability of Archie, people searching for a topic had to know the exact IP address of the computer on which it was located. With Archie, people typed in keywords and Archie returned locations in the UNIX format that identified the host name, the file location and the directory name. Users would then use FTP to transfer files identified by Archie. Another of these programs, Gopher, while more menu driven, still relied on knowledge of UNIX commands but allowed for a rudimentary form of bookmarks to go directly to a file. In addition to being difficult to use, searches were limited to university- and government-sponsored sites and results were not context sensitive.

Once the World Wide Web and browsers were available, more user friendly search engines were developed and the number of sites that could be searched mushroomed. Early search engines Lycos, Yahoo! and WebCrawler started operating in 1994. In 1995, Excite, AltaVista and Infoseek (now part of Go.com, owned by Disney) debuted. AltaVista originally was owned and developed by Digital Equipment Corporation before it was bought by Compaq, who later sold it to CMGI. AltaVista was very fast for its time and was the first search engine to use natural language. It could understand queries with terms such as what if. It further included instructions for using Boolean terminology to refine searches—and, if and or terms used for computer logic. (Boolean logic is named after a 19th century mathematician.)

However, many of these search engines listed the names of thousands of sites when users requested searches. Often the sites in the list were not relevant to the topic and the list contained no site descriptions. Newer search engines use sophisticated methods to rank sites and to determine site relevancy. Inktomi innovated the use of clustered work stations rather than standalone computers to achieve faster searches. Servers in clusters can communicate simultaneously so that searches can be completed faster than with single servers.

Search Engines Today

Popular search engines include Ask Jeeves, Inc., Northern Light, HotBot, AltaVista, Google and LookSmart. Many of the largest search engines such as Excite and Yahoo! are portals as well with features such as news, entertainment information and weather services. Most of the major search engines license their technologies to portals and Internet service providers. For example, Yahoo! uses the Google engine. AOL Search, HotBot and iWon use Inktomi as their search engines.

There also are specialized information service providers on the Internet that charge for their services and offer more specialized information. For example, Northern Light Technology, Inc. offers search services and news information to businesses. EoExchange, Inc. also offers premium search services on specific topics.

How Search Engines Work

Search engines create databases of either the first page of a Web site or all of the sites' pages through automated software programs called spiders or bots (short for robot). (These are different terms for the same process.) A *spider* will "crawl" from site to site looking for key phrases or URLs. When it completes the search, it creates indexes (lists) of the pages. When people do searches, it lists them in a particular order using proprietary algorithms. The order in which pages are listed is called *ranking*. Factors used in ranking include how frequently terms are used, location of terms within the document (in the title or in the headers, etc.) and the number of pages at a site that use the term searched for. Other external factors may be used such as how many other sites link to the site, how often visitors "click" on a site (visit it) and placement fees. Pay-for-placement, which was pioneered by GoTo.com, is now a factor at America Online, Lycos, AltaVista and parts of Microsoft's MSN and others. LookSmart and Inktomi also charge a fee if companies such as retailers want individual pages listed for particular products.

Search engines are either meta-based, use spiders or are natural language–based.

- Meta-based search engines, also called metasearch sites, such as Dogpile.com, Mamma, SavvySearch and MetaCrawler search multiple search engines and compile them into a list for searchers.

SEARCHING ON THE WEB—GOOGLE

Larry Page and Sergey Brin, the founders of Google Incorporated, met when they were PhD candidates in the computer science department at Stanford University. Page was looking at how sites link to each other and Brin was looking at data mining—what information is available and how to find it. They shared a feeling that Web searching needed to be improved and devised a new approach to sorting results. They took their ideas about searching for information to other search engine companies. However, they found that other companies' strategies were focused on expanding into areas such as media portals and adding functions to search engines to keep people at their sites.

Brin and Page wanted to concentrate on search techniques and information retrieval so they decided to found their own company and successfully sought venture capital funding for their endeavor. Because their searches are fully automated, they operate with only 200 employees, half of whom are engineers or technical people. Over 40 have PhDs. Traffic to their site increases 20% per month although they do no advertising. According to Google, users hear about them by word of mouth. They perform 100 million searches per day, over 55% for users outside of the United States. They currently have sites in Canada, France, Germany, Italy, Japan, Korea and the United Kingdom as well as the United States. People can restrict their search to Web pages written in 26 distinct languages or search using an interface of one of 36 languages.

Google uses two techniques in its searching, page ranking and mathematical algorithms. The page ranking system looks at other pages that link to particular sites. For example, if someone does a query on restaurants in Spain, the Google engine looks at and ranks restaurants based partially on how many sites link to it and the type of sites linking to it. For example, a *New York Times* link ranks higher than a link from a personal Web page. The proprietary mathematical equation analyzes the links to the page as well as looking at the text on the page—the headlines, bolding and the proximity of words to each other for relevancy of text or data on the page. This validation is important because it eliminates the possible "spam" effect of sites sending thousands of the same messages to a site.

SEARCHING ON THE WEB—GOOGLE *(continued)*

When users request a search at Google, they are actually searching Web pages located on Google's 8000 Linux-based computers. The computers are located in clusters at five server farms at hosting sites in the Internet. Google "crawls" the Web continuously looking for new and updated Web sites. (*Crawling* is the use of a software program to automatically search the Web.) Google believes it has the largest index in the world with 1.3 billion uniform resource locators (URLs). (A *URL* is the Web address for Internet sites.) It performs 100 million searches per day and has most of the Web pages for the useful sites in its index. It doesn't keep URLs for password-protected or personal Web pages at its site.

Google, which predicts it will be profitable by year-end 2001, has two sources of revenue, context-sensitive advertising on its site and licensing its search engine. The context-sensitive advertising brings up ads related to products and services for which users request searches. It licenses site search and Web search products. Its Web search product is licensed to Yahoo!, Vizavvi (part of Vivendi), China Netease.com (the second largest ISP in China), Sprint, VirginNet and others. Companies such as Cisco license Google's site search product. Google initially provided its Web searching software without a charge to gain visibility at sites such as portals.

Google focuses on making information universally available. It is developing interfaces so that wireless devices such as Japanese I-mode handsets and Palm VII wireless devices can be used for Google search. A test pilot is being conducted with BMW using speech recognition to search by voice. Searches can be done for PDF documents and development is underway to search for other image files such as JPEG files, which users may wish to use for PowerPoint presentations.

- Spider-based search engines perform searches using automated software programs. The Northern Light, Inktomi, HotBot, AltaVista, Google and LookSmart search sites use spiders.

- Ask Jeeves is a natural language search engine where people can ask questions in everyday sentences or phrases. Ask Jeeves keeps templates of commonly asked questions.

INTERNET ADDRESSES ....

Uniform resource locators (URLs) such as www.Yahoo.com represent addresses for sites on the World Wide Web. The Internet protocol, the system for addressing Internet packets, translates URLs to 32-bit IP addresses (e.g., 123.444.52.323) so they can be routed to their destination. To avoid duplication, most of the URLs are administered by central organizations.

The international Internet Corporation for Assigned Names & Numbers (ICANN) is an international nonprofit organization created by the United States government in 1998 to oversee Internet naming and numbering matters. ICANN appoints organizations to assign and keep track of URLs and approves the creation of new top-level domain names. Top-level domain names can be generic such as .com or country-specific such as .uk for the United Kingdom. ICANN approves companies to be registries and registrars.

- *Registries* manage the entire database for a top-level domain name such as. org. They may also sell domain names to end users. There is only one registry per top-level domain name.

- *Registrars* sell domain names to end-user customers. However, they don't manage the database for all of a particular top-level domain name. There are many registrars for each top-level domain name.

Registries—Management of Entire Top-Level Domains

Registries keep track of and manage databases of URLs. VeriSign manages the registry of top-level domain names .com, .net and .org. It operates the shared registration system (SRS), a database of .com, .net, .org, .tv, .bz, .nu and .cc top-level domain names. For example, if an organization or individual requests a particular domain name, the registrar checks the SRS for availability. The SRS contains information about networks, domain names and the contacts for each domain name. VeriSign's .net registry agreement with the U.S. Department of Commerce expires June 30, 2005. It will divest its .org registry in 2002 after which time ICANN will assign a non-profit organization as the registry.

ICANN has assigned the rights to keep registries of names in the following new top-level domains:

- .edu to EDUCAUSE
- .biz to NeuLevel
- .name to Global Name Registry Ltd. (GNR) in London
- .info to Affilias, LLC

Registry companies are trying to avoid disputes about trademarked organization names.

Registrars

Companies called registrars have been approved by ICANN to buy banks of names at a discount from registry organizations. One hundred forty-eight companies worldwide are accredited to date as registrars. Registrars are responsible for gathering the technical information on which each domain name they register is located. They pay fees of about $6 to companies such as VeriSign and NeuLevel for each address they assign within a domain. Customers pay an annual fee to registrars to keep their domain registration up to date.

VeriSign is both a registrar and a registry. The Department of Commerce audits VeriSign to ensure fair treatment of registrars by VeriSign. It requires that VeriSign operate its own registrar service that it provides to end users separately from the service it provides to other registrars.

Numeric IP Addresses

Numeric IP addresses are assigned separately from URLs. ISPs and other organizations are assigned numeric IP addresses by registry bodies such as American Registry for Internet Numbers (ARIN), which assigns numbers in North and South America, the Caribbean and sub-Saharan Africa. ISPs keep lists of IP addresses that they use to route traffic to their customers that is not directed to a customer's domain name (username@AOL.com). Asia Pacific Network Information Center (APNIC) and Reseaux IP Europeens (RIPE) manage numeric IP addresses for Asia and Europe, respectively.

The Structure of Internet Addresses and Adding Capacity for More Addresses

Email addresses demonstrate the structure of IP addresses. To the left of the @ sign is the user's name. For example, JohnDoe@. To the right of the @ sign is the domain name. The domain name is the name of the computer at which the email address is located. Corporations use their name or an abbreviated form of their name for their domain name. To the right of the computer or organizational name is a description of the type of organization using the address. This is a top-level domain. The following are six generic top-level domain names:

- .com—Commercial businesses worldwide
- .org—Nonprofit organizations worldwide
- .net—Network providers worldwide

- .edu—Educational institutions in the United States
- .gov—United States governmental bodies
- .mil—Branches of the United States military

The current 32-bit IP addressing scheme has a capacity for 4 billion addresses. (A 32-bit code has 2^{32} permutations.) There is concern that use of IP addresses for data-equipped wireless service will deplete the number of available addresses. In addition, demand for Internet addresses in countries such as Japan, India and China is expected to increase. Currently, North America has 74% of the world's IP addresses, Europe has 17% and Asia/Pacific has 9%. A total of 400 million public IP addresses are in use.[1] (Public IP addresses point to an organization. Private IP addresses specify particular users or devices within organizations.) A new 128-bit protocol, IPv6, has been approved that will greatly increase the number of available public Internet addresses. However, Internet equipment such as routers and servers need to be upgraded to work with Ipv6. Major manufacturers such as Cisco, Microsoft and Sun have announced plans or started to produce IPv6-compatible routers, servers and operating systems.

New Generic Top-Level Domains (gTLDs)

Generic top-level domain (gTLD) names are not associated with a particular country or territory. ICANN, the Internet Corporation for Assigned Names and Numbers, which is responsible for approving new top-level domain addresses, has approved the following seven new generic top-level domain names.

- .biz—For businesses and corporations
- .info—For information-based services such as newspapers, libraries, etc.
- .name—For individuals
- .pro—For professions such as law, medicine, accounting and so forth
- .aero—For services and companies dealing with aviation
- .coop—For business cooperatives
- .museum—For museums, archival institutions and exhibitions

---

1. These statistics were reported in the article, "Introducing a New Internet Protocol to Fix Traffic Problems Faces Criticism, Apathy," published in *The Wall Street Journal* WSJ.com, 14 May 2001, by Dan Goodin.

Country Code Top-Level Domain Names (ccTLDs)

Countries outside of the U.S. use country-specific, geographic, top-level domain names referred to as country code top-level domain names (ccTLDs). For instance, .jp is for Japan, .cn is for China and .uk is for the United Kingdom. Sites may use generic domain names preceding the country code top-level domain (ccTLD) name. Country-specific top-level domain names are approved by ICANN in Latin character sets only. Many Asian countries have requested ICANN approval of top-level domain names in non-Latin characters as more of their populations acquire Internet connections. ICANN, however, usually follows Internet Engineering Task Force (IETF) recommendations, which has indicated it may soon set standards for non-Latin characters. VeriSign is testing the use of non-Latin characters.

Alternative Domain Naming Services

Some Asian countries are developing an alternative set of domain name servers in non-Latin characters. China has announced it is developing its own domain naming system. China states that it considers it its sovereign right to control domain names in Chinese characters. Because these names are in a different set of master directories, users must download special plug-in software with unique domain name system settings. The Chinese government has made free software available for routing traffic to its domain names. A Singapore-based company, iDNS Ltd., also has its own domain naming system.

ELECTRONIC COMMERCE AND ADVERTISING ON THE WEB ....

The World Wide Web is an important element in commerce, entertainment, advertising and marketing. However, it is still in its infancy. In 2000, the dollar volume of retail products and services sold via the Internet was about 1.7% of total retail sales. This is up from 1.1% in 1999. In addition, the number of online residential users is growing. In the United States, 16 million users—58% of the population—accessed the Internet in April 2001 compared to only 6.8 million in April 2000. Email and Web surfing are the main reasons people use the Web. Web surfing influences purchase decisions. The article, "More People Went Online to Talk and Send Greetings Than Shop," published in *The New York Times On the Web*, 8 January 2001, by John Schwartz, cited statistics gathered by the Pew Internet and American Life Project. They found that 32% of online users compared prices online even though they made their purchase offline.

Factors holding back electronic commerce on the Web include:

- Consumer concerns about security.
- Consumer concerns about privacy.
- Uneven customer service for online transactions. Numerous surveys have reported customer dissatisfaction with late shipments or incomplete shipments, poor Web page design and difficulty contacting customer service representatives. Organizations with experience in catalog sales generally receive higher customer ratings due to their pre-existing back office and customer service infrastructure.
- After working all day, some people do not want to turn on their computer. They like the one-way entertainment found in television.
- Consumers' slow-speed analog modems. Only 12% of the United States population has high-speed cable, DSL or satellite connections to the Internet. According to a Government Accounting Office (GAO) report issued October 2000, high-speed Internet access is available to 52% of the users of dialup modems. To date, these users don't see a compelling need to spend the extra fees for high-speed access. The GAO report noted that two fifths of broadband users had incomes of $75,000 or more. This is not surprising with the cost of DSL and cable modems rising to levels of $50 per month. With the exception of South Korea, high-speed access in the rest of the world is lower than in the United States.

Advertising on the Web— A Source of Revenue

Advertising first appeared on the World Wide Web in 1994. Web-based advertising takes the form of banner ads, rich media ads with sound and moving images and pop-up ads that appear on users' screens and have to manually be closed. In the early days of the World Wide Web, experts believed that the Web would operate similarly to television where ad revenue paid for programming. That model is losing credibility.

One way to measure advertising effectively is "click-through" rates on ads that link visitors to advertisers' home page purchase offers. However, in 2001 click-through rates had declined to .1% to .5%, down from 2% to 3% in 1997. Many dotcom companies built their strategy around advertising revenues, which failed to materialize for many of them who went out of business. This was a blow to the Internet because dotcom companies accounted for over half of the advertising on the Web in 2000. In addition, low click-through rates caused a drop in advertising rates and total revenue. Merrill Lynch & Company predicted that online ad revenues would decrease by 25% in 2001. Suein L. Hwang reported this statistic in the article, "Ad Nauseum," published in *The Wall Street Journal WSJ.com*, 23 April 2001. Most Internet sites are looking for strategies in addition to advertising to earn profits. The article, "Monitise This," published in *The Economist* print edition, 22 February 2001, by Suein L. Hwang, states:

> *Those that cannot find revenue sources beyond advertising will either go bust or be forced to admit that their site is a non-profit enterprise. If truth-in-advertising rules were enforced, most dotcoms would be dotorgs.*

Because studies have indicated that people ignore banner ads, there is now more emphasis on pop-up ads, larger animated ads, and ads inserted before, between or at the end of audio and video streaming broadcasts. For example, an ad can be placed in a box in the on-screen player in which a video is being showed. An audio message can be inserted before music is streamed. However, there is a concern that ads that are too aggressive will alienate potential customers. To date, Internet ads are not as entertaining as TV commercials that often have catchy tunes, amusing animation and alluring models. However, some marketing people think that Internet ads serve a purpose, they promote brand awareness and long-term awareness.

The electronic aspect of online advertising lends itself to use as a market research tool. New technology enables sites to tailor ads based on the person viewing the ad. For example, the ad might look at where the user was previously. In addition the site might identify the profile of the person based on online registration associated with the user's "cookie." A *cookie* is a small software file sites place in the user's browser that identifies a user but does not reveal email addresses or user names. (Some sites use cookie information to eliminate customers' re-entering passwords.) Moreover, because advertising effectiveness can be measured quickly, ads can be quickly altered and tested again to make them more effective.

Online Commerce—What Is Profitable and Sells?

The Internet, while still accounting for a small percentage of total retail sales, is a decision factor in many purchases and in certain industries a key ingredient in overall sales. Computers, books, travel and music each represent over 5% of retail sales in their category. The online commerce industry is at a crossroads where many services are popular but profits are often elusive.

Consider the following:

- Many consumers research products online but make the actual purchases in person or over the telephone—hotels, resorts, mutual funds, stocks, entertainment and restaurants all lend themselves to online research.

- The online sale of books, computers and free downloading of music have all impacted sales at retail outlets.

- Consumers make travel arrangements online in hopes of finding lower airfares.

- Online recruitment ads have taken a large chunk of revenue from newspapers.

- Purchase orders, bills and sales proposals are transmitted via the Internet but are not counted toward any tally of sales.

- Independent and large book chains and a computer retailer all stated publicly in 1999 that their sales were hurt by online retailing.

- Business customers routinely research a company on the Internet. Company Web pages influence their purchase decisions.

Pornography sites have been consistently profitable. In the article, "Few Talk About It, but Porn Plays Big Role in Web Economy," published in *The Wall Street Journal WSJ.com*, 21 March 2001, by Lewis Perdue, research firm DataMonitor predicted that adult sites would earn 69% of all the Internet-based revenue for premium services in 2001. The same article cited statistics from traffic-measuring firms Netratings and Jupiter Media Metrix that 25% of U.S. Web surfers visit adult sites in a given month. More important than the number of visitors is the fact that most of these sites are profitable. They have a compelling product and people are willing to pay for it. Furthermore, users view adult sites in the privacy of their home. (Only their credit card companies and market research firms know their identity.) Interestingly, these sites use streaming video and audio, which are greatly enhanced by higher speed Web access.

The companies that have attracted the most customers on the Internet have added something unique, not available at retail sites. For example, Amazon enhances their site with purchasers' reviews. In addition, it offers, as do many e-retailers, the ability to easily sort offerings by topic. However, Amazon.com has an enormous amount of debt, $2.1 billion as of June 2001. It has stated that it will be profitable by year-end 2002 excluding debt payments. Entertainment and access to specialty items not easily found elsewhere are factors in the popularity of iWon (sweepstakes), eBay (auctions), X10.com (networked electronics and surveillance systems) and Flipside (games) sites.

eBay is one of the few profitable online businesses. It charges a fee to both sellers and buyers. eBay initially offered only collectibles from individuals but now acts as a sales channel for other retailers and liquidators. These companies use eBay as a channel for returned goods, refurbished electronics and other unsold items. Another profitable e-business is publicly traded eDiets.com. eDiets sells subscription-based diet services consisting of online tools to track weight loss and plan diets. Subscribers also can chat with other subscribers, registered nutritionists and psychologists. This is an interesting example of people paying for information that is important to them and that they can use conveniently in the privacy of their homes.

Many organizations are still learning how to conduct business online. Borders.com and Toys "R" Us, both of whom had large losses in their online operations, signed an agreement with Amazon.com to manage their online operations. Amazon.com's competence in online systems, distribution and billing made them a suitable choice. Expertise in order fulfillment and customer service are important ingredients. For example, Lands End and L.L.Bean both have profitable Web operations. Unlike Amazon.com, they did not have the expense of building new order fulfillment systems for their online operations. The steep discounts Amazon.com offered also cut into profits.

The following are some of the reasons consumers and organizations "shop online:"

- To save money
- To save time
- To compare prices quickly
- For faster access to information
- To track orders online
- To research products more quickly

Automating Business-to Business E-commerce—E-commerce Enablers

Overall, e-commerce systems are in their early stages of development. No product automates all of the e-commerce steps. Moreover, dissimilar tax systems, language hurdles and currency issues hurt commerce among companies in different countries. To date, the biggest impact of the Internet on commerce is the ability that email provides to communicate across time zones and send documents as attachments.

Sales of systems that support direct business-to-business electronic transmissions have been hurt by the slowdown in the economy in 2000 and 2001. In addition, acceptance of systems to select suppliers through bidding processes and online exchanges have been hurt by purchase managers wishing to use personal relationships, quality and the supplier's delivery record in making decisions. Intelligence to enable software to evaluate these "soft" factors is not available. The software that bridges disparate systems between organizations is XML. (See "XML—For E-commerce" earlier in this chapter.)

Systems that automate the creation, the process for obtaining approvals on and the transmittal of purchase orders (POs) to suppliers are available. For example, employees that want to make a purchase access a purchase order form on their intranet. After they've filled it out, the PO is sent automatically up the chain of command within the organization for the appropriate approvals. It is then, depending on the supplier's capability for receiving the PO, automatically faxed, sent by email or transmitted electronically to the supplier. At the supplier's order entry system, direct electronic transmittals don't have to be keyed in by the supplier. These systems make the purchasing department more efficient by freeing up purchasing departments for higher level tasks. However, unless the purchase order is transmitted directly to the supplier's order entry system, e-commerce is not automated between supplier and purchaser. Ariba and CommerceOne offer these types of products.

Supply chain and manufacturing software products contain information so that the correct quantity of components needed to manufacture products can be ordered and tracked. Companies that use supply chain and manufacturing software transmit forecasts to suppliers so that parts needed for manufacturing will be available. These packages have the capability through XML software to link to internal manufacturing systems. Managers load in a manufacturing plan and receive back the number of different types of parts needed to manufacture the end product. Agilent Software and i2 Technologies produce supply chain systems.

Collaborative design packages support links between engineering design firms and manufacturing companies often in different continents. The purpose is to obtain feedback from manufacturers as to how to improve the design to work with the manufacturers' processes. PTC and MatrixOne are leaders in collaborative design packages. Oracle and SAP offer packages for all of the preceding categories.

PRIVACY ON THE WORLD WIDE WEB....................

Numerous studies have documented that concerns about privacy violations hamper online commerce. There are valid reasons to be concerned about privacy on the World Wide Web. The proliferation of telecommunications links to computers that contain databases about consumers and the lower cost of hard drives to store large databases have resulted in lower cost, more sophisticated snooping tools.

- *Cookie software*—A site visited by a user can add a small text file to the visitor's browser that identifies the user to the site. The cookie is used for password authentication so that people are not required to type in passwords each time they visit sites to which they subscribe. They are also used, if a site has the person's email address, to send personalized research or news leads to users based on their cookie. The cookie, however, does not divulge site users' email addresses. Those are provided voluntarily via online registration, purchases or contests.

Cookies can be used to track customer behavior at multiple sites. The information is used to create profiles of sites users visit and browsing habits. Advertising companies like DoubleClick that sell banner ads to many sites enable this capability. A unique number is placed in the cookie and tracked from site to site. If the visitor fills out a registration form at one of the sites, the ad network associates the user information (e.g., name and address) with the profile.

- *Online registration and contest forms*—Telephone numbers, email addresses, and home and business addresses are collected from online forms. These are frequently put into demographic databases by companies and sold to direct marketers.

Cable TV and satellite TV providers have the capability to monitor and capture information about the viewing habits of their customers that have personal video recorders such as ReplayTV and TiVo. Personal video recorders are set-top devices with hard discs that let users record and schedule recording of television shows and play back the shows minus the commercials. (See Chapter 7 for personal video recorders.)

Record companies can monitor and keep lists of listening habits of people that download music at their sites.

Email "bugs" can be embedded in HTML email (described previously), which enables marketers to send email with the look and feel of Web pages with multimedia formats. The software bugs tell marketing companies if users opened the email message. The bugs also send marketing firms copies of the email and comments added to it if it is forwarded to others. The bug can be planted in email that looks like it is plain text only also. Thus, a business associate could know, for example, about any comments added to a proposal sent to potential clients. (Users can disable this JavaScript feature in their Netscape or Explorer browsers but they will lose the ability to receive mail in the HTML format.)

- *Powerful databases*—Companies such as Acxiom, 7/24 and Abacus Direct (part of DoubleClick) offer online services where, for a fee, direct marketers purchase personal data about consumers.

- *The "wired" universe*—The rise in communicating computers makes databases available to anyone with an Internet connection and a PC. People buy access to lists or they hack into computers containing personal information. As systems acquire more sophisticated security, hackers increase their own break-in capabilities. In 2000, hackers broke into Western Union's Web site and stole debit card and credit card information about

15,700 users. Consumers are aware that computer systems are vulnerable to hackers and are leery of leaving private information on the Internet.

Opt-out vs. Opt-in—Different Approaches to Protecting Privacy

Some Web sites give users an option to request that locations not collect or sell information about them collected at their site. This is called an opt-out opportunity. The problem is that this choice is often buried deep within a site's privacy statement. Even if a user opts-out, it may not apply to every banner on the site. For example, large advertisers that place ads for many companies use special cookies (described above) that track and link users' behavior at many sites. In these instances, opt-out forms need to be filled out at every site containing the banner ad from the advertising network's, for example DoubleClick's site. Opt-in, which most sites don't offer, means that the site does not gather personal information about visitors unless they authorize it by filling in an opt-in form.

Privacy safeguards are stricter in Europe than in the United States. This created problems for companies with sites that spanned both continents. The Commerce Department and the European Union signed a treaty called Safe Harbor to eliminate this barrier. Under the terms of the agreement, companies that meet Safe Harbor privacy rules will be issued a mark for their site by privacy watchdog TRUSTe. Because the program is voluntary, the extent of compliance is not clear. The standards that must be met to receive the TRUSTe stamp are:

- Web sites tell visitors what information is being collected about them: what the information will be used for and with whom the information will be shared

- Consumers must be able to choose whether or not personal information should be shared with other organizations

- Consumers must have the right to view and correct information collected about them

The advertising industry, under pressure from privacy groups and to avoid legislation mandating privacy, has set up a site users can go to where they can request that information or profiles about them not be set up of their browsing or online shopping patterns. The site is www.networkadvertising.org. They have also set up a site to be managed by independent accounting firm Andersen where users can make complaints about companies that fail to comply with opt-out requests. This site is www.andersen-compliance.com. Critics feel that this effort will have little impact, as most users don't realize they're being profiled and don't know about the opt-out site.

LEGAL ISSUES ....

The Internet has changed the nature of entertainment and information distribution. Prior to the Internet, people illegally copied music from each other and "mixed" their own tapes with selections from multiple sources. They also shared books and copied articles for each other. These copying efforts were done one at a time. Currently songs, databases and computer source code posted on the Internet are available to millions of people as opposed to one by one. Thus infringements on copyrights can have an enormous impact. The question of what constitutes property in cyberspace is at the center of Napster, Mp3.Com, Incorporated and other law cases encompassing information and databases on the Internet.

The MP3 case involved MP3.com copying music on its servers and letting millions of users who already owned the music listen to it free on computers or devices capable of playing MP3 files. For example, owners of CDs played the CDs to prove they owned a copy and then MP3.Com gave them access to play the same titles from any location. However, the Record Industry Association of America (RIAA) sued MP3.com and claimed that people could get around the requirement that they must own the CD to download it from the MP3.Com site. The courts ruled against MP3.com and fined it $25,000 per disc it copied for copyright piracy. After the judgment, MP3.com made agreements with the four largest record companies to sell and store CDs online. It also offers a free service for users willing to listen to ads. By 2001, it was operating at a loss and was acquired by music and entertainment company Vivendi Universal SA, which plans to use its technology for a new online music subscription service called pressplay. Smaller independent music companies that did not participate in the preceding suit are suing MP3.com for copyright infringement.

The Napster case was different than the MP3 case because Napster did not directly copy music. It enabled others to download music using Napster's file-sharing program. It operated similar to a search engine that enabled people to find free music from many sources. Napster kept a centralized list of music available on other people's computers. People at the Napster site could download music from any computer in the central catalog that was turned on.

In 1999 the Recording Industry Association of America and, in 2000, two recording artists sued Napster for copyright infringement. The courts ruled against Napster, which had claimed because it was acting as an Internet service provider and because it was not making copies, was exempt from the copyright infringement rules. The court ruled that Napster must stop enabling music files to be shared. The record companies are now suing other file-sharing companies such as Gnutella and Aimster whose file-sharing services do not keep central catalogs of music on other's computers.

According to Stephen Chow, a partner at the Boston law firm of Perkins, Smith & Cohen, LLP, the Napster case has privacy implications. Both copyright owners and pirate-catching services are sniffing (monitoring) the IP (Internet Protocol) addresses of people using Napster-like music services. In Belgium, police went after people for illegally downloading music. Copyright owners have asked Internet service providers to block service to music-sharing sites under the Digital Millennium Copyright Act (see "The Digital Millennium Copyright Act (DMCA)—Royalties for Radio over the Internet" for details on the act).

Post-Napster Music Industry Online Efforts

Edgar Bronfman, Jr., vice chairman of Vivendi Universal, testified before the United States House Subcommittee on Intellectual Property that the industry had been hurt by free peer-to-peer music from sites such as Napster. No statistics have been published to prove Mr. Bronfman's claim. According to Recording Industry Association of America statistics, revenue of CD singles decreased 35.8% from 1999 to 2000 from $222.4 million to $142.7 million. However, revenue of CD albums increased 3.1% from $12.8 billion to $13.2 billion in the same period. Moreover, sales of singles, which accounted for less than 1% of music sales in 2000, started dropping in 1998, before Napster's May 1999 founding.

Music critics and newspaper columnists have stated that high prices and the fact that albums often contained only a few popular songs hurt CD album sales. The model of distributing music from the Internet is having a major impact on business plans. The largest music companies are starting Internet-based digital distribution organizations. The following three arrangements have been announced:

- Bertelsmann agreed to a partnership with Napster where users pay to download music from **Napster's** site.

- AOL Time Warner, Bertelsmann's BMG unit, RealNetworks and EMI Group started **MusicNet** to sell music online using encryption and compression from RealNetworks, Inc. and distributed via AOL and RealNetworks. Only music from these companies, about 40% of the market, will be available with MusicNet.

- Vivendi Universal and Sony have started **pressplay**, which will be distributing music on Yahoo!'s site and other sites that license its technology. Pressplay will use MP3.com's technology. Only Vivendi and Sony music, about 47% of the market, will be available.

Because this is a new form of distribution, new terms need to be set up with artists. Agreements with individual performers, songwriters and music publishers are being worked on by the preceding companies. However these agreements are structured, digitally downloaded individual songs will give consumers more choices on which songs to collect. It also gives them an opportunity to inexpensively listen to new artists. The industry has a new way to promote and distribute new recordings.

The Digital Millennium Copyright Act (DMCA)—Royalties for Radio over the Internet

In October 1998, the U.S. Congress passed the Digital Millennium Copyright Act (DMCA). The Act was designed to implement World Intellectual Property Organization (WIPO) agreed-upon issues. It also requires Webcasters to pay royalties for music broadcast over the Internet. It made it a crime to circumvent anti-piracy measures built into commercial software.

It also includes a provision that Internet service providers aren't liable for customers who use their network service to illegally copy files. It granted "safe harbor" to Internet service providers that provide the network over which users illegally copy files. However, the act has a provision whereby copyright owners can obtain a subpoena ordering a service provider to disclose the identity of a subscriber allegedly engaging in infringing activity. The service providers must also terminate accounts of repeat infringers. ISPs are not liable for penalty as long as they don't know of copyright infringement activities and don't profit from them. In the Napster case previously described, Napster claimed that it was an Internet service provider and thus not liable for infringements by people that used its software.

The Digital Millennium Copyright Act also includes provisions related to songs broadcast by radio stations over the Internet. The Act limits the number of songs by specific artists and albums that Webcasters can play within given blocks of time. The DMCA also prohibits Webcasters from telling listeners the name of the next song to be played.

Anti-pornography Laws and Freedom of Speech

Freedom of speech rights sometimes clash with people's desire to protect children from pornography on the Web. For example, the 1998 Child Online Protection Act (COPA) makes it a crime to place objectionable material on the Web where a child may view it. The law specifies that the material can be on the Web but that sites must require users to use a credit card or access number as proof of age to view the material. The law has never been put into effect because a lower court granted the American Civil Liberty Union's request to prevent its taking effect. The United States Supreme Court will rule on the constitutionality of the law in October 2001.

Another Act where freedom of speech intersects with child pornography issues is the Children's Internet Protection Act (CIPA), which the United States Congress passed in 2000. It requires that schools and libraries that participate in certain federal subsidy programs install "technology protection measures" to block access to obscenity, child pornography and material harmful to minors on all of their Internet access terminals. The Act also requires Internet safety policies preventing minors from accessing email, unlawful activities online and chat. The American Civil Liberty Union (ACLU) and the American Library Association (ALA) have stated their intention of challenging the constitutionality of CIPA. (The ACLU has stated that they may only initiate action against the library regulations because schools have a quasi-parental role.) A three-judge panel appointed by the Third Circuit Court of Appeals will hear the case in the December 2001 time frame. If CIPA is declared constitutional, libraries and schools have until July 2002 to implement CIPA requirements. They must declare that they will participate in the blocking or evaluate if they will participate by October 28, 2001. If the law is put into force, libraries that don't implement filtering will lose federal funding.

In expectations of this Act, Peacefire, a civil liberties group based in the United States, tested the most widely sold censorware programs in October 2000. It found error rates of between 20% and 80% where the programs blocked sites that did not contain pornography. One problem with filters is that they cannot determine the context in which language is used. The filters block topics such as anatomy discussions and medical treatments as if they are pornography.

Some countries have broad Internet restrictions. For example, in Saudi Arabia, all residents are denied access to pornography and defamatory statements about the royal family. Singapore and the United Arab Emirates monitor Internet traffic by forcing it all to go through a central gateway. These countries and other countries block traffic from certain Internet addresses. According to the article, "Punching Holes in Internet Walls," published in *The New York Times on the Web*, 26 April 2001, by Jennifer Lee, 20 countries significantly restrict Internet access. Residents of these countries often find ways to access these sites by signing up with ISPs such as SafeWeb that encrypt data to and from SafeWeb servers.

Having to create different Web sites for a variety of countries is a problem particularly for portals that appeal to residential consumers. The following is a quote from Vermont Democratic Senator Patrick J. Leahy, Chairman of the Senate Judiciary Committee, about the best way to regulate the Internet internationally. The quote appeared in the article, "Continents Clash on Content," published in *The New York Times on the Web*, 18 April 2001, by Amy Zuckerman:

> *The temptation of government is to apply rules on the Internet that they wouldn't do otherwise. With so many countries over there, you're not going to get consensus by accident. We have to be technologically neutral the way we have with telephone lines and digital signatures, but when you get into the area of content there's a major problem of the differences from country*

to country… The bottom line is, if you have criminal content, nail the criminal. Don't close down the Internet.

Filtering Software—Policing Corporate Browsing and Email

To ensure that employees use the Internet for work-related tasks, organizations as well as governments block particular Web sites. They use software that blocks URLs to known pornography, hate/racism, sport, gambling, religion and weapons sites. Suppliers of Internet filtering software use automated search tools that find sites with pornographic pictures, racist symbols and Web content related to the preceding topics. Other filtering software screens incoming Web pages and sends warnings to staff that pop up on their computer screens while they are viewing, for example, a travel site. The message on the screen tells the employee that the site they are viewing is not an appropriate work-related site.

In addition to blocking and screening Web sites, enterprises such as financial institutions use software to monitor email for compliance with Security and Exchange Commission (SEC) compliance. For example, they look for insider trading and other illegal activities. Compliance with Equal Employment Opportunity Commission (EEOC) requirements is another reason organizations filter out offensive Web sites. For example, in May 2001, the EEOC ruled that a Minneapolis library exposed staff to a hostile work environment by allowing patrons to access pornography.

OPEN CABLE—CABLE COMPANIES AS BOTH ISPS AND NETWORK SERVICE PROVIDERS ....

Most cable TV companies in the United States use either Excite@Home or Road Runner for the Internet service provider function for their cable modem customers. ISPs provide email, hosting and Web content. Cable TV operators are starting to allow other ISPs, such as AOL and Earthlink, to offer service for cable modem subscribers.

ISP Service for Cable TV

Road Runner and Excite@Home (see Table 8.2) furnish the connections to the Internet backbone as well as content and email service for the majority of cable modem customers in the United States. Excite@Home is made up of two divisions: the backbone network and the ISP functions. At Home provides backbone connections to the Internet, the access network. Excite furnishes the ISP, email, home page hosting and content functions. For example, Excite currently operates email service for Comcast

Table 8.2   Road Runner and Excite@Home

High-Speed Access Provider	Owners	Comments
At Home Corporation does business as Excite@Home	Controlled by AT&T Broadband.	Excite@Home service to 3.2 million customers offered through 20 U.S. cable providers. Has service in Australia, the Netherlands and Japan. It owns electronic gree†ting card site Bluemountain.com. At Home Corporation may sell the Excite portal part of the business.
Road Runner	Controlled by Time Warner Cable.	Road Runner has 1 million subscribers.

cable modem subscribers. The first page customers see when they log on to the Web is managed by Excite. At Home operates the backbone network of Excite@Home. The backbone network carries signals from individual headends to cable TV data centers and to the Internet. Headends are the point from which cable TV operators transmit television signals and operate transmission systems that convert radio frequencies to signals compatible with the Internet.

Road Runner and Excite@Home own and operate the routers, servers and optical lines connecting cable company headends with regional data centers. The regional data centers are connected to the Internet or to larger data centers. Road Runner has service in 25 states as well as in Newfoundland, Canada. At Home has super nodes throughout the United States where it stores customers' Web pages, email and media partners' Internet content such as sports scores, travel services, games and shopping information. Some cable TV overbuilders such as RCN, WideOpenWest LLC and Digital Access, which compete with the incumbent cable companies, provide their own content and access to the Internet. They operate their own ISP service.

Open Cable Service—Trialing Connections to Other IPS

Cable modem providers require that customers use the cable TV's own ISP service as well as their cable modem connections. This is different than dialup services where local telephone companies offer the telephone service but customers can choose from a variety of ISPs such as MSN, Juno (part of NetZero) and EarthLink. Until the AOL

Time Warner merger, the FCC did not require that cable companies unbundle their network access service from their ISP service because cable companies are regulated as cable TV, not common carrier companies. This creates problems for users as they must either change their email address or continue to pay for their dialup account to preserve their former email address when they change to cable modems. It also locks smaller ISPs out of the cable modem ISP market.

When AT&T bought TCI, Internet service providers such as AOL and Mind-Spring (now part of EarthLink) protested to the FCC that AT&T and the cable companies would have monopolistic powers on Internet access. Furthermore, the Regional Bell Operating Companies (RBOCs) stated that cable companies should have the same unbundling requirements to open their networks as common carriers. AT&T, who did not want to lose any ISP revenues, countered that opening cable connections to competitive providers would jeopardize its investment in upgrading TCI's network for cable modem and telephone service. The government, which wants to encourage local competition, did not require the cable companies to unbundle their network connections to the Internet.

However, by December 1999, AT&T pledged to open its network to other ISPs by 2002 when its exclusive contract to use At Home ends. Cox Cable also has pledged to open its network to other ISPs. Portland, Oregon; Broward County, Florida and four towns in Massachusetts sued AT&T in separate cases to open its networks to other providers. AT&T won each of these cases. However, the FCC is reviewing its policy on open cable. In the meantime, AT&T is conducting a technical trial of open cable for 500 residents of Boulder, Colorado with eight Internet service providers.

With open cable, when customers log on to the Web, they send a signal to AT&T identifying their ISP and AT&T sends their traffic to the selected ISP. In order for this to work, the ISP and the cable TV company need peering arrangements as in Figure 8.4 where they exchange traffic. (See "Peering—A Way to Exchange Data Between Networks".) The cable TV providers have expressed concern that ISP traffic will clog their local networks. For example, large amounts of streaming video could create traffic jams. The United States Internet Industry Association (USIIA) has expressed concern about getting fair treatment from cable TV providers. For example, when negotiations between Time Warner and ISPs were initiated, Time Warner sought 75% of ISPs' Internet access fees and 25% of their ad revenues. Time Warner also asked for rights to approve ISP's start-up pages and a spot for Time Warner on each start-up page.

Cable providers point out that telephone companies that provide DSL use mainly their own ISP service. For example, as of 2001, 85% of SBC's DSL service was handled by SBC's own ISP service. Verizon Online, the Verizon ISP, handled 90% of Verizon's DSL traffic. However, in the former GTE area, GTE's ISP entity handled only 45% of its DSL traffic.

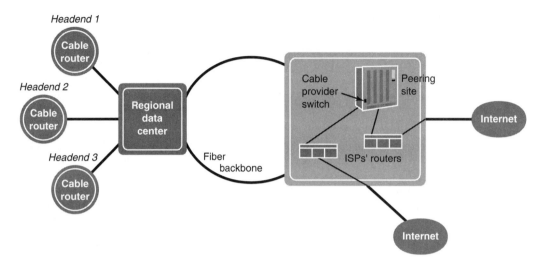

Figure 8.4
Open cable service.

The AOL Time Warner Open Cable Agreement

As a provision of approval for its merger, the Federal Trade Commission (FTC) required that AOL Time Warner open its networks to other ISPs and accept continued monitoring of these efforts. The FTC responded to concerns by small competitive ISPs that they would be locked out of the broadband Internet access market. The following is a summary of the FTC rules:

- *Open Access*—AOL Time Warner is required to make its network available to at least one other ISP before it can offer its own service and at least three other ISPs within 90 days.

- *Content*—AOL Time Warner must notify the FTC of notice of complaints that it fails to carry interactive content, signals of television programmers.

- *DSL Marketing*—AOL Time Warner must offer, market and price AOL DSL service the same way in markets with AOL Time Warner cable modem services as in areas without cable modem service.

AOL Time Warner currently has agreements with Juno Online Services and EarthLink, Inc. Open cable trials are underway in Columbus, Ohio. Initially, Time Warner will be responsible for billing and customer service for Juno customers who choose cable modem access.

INTRANETS AND EXTRANETS...............................

An *intranet* is the use of World Wide Web technology within organizations. Extranets extend the reach of intranets from internal-only communications to sharing documents and information for business-to-business transactions.

Intranets—Impact of Web Technology on Internal Operations

In essence, an intranet is a private Internet with a browser interface to corporate information. Employees use browsers on their PCs for applications such as collaboration on projects and looking up employee extension numbers. An intranet provides employees access to internal information. However, unlike the Internet, outside users cannot access intranet applications. Security is built into these applications such that only authorized users have access to the internal databases and documents. Internal users can access the public Internet through their browser.

The adoption of Web technology for corporate intranets is one example of the Internet's impact. New software commonly uses browser interfaces for administration. It makes training on using the software easier. Intranets have enabled enterprises to add new software without downloading the client piece of the software to each desktop (each PC). For example, users click on applications located on Web servers to access the program. This makes it faster for IT staffs to add applications.

The following are ways that organizations use intranets:

- Project monitoring and updates
- Publication of regulatory manuals and Internal telephone books
- Internal job postings
- Searching for information within the organization
- Postings of sales presentations
- Information on R&D projects
- Postings of white papers (explanations of technology)
- Newsletters
- Benefits information
- Distribution of custom-made software applications
- Distribution of training schedules
- Conference room scheduling

Portals are being developed for enterprises that organize information content for users in a similar fashion as public portals. However, access to corporate information is controlled by software restriction. Not everyone has access to all files.

Intranets add more traffic to already congested commercial, government and nonprofits' internal networks. Browsers are "bandwidth hogs." They have color, sound and graphics capabilities. They add traffic to local area networks (LANs), campus connections between LANs and connections between LANs across countries and worldwide.

Extranets—Using Internet Technology with Customers, Partners and Vendors

Typically, extranet transactions are conducted with suppliers, vendors and trading partners. Placing orders is one application for extranets. Access to extranets is generally password protected.

Customers use passwords to log into suppliers' databases to check on availability and rates for products. They also place and check the status of orders via the Web. New business-to-business applications enable orders to be transmitted directly to order entry systems. The absence of human intervention eliminates the possibility of human errors in input.

Benefits of Web technology for extranets:

- *Decreased labor costs*—Customers place their own orders.
- *Savings on paper*—Customers print their own orders.
- *Shortened ordering cycles*—Customers can access pricing, rates and delivery dates without waiting for salespeople or customer service representatives to give them the information.

Trouble ticket reporting is an example of an extranet function. Large organizations give customers the ability to report repair problems via the Internet. After a customer logs in with his customer ID and password, he fills out a form describing the repair problem. The trouble ticket assigns him a trouble ticket number for tracking purposes. Both the customer and maintenance organization now have an electronic timestamp of when the trouble was reported. The trouble ticket is automatically sent to the dispatch staff to be resolved.

A concern with extranets is security. Extranet applications give outside organizations access to portions of organizations' databases. Three ways that security issues are addressed on extranets are:

- Authentication assures receivers that senders are who they claim to be and not hackers.

- Integrity checks assure the sender that no third party has inserted third-party data such as viruses that damage corporate data. Integrity checks ensure that the data is what it claims to be and not something that can harm computer files.

- Encryption scrambles the data sent so that no one except the intended recipient can read the data.

Because of these security concerns, many extranets are located at Web hosting sites. The customer has its own computer or a host-supplied computer located at the hosting company. High-speed T-3 or various OC-speed lines connect the hosting company to the Internet backbone. Often companies remotely upload or download information to their host-located computer via T-1 lines. T-1 lines run at 1.54 million bits per second (bps), T-3 runs at 44 million bps and OC (optical carrier) speeds start at 52 million bits per second. (See Chapter 6.) In addition to hosting companies such as, Genuity, Digex and Exodus, carriers such as Global Crossing, AT&T, Sprint and WorldCom offer hosting and extranet services. Application service providers also sell extranet services.

SECURITY ON THE WORLD WIDE WEB—
ESTABLISHING TRUST ....

The face-to-face and telephone-to-agent interactions that provide assurances to customers are absent on the Internet. People who shop in stores have a personal encounter with clerks. They assume the salesperson that takes their credit card is trustworthy because they see her. They know that person is authorized to take their money, debit card or credit card. People who shop on the Internet need to find a way to establish trust with the organizations with which they do business. Establishing security on the Internet will help increase its utilization for electronic commerce.

The security tools discussed next are installed in corporate servers, application service providers (ASPs), ISP servers, hosting companies and carriers that provide virtual private networks (VPNs). (See Chapter 5 for VPNs.) For corporations, the largest threat to computer security comes from internal employees. Acts of sabotage from disgruntled employees or employees that have been laid off cost businesses millions of dollars. Some companies purchase intrusion detection software before conducting lay-offs.

Public and Private Keys and Digital Certificates

Tools that are used for security on the Internet are used in private networks as well. These tools are public key encryption, private key encryption and digital certificates. *Digital certificates* verify that the vendor is who they say they are. *Private* and *public key encryption* ensure that only the intended recipient can read confidential information such as credit card numbers.

Encryption scrambles documents using mathematical algorithms so that only the intended recipient can decrypt and read the document. Public and private key encryption work together to create and read secure documents. Complementary mathematical algorithms called public and private keys are used to encode documents. A document scrambled by a private key can only be read by a recipient with the complementary public key. A public key can't read a document created by the same public key and a private key can't decipher a document created by the same private key. Thus, public with private key encryption is asymmetric. Different keys perform the encoding and the decoding.

When someone shops, for example, at Amazon.com, Amazon.com sends the shopper a unique public key that scrambles the user's credit card number and order. The Amazon.com site uses its complementary private key to decode the order. The advantage of asymmetric public key cryptography is that the public key can be given out freely without corrupting the security because only the owner of the key has the private key.

Digital certificates with digital signatures are used to authenticate vendors. Web sites contain digital certificates that verify they are who they claim to be. The digital certificate is provided by a trusted third party who has done a background check on the vendor. The digital signature verifies that people are who they claim to be by sending a digital summary of the data sent. The receiving end receives the digital signature and makes a mathematical summary of it. If the receiving end's summary exactly matches the sending end's summary, the identity of the sender is verified. Security software made by VeriSign, Inc. and installed on browsers reads the digital certificates that authenticate vendors. Browsers have a normally open padlock icon that shuts during a secure transaction. This is extremely important because the padlock indicates that the site uses encryption technology such as Secure Sockets Layer (SSL) that uses a 128-bit code for encryption. This means it uses a code-based 2^{128} encoding technique.

Firewalls and Tunneling

Security tools, known as firewalls, are installed in corporate and Internet service provider computers in front of corporate databases. Firewalls screen transmissions before allowing them to reach corporate computers. The firewall verifies the integrity of the data and the sender. The firewall may screen users by their email address. This is called address filtering.

Some companies install demilitarized zones (DMZs) between their firewall and the Internet. DMZs isolate internal traffic from external and Internet traffic. The DMZ takes a more detailed look at traffic than just the address. It also looks at the application itself in case it has a virus or has other characteristics that would harm the internal network.

Many firewalls contain proxy servers. A proxy server provides an extra level of security by not letting outside people connect directly to internal resources. When someone from the outside communicates with the company, he is routed to the proxy. The proxy server wraps new headers around messages from the outside and sends it to the internal device. The proxy acts as a relay service, preventing external users from directly connecting to internal resources such as databases and secure information.

Many organizations outsource their Internet applications to Internet service providers. When they do, they want assurance from the Internet providers that the outsourced applications are secure. Firewalls and proxy servers are installed extensively at Internet service providers as well as end-user sites.

Making the Internet a Trusted Place to Do Business

Virtually all 100,000 e-commerce sites use VeriSign, Inc.'s digital certificate and public key software when they ask for credit card information. The company feels that the widespread acceptance of public keys and digital certificates has helped make the Internet a safer place for e-commerce and business transactions. Businesses use the Internet to transmit a variety of confidential data. For example, Intel transmits designs for its chips; banks move money through the Internet; hospitals exchange patient records; and the automotive industry does business with its entire supply chain through the Internet. Credit card companies cover losses of credit cards over $50. Intel's potential damage if someone hacks into and steals its chip designs is much larger. An additional form of encryption security is tunneling. *Tunneling* encapsulates packets within other protocols for added security when traffic is carried on virtual private networks. Tunneling separates and keeps private transmissions from multiple customers. Tunneling allows new protocols to be packaged and transmitted within older protocols. They are "unwrapped" when they are received by remote firewalls at extranet and intranet sites.

CONCLUSION ....

It appears that technology for making the Web fast and building infrastructure to keep up with large amounts of traffic is more advanced than business models for earning profits on the Internet. Internet service providers, online retailers and portal operators, among others, are struggling to build new infrastructure, attract customers and capital and eventually make a profit.

One unknown about the acceptance of the Internet as a medium for entertainment and consumer commerce is the rate at which populations adopt high-speed Internet access. It's also unclear if consumers see the Internet as just an extension of using a computer at work and want to watch television to relax in their off-hours rather than browse the Internet. As youngsters that take for granted using computers for chats and games grow up, this attitude may change. In addition to high-speed access, consumers often do not have browsers with the capability to receive some types of streaming video and audio. Nor do they always have the ability or know how to download Adobe Reader to take advantage of documents presented as portable document format (PDF) files.

Interestingly, South Korea has the highest percentage of people with broadband access to the Internet. They access streaming video and audio more than any other country, which makes them more likely to use the Internet for entertainment. Two important factors led to South Korea's high rate of high-speed access. Most of their population lives in densely populated cities. Laying new fiber optic lines in these areas results in faster financial returns than in rural areas. In dense cities, more potential customers create larger revenue streams per strand of fiber. In addition, the South Korean government licensed only a limited number of facilities-based carriers. Thus, investments and profits are concentrated among fewer companies with the necessary capital to invest in infrastructure.

Regardless of the speed of consumer acceptance of the Internet, it's clear that the Internet has had an enormous impact on business. In particular, global transactions take place at a faster pace than ever before. Companies send each other email and attachments regardless of time zones. Moreover, corporate Web sites are important public relations and marketing vehicles. Potential customers and suppliers "check out" each other's Web sites often prior to making initial contacts. Press conferences, consultant briefings and corporate financial reports all can be presented through a variety of means including streaming audio presentations and audio conferences combined with online presentations.

9 Wireless Services

In this chapter...

Cellular service is the single-most important technology bringing basic telephone service to large parts of Asia, Latin America and Africa. For vast numbers of people in these regions, a mobile telephone is the first telephone service they will have. The number of cellular telephones outnumber fixed landline service in many Asian and Latin American countries such as Chile, Japan, Mexico, Paraguay and Venezuela.

Wireless paging, mobile data communications and cellular services have changed the way people communicate. Being tethered to a cord is no longer acceptable. Unfortunately, incompatible cellular services were implemented throughout the world and by carriers within the United States.

The first form of cellular service, analog cellular services, also known as advanced mobile phone service (AMPS), was widely deployed by the late 1980s. It was implemented in a standard format developed by AT&T so that all telephones worked on all analog cellular networks in the U.S. Interestingly, there were seven different, incompatible analog types of cellular service implemented at the time in Europe. Analog cellular services became so popular that capacity, particularly in metropolitan areas, was inadequate.

Digital cellular was deployed in the United States in the 1990s to overcome capacity limitations. However, by this time, AT&T had lost its monopoly on local service so that local Bell operating companies implemented incompatible digital technologies. In the U.S., the Telecommunications Industry Association (TIA) settled on a standard using time division multiple access (TDMA). However, shortly thereafter, many of the Bell telephone companies decided to use a newer access method, code division multiple access. Code division multiple access (CDMA) has more spectral efficiency than time division multiple access. It handles more traffic in the same amount of spectrum (range of frequency).

Thus, the U.S. started down the road with two different standards, TDMA and CDMA, both different than Europe's GSM service. In 1987, the European Union chose a standard called global system for mobile communications (GSM) for delivering digital wireless telephony uniformly throughout Europe. Handsets cannot operate on networks with different frequencies unless they have chips that work on multiple frequencies and multiplexing schemes. All digital cellular services use multiplexing to enable devices to share wireless channels. The multiplexing is the air interface, the way a cellular call is carried between the handset and the cellular carrier's antenna.

In addition to air interfaces, cellular networks often operate on different frequencies. The Nextel TDMA service works on a different frequency than that adopted by other carriers and is incompatible with other digital services. Even GSM service is used on different frequencies throughout the world. Table 9.1 lists the frequencies used for cellular service in much of the world. Personal Communications Services

Table 9.1   Wireless Services Offered in the United States and Canada

Service	Frequencies	Features	Comments
Advanced mobile phone service (AMPS)	824 to 849 MHz 869 to 894 MHz	Analog, first type of cellular technology. Provides basic calling and voice mail. Implemented in the late 1980s. More capacity than non-cellular previous service.	Two providers, the local telephone company and a competitor, originally served each metropolitan area. All telephones were compatible with all services.
Digital-advanced mobile phone service (D-AMPS)	824 to 849 MHz 869 to 894 MHz	Digital service has more capacity than analog service. Provides advanced features such as caller ID and short messaging service.	Both CDMA and TDMA air interfaces operate on D-AMPS. Verizon Wireless and Cingular Wireless are the largest D-AMPS providers.
Global system for mobile communications (GSM)	450 MHz 890 to 960 MHz 1.8 GHz 1.9 GHz	A cellular digital technology. The same handsets can be used in all countries that use GSM multiplexing.	Standard used in Europe, the Far East, Israel, New Zealand and Australia. Also used by VoiceStream and soon AT&T Wireless and Cingular Wireless in the U.S.
Personal communications service (PCS)	1.8 to 1.9 GHz	PCS refers to the spectrum used in some cellular networks. PCS networks have the same features as other digital cellular networks but need more closely spaced, smaller antennas.	Sprint Cellular, Verizon Wireless and AT&T Wireless all have parts of their networks on PCS frequencies.

Table 9.1   Wireless Services Offered in the United States and Canada *(continued)*

Service	Frequencies	Features	Comments
Nextel and other specialized mobile radio (SMR)	816 to 866 MHz	Offerings include packet data from Cingular Interactive and Motient Corporation and wireless digital telephone service from Nextel.	Originally used for analog, two-way voice dispatch services. Nextel's service is based on i-DEN time division technology developed by Motorola to support voice, paging and messaging on the same telephone.
Cellular digital packet data (CDPD)	824 to 894 MHz 1.8 to 1.9 GHz	CDPD is used for short, bursty data communications applications such as email, dispatch, alarm monitoring and credit card verification. The top speed is 19.2 Kbps.	A wireless data communications standard using the Internet Protocol (IP). Operates on spare capacity of D-AMPS and PCS networks.

•CDMA and TDMA are explained in more detail at the end of this chapter.

(PCS) uses still other, higher frequencies or portions of the airwaves to transmit signals. PCS requires smaller towers spaced closer together. PCS service was implemented in the late 1990s to compete with digital and analog lower frequency services sold by Bell telephone companies and their competitors. Some similarities and differences between PCS offered by companies such as Sprint PCS and AT&T Wireless and digital cellular already implemented are:

- Both are compatible with either code division multiple access or time division multiple access.

- Both provide the same enhanced calling services such as caller ID, paging and short messaging services via a liquid crystal display on handsets.

- Both are difficult to eavesdrop on because the multiplexing scrambles the voice signals.

- PCS towers are smaller and must be spaced closer together. PCS vendors call their towers' antennas because of their small size.

Competition for digital cellular and personal communications service (PCS) led to price decreases and affordable cellular service for residential and business consum-

TDMA, CDMA AND GSM FOR DIGITAL CELLULAR NETWORKS

TDMA, CDMA and GSM operate on all frequencies used in cellular networks. See Table 9.1. They are *air interface methods*—ways to transmit calls between cellular handsets and the cellular carrier's equipment. They significantly increased capacity on analog cellular networks by enabling multiple handsets to share frequencies.

- TDMA (time division multiple access) is based on time division multiplexing. Each call is assigned a time slot. TDMA is used in Cingular Wireless and AT&T Wireless networks.

- CDMA (code division multiple access) divides up the airwaves by associating a unique code to each call. It is used in Verizon Wireless and other networks worldwide in Israel, Asia and Latin America.

- GSM (global system for mobile communications) is the most widely used air interface method. It uses a different form of time division multiplexing than that used in TDMA service. GSM was first used in Europe. VoiceStream in the United States operates a GSM network.

ers. In 1998, for the first time, the sale of digital handsets exceeded those of analog handsets. A major challenge for digital cellular is improving network quality. PCS providers such as AT&T Wireless and Sprint PCS are still building out their networks. Although Cingular Wireless and Verizon Wireless have nationwide networks, they both have pockets where they don't have service or roaming agreements with other carriers. Roaming is the use of cellular phones by subscribers on other providers' networks. There are also areas in large cities where tall buildings and congestion lead to dropped calls and poor service.

Another wireless technology is specialized mobile radio (SMR), which was used originally for dispatch services in businesses such as contracting. The airwaves on which these channels were used were later deployed to transmit data for transportation, field maintenance and delivery organizations. Motient Corporation (formerly ARDIS) and Cingular Interactive (formerly RAM and BellSouth Data) developed specialized networks for transmitting wireless data. These networks are now used for two-way email service for Palm and RIM's Blackberry hand-held devices. Finally, Nextel, a user of these frequencies, changed its analog data network services from an all-data network to a digital voice and data network. It sells digital telephone services and offer phones capable of operating on GSM as well as Nextel networks. (Refer to Table 9.1 for a comparison of various wireless services available.)

Sales of paging services have slowed considerably as more users switch to digital cellular service whose prices have dropped and coverage, while not perfect, is improving. To counteract the slowdown in sales and to take advantage of the large two-way paging networks in place, manufacturers have developed two-way email service on pagers.

Wireless functionality is expanding into more data services. Satellites have the advantage over cellular and landline services of reaching remote areas. They are starting to be used for two-way Internet access. The biggest investments for high-speed data services are for 3G and 2.5G service. To date, billions of dollars have been invested in spectrum and equipment. It is unknown what the impact of health and safety concerns as well as costs to upgrade networks will be on the growth of cellular service for voice and data.

HISTORICAL BACKGROUND OF MOBILE AND CELLULAR SERVICES ....

Prior to the first deployment of analog cellular car telephones in 1984, users who wanted to place telephone calls from their cars used mobile non-cellular telephone networks that had connections to the public switched network. The first mobile telephone system was started in 1946 in St. Louis, Missouri. Costs for car telephones were high, between $2000 to $2500, and capacity was limited. The local telephone company in each city operated one transmitter and receiver for the entire area. Thus, the entire area covered by the one transmitter shared the same channels. This meant that only a limited number (25 to 35) of simultaneous calls could be placed on each city's mobile system. In addition to limited capacity, the quality of service was spotty with considerable static and breaking up of calls.

Mobile radio service was more widespread than mobile telephone service prior to the mid-1980s. Mobile radio is a "closed" service without connections to the public switched network. Mobile radio operators can only reach people on their closed network. For example, users on one taxicab service's system cannot call users on another cab's system. Police departments were early pioneers of car radios. The Detroit police department used mobile radio service in 1921. In the 1930s, mobile radio use spread to other public safety agencies such as fire departments. Mobile radio systems are now used for aviation, trucking, taxis and marine applications.

Mobile radio is half-duplex: Calls are two-way but only one user at a time can transmit. For example, when one person is done speaking, he uses a convention such as "over and out" to let the other person know he is finished talking. People using mobile radio push a button to talk.

SPECTRUM ALLOCATION ....

Aviation, marine, trucking and emergency public agencies all use different portions of the spectrum, or airwaves, to communicate over wireless radio frequencies. The term *spectrum* refers to a range of frequencies or the portion of the radio waves allocated for particular applications such as satellites or cellular service. A *frequency* is the number of times each second that each radio wave completes a cycle. As mentioned in Chapter 1, each cycle looks like a resting letter S. A cycle is complete when a radio wave passes through the highest and lowest portions of the wave. The term *hertz* refers to one cycle of a radio wave.

The allocation of spectrum is administered on both an international and national level. The International Telecommunications Union (ITU) manages the allocation of spectrum for services such as satellite and television because these services cross national borders. Individual countries allocate spectrum for their own areas. For this reason, countries have assigned different frequencies to fixed wireless service. This drives up manufacturing costs as fewer economies of scale are achieved.

In the United States, the FCC has broken up spectrum into bands and assigned it for particular purposes. For example, residential cordless phones are assigned to the 800 million cycles (hertz) MHz per second, and 2.4 gigahertz bands. Citizens band radio is assigned to the 27, 462 and 467 MHz, or million hertz bands. The very high frequency (VHF) bands for TV channels 2 through 12 and mobile radio services for police and fire dispatch use are in the 30 MHz to 300 MHz range of frequencies. Thirty MHz means that each wave has 30 million cycles or hertz per second. It completes 30 million cycles; 30 million resting Ss in one second.

Higher frequencies have shorter wavelengths. (A *wavelength* is the distance between the highest point in one wave to the highest point in the next wave.) For example, a 3000-Hz wave has a longer wavelength than a 3,000,000-Hz wave. Small wavelengths are more susceptible to rain and weather conditions. A rain droplet can destroy a smaller wave more easily than a larger one. The raindrop is bigger in relationship to a small wavelength than to a large wavelength. Therefore, high-frequency microwave systems are more susceptible to weather conditions than lower frequency systems. Signals on higher frequency services such as personal communications services (PCS) also cannot be transmitted as far as lower frequencies before they fade. Therefore, PCS towers and antennas must be closer together than lower frequency, traditional cellular services. This is the reason that 3G (third generation) advanced wireless networks that use higher frequencies will need to add many more cellular towers. The towers will need to be closer together to accommodate short wavelengths.

If frequencies were not allocated to specific companies for specific uses, transmissions would overlap or interfere with each other. For example, if two telephone calls took place in the same airspace at the same frequency, the callers would be able to hear each other's conversations. This is interference.

The limiting factor in cellular network is spectrum. The advent of cellular and digital technologies discussed later enabled a fixed amount of spectrum to be used more efficiently by many more users. This is called *spectral efficiency*, the capability of using the same spectrum for more subscribers.

Spectrum for Higher Speed 3G Services

The World Radiocommunication Conference (WRC) 2000 of the International Telecommunications Union identified three bands of spectrum on which third generation cellular (3G) service should operate. (3G service for advanced voice and data services is reviewed later.) However, available spectrum is scarce in the United States and most of the spectrum in these bands is already occupied by other services:

- 806 to 960 MHz—Cellular and specialized mobile radio.
- 1710 to 1885 MHz—1850 to 1885 MHz is used for personal communications service (PCS), a form of digital cellular. The Department of Defense is the primary user of 1755 to 1850 MHz. The Commerce Department has stated that 45 MHz could be cleared in these ranges at a cost of $2.1 billion.
- 2500 to 2690 MHz—Instructional television and Multipoint Multichannel Distribution Service (MMDS) for fixed wireless.

PCS frequencies were auctioned off in 1996 to NextWave Telecom Inc. and Metro PCS. Both of these companies filed for bankruptcy and to date have not used the spectrum. The FCC repossessed the licenses and held a new auction for the licenses won by NextWave. Companies backed by Verizon, VoiceStream Wireless, Dobson Communications, AT&T Wireless and Cingular submitted the highest bids. However, in June 2001 the courts ruled that the FCC had no right to reclaim the licenses. Moreover, a bankruptcy court refused to allow the government to repossess the Metro PCS licenses. It's not known if the government will appeal these decisions or if NextWave and Metro PCS will sell the licenses to other cellular companies. NextWave announced in July 2001 that it has contracted with Lucent Technologies to build a cellular network.

The lack of unassigned, usable spectrum is an enormous problem in the United States. Spectrum in lower frequencies was given out to public service agencies, television, police and radio. As higher frequencies became usable, they were assigned for applications such as fixed wireless and very small aperture terminal (VSAT) satellites without adequate planning. Moreover, free spectrum was given to television broadcasters for digital television. Broadcasters have spectrum they currently use for analog television plus spectrum for digital television. The government is planning to auction, for wireless service, the frequencies used for UHF (ultra high frequencies) channels 11 to 69, which TV broadcasters are scheduled to give up by 2006.

The auctions are scheduled to start with parts of channels 60 to 69 that are not in major markets in 2001. However, cellular providers prefer to wait until and if spectrum in major markets opens up. President Bush has proposed a two-year delay on these auctions, which cover the 700 MHz range.

The ITU has stated that each country is free to select the spectrum to be used for 3G. However, devices for roaming service will be simpler to manufacture if they operate on the same frequencies worldwide. The FCC originally stated that it would identify spectrum for 3G systems by July 2001 and hold an auction by September 30, 2002. In June 2001, it announced that it would not meet the July 2001 date and would continue working on the matter.

CELLULAR TELEPHONE SERVICE— TECHNOLOGIES..

The first generation of cellular services introduced in the 1980s was analog. These were later upgraded to digital. The most important advantage of digital cellular is its improvement in capacity. Second generation digital cellular used in existing digital networks supports three to ten times the capacity of analog cellular.

Advanced Mobile Phone Services (AMPS)

Advanced mobile phone service (AMPS) is the analog cellular telephone service provided in the United States. (All two-way wireless handsets are in reality radios with transmitters and receivers. Radios transmit energy into the air.) Cellular service increased capacity of mobile technology because it reuses frequencies in hexagonal-shaped cells, as depicted in Figure 9.1. With analog cellular service, each cell carries up to 57 conversations. If carriers need more capacity, they split cells into smaller sizes and reuse frequencies in the newly created cells. More cells equal more capacity.

The concept of cellular telephone service originated in 1947 at AT&T's Bell Laboratories (now part of Lucent Technology) with trials conducted in Chicago and Baltimore in late 1983. The FCC set aside radio spectrum for cellular service at 825 to 890 MHz and decided that each of the 306 Metropolitan Statistical Areas and 428 Rural Service Areas were to have two cellular service providers. The local wireline telephone company was assigned the B block of frequencies and a non-telephone company was assigned the A block. The FCC hoped to foster competition by having two providers in each area.

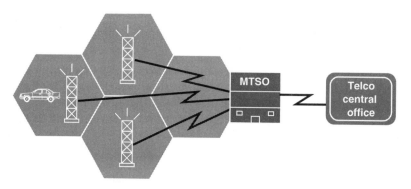

Figure 9.1
The mobile telephone switching office (MTSO) connects the cellular network to the public switched telephone network.

Other than the 30 largest metropolitan areas, cellular frequencies in the A block were given out by an FCC lottery to qualified vendors. Initially, cellular service was purchased for salespeople and business executives who justified the high cost of telephone calls by their ability to use their time more effectively. The cost of each call was roughly equivalent to the cost for an operator-assisted call. Telephone bills for corporate users such as salespeople were typically $200 per month. Although usage fees remained high, handset costs dropped. Telephones were often provided at no cost or at a minimal fee to attract new customers.

Digital-Advanced Mobile Phone Service— D-AMPS

Cellular providers such as Verizon Wireless and Cingular Wireless offer digital cellular service over the same frequencies as their analog cellular services. Depending on the digital technology, digital cellular has three to ten times more capacity than analog service. Cellular carriers set aside channels for digital service, which use either time division multiple access or code division multiple access. (A more detailed explanation of these access schemes is provided later.) Carriers designate a portion of their total channels to transport calls in digital format.

Initially, carriers added capacity by breaking cells up into smaller sizes. However, adding small cells has its problems. Smaller cells lead to more dropped calls and dead areas where calls cannot be made because of problems of overlapping into adjacent cells.

In addition to capacity, carriers hoped for extra revenue from enhanced features such as messaging on handsets. They also wanted to stay competitive with PCS service. D-AMPS supports the same features as PCS: caller ID, alphanumeric paging, voice mail notification, short messaging, a longer battery life and services such as call return.

Privacy also is improved on all forms of digital cellular service. Snoopers with scanners easily listen in on analog cellular signals. Eavesdropping on digital transmissions is more difficult because the digital bits are scrambled when they are multiplexed using time division multiple access (TDMA) and code division multiple access (CDMA) schemes. Sophisticated scanners can be used to listen in on calls carried on digital service; however, the scanners are more expensive and less readily available than analog scanners. Many vendors of digital scanners claim they only sell them to law enforcement agencies.

Digital signal processors in handsets decode the digital bits representing caller ID numbers and paging messages into alphanumeric characters displayed on handsets' liquid crystal displays. Digital signal processors (DSPs) are specialized, very high-speed computer chips. See Chapter 5 for an explanation of digital signal processors. The DSPs also code and decode the voice signals, converting them from analog to digital at the sending end and from digital to analog at the receiving end. Most digital cellular handsets are dual or tri-mode mode. Tri-mode cellular phones operate in for example, PCS, TDMA and analog cellular markets. When callers are in analog areas, they lose caller ID and other advanced features associated with digital cellular.

PCS—Personal Communications Services

Personal communications services (PCS) were conceived as a way to provide a low-cost, feature-rich wireless telephone service. Pricing was to be low enough for the service to be affordable to a wide segment of the population. The handsets incorporate two-way paging, short messaging service on the liquid crystal display and voice messaging. PCS services operate on a different portion of the airwaves (the 1.8 to 1.9 Gigahertz frequencies) than the earlier analog and digital cellular services (AMPS and D-AMPS). The major difference between D-AMPS and PCS is that because of the higher frequencies, PCS networks have a larger number of and smaller antennas. Because of the shorter wavelengths associated with these high frequencies, antennas need to be spaced closer together.

In 1993, the FCC announced plans to auction off portions of the 1.8 to 1.9 Gigahertz personal communications services spectrum. Six chunks of spectrum for PCS service were defined as A, B, C, D, E and F blocks. The A and B blocks were for the 50 MTAs (Major Trading Areas), which are regions that include multiple cities or states. C through F channels were in each of the 450 Basic Trading Areas (BTAs), which include only one metropolitan area. Blocks A, B and C have 30 MHz of spectrum and blocks C, D and E have 10 MHz each. The rules forbade incumbent cellular providers from bidding on frequencies within their own regions. They were not allowed to bid in areas where there was a 20% or more overlap with the PCS area in their existing cellular coverage.

The federal government's goals in promoting new use of the airways were to encourage competition and raise money for the U.S. Treasury. By dividing up the country into six groups of frequencies, each area could have six PCS competitors plus the two existing cellular providers. Competition from PCS services has driven prices down for all cellular service and encouraged growth in new wireless services. (See Table 9.2.)

Table 9.2   The Largest Cellular Providers in the United States

Cellular Provider	Number of Customers as of 2001*	Comments
Verizon Wireless	28 million customers	Vodafone, largest wireless company worldwide, owns 45%. Verizon Wireless was formed by the combination of Vodafone AirTouch, GTE and Bell Atlantic Wireless assets. It includes AirTouch, PrimeCo and AirTouch paging assets.
Cingular Wireless	20 million customers	A joint venture of BellSouth and SBC's (CellularOne) cellular assets.
AT&T Wireless	15 million customers	IPO completed July 2001. NTT DoCoMo, the largest wireless company in Japan, owns 16%. AT&T Wireless owns controlling interest in Rogers Wireless of Canada.
Sprint PCS	11 million customers	Service covers 50 states plus Puerto Rico and Virgin Islands.

Information on number of customers from company-provided information.

GSM Service

GSM is the digital cellular standard that was originally decided on by European governments and was first deployed in 1990. According to market research firm, Gartner Consulting, as of April 2001, 62% of cellular service was based on GSM. The reason for its popularity is its worldwide compatibility. GSM service offers the same functionality as PCS and D-AMPS networks. It operates in four ranges of frequencies listed in Table 9.1. It uses a time division multiple access scheme similar to that used in the United States by Cingular Wireless.

GSM phones have Subscriber Identity Module (SIM) cards that clip on them for storing user identity. Most GSM phones are either dual or triple mode and are capable of operating on various GSM frequencies. Alternatively, the SIM card can be used when people roam on different networks.

Specialized Mobile Frequencies for Voice— Nextel

Nextel was founded in 1987 and initially offered data communications over analog radio facilities. Nextel's newer wireless telephone service is carried over digital facilities in its 800 to 900 MHz spectrum. The service is used with Motorola telephones and is geared toward small and medium-sized businesses. In early 1999, Nextel upgraded its network to support browser-equipped Motorola telephones. It targets commercial, not residential, customers. Motorola Corporation and the McCaw family each own 20% of Nextel. (The McCaw cellular company was purchased by AT&T in 1993.)

Nextel phones have a liquid crystal display that can be used for text and numeric paging. Nextel coverage is in 185 of the top 200 markets and within reach of 77% of the U.S. These areas are largely metropolitan locations. Vast areas of sparsely populated sections of the country will not be covered. Nextel is accessible from major interstate highways. However, it will not have towers or service in remote locations with few businesses such as North Dakota and Montana.

In addition, Nextel offers Nextel Direct Connect. This service enables employees in the same company to have direct connections to each other by pushing a button on their telephone.

Because Nextel service does not work on the 1800 to 1900 megahertz frequencies, it did not have to participate in costly bidding for new frequencies. However, it has a limited amount of spectrum. Nextel offers the same features as PCS service such as short messaging text paging, email and voice mail. These phones use a technology, iDEN (integrated Digital Enhanced Network) developed by Motorola that breaks each 25 kilohertz channel into up to six time slots able to carry voice, paging traffic, data and dispatch messages. It compresses the voice small enough so that it can fit into one of the six time slots.

High-end Nextel phones have email capability embedded in them that works with Microsoft Outlook and Lotus as well as email provided by Internet service providers. The Nextel email server converts these email formats to that compatible with Nextel. Subscribers access their email by pressing the email button on their telephone and entering their password. A cookie in the phone sends the user name and email account information. The phone can be set up to receive all or some email messages. This functionality doesn't work when roaming. A cable is available to connect the phone to a laptop computer so that email can be stored on a computer.

Nextel offers a dual mode, GSM and 900-megahertz TDMA Motorola telephone that operates in over 60 countries with which it has roaming agreements. Nextel sells service directly and through Nextel Partners, an affiliate who sells in small to medium-sized markets in 30 states within the United States. Its single mode phone operates in parts of Canada, Latin America and the Philippines where Nextel International operates networks in the same frequency and access methods as those in the United States. Nextel's lower frequency network requires fewer towers because lower frequency, longer wavelength signals travel farther without deteriorating than PCS signals at higher (1900 megahertz) frequencies.

CELLULAR VENDORS ....

Companies such as AT&T Wireless and Sprint PCS are enlarging their networks to attain a nationwide footprint. Massive investments have been made to acquire air space for PCS service, market services and build cell sites. Cable TV companies, long distance companies and Bell companies formed joint ventures to offer PCS service. Sprint PCS was originally a joint venture of Sprint Communications and three cable companies: TCI, Comcast and Cox Communications. It was conceived as a way to jointly offer wireless and telephone service. The cable companies later divested their ownership of Sprint PCS. International and enhanced data services are focuses of all the large cellular companies in the United States.

Verizon Wireless

Verizon Wireless was formed by a merger with Vodafone AirTouch. Vodafone owns 45% of Verizon Wireless and Verizon Communications owns the rest. In 1999, Vodafone Group PLC purchased AirTouch. At the time, AirTouch was the third largest D-AMPS provider. Prior to the formation of Verizon Wireless, Bell Atlantic purchased GTE, whose wireless assets are part of Verizon Wireless. Verizon Wireless operates CDMA networks in the PCS frequencies as well as its digital and analog service in the 800 frequencies. This is a problem for customers that might want one-number service internationally because Vodafone operates GSM networks.

Cingular Wireless

The merger of SBC's CellularOne operation and BellSouth's cellular arm formed Cingular Wireless. SBC had previously purchased Ameritech, Pacific Bell and Southern New England Telephone in Connecticut cellular service. They converted Ameritech's CDMA to TDMA to make it compatible with CellularOne's TDMA structure. Bell-

South has a mix of CDMA and TDMA air access. SBC owns 60% and BellSouth owns 40% of Cingular Wireless.

AT&T Wireless

AT&T Wireless got its start in cellular service with its purchase of the (at that time) largest cellular carrier in the U.S., McCaw Cellular Communications, Inc., for $12.6 billion in 1993. Interestingly, when McCaw was bought by AT&T, it had never made a profit.

AT&T Wireless has a strategy of buying existing cellular networks, forming alliances with cellular providers and building new PCS services from scratch. In 1998, it purchased independent cellular provider Vanguard Cellular. AT&T purchased PCS spectrum from FCC auctions wherever McCaw did not provide its AMPS service. AT&T service is based on TDMA. It introduced PCS spectrum in its non-McCaw territory. It sells tri-mode telephones that adapt automatically and work on analog cellular AMPS, TDMA D-AMPS and 1.8 to 1.9 GHz PCS frequencies. It is adding GSM service to its network.

GSM Providers

The largest provider of GSM service in the United States is VoiceStream Wireless, which has purchased or owns through purchases of other companies: Omnipoint Corporation, Powertel, Inc., DiGiph PCS, East/West Communications and Aerial Communications. Deutsche Telekom purchased VoiceStream in 2001. VoiceStream has 5.4 million customers and offers service in 38 of the United States' 50 states. It will be part of Deutsche Telekom's T-Mobile subsidiary. Both companies' subscribers will have one number, one bill roaming throughout each other's areas. T-Mobile owns cellular providers One2One in the UK and max.mobil of Austria.

The desire for one-number international roaming for corporate clients is providing the impetus for AT&T Wireless and AT&T Rogers Wireless, Inc. to add GSM service to all of its cell sites. This will give AT&T Wireless a larger GSM footprint than VoiceStream. It hopes to sell cellular service to multinational customers with staff in both the United States and abroad. AT&T Wireless plans to sell general packet radio service (GPRS) data service on its GSM platform. It will keep residential customers and customers that don't purchase advanced services on its TDMA service. GPRS is an "always on" packet service with higher speeds than currently available TDMA networks. AT&T Wireless will focus on high-speed data services to corporate clients. It will heavily promote either WAP or i-mode–type Internet access plus two-way messaging service. Cingular Wireless has also announced that it is upgrading some areas to the general packet radio service (GPRS) GSM platform.

Sprint PCS

Sprint PCS has licenses for PCS spectrum in all 50 states. It has added numerous cell sites in 2000 and 2001. One of its advantages is its billing system, which is newer than that of many of its rivals. It markets service to business and consumer customers. It reaches residential customers through its distribution by Tandy Corporation's Radio Shack retail chain. Sprint PCS operates on code division multiple access (CDMA) technology. Sprint is investing heavily in cdma2000 3G service that it will use as a platform for two-way messaging, short messaging service and other data services. (3G high-speed data services are discussed later.)

Virgin Mobile, a unit of UK-based Virgin Group, has announced that it will use the Sprint PCS network over which to sell its own brand of cellular service. Virgin Mobile will provide the sales, marketing, customer service and billing for the service. Virgin Mobile is known as a *virtual operator*. It supplies service but has none of its own cellular network infrastructure.

The Structure of Cellular Networks

Cellular networks are composed of the following equipment and software. See Figure 9.2. Various vendors have different labels for these devices:

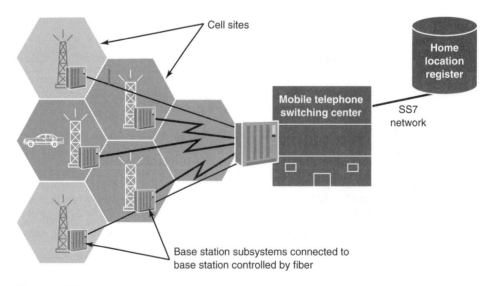

Figure 9.2
A cell site, mobile switching center and SS7.

- *The base transceiver station (BTS) or base station subsystem (BSS)*—The base transceiver station is connected to the antenna. It transmits and receives mobile calls from the cell site's antenna and amplifies (strengthens) signals. A base station consists of a BTS plus the antenna. The base stations are the costliest part of a cellular network's hardware.

- *The base station controller (BSC)*—The BSC is the traffic cop of the mobile network. It does the pre-call setup (e.g., it assigns calls to radio channels in the base station transceiver, sends ringing to the correct channel and measures signal strength). The base station controller can be located at the base transceiver station or one controller can manage many base transceiver stations (BTSs).

- *The mobile switching center (MSC), also called the mobile telephone switching office (MTSO)*—The MSC is analogous to a PBX or central office switch. It switches calls between cellular networks and the public switched telephone network. Mobile switches have Signaling System 7[1] (SS7) links to databases that contain billing and roaming information. (See Chapter 5 for SS7.) Mobile switches control up to 255 cell sites. New ones control up to 1024 sites.

- *Databases*—Home location registers (HLRs) contain information service and billing information on subscribers. The HLR also keeps track of the status and location of subscribers within its area. Visitor information is located in the visitor's location register (VLR). The United States has a nationwide Signaling System 7 cellular network operated by a consortium of cellular companies. It was started by AT&T.

- *Connections to the public switched telephone network*—Mobile telephone switching offices are connected to landline public networks by high-speed 45 megabits per second (Mbps) T-3 links.

THE CELLULAR MARKET ....

Competition has benefited customers by triggering price decreases and wider availability of service. The Cellular Telecommunications Industry Association statistics in Table 9.3 indicate that the number of cellular subscribers grew by 24 million users from 86 million in 1999 to 110 million in 2000 in the United States.

Annual revenue in 2000 was close to $52.5 billion. For the past two years, average monthly bills have increased. From 1988 when the statistics were first published

---

1. Short message service, information displayed on handsets and enhanced features such as caller ID and repeat dialing, are made possible by Signaling System 7 links to databases.

Table 9.3 Annualized Cellular Subscribers and Revenues in the United States

Date	Subscribers	Revenues ($)	Monthly Bill
December 1988	2,069,441	1,959,548	$98.02
December 1989	3,508,944	3,340,595	$83.94
December 1990	5,283,055	4,548,882	$80.90
December 1991	7,557,148	5,708,522	$72.74
December 1992	11,032,753	7,822,726	$68.68
December 1993	16,009,461	10,892,165	$61.48
December 1994	24,134,421	14,229,920	$56.21
December 1995	33,785,661	19,071,966	$51.00
December 1996	44,042,992	23,634,971	$47.70
December 1997	48,705,553	25,575,276	$43.86
December 1998	69,209,321	33,133,175	$39.43
December 1999	86,047,003	40,018,489	$41.24
December 2000	110,040,541	52,466,020	$45.27

Source: The CTIA Semi-annual Data Survey. Used with permission of CTIA.

to 1998 they decreased each year from a high of $98.02 in 1988 to a low of $39.43 in 1997. The penetration of cellular telephones is lower in the U.S., 39% according to the FCC, than in Europe. In Finland, more people have mobile phones than landline phones. The fact that more people don't have cellular phones, and the ones who do have low monthly usage, can be attributed to the following factors:

1. In the United States, as opposed to other parts of the world, callers pay for calls they receive as well as those they make. Thus people are reluctant to give out their cell phone numbers.

2. Many consumers are cost-conscious and purchase the telephones more for safety reasons than the need to make daily calls.

3. Most residential users have landline service that allows them an unlimited number of local phone calls. In other parts of the world, consumers pay by the minute for each local call.

Pricing structures and elimination of roaming fees have resulted in increased usage. Complicated roaming fees are being eliminated for customers who use digital cellular service. Most providers offer calling plans where subscribers can purchase "buckets" of, for example, 200 minutes for $30. Because more carriers have networks across the country, they can offer fixed-price national plans that include an allotted number of minutes. Nextel was the first provider to drop its roaming fees in January of 1997. Roaming services allow customers to use their cellular telephones in other than their home regions. Vendors such as Sprint PCS and AT&T Wireless followed suit. Another way that cellular providers promote usage is "family" plans that offer discounts to members of the same family that purchase cellular service.

Efforts to Improve Service— Antenna Improvements

Caller dissatisfaction with quality of service leads to *churn*—customers discontinuing service or changing carriers. Major challenges facing cellular providers are the lack of a uniform national cellular network and uneven quality in service particularly in rural areas and large cities. The sparse nature of population densities in areas such as western states and far northern regions make it difficult to economically deploy service. In addition to gaps in coverage, congestion in large urban areas such as San Francisco and New York is a problem. Many customers complain about choppy calls and locations where their telephones do not work. Tower spacing, capacity and interference in the form of tunnels and low-lying areas are challenges. Cellular providers are faced with the challenge of fine-tuning their transmitters to eliminate dead zones and holes in coverage.

John Catlin, Manager of Wireless Information Services for Agilent, maintains that the biggest challenge is being able to balance capacity for voice with that for data services while maintaining signal strength in data calls, which need a much better signal. For example, if voice is compressed to leave more capacity for data, how will this impact voice quality? The challenge on data is especially acute inside buildings where coverage is often uneven. Agilent offers a service where automatic dialers inside vans are driven through various regions while they make continuous test calls on as many as eight networks simultaneously. In 2.5 generation TDMA and GSM networks, higher speed data uses capacity previously allotted for voice traffic. Mr. Catlin, who has been conducting studies since 1998, has noticed the growth of the footprint of networks, particularly in smaller and mid-sized cities.

New "smart" antenna systems are being implemented that increase spectrum capacity by providing multiple beams of energy into from three to six sectors (sections) of a cell. Antennas transmit radio frequencies in cell sites in 360-degree circles. With new antennas, sectors can be adjusted through software so that higher percentages of spectrum are beamed to busy sectors. This is one way carriers transmit greater amounts of traffic with a limited amount of spectrum. Smart antennas increase capacity by 35% to 50%.

Repeaters are used in rural areas with lower densities of traffic. They extend, "repeat" the signal, making it stronger, so that it can be sent longer distances before fading. This obviates the need for adding more cell sites. It does not increase the amount of traffic that a given amount of spectrum can handle. It makes sense in low-traffic areas where carriers want to cover large areas.

In-building Antenna Systems—Adding Coverage to Skyscrapers

Large buildings in cities are particularly hard places in which to provide cellular service. It's extremely difficult to penetrate walls without turning up power too high. The height of buildings also is a problem. Putting antennas in top stories gives coverage there but the signal is too weak for street-level traffic. One solution is to install a cell site within buildings with small antennas on every floor. A base unit is connected by fiber strung through the building's riser to hubs on each floor. Each hub is connected to antennas on the same floor. The base station in the basement or outside a building is connected to the cellular provider's network via cabling. The same system in a building can support many air access methods simultaneously (e.g., TDMA, GSM, Nextel, paging and CDMA). Carriers pay for the in-building cell site and may share a percentage of the cellular revenue with the landlord. These systems are used to provide service in subway tunnels, convention centers and skyscrapers.

Health Concerns

The increasing proliferation of cellular telephones worldwide is prompting concerns about their impact on health. According to Needham, Massachusetts research firm, Tower Group, there were 585 million mobile phone users worldwide in 2000—115 million of them in the U.S., where 3 million more are being added each month. The U.S. General Accounting Office (GAO) reported in May 2001 that:

> *"Current research doesn't show that energy emitted by cellular phones has adverse health effects, but there is not yet enough information to conclude that they pose no risk."*

Cell phones emit radio waves, which produce low levels of radiation, mostly from the antenna. In 1996, the Federal Communications Commission (FCC) established a level of 1.6 watts per kilogram of human tissue as the highest amount of radio waves a device can safely emit when held against the body. The measurement of the amount of radio frequency energy absorbed by the body is called specific absorption rate (SAR). The GAO has urged the FCC to standardize testing procedures since there are many testing variables that can affect results. Manufacturers include SAR rates and safety information in booklets included with new cellular devices. The information is not included on the cell phone's packaging. Thus consumers must ask an employee to open multiple boxes if they want to compare radio frequency absorption levels.

In an attempt to determine their health impact, in June 2000 the Food and Drug Administration (FDA) entered into a partnership with the cellular industry in which new research will be funded by the industry but the FDA retains the right to choose the researchers and the subjects investigated. Some experts outside the industry are critical of the fact that studies are being financed by industry.

In the UK where more than half the population uses mobile phones, the government commissioned a group of independent experts to study safety issues. The Independent Expert Group on Mobile Phones issued their report in May 2000. The group chaired by Sir William Stewart concluded that:

- The balance of evidence to date does not suggest that emissions from mobile phones put the health of the UK population at risk.
- There is now some preliminary scientific evidence that exposures to radio frequency radiation may cause subtle effects on biological functions, including those of the brain.
- A precautionary approach to the use of mobile telephone technologies should be adopted.
- The use of mobile phones while driving can have a detrimental effect on the quality of driving.
- The widespread use of mobile phones by children should be discouraged.

Committee members called on the industry not to target children under 16 in their marketing campaigns. Panel member Colin Blakemore, an Oxford brain development expert said,

> "We can't say that there is any risk for children—but if it later emerges that cellular phones cause harm, children may be more vulnerable because their nervous systems are still developing. They have thinner skulls and smaller heads and would have a longer life time exposure to the radiation."

The preceding quote appeared in the AP article, "UK Panel Eyes Risk of Cellular Phones," published in *The Boston Globe*, 12 May 2000, page A20, by Emma Ross.

Safety on the Road

In addition to health impacts, there is a concern that driving while talking on a cellular telephone may be dangerous. Limiting cellular telephone use by drivers has gained worldwide support. At least 23 countries, including Japan, Italy, Spain and Israel, have adopted various bans. In the United States, the National Highway Traffic Safety Administration estimates that 85% of cellular telephone owners use them while driving. New York is the only state that currently bans talking on handheld cellular phones while driving. In May 2001 bills were introduced in the U.S. House and Senate to ban or limit cellular telephone use while driving.

There has been a growing grassroots movement for legislative action led in large part by families of victims of cellular telephone–related accidents. Eleven municipalities including Marlboro, New Jersey and Brookline, Massachusetts have enacted legislation limiting driver use of mobile phones. Illinois and Connecticut are seriously considering legislation and bills have been introduced in several states throughout the country.

A 1997 study published in the *New England Journal of Medicine* concluded that cellular telephone use by drivers was a major distraction that quadrupled the risk of an accident. In the U.S., there are no reliable statistics as to how many accidents are related to talking on the phones. In the article, "First You Dial, Then You Crash," published in *Salon.com*, 7 December 2000, by Dawn Mackeen, Tom Dingus, Director of the Virginia Tech Transportation Institute, estimates between 600 to 1000 people die each year in cellular telephone–related crashes in the United States.

On February 7, 2001 the University of Montreal's Transportation Safety Laboratory, in its official report, "Using Mobile Phones Increases Risk of Accidents on the Road" concluded that cellular telephone users had a 38% higher risk of accidents than non-users, and the risk increased with the frequency of calls. This study by Dr. Claire Laberge-Nadeau, compared questionnaires to telephone and accident records of 36,000 subjects. One male out of three and one female out of two said that cellular telephone use significantly interfered with their driving.

Deputy Administrator of the National Highway Traffic Safety Administration (NHTSA), Rosalyn G. Millman, on July 18, 2000, announced that the NHTSA's consumer information would include the following advice:

> *"Growing evidence suggests using a wireless phone or other electronic device while driving can be distracting and drivers should not talk on the phone or use other devices while their vehicles are in motion.... NHTSA's preliminary review and assessment suggest that existing laws are not necessarily adequate to limit distractions from wireless phones or other electronics."*

Deputy Administrator Millman's statement also cast doubt about the safety of using hands-free devices while driving, "Hands-free, depending upon the equipment, may reduce both manual and visual distraction—but it will not affect or reduce cognitive distraction."

The industry has taken the discussion of safety issues seriously. Verizon Wireless, the largest wireless provider in the United States, has indicated that it will sup-

ENHANCED 911 FOR CELLULAR CALLS

Thirty-three percent of all calls to 911 are from cellular telephones. However, people who call 911 often can't tell emergency operators their exact location. The lack of information on a car's location causes delays by emergency units in reaching people. To solve this problem, in October 1996, the FCC mandated enhancements to the information that cellular carriers are required to transmit to public safety access points, the people and equipment that handle 911 calls. This order makes enhanced 911, the ability for public safety agencies to receive caller ID and location information, mandatory.

Phase 1 of the FCC order on enhanced 911, which commenced on April 1, 1998, ordered that callers' numbers and section of the cell site from which the call is sent, must be transmitted. It further required that cellular carriers transmit 911 calls for non-subscribers as well as subscribers. The cellular number is sent so that the public safety group, as mandated, can call back the cellular phone if the call is dropped. The exact location of the caller within the cell site must start to be phased in by October 2001.

Categories of systems include those that operate with technology embedded in handsets; in cellular networks, from satellite signals or a combination of these categories. In the handset system type, all of the location intelligence resides in chips in the handset. If this approach is taken, a battery or some type of device has to be attached to older handsets to make them compatible with the location technology. Accuracy on handset-type systems must be within 54.5 feet (50 meters) of the location of the cellular telephone for 67% of calls and within 163.5 feet (150 meters) for 95% of calls.

In contrast to handset-based systems, with network-based systems, all of the intelligence is in the provider's cell site. Both network-based and handset-type systems rely on the 24 global positioning system satellites (GPS) launched by the federal government for military tracking purposes. Chips in handsets transmit location data to three satellites at a time. In network- and handset-based systems, cars stuck under tunnels present a problem as line of site needed for communications to the GPS system is blocked. Because of these difficulties, the FCC requires that network-based solutions must be accurate for 67% of calls with a 328-feet (100-meter) radius and 95% of calls within a 984-foot (300-meter) radius.

The FCC ordered that by October 1, 2001, all cellular providers must be able to pinpoint the longitude and latitude for at least 50% of the public safety provider's coverage area six months after requested to do so by a public safety access provider. Software translates latitude and longitude information into street names so that public safety staff can dispatch police, fire departments and ambulances by street names. These rules apply to calls made for roaming as well as in-home territory calls. Cellular providers have requested extensions of the October deadline.

port laws requiring the use of hands-free devices such as headphones when talking on cellular telephones while driving. Until Verizon's announcement, most carriers had stressed the "education not legislation approach." Indeed, in the article, "Verizon Breaks Ranks, Backs Ban of Cell-Phone Use While Driving," published in *The Wall Street Journal WSJ.com*, 26 September 2000, by Nicole Harris and Jeffrey Ball, lobbyists from the cell phone industry have helped defeat legislative initiatives across the country. Safety advocates, while applauding Verizon's announcement as a start, remain concerned because studies have indicated that talking on a cellular telephone even with a hands-free device remains a dangerous distraction.

Liability concerns are becoming a front and center issue at commercial organizations. The article, "Workers Told to Stay off Cell Phones," published in *USAToday.com*, 26 September 2000, by Stephanie Armour, discussed the growing awareness of employers that they could be held liable for a crash. Employment lawyers are urging companies to have a cell phone policy and to discourage employees from using the phones while driving.

Privacy and Advertising Intrusions on Cellular E911

Databases located in carriers' networks track location information about users when their cellular phones are turned on. Privacy experts are concerned that if carriers share tracking information, marketing organizations will know people's shopping habits and driving routes and collect this information in a database. These worries are not limited to information gathered from cellular telephones. They cover tracking habits of people that use Blackberry email pagers, in-car navigation systems such as GM OnStar, personal digital assistant devices and laptops equipped with radio modems or Bluetooth chips.

Carriers have expressed an interest in linking information in their databases to services. These services could be notices of specials, yellow pages, weather information and automobile navigation systems. This could make cellular phones liable to receive unsolicited advertisements such as coupons for stores located near the subscriber. Carriers are making large investments in tracking systems and no provision is in the ruling to compensate them for the cost of buying, installing and maintaining them.

Congress, in the Wireless Communications and Public Safety Act of 1999, Section 222, required that cellular providers not give out information from E911 service to any other concern without a user's express prior permission by use of "opt-in" features. It also required providers to let users know when information about them was to be collected and the intended purpose of that information. The Center for Democracy and Technology (CDT) in their April 6, 2001 "Comments of the Center for Democracy and Technology" by James X. Dempsey made the following statement before the Federal Communications Commission. (The Technology and Public Policy Clinic of the University of California Berkeley School of Law co-wrote the report.)

> *"The portability of mobile devices and the ubiquity of their applications coupled with their ability to pinpoint the location of individuals and reveal it to others could, in the absence of clear privacy rules, produce a system where the everyday activities and movements of individual consumers are tracked and recorded. Wireless location technology has the potential to take data collection to new heights, allowing records to be compiled not just about discrete transactions but about individual's whereabouts."*

Many of the E9111 systems do have the ability to allow users to opt-out of having their location records transmitted without the user's consent. The Snaptrack (owned by Qualcomm), E911 handset-based system, lets users program their telephones so that only 911 calls transmit location information. To date, the carriers have not made public statements about how they will ensure privacy. The Cellular Telecommunications Industry Association has asked the FCC for a rulemaking that will clarify the privacy requirements related to E911.

Called Party Pays—An Impediment to Cellular Usage

In most of the world, cellular users do not pay to receive cellular telephone calls. Fees for incoming calls prevent cellular service from being a viable alternative for local telephone service. It keeps cellular costs high and is a factor in slowing cellular growth. Table 9.3 shows that while cellular service is growing, the average bill is low. Many consumers have cellular phones for safety and emergency use but are reluctant to give out their telephone number because of usage charges for receiving cellular calls. The FCC has stated that it will study the issues involved in caller pays services.

If calling party pays is implemented, consumers need to be alerted that they are about to make a toll call. The charge covers the cost of carrying traffic from the landline network to the wireless network. Possible options for uniformly alerting callers to the fact that they are about to be charged for a call when they call a wireless phone are:

- Using special prefixes or area codes such as 500 set aside for cellular calls. (Canada has set aside the 600 area code for cellular service.) The wireless industry in the United States does not support this option because it doesn't want to disadvantage cellular service by giving it separate blocks of numbers.

- The use of intercept announcements telling people they are calling a cellular number for which toll charges apply.

- Audible tones to alert callers that the call is non-standard.

If calling party pays is implemented, billing settlements between the wireline providers and wireless providers will be another open question. For example, should

FRAUD ON CELLULAR NETWORKS

According to Kate Strong, Product Marketing Manager for Lightbridge, Inc.'s fraud products, there is $12 to $14 billion of cellular fraud worldwide. This is an enormous problem and represents 4% to 10% of carriers' revenue that they write off as bad debt. The three main types of cellular fraud are customer acquisition fraud, technical fraud on cell phones while they're in use and internal fraud.

The largest amount of fraud, customer acquisition fraud, occurs when people sign up for cellular service using false information such as stolen credit cards and false addresses. If they're approved for service, they might then call the cellular provider and falsely claim that they moved during the first 30 days of service and thus did not receive a bill. They want to prevent the provider from cutting off their service when the person from whom they stole identification receives the bill and notifies the carrier that the service was obtained fraudulently. To prevent subscription fraud, carriers use databases from companies such as Lightbridge and IDT Wireless to verify identity. They ask callers questions about information not usually found in people's stolen wallets. These questions include date of birth, home and telephone phone numbers, social security number, mother's maiden name and whom they have their mortgage with.

Technical fraud occurs when thieves use equipment to copy mobile identification numbers (electronic serial numbers) transmitted when people make cellular calls. The thieves clone these numbers onto their own handsets and make calls until the carriers notice unusually high usage and cut them off. Carriers also track these thefts by noting when the same mobile identification number is used in two different parts of the country a few minutes apart. This type of fraud is declining because digital networks scramble signals so that it is more difficult to steal identification numbers. Technical fraud occurs most frequently when users roam on analog networks.

The area of fraud growing most quickly is internal fraud. With internal fraud, crime rings infiltrate billing, operations and customer service departments. In all of these departments, the criminal sets up service for unapproved users. Carriers are tightening their internal controls so that the credit department, customer care and implementation staff share information on the customer acquisition process. For example, ongoing checks need to be made such that credit checks and subscriber verifications were actually completed for all new service.

the wireline or wireless carrier bill the person who makes the call? If the wireline carrier bills the call, how much will the wireless carrier pay for the billing service? The organization that bills for calling party pays would have to deal with irate consumers who are not used to paying usage on local calls.

Another problem is leakage. Leakage is defined as calls that cannot be billed. These might include calls from pay phones, hotels, prisons and college campuses or calls originating out of the local area. One consideration is to require that these calls be billed to credit cards. All of these issues point to the importance of a clear and uniform way for handling calling party pays. Countries such as Israel that have calling party pays have a higher penetration of cellular service than the United States.

The FCC is considering national rules on standard ways to alert callers to calling party pays and whether there should be rules to protect consumers from excessive calling party pay rates. In an attempt to fashion a uniform nationwide policy, it has declared that states cannot promulgate rules about calling party pays.

Limited Mobility Wireless for Local Telephone Service

For large groups of the world's population, cellular service has the possibility of being the first type of telephone service they obtain. Fixed wireless service is the use of wireless technology for local telephone service. Traditional wireless local loop service, discussed in Chapter 4, consists of a dish in a neighborhood that beams service to small dishes on people's homes and businesses. The neighborhood dish is connected to the central office by fiber optic cabling. Telephone service via fixed wireless local loops is different than cellular service because it only works at the customer's site. Fixed wireless service also is connected to a public switched network central office rather than a mobile central office.

It was thought that fixed wireless service would be adopted in developing countries and by CLECs in the rest of the world as a low-cost alternative to digging up streets and laying new cabling to every customer. It was also a way to avoid obtaining rights of way to use public streets for fiber cabling. To date, because of high startup costs, wireless local loop technology is being implemented at a slow pace.

A new service called limited mobility cellular service is a way to provide local service using cellular technology. Like wireless local loop service, digging up streets and procuring rights of way are eliminated. Limited mobility cellular service as offered on CDMA networks can limit mobility to a subscriber's town or neighborhood. For an extra fee, service can be purchased to include a larger geographic region. It is based on the location-tracking technology described for E911 service. Chips in users' handsets transmit subscriber identification to the base station where the ID is matched to a database (home location register) with information about the mobile telephone's allowed calling area and services to which they subscribe.

Wireless Number Portability—Keeping the Same Number When Changing Carriers

Wireless local number portability enables subscribers to keep their cellular telephone number when they change from one wireless provider to another. This is significant for users that want to keep their cellular phone number when they change carriers. According to the Cellular Telecommunications Industry Association (CTIA), 4 million customers—28% of subscribers—disconnect service annually. It's not known how many of them change to another carrier. The largest impact of cellular number portability will be on business customers who often give out their number to customers and vendors. Many business users are reluctant to change cellular carriers because of the current requirement to change their cellular telephone number.

The Telecommunications Act of 1996 required wireless number portability in the United States by June 30, 1999. The cellular industry requested and received a delay until November 24, 2002 to work out the technical details. The way portability will work is that the mobile identification number (MIN) that now is the same as users' 10-digit mobile directory number will no longer necessarily be the same. Under wireless number portability, when someone calls the mobile directory number, the wireless carrier will perform a "data dip" at a national database. The national database will correlate the 10-digit directory number to a 10-digit mobile subscriber identification number, which will identify the mobile carrier assigned to the directory number.

Wireless number portability will be significant if more people start using their cellular service as a replacement for wireline service. It will provide truly geographic number portability in the same manner as toll-free service.

Limitations of Circuit-Switched Cellular for Data Communications

The analog cellular network was designed in the 1970s by AT&T for voice services. The major impediment to sending data over existing second generation cellular services is the change in signals and the errors introduced during the handoffs between base stations and when the signal is transmitted between the mobile portion of the network and the landline-based portion of the network.

Because of the delays and constant retransmissions due to errors, cellular modems rarely transmit at their top speed of 14.4 Kbps. The most common speed tends to be 9600 bps, far lower than speeds generally achieved over wire lines.

CDPD—Cellular Digital Packet Data, IP Wireless

Cellular digital packet data (CDPD), also called IP wireless, was developed by IBM as a way to transmit wireless data over spare capacity in cellular providers' analog networks.

It was first offered in 1995. It is a way to transmit short, bursty messages such as electronic mail, credit card verification, alarm monitoring and dispatch communications. Because it uses spare voice channels in cellular networks, it was planned as a low-cost solution for people who need to transmit short messages from multiple locations. AT&T Wireless, Verizon Wireless and Alltel are among the carriers who offer CDPD.

Cellular Digital Packet Data (CDPD) is not widely used. The speeds are slow. The top speed is 19,200 bits per second. However, throughput, the number of actual user bits sent, is 14,400 bps. Overhead bits used for addressing, billing, source address, error correction and encryption cut down on the number of user bits sent per second. Another factor holding back broad acceptance of cellular digital packet data is the lack of universal coverage.

The CDPD network is an overlay network. It works "over" the standard cellular networks using spare voice channels. Providers reserve channels, often from one to three, in each cell site for IP wireless traffic. If no capacity is available, they "channel hop" to spare channels in adjacent cells. CDPD modems encrypt the data before it is sent. CDPD modems are available for certain Palm and Compaq Pocket PC devices. Cellular data is subject to the variations in coverage and quality that affect voice service.

THE TRANSITION FROM SECOND TO THIRD GENERATION CELLULAR NETWORKS ....

First generation cellular networks were analog. Carriers upgraded networks to second generation digital cellular technologies to add capacity without adding spectrum. TDMA, GSM and CDMA are air interfaces used to transmit signals between handsets and antennas at base stations. As cellular service became even more popular, carriers wanted to increase capacity for voice traffic and offer higher speed cellular service for data and multimedia capability. As noted previously, the throughput of second generation digital cellular is 14.4 kilobits per second on TDMA and CDMA networks and 9.6 kilobits per second on GSM networks. Carriers also wanted to create a standard so that subscribers could use their cellular telephone number and handset worldwide.

The International Telecommunications Union started an effort called IMT-2000 (International Mobile Telephone) to define one advanced digital standard for high-speed data on cellular networks. Unfortunately, because of political pressure from manufacturers, the International Telecommunications Union (ITU) subcommittees endorsed two third generation techniques. See Tables 9.4 and 9.5. Ericsson backs one, W-CDMA. Qualcomm supports the other, cdma2000. Qualcomm receives royalties on all W-CDMA and cdma2000 service. It supplies chips for cdma2000 handsets as well.

- W-CDMA (wideband CDMA) is the third generation technology that most GSM and TDMA cellular providers have stated they will use. W-CDMA is also known as Universal Mobile Telecommunications System (UMTS). W-CDMA has not been standardized as of June 2001.

- cdma2000 is the technology that most CDMA providers and some providers in newly developing countries such as China (China Unicom Ltd.) and India have stated they will use.

Table 9.4   3G Cellular Services

W-CDMA, cdma2000 and EDGE are collectively known as IMT-2000 International Mobile Telecommunications for the year 2000. IMT-2000 is an ITU initiative.		
Service	**Other Designations for the Service**	**Comments**
W-CDMA Wideband code division multiple access	Also known as Universal Mobile Telecommunications System (UMTS). European Telecommunications Standards Institute (ETSI) is reviewing proposals for a UMTS standard.	Ericsson and Nokia supports this 3G technology for higher speed data. Most GSM networks have stated they will evolve their networks to W-CDMA.
cdma2000	An upgrade from CDMA IS-95A and IS-95B service.*	Qualcomm supports this 3G technology.
The following are three different cdma2000 3G platforms.		
1xRTT First generation candidate radio transmission technologies	IS95C 1xMC (first generation multi-carrier).	First "generation" of cdma2000 service that doubles voice capacity and increases data speeds.
1xHDR First generation high data rate	1xEV-DO (first generation evolution data only).	Higher data speeds but no increase in capacity for voice traffic.
3xMC Three multi-carrier		Bonds three channels together to achieve higher data speeds.
IS-95A is the CDMA technology used in most of the world. IS-95B is an upgrade that provides packet data service. Most carriers are migrating from IS-95A to 1xRTT.		

Table 9.5 *Transitional 2.5G and 3G Cellular Services*

Carriers with GSM and TDMA networks implement these technologies before installing more costly W-CDMA networks.		
Service	**Other Designations for the Service**	**Comments**
GPRS General packet radio services		This is a 2.5G platform for sending packet data in spare voice channels of cellular networks.
EDGE Enhanced data rates for GSM evolution	UWC-136 Universal Wireless Communications.	More suitable for American TDMA networks because it uses spectrum for data in smaller chunks than GPRS. Depending on implementation, either 2.5G or 3G.

The Transition to W-CDMA - GPRS—Data Carried as Packets in 2.5G Networks

Because of the lower cost, most TDMA and GSM carriers will upgrade their systems to 2.5G general packet radio services (GPRS) prior to upgrading to 3G, W-CDMA. GPRS is a packet data service based on the IP protocol. It can be used on North American TDMA as well as GSM networks in Europe and elsewhere. GPRS is a data-only service with a peak speed of 115 Kbps. Interference, noise and possible network congestion cause the typical speed to be closer to between 20 Kbps and 80 Kbps rather than the peak GPRS speed of 115 Kbps. However, GPRS service has the advantage of being "always on." It is not necessary for users to dial into the network.

GPRS is a data overlay network because data is "overlayed" by adding software and hardware to base transceiver stations and base station controllers as well as software in mobile switches. GPRS packets, which have a peak speed of 115,000 bits per second, are transmitted in spare voice channels. Two spare data channels must be bonded together to achieve the top 115-Kbps speed. This is the major disadvantage of GPRS; it uses voice capacity for data, which is a problem in congested areas.

Some carriers such as British Telecommunications have added compression to networks to increase throughput on GPRS networks. The higher throughput enables more data to be sent in a given time period by "shrinking" the amount of data sent. Compression, as discussed in Chapter 1, eliminates white spaces and shortens common characters so the time required sending data is decreased. The user has the impression that speeds are increased.

EDGE-Enhanced Data Rates for GSM Evolution

EDGE is considered a 2.5G technology or a 3G technology, depending on the type of EDGE service deployed. Most carriers considering EDGE plan to use it as an intermediary overlay for higher speed data. Enhanced data rates for GSM evolution (EDGE) offers higher speed data rates than general packet radio services (GPRS), up to a peak 384 kilobits per second but 60 to 180 kilobits per second achievable depending on network conditions. Upgrading to EDGE requires new hardware and software. EDGE is more suitable than GPRS for TDMA networks because it requires smaller chunks of spectrum than GPRS. It more closely matches the way spectrum is allocated in second generation TDMA networks such as that of Cingular in the United States.

Upgrades to W-CDMA from GSM—Costly

Because W-CDMA is based on code division rather than time division access, upgrades on GSM networks (based on time division) to full 3G service will require an almost new infrastructure. New controllers must be added as well as hardware and software to the base transceiver station. The use of new, higher frequency spectrum will necessitate more antennas and more base transceiver systems than those used in 2G and 2.5G networks. In addition, hardware and software upgrades for mobile switching offices will be needed. Finally, new billing and back office systems will be required. Cellular companies that have collectively spent more than $100 billion for spectrum are taking the following steps to underwrite the cost of building 3G networks:

- Creating partnerships with other providers to share the cost of constructing and maintaining 3G network infrastructure. This happened in Germany and Britain with Deutsche Telekom and British Telecommunications PLC.

- Requesting vendor financing for new equipment. European carriers have requested that Alcatel and Ericsson loan them the money to purchase 3G gear.

- Selling subsidiaries in other countries to raise cash.

- In Europe, carriers that purchased 3G spectrum in areas where they don't have 2G networks are considering reselling cellular service on other carriers' 2G networks while they build 3G capabilities. This saves them the expense of building second generation service.

- There is some thought that in countries such as Germany and England, where the government reaped enormous amounts of money from spectrum auctions, the government should refund some of the fees. An alternative would be to allow carriers to take over other providers without returning the merged carrier's license.

- Requesting that governments from which they purchased costly spectrum relax the terms of the license. For example, Spain is allowing operators to delay the start of 3G networks until June 2002 from August 2001.

An ETSI group, the UMTS forum is working on final 3G standards for GSM operators. 3G service is not expected to be available on a large scale in the near future.

DoCoMo in Japan is the first carrier in the world to upgrade to third generation W-CDMA. However, its implementation is a little different than the W-CDMA planned for the rest of the world. It is called J-WCDMA. Its implementation is delayed because of difficulties in handing off calls between cell sites as people move from cell to cell. In addition, the phones, because they use more power, tend to overheat. Japan, like other parts of Asia, did not hold auctions for spectrum for 3G service. Rather, the governments awarded spectrum based on "beauty contests" of carriers' qualifications. The lack of requirements to spend huge sums on spectrum has left Asian companies with more resources to upgrade their networks.

The Transition to cdma2000—1xRTT (First Generation cdma2000) and HDR (High Data Rate)

Upgrades to third generation service on CDMA networks are less costly and complex than those for TDMA and GSM networks. This is because second and third generation CDMA networks are already based on code division multiple access. The major incentive for upgrading to third generation cdma2000 is the increased voice capacity.

cdma2000—1xRTT

The first phase of third generation cdma2000 provides "always on" data rates up to a peak data rate of 144 kilobits per second and additional voice capacity. As in GPRS, achieved data speeds will be lower than peak data rates, anywhere from 18 Kbps to 71 Kbps. Korea Telecom achieved an average data rate of 71 Kbps. All that is required for upgrades to 1xMC are new cards in the base transceiver system and software in the mobile switching center. Routers, billing, authentication and authorization systems and connections to IP networks will be required for the data services.

Handsets for earlier CDMA technologies will work on 1xRTT systems but the increased capacity for voice calls will not be totally achieved. Qualcomm believes that voice capacity can be doubled if all users have 1xRTT phones. The new handsets also will be required for 1xRTT packet data service. 1xRTT handsets used in South Korea have double standby time (when the phone is on but not used) because they "wake up" faster but 10% to 20% less talk time.

Carriers in South Korea implemented the first generation (1xRTT) of cdma2000 in October 2000. According to Qualcomm, 45,000 cell sites will be added in China in 2002. CDMA carriers in the United States and Canada also have committed to cdma2000. However, overall to date, it appears that the large majority of cellular providers will upgrade to W-CDMA because of the prevalence of GSM worldwide.

High Data Rate (1XHDR): cdma2000

Network providers who already have the first stage cdma2000 can upgrade to higher data speeds by adding software for High Data Rate (HDR), also referred to as 1xEV-DO (data only). High Data Rate service is a data-only enhancement with a stated capacity of 2.4 megabits per second. No capacity is gained for voice traffic. In areas with high data traffic, the speeds are expected to be about 130 Kbps. High Data Rate service can be mixed with first generation 1xRTT equipment so that only areas with high demand for data need be upgraded.

3xMC: Third Generation cdma2000

A third generation of cdma2000 has been announced, called 3xMC (third generation multi-carrier). It uses spectrum more efficiently for voice and data. The expected "real" capacity for data is 1 megabit per second but this has not been tested. Hardware as well as software upgrades will be required. Qualcomm expect carriers to use 1xHDR rather than 3xMC.

Upgrades to cdma2000 on TDMA Networks

TDMA cellular operators that upgrade to cdma2000 rather than W-CDMA will need entirely new base stations and base station controllers, new handsets for users and billing systems as well as routers and connections to IP data networks. If they use their existing spectrum, they will not need to add new cell sites and antennas.

A Comparison Between W-CDMA and cdma2000

A major advantage of cdma2000 is the low startup costs for carriers such as Sprint PCS that have pre-existing code division multiple access networks. Sprint PCS has stated that it spent $1.5 billion to upgrade to first generation 3G service, which did not require new spectrum and provided additional voice capacity. That gives Sprint an enormous advantage over carriers that spent billions on 3G spectrum. These services won't be deployed on a large scale for three to five years. Moreover, GSM and TDMA upgrades to 2.5G service do not provide any additional voice capacity. Voice traffic represents the major portion of carriers' revenue.

Qualcomm claims that cdma2000 technology is superior to W-CDMA because it handles more voice calls with a given amount of spectrum, requires less power for handsets and supports superior handoffs between cell sites. Cell site handoffs are the process of transferring calls to adjacent cells as drivers and pedestrians move locations.

The major advantage of W-CDMA is the large installed base of GSM networks. The majority of the world's cellular networks are based on GSM. If all these networks as well as TDMA-based networks upgrade to GPRS and W-CDMA, roaming will be expedited. Qualcomm has stated that by 2002, it will produce chips for handsets that will support all of the following in one chip: W-CDMA, cdma2000, CDMA, GPRS, GSM and analog services.

Handsets for 3G and 2.5G Services

When carriers sell handsets to subscribers, they offer them at below their own cost as a way to attract customers. For example, a carrier might pay $350 for a handset that they sell to customers for $250. The feeling is that usage revenue will offset handset costs. Therefore handsets represent a major expense in upgrading cellular networks. In all of the above cases, new handsets are required to take advantage of higher speed data, longer battery life and more capacity for voice traffic.

New handsets are being developed with chips that allow people to roam between all of these types of networks. Many of them have color screens and dialing pads with software called T9 that predicts the words people wish to spell based on the context of the other words they've already entered. Other enhancements include voice recognition and large screen displays. The shape and size of phones is called *form factor*. Chips compatible with 2.5G and 3G networks will be embedded in palm-held computers, personal digital assistants and laptop devices.

The availability of telephones that work on 3G W-CDMA networks is a problem. These handsets require more power and complex software. They are, in effect, small computers with voice and data capabilities. TTPCom Ltd., a UK handset-technology company, predicts availability at the end of 2004. Nokia, however, has stated it will deliver millions of 3G phones by the end of 2002. These opinions were stated in the article, "Mobile Telecom Firms Question Benefits, Price of 3G Technology," published in *The Wall Street Journal WSJ.com*, 20 February 2001, by David Pringle and Kevin J. Delaney.

All-Packet Cellular Networks for Voice and Data

Cellular networks are evolving from circuit switched to packed-based technology in a similar way to landline networks. One example is that of AT&T Wireless in the United States. After it upgrades to 3G, it plans to implement IP within its own backbone network between its base stations and base station controllers and between its mobile central office switches. Its next stage after the backbone implementation will be to upgrade all of its mobile switches from circuit to IP-based platforms. It intends to keep its fiber connections between its sites because of fiber's greater-than-wireless capacity.

4G—Futures

4G service is a proposed upgrade to cellular networks using IP protocols to greatly increase the speed of data sent over cellular networks. It is at least five years away from implementation. As it is envisioned, 4G would use a technique called orthogonal frequency domain multiplexing for its air interface (OFDM). OFDM divides the frequency into a large number of smaller channels called subchannels. It is a technology based on frequency division multiplexing where the frequency is shared by many users and depends on very fast digital signal processors. OFDM is used now for stationary applications such as high-frequency definition television in Europe and Digital Audio Broadcasting (DAB).

MOBILE INTERNET ACCESS, MESSAGING SERVICES AND BLUETOOTH...

Email is the most popular data application for cellular devices. A device capable of accessing a cellular network is referred to as a Mobile System (MS) or a Mobile Subscriber Unit (MSU). Cellular service can be accessed by a multitude of devices including two-way email pagers, personal digital assistants and Palm computers as well as voice-only devices. In surveys, consumers have expressed little interest in mobile Internet access. Those offered by the major carriers have not gained a great deal of acceptance. However, carriers and application developers are moving ahead with new services that they believe will gain more acceptance, particularly from the business community, on higher speed data networks they are implementing. They are hoping to generate additional revenues from these services.

Data-enabled wireless devices provide the means for users to access computer data and Internet information from remote locations. Wireless ISPs such as GoAmerica have agreements with cellular carriers to connect the carriers' subscribers to the Internet via GoAmerica. In addition, GoAmerica also has an agreement with RIM, which manufactures the Blackberry device, to embed the GoAmerica browser on Blackberry devices.

Microsoft, Palm and Symbian are promoting their operating system for mobile subscriber units with voice and data capability. Operating systems are used for functions such as organizing information and determining how applications are viewed on "desktops" of computers. The Palm operating system is an example. Use of these operating systems will make it easier to access Internet information from wireless devices. Symbian PLC, jointly owned by Ericsson, Motorola, Psion, Nokia and Matsushita, is developing the Pearl operating system for mobile computing devices. The goal of the companies is to use the operating system on hand-held computers and wireless handsets for Internet access. Sony has licensed the Symbian operating system for its devices.

Microsoft is developing a competing operating system called Stinger in conjunction with Samsung. Microsoft is using its strength in email server packages to promote Stinger. It has announced that it is including Stinger with Microsoft Exchange email server software.

Mobile Commerce

Mobile commerce, using mobile devices for purchases and entertainment, is in its infancy. Slow networks and lack of consumer interest have held it back. Developers are working on applications for enterprises such as real estate listings. Other applications are streaming music and pornography accessible by Palm-type devices. New methods of paying for services are being devised to eliminate users having to key in credit card information. For example, e-wallet sites have been set up, which hold a consumer's credit card information. The e-wallet data is used to make online purchases without entering credit card data. For all of these applications, gateways called mobile servers are located at the edge of the Internet to convert cellular protocols to those compatible with the Internet.

Short Messaging Service (SMS)

Short messaging services are 160-character-long paging type messages that can be sent to and from most digital telephones. They are different than email messages, which are stored at email servers located at Internet service provider data centers and at corporate sites. Attachments and HTML formatting with colors and images are not supported by current SMS. Short messaging service is hugely popular in Asia and Europe, particularly among teenagers. In the article, "Java and SMS," published in *Business & Technology Wireless*, Premier 2001 Spring issue, page 74, by Keith Douglas reported that Vodafone receives more revenues from short messaging service than voice services.

Short messaging services are being enhanced. VoiceStream and other carriers have integrated instant messaging with short messaging service. (See Chapter 8 for instant messaging.) Moreover, many digital phones have T9 predictive text capability previously described. (T9 was developed by Tegic Communications, part of Microsoft.) Enhanced SMS will be available by the end of 2001. It will enable SMS messages to be sent with different typefaces, images, animation and melodies embedded in them.

The limitation for SMS in the United States is that messages can only be sent between users on the same network.

Bluetooth

Bluetooth is a standard for special software on radio chips that enables devices to communicate with each other over a short-range radio link. The link can operate over distances up to 10 meters (32.8 feet). It uses the same frequency, 2.4 GHz, as 802.11 wireless LANs and cordless phones. The FCC is looking at ways to eliminate interference between 802.11 LANs and Bluetooth devices. (See Chapter 2 for wireless LANs.) Bluetooth enables devices such as printers, laptops, headsets and fax machines to communicate. With the Bluetooth chip, travelers will not have to bother carrying cables with them for mobile communications, for example, when using a laptop with a cellular telephone. A special interest group made up of Ericsson, Toshiba, IBM, Intel and Nokia developed Bluetooth.

Bluetooth-equipped devices emit high-frequency radio signals. Bluetooth devices within range of these signals can communicate with each other. For example, a hand-held personal digital assistant could synchronize and exchange data with a computer without using cables. There are nine different protocols called profiles for Bluetooth, each of which supports different types of applications. For example, one profile enables headsets to communicate with cell phones and computers. Another application links laptops or desk PCs to an access point that can be used for Internet access. Bluetooth supports links for voice and data. The first shipments of Bluetooth-enabled devices, which are planned for 2001, will be for headsets, telephones and circuit cards for PCs.

The Wireless Application Protocol (WAP)

WAP is a proposed standard designed for wireless Internet access. People with WAP-enabled cellular phones access Internet sites, which are written in a special programming language. The object is to make information downloaded from the site fit into cellular devices' small screens. The Wireless Application Protocol is a menu-driven method for downloading information such as flight schedules and bank balances to cellular phones from the Internet. WAP service was introduced in Europe in 2000.

However, its slow speed, incompatibilities with some phones and technical glitches resulted in user dissatisfaction. In addition, there were not a great many sites available where operators had taken the trouble to re-write them for WAP access.

In addition to the preceding, WAP is a "dialup" service, and connection and download speeds are slow. It is possible that as networks are upgraded for packet data service and WAP technology is improved that WAP services may become more popular.

i-mode Service Worldwide

i-mode service, developed by NTT DoCoMo, enables subscribers to download Internet information, email and entertainment from cellular networks. It is enormously popular in Japan (see Chapter 10) and DoCoMo plans on introducing it in Europe through joint ventures with Telecom Italia and KPN NV. The European service will operate on WAP as well as i-mode platforms. DoCoMo also announced that AT&T Wireless will offer i-mode service over its upgraded GSM service, which will have general packet radio service (GPRS) data networking capability. Email, financial information, restaurant and movie listings are examples of possible i-mode services. Services will either be based on monthly flat fees or per-packet basis.

Unlike WAP, i-mode service is transported as packet over IP–based digital cellular networks and no dialing is needed for accessing the network. It is "always on." In addition, i-mode Web sites are easier to design because they are based on a variation of Hypertext Markup Language (HTML), which is used to program Web sites accessed by landline devices.

SPECIALIZED MOBILE RADIO—ORIGINALLY VOICE, LATER DATA..

Initially, the 800 to 900 MHz range of specialized mobile radio spectrum was used for voice applications. Examples of customers who use these services are contractors and concrete companies. They push a microphone button to talk. Conversations between the mobile units and from mobile units to a central site are private. These systems have no interconnection with the public switched telephone network. This spectrum was later used for analog data-only service by ARDIS, now merged with AMSC (American Mobile Satellite Company) and RAM, now part of Cingular Wireless. Eventually, companies such as Nextel Communications used the spectrum for digital services to sell voice, data, paging and short messaging services.

Organizations that provide delivery services, field service and installation and transportation services use these services for mobile employees. Consider companies that send out telephone repair people to fix phone systems. The hours that a technician is on-site are entered into a portable computer by the technician so that the customer is billed accurately. Giving technicians the capability of entering hours at customer locations translates to more accurate time and material billing.

Private Networks over Mobile Radio Frequencies

In the late 1970s, companies started using radio frequency networks to transmit data from mobile workers. A prime example of an organization using wireless for private data communications is FedEx. FedEx's early implementation of its private data communications network gave it a major edge over competitors. The service is used to track the location of packages. Each package has a bar code; when the package is picked up or dropped off for delivery, its bar code is scanned into FedEx's computer system at the drop-off site or by a driver's hand-held device. The hand-held device transmits the bar code to FedEx's computers. The scanning is repeated at each strategic point in the delivery system and transmitted to FedEx's computers over the radio frequency network; thus, FedEx knows where each package is in each step of its journey.

A complementary technology that helped spur the use of radio networks for mobile workers is the availability of portable computers and hand-held devices and scanners for data entry. Improvements in flash memory, developed by Intel, allow computers to hold information in memory while computers are turned off. In addition, lighter batteries and micro-circuitry make portable computers and scanners lighter and smaller so that technicians and delivery people can easily carry them.

Specialized Mobile Radio—Packetized Data Networks for Two-Way Email and Field Services

Specialized mobile radio networks cover the major urban centers in the United States. These data-only packet radio systems have been available since 1984. Other than Nextel, they do not connect to the public switched telephone network. They operate at a top throughput speed of 14.4 Kbps. Hand-held devices such as the Palm, Blackberry and Handspring use these networks for wireless access to email. The Blackberry wireless device is used with the Motient DataTAC networks in the United States and Canada as well as the Bell Mobility data network in Canada.

Rather than develop their own private radio networks, companies often lease specialized mobile radio networks from companies such as Cingular Interactive (formerly BellSouth Mobile Data) and Motient Corporation (formerly American Mobile Satellite Company, which purchased ARDIS). They were originally used mainly for trucking, field service and dispatch services and communications from mobile workers. Cingular Interactive is part of Cingular Wireless.

The underlying packet technology used in the Motient network is called DataTAC® (Total Access Communications). SMR (specialized mobile radio) uses FCC-allocated spectrum in the 800 to 900 MHz range, close to the spectrum set aside for cellular telephone service. SMR was initially analog, but carriers have upgraded to digital facilities. Nextel Communications, located in Reston, Virginia, is an interesting example of a specialized mobile radio carrier upgrading its facilities to digital and expanding its reach of services from data communications over analog facilities to digital voice communications.

Mobitex—Packet Access Method for Personal Digital Assistants (PDAs) and Blackberry Devices

Hand-held devices such as Palm and Blackberry access and send email over Mobitex packet networks. Mobitex is a packet data network technology based on a cellular structure. It was originally developed and put into trials in 1983 by Swedish Telecom Radio and developed further by Eritel, then jointly owned by Swedish Telecom and Ericsson. Eritel later relinquished all rights to Ericsson. Mobitex is the packet technology used in the Cingular Interactive packet data network. There are 30 Mobitex networks in 23 countries worldwide. Because European Mobitex networks operate at 400 MHz and the North American and South American networks operate at 900 MHz, devices that operate on U.S. Mobitex networks in the United States can't be used on other Mobitex networks.

In the late 1990s, Research in Motion developed a radio modem for a pager to support two-way electronic mail and Internet access. Manufacturers also developed integrated internal radio modems for personal digital assistants like Palm and Handspring. The Research in Motion (RIM) hand-held device weighs less than 5 ounces and the smallest one is only 2.5 inches long by 3.5 inches wide with a 6- or 8-line display and keyboard. The ones sold by AOL and EarthLink are preconfigured with email from these ISPs. The Blackberry devices sold to enterprises can receive email from enterprise email systems such as Lotus Domino and Microsoft Exchange. The Blackberry two-way email pager is also available from UK cellular provider BT Cellnet and Canadian Mobitex operator Rogers™ AT&T® Wireless. Unlike the Palm where the user must manually check for messages, the RIM is an "always on" device. Email is automatically sent when there are messages.

PAGING SERVICES ....

Motorola Corporation first introduced tone-only pagers in 1956. Tone-only pagers send a tone to a person's pager. People who are paged call a paging operator or an answering service to find out the telephone number and possibly why a person was trying to reach them. Physicians, plumbers and people who needed to be reached in emergencies were early users of tone-only pagers.

Pager sales boomed from the time they were introduced in 1956 until 1998, when growth slowed. When cellular telephone service was introduced in the late 1980s, many industry experts thought that this would be the death knell for paging because cellular is a two-way service. However, paging sales continued to grow strongly until competition in the cellular industry caused prices for cellular phones to drop. Not only did the prices of cellular phones drop but also paging capabilities were added to the phones. People found that they could carry one device capable of paging, short messaging and two-way telephoning. In 1997, for the first time, the number of cellular telephones exceeded the number of pagers in service.

By the late 1990s and early 2000s, paging companies were merging and going into bankruptcy. The two largest paging companies in the United States are Arch Wireless, Inc. and Metrocall. Both are in shaky financial condition.

Paging vs. Wireless Telephone Service

Many customers, particularly business people, use their cellular phones for both paging and telephone calls. PCS and traditional digital cellular both support paging and short messaging services in the form of brief email messages to users with digital handsets. The gap between functionality in paging and cellular services has narrowed.

The difference in cost between paging and cellular service is narrowing as well. However, paging is still cheaper than cellular service; monthly fees range from $7 to $13 and often include usage. Moreover, pagers are easy to use, convenient and small. A pager fits on a person's belt. Another important advantage of pagers is the length of their battery life. Paging batteries, usually AA, often last for a month or two. PCS batteries last up to about two weeks on standby.

Two-Way Paging Using Narrowband PCS

Paging services utilize PCS spectrum for advanced features and product innovations such as two-way advanced messaging services. For example, two-way pagers allow users to receive pages and short messages and respond to pages with canned messages preprogrammed under buttons of a pager (e.g., "stuck in traffic"). Second generation two-way pagers incorporate keyboards and can be used to send and receive email. For example, to send a message to a pager, someone logs into the paging network's Internet site and sends a page using the recipient's PIN as part of the address. The reply can be sent to a variety of devices such as a cell phone, another pager or a standard email address. If it's sent to a cellular telephone without text messaging support, some services convert the message to synthesized voice. Motorola offers a pager that can receive email from corporate Microsoft Outlook email servers. Some carriers who purchased narrowband spectrum are using PCS frequencies to deliver Internet information such as stock quotes and sports scores.

Two-way paging uses two narrow slices of the PCS spectrum that the FCC started auctioning off in 1994. One channel is used for sending the page and the other for responding to pages. Paging companies are interested in narrowband paging, not only for its two-way capability, but also for its ability to provide additional capacity. Non-PCS pagers send pages using a technique called Simulcast. Simulcast sends each page through every tower in the paging carrier's network. This uses up capacity inefficiently. Narrowband PCS, on the other hand, sends each page only to the same place as the last transmission. This is correct in 90% of the pages.

SATELLITES..

Geosynchronous satellites orbit 22,300 miles above the earth's surface. Because they are so high in the sky, the area to which each satellite is capable of beaming signals is large. This is analogous to a flashlight beam. Holding a flashlight higher in the air extends the amount of area the light illuminates. Lowering the flashlight lessens the amount of area the light covers.

Because they are so high from the earth, geosynchronous satellites introduce a few-seconds delay on voice and data transmissions. Consider voice telephone calls placed in locations where fiber optic cabling is not in place. People who placed calls to international locations in the 1970s and 1980s often experienced clipping and delay. If two people on a telephone call spoke at the same time, parts of words were "clipped" off. The quality of these calls was notably degraded by delays in transmission. The same problem exists in interactive, two-way data communications over satellites.

The reach and broadcast nature of satellite service makes it suitable for paid television service. However, to date the leader in the United States, Hughes' DirectTV service, has only 10 million customers and the next largest provider, EchoStar, has about half that number. By year-end 2000, cable TV had 69 million customers. Direct-TV has an additional 3 million customers in Latin America. EchoStar has made an offer to purchase Hughes Electronics from its current owner General Motors.

Low earth-orbiting satellites (LEOs) solve the delay problem because they are positioned from 435 to 1500 miles above the earth. However, placing satellites lower in orbit decreases each satellite's coverage area. Because they are lower in the sky, LEOs cover a smaller area than geosynchronous satellites. Thus more of them are needed for worldwide reach. The requirement for a greater number of satellites increases the cost of LEOs.

Geosynchronous satellites orbit the earth in fixed orbits. In contrast, low earth-orbiting satellites are non-stationary. Therefore, calls need to be handed over to other satellites or points on the earth rather quickly. An advantage to LEOs is that their low position relative to the earth means that lower power is required on the devices and handsets used with LEOs. Lower power translates to lower costs. Regardless of the type, all satellites have a limited life, 7 to 15 years before they "decay" and must be replaced. One service, Teledesic, conceived by Craig McCaw and backed by both McCaw and Microsoft's founder Bill Gates, initially planned to use 840 satellites, but scaled back to 288.

A third type of satellite is called middle earth-orbiting satellite, or MEO. MEOs orbit the earth at 6000 to 13,000 miles up. The 24 GPS satellites owned by the United States government are MEO satellites.

VSAT Service—Small Satellite Dishes

Very small aperture terminals (VSATs) are small satellite dishes that contain antennas that receive and transmit signals between computers and satellites. The dish ranges in size from 24 inches high by 36 inches wide for VSATs used for data communications to 18 inches wide for those used for direct broadcast television. Their small size is possible because of highly focused beams generated from antennas on satellites and the fact that the service is offered at high frequencies, which have shorter wavelengths. The development of VSAT technology in the late 1980s made satellite service affordable for commercial applications where many branch locations transmit back to a central location. These applications include gas stations for transmission of credit authorizations and daily receipts and retail chains for inventory and pricing updates and sales results. The implementation of VSAT networks obviated the need for organizations such as retail chains and postal services to main complex networks of private lines.

Satellite networks are composed of a hub, satellites and receiving antennas on dishes. Receiving antennas also are called *ground stations*. Receivers on antennas convert airborne signals to electrical signals. The transmitter on the antenna converts electrical signals to airborne (radio frequency) signals. The point from which broadcasts originate is the hub. The hub has a large dish, routing equipment and fiber links to either the enterprise's headquarters for commercial customers or the Internet for Internet access applications. The hub site also is called the network operations center (NOC). For Internet access applications, the NOC has the ISP services such as email and home page on servers. All communications broadcast from the hub travel up to the satellite and then down to the ground stations.

Satellite transmissions consist of broadcasts from the satellite to customers. The downlink from the satellite to the VSAT is relatively simple. All of the signals are broadcast to everyone and each customer takes off data addressed to them. Systems with two-way communications capability have more complexity. The uplink communications from the customer to the satellite are more complex because thousands of

SATELLITE SERVICE FOR TWO-WAY INTERNET ACCESS

Gilat Satellite Networks, an Israeli company, developed hardware and software to make two-way Internet access via satellite affordable for residential consumers. It developed manufacturing methods to lower the costs of modems and outdoor equipment. In addition, it created sophisticated algorithms to work with the Internet suite of protocols, TCP/IP. The protocol uses a mathematical algorithm for collision detection at the hub. The algorithm resolves collisions and very quickly allocates bandwidth to many modems at different times. Gilat also perfected proprietary algorithms that eliminate the Internet protocol's requirements for acknowledgments for each group of packets. Because each acknowledgement has to travel 20,300 miles to the satellite and another 20,300 miles to the ground stations, they create delays. Finally, Gilat created a protocol to speed up downloading media-rich HTTP Web pages.

The two-way Gilat VSAT and modem service is sold by ISP StarBand, which charges $70 monthly for Internet access and between $650 and $900 for installation. (Microsoft, Echostar and Gilat jointly own Star-Band). If the consumer opts for 150 channels of television in addition to Internet access, the monthly fee is $100. For residential customers that can't get cable modem or DSL high-speed access to the Internet, two-way satellite service is an expensive (but often their only viable) option. StarBand customers receive a VSAT satellite dish and a modem. (See Figure 9.3.) The dish is usually installed on their roof but can also be put on a pole or mounted on an outside wall of the home. The USB or Ethernet-compatible modem is connected to the VSAT dish. The modem takes data from the antenna and converts it from satellite signals to digital signals for PCs. It translates the data to radio frequency on the way out. The StarBand service offers speeds of 150 kilobits per second on the uplink to the satellite. The downlink speed is 48 megabits but it is a broadcast stream shared by all residential Internet access customers.

The service is available throughout the United States through Radio Shack, directly from the StarBand Web site and from DISH network retailers. The DISH network is an Echostar channel of 23,000 retailers. The National Rural Telecommunications Cooperative (NRTC) also sells the service through its 1000-member independent telephone and utility company members. Gilat is forming StarBand operations in Asia, Europe and Latin America. WildBlue, using Echostar satellites and Spaceway, using Hughes satellites, also are planning to offer two-way satellite service to consumers.

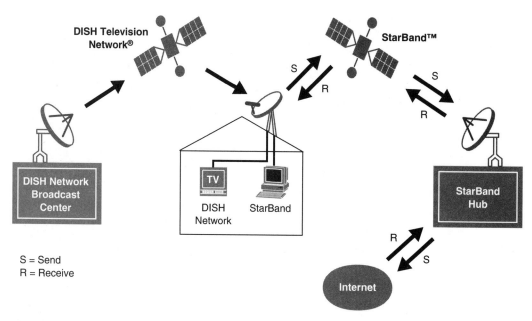

Figure 9.3

Two-way Internet access via satellite. The DISH network broadcasts TV signals
and the StarBand service is for Internet access. Figure courtesy of StarBand
Communications Inc.

users transmit at the same time. The hub needs complex software to be able to manage
receiving data from thousands of users without introducing delay.

The two-way VSAT satellite service developed for commercial applications was
initially too costly to be offered for residential customers. When customers first used
satellites for Internet access it was one-way only. People used a telephone line to send
messages to the Internet and the satellite link for receiving Internet data.

Vendors of LEOs

The proliferation of cellular service and the growing availability of transcontinental fiber links have hurt low earth-orbiting satellite networks. In addition, implementation
and construction of LEOs requires a long lead time during which user requirements
and competitive technologies are developed. To date, none of them have been success-
ful. Teledesic had funding from the former owner, Craig McCaw, of McCaw Cellular.
Bill Gates of Microsoft added $10 million and Motorola at one time also invested in
the endeavor. Teledesic has combined assets with ICO Global Communications. The
combined endeavor, ICO-Teledesic Global Limited, will sell Internet access, mobile
voice and data communications to industries such as gas, oil, transportation and con-

struction starting in 2003. ICO service operates with middle earth-orbiting satellites. It's unclear how the two different types of satellites will operate with each other.

Two other LEO providers are Globalstar and Orbcomm. Orbcomm focuses on paging, messaging and tracking services. The satellites are capable of sending two-way data in packet-data format. Its monitoring services are aimed at oil pipeline, gas companies and utility companies for meter reading. Its satellites also are used to track vehicles. Neither company is profitable and Globalstar has said that it might file for bankruptcy. Iridium, which was started by Motorola, filed for bankruptcy in 2000 and was purchased by a private company later in 2000 for $25 million. Seven billion dollars had been invested into Iridium.

TIME DIVISION MULTIPLE ACCESS, GSM AND CODE DIVISION MULTIPLE ACCESS AIR INTERFACES ....

All digital wireless services use multiplexing techniques to carry more calls on the same amount of spectrum as analog cellular service. Multiplexers are devices that transmit signals from two or more devices over a single channel. Thus, while all digital services have more capacity than analog cellular, the ways they add capacity are incompatible with each other. That is why callers cannot necessarily use their cellular telephones when they travel. The three most prevalent multiplexing techniques in the world are time division multiple access (TDMA), code division multiple access (CDMA) and Global System for Mobile Communications (GSM). When used in wireless networks, multiplexing techniques are referred to as *air interfaces*. They are methods used to access (share) spectrum between the wireless device (handset or wireless computer) and the provider's base station.

These different multiplexing schemes are:

- CDMA (code division multiple access) used by Sprint PCS, Verizon Wireless and South Korea Telecom and other parts of Asia. Thirty percent of cell phones in the U.S. and Canada operate on CDMA.

- TDMA (time division multiple access), implemented by digital cellular providers such as Cingular Wireless and AT&T Wireless.

- GSM, originally Groupe Speciale Mobile, but now known as Global System for Mobile Communications. A standard set by the European Union and used in Europe, the Far East, much of South America, New Zealand and Australia. The AT&T Wireless TDMA scheme is similar to GSM's TDMA. In the U.S., VoiceStream uses GSM and AT&T Wireless and Cingular Wireless are in the process of installing it alongside their existing TDMA service.

Code Division Multiple Access

U.S.-based Qualcomm developed CDMA, which was invented by the company's founder, Irwin Jacobs, in the late 1980s. The promise of more capacity and a requirement for fewer base stations made by CDMA proponents steered many U.S. digital wireless companies, particularly the Bell telephone companies and Sprint Communications, away from the time division multiple access (TDMA). The Telecommunications Industry Association in 1989 agreed upon the TDMA standard. Qualcomm was started in 1985 and introduced code division multiple access in 1989. Service using CDMA was targeted for implementation in 1992. However, technical glitches delayed actual implementation until 1996.

Code division multiple access is a "spread spectrum" technology. Each conversation transmitted is spread over multiple frequencies as it is sent. This is accomplished through the use of unique 40-bit codes assigned to each telephone transmission. These codes are called Walesh codes. Having a unique code assigned to each data or voice transmission allows multiple users to share spectrum or air space. CDMA has more capacity than TDMA.

In addition to capacity, CDMA handsets use low amounts of power. This can be significant in light of consumer concerns about cellular handsets causing cancer. Lower power emissions translate to less threats of wireless service causing cancer. Finally, calls are transferred (handed off), from cell to cell by a soft handoff method superior to TDMA and analog cellular's handoff. With a soft handoff, a call is rarely dropped during the handoff. For a short period of time during the handoff or transfer, the call is held as it is received and as the cell hands it off. Unfortunately, the decision to use what they perceived as a superior multiplexing method cost many carriers in the U.S. a high price in lost compatibility.

Time Division Multiple Access and GSM

The standard that had been agreed upon by the TIA when CDMA was promulgated is time division multiple access, or TDMA. In TDMA, the transmission channel is broken into a number of time slots—for example, six. Three of the time slots carry traffic from three devices, and three are not used. The three unused time slots ensure that there is no interference between traffic on the time slots carrying traffic. Time division multiple access has three to five times the capacity of analog cellular service.

While time division multiple access is used both in the U.S. and the rest of the world, the methods do not interoperate with each other. The standard in Europe and most of the rest of the world is called GSM (Groupe Speciale Mobile). GSM works by dividing channels of 200-kilohertz spectrum into eight time slots. Seven of the time slots carry traffic and the eighth carries control signals. The U.S. has settled on a standard called IS-136.

10 Globalization

In this chapter...

This chapter focuses on the largest markets in Europe, Asia and Latin America. Deregulation and improvements in telecommunications have created intense competition for long distance, high-speed access to the Internet, Internet services for business and cellular calling. For the most part, monopolies still control local services.

Many carriers and equipment suppliers have expanded their operations.

- SBC has investments of more than $25 billion in 23 countries in Latin America, Europe, Asia and Africa. Spain's Telefonica controls a large part of the infrastructure in South America. NTT DoCoMo owns 16% of AT&T Wireless. Cable & Wireless PLC owns one of the world's largest Internet backbones, which stretches across the world from Asia, to Europe and North America.

- AT&T, WorldCom, Level 3, France Telecom, Qwest, Telecom Italia, Deutsche Telekom, NTT Japan, BellSouth and Vodafone are other network service providers whose scope is global.

Prior to deregulation, telephone companies were often owned by the state and controlled by the same agency that ran the postal service. Thus, the name PTT, which refers to Post Telephone & Telegraph, is often used to refer to the incumbent telephone company or telecommunications regulatory agency. In China, in addition to the Ministry of Post and Telecommunications (MPT) network, the Ministry of Railways (MoR) built a fiber optic network alongside its tracks that it operates for telecommunications. In Japan, three railroad companies also built a network along their railways. Japan Telecom is the carrier that grew out of that venture. It is the third largest carrier in Japan.

In North America and the rest of the world, lower cost technology made it feasible to build new networks and services that undercut incumbents' prices. Interestingly, the first competitive efforts arose as a result of innovation in wireless services. In the United States, microwave made it cost effective for MCI to build and sell private line service without laying costly copper wires. Elsewhere in the world, the explosion of cellular led to wireless network services parallel to landline networks owned by governments and operated by incumbent carriers. Wireless services of all types, including those for fixed wireless local service, enable providers to install networks without digging up the street, laying conduit and obtaining rights of way in individual streets and cities.

Technologies such as fiber optics, digital signal processors (DSPs) (see Chapter 5) and low-cost computer chips are bringing down the cost of building switches and backbone networks. The availability of new technology and the lure of opening new markets attract investments in new and established carriers. More competition results in lower prices and tighter margins and less traffic per carrier. This can result in less revenue to pay off the high percentage of fixed costs for hardware, fiber optic lines and cellular equipment. It costs little more to maintain a network at 75% capacity than one at 25% capacity. The key in this equation is increased usage because of lower prices. This is a particular problem in countries with high poverty rates and small middle classes or a small base of business customers.

In Europe, construction of data and long distance networks has resulted in a glut of capacity between metropolitan areas. One illustration of the over-supply of bandwidth is the phenomenon of bandwidth trading discussed in Chapter 4. Instead of building new fiber routes, carriers bid on spare capacity in existing routes in exchanges such as Band-X's, located in London, and Germany. Routes where capacity between cities are bought and sold are: London/Amsterdam, London/Paris, Frankfurt/Berlin, Paris/Madrid and Paris/Milan or Rome. Band-X posts lists of speeds and routes available and carriers bid to use them.

THE IMPETUS TO DEREGULATE ....

Parts of Europe were deregulated in 1997 and Asia, including Japan and Singapore, are just opening their markets as is Australia. Latin America began opening its markets in 1997. Two factors are pushing deregulation: the desire to be part of the World Trade Organization (WTO) and the prospect of upgraded network infrastructures. A requirement for joining the WTO is that countries liberalize their market for imports and foreign companies. WTO members derive benefits from having more companies to buy and sell services with on a *quid-pro-quo* basis.

Many countries created telecommunications monopolies to ensure the presence of secure telecommunications. Given the availability of new technologies, this is no longer required. However, over the years, incumbent telephone companies had no incentive to upgrade networks, improve customer service, lower prices or improve technology. Many countries looked to events in the United States where free market conditions in the 1980s and 90s resulted in innovation, lower prices for long distance and more choices for end users.

Steps in Deregulation

In some areas of the world, particularly Latin America, incumbents were first privatized but given a period of time in which to prepare for competition. In addition, governments raised money from the sale of shares in incumbents. During the period after they were privatized but before competition was allowed, they improved infrastructure and balanced prices. Previously, long distance prices were high to subsidize local services. With balanced prices, long distance costs were lowered by incumbents to compete with potential new carriers who were expected (and, in fact, did) offer lower prices for these services when they were given licenses to provide telecommunications.

After a period of time, licenses generally were issued to both foreign and domestic carriers for long distance, cellular and data networking products. In Latin America and Asia, this period was longer than in Europe where the network infrastructure was more modern.

Challenges

Telecommunications networks in much of the Middle East, Africa and Asia are run by incumbents with monopolies in telecommunications. Elsewhere, British Telecommunications PLC in the United Kingdom (UK), Deutsche Telekom AG in Germany, Telebras in Brazil and NTT in Japan, are losing market share in their long distance and data communications networking markets. They all, however, continue to dominate their markets for fixed-line and local services.

Opening local loops for competition requires multiple connections to central offices, billing systems and copper facilities in locations where competitors don't have their own fiber or fixed wireless facilities. Incumbents that have often lost market share in long distance and other service are reluctant to cooperate with companies that are in competition with them. Each of these connections requires fees as well as technical agreements. Incumbents argue that fees are too low and competitors feel that they are too high to allow for profits. In the UK, most of the companies that are conducting trials of digital subscriber line (DSL) connections backed out of DSL service. They cited British Telecom's high interconnection fees and the fact that British Telecom is not making central office space available for placement (collocation) of local competitors' equipment.

Establishing long distance service is much less complex than competing for local service. Connections for long distance and international service generally only require connections in a few central offices per metropolitan area as opposed to interconnections and resale of many different pieces of the incumbent's network in order to reach customers to sell local services.

Trends in Global Markets

Voice over IP, cellular and prepaid cellular services are key technologies driving competition and enabling more populations worldwide to have access to telephone service. In addition to making services more widely available, they have lowered the cost of telephone calls.

VoIP

Voice over IP (VoIP) is a driving force in opening up competition in emerging markets. Alternative methods of making calls often are present before markets are officially open. In some cases, people find ways to make calls at a lower cost using, for example, voice over IP, call-back for international calls and prepaid calling cards to save money on long distance to other parts of the world. In China, people started making calls from their computers before other carriers were ostensibly allowed to provide service. This is happening in Africa and the Middle East as well as Thailand and Peru. People with a computer equipped with speakers and a microphone use their Internet connections to place low cost long distance calls. Small operators in these countries also carry voice over IP calls for customers.

Prepaid for Cellular

Because of the lack of credit, most new cellular subscribers sign up for prepaid service. However, revenues per subscriber for prepaid services are lower than those for monthly subscribers. According to Q4 2000 *Business Monitor*, published by Business Monitor International, page 35, in Brazil, prepaid phones account for 52% of the mobile service.

Cellular and Fixed Wireless

According to the International Telecommunications Union (ITU), by December 2000, there were more mobile than landline phones in Hong Kong, Japan, the Republic of Korea, Singapore and Taiwan. A key contributor to cellular growth is that in most of these countries, callers pay only for cellular calls they make. Customers do not pay for calls they receive. Therefore, they are not reluctant to give out their cell phone numbers and use their mobile phones more frequently often as a replacement of their fixed-line phones.

A key factor driving growth in cellular service and fixed wireless service is the lower costs to build wireless infrastructures compared to laying cable to each subscriber. After paying for spectrum, carriers install central offices and cell site antennas and controllers. The only fiber they need are in backbone connections between their switches and for connections to other carriers. Costs for these backbone connections are lower than laying cable to each customer location.

Because cellular margins are being squeezed and third generation (3G) licenses are costly in most countries, carriers are exploring joint ventures with each other to share the expense of upgrading infrastructure for broadband mobile service. The article, "Viag Interkom Seeks Cooperation from Rivals on Mobile Networks," a *Wall Street Journal* News Roundup, published in *WSJ.com The Wall Street Journal*, 27 February 2001, reported that Viag, owned by British Telecom, is exploring joint efforts with other carriers to share the cost of creating new infrastructure in Germany.

LATIN AMERICA...

Although most countries in Latin America have privatized their telecommunications industries, competitors have a small share of the fixed-line market. Major competitive focuses are on high-speed Internet and intracompany data connections for businesses and cellular services. The three largest countries in Latin America are Brazil, Mexico and Argentina. Table 10.1 indicates the low penetration of telephone lines and mobile phones in these three countries in 1999. In Paraguay (60%) and Venezuela (57%), more people have cellular than fixed-line phones.

Telefonica SA, the incumbent telephone company in Spain, has the largest presence in Latin America of any single company. In November 1999, it owned one of three phone lines in Latin America. It owns Telefonica de Argentina SA, Telefonica del Peru SA, Telesp Participacoes SA of Sao Paulo and pending approval, half of the cellular users in Brazil jointly with Portugal Telecom. In addition, its subsidiary, Emergia Holding, is planning to construct an undersea fiber optic cable between Latin America and the United States. Half of Telefonica's revenues are generated in Latin America.

BellSouth International, under the brand names Movicom BellSouth and BCP Telecommunicoes, S.A. with over 6 million cellular customers as of March 2000, has a major presence in Latin America. According to the article, "The Crafty Globalizer," published in *Forbes*, 20 March 2000, page 81, by Peter Spiegel, BellSouth's international revenues account for 10% of total revenues. It has cellular operations in 10 Latin American countries and Internet service in most of these. It launched operations in Latin America in 1989 in Buenos Aires, Argentina with its wireless carrier, Movicom BellSouth. In 2000, it launched a major branding strategy to identify its cellular holdings as BellSouth. Its goal is to gain business travelers' roaming traffic when they travel in South America. See Table 10.2 later in this chapter for key carriers.

While not as large as Brazil, Mexico and Argentina, Chile was the first country in Latin America to open its markets to competition. It has a large number of digital central office switches and many competitors. Argentina also privatized and deregulated telecommunications early compared to the rest of Latin America.

Brazil

Brazil is the fifth largest country in the world. It covers almost half the territory of South America and has 20 states within its boundaries. The largest city in Brazil, Sao

FIDELITY INVESTMENT'S TELECOM VENTURES

Back in the 1970s, top management at Fidelity Investments recognized the importance of telecommunications in its own company and early on saw opportunities in telecommunications. Fidelity, a Massachusetts-headquartered mutual funds company, was an early investor in telecommunications pioneers MCI, local fiber network provider Teleport Communications (now part of AT&T) and other companies. Fidelity Investments saw the need of large financial institutions and major corporations for higher bandwidth services for call centers, financial transactions and data communications.

Teleport supplied high-speed optical links from customers to long distance carriers that undercut incumbent telephone company prices. At this time, fiber was not available in metropolitan areas and implementation of T-1 over copper cabling took months.

As telecommunications in the United States became more competitive, Fidelity saw opportunities in Europe where markets were wide open for metropolitan area data networks. In 1992, it founded City of London Telecommunications, now called COLT Telecom Group PLC, in London. When long distance was deregulated in the UK and later throughout Europe, Fidelity already had a presence and began selling long distance service. COLT expanded in the 1990s into Germany, Austria, France, Switzerland, Spain, Italy and the Netherlands. Fidelity successfully took COLT public in 1996 and added Internet services to its offerings by purchasing French ISP Imaginet. It linked its metropolitan networks together into a European-wide network that it is jointly building with Level 3 Communications.

Fidelity formed two other companies, KVH in Japan and MetroRED in Argentina, Brazil and Mexico that it operates similarly to COLT. KVH and MetroRED are building fiber networks within large cities. They plan on connecting the networks in individual cities to each other and to undersea cables. MetroRED is connecting together its fiber networks across Latin America. KVH and MetroRED's strategy is to differentiate themselves by the data services they sell over their fiber networks. One of their focuses is on application infrastructure provider (AIP) services. In conjunction with their fiber connections, the AIP offerings include data center services such as network management, billing, hosting and firewalls for application service providers and large enterprises.

Table 10.1 Latin American Telephones Per 100 Inhabitants—1999

Economy	Total Population (M) 1999	Per Capita (US$) 1998	Telephone Lines Per 100 Inhabitants 1999	Mobile Subscribers Per 100 Inhabitants 1999
Brazil	167.99	4675	14.87	8.95
Mexico	97.36	4330	11.22	7.94
Argentina	36.58	8257	20.11	12.12
Chile	15.02	4912	20.70	15.05

Source: ITU data for population was provided to the ITU by the United Nations and per capita figures were supplied to the ITU by the IMF, the Organization for Economic Cooperation and Development (OECD) or the World Bank.

Paolo is the third largest city in the world. Brazil is the most industrial of the Latin America countries. According to a U.S. Department of Commerce report, "Latin America Business Development Mission February 11–19 2000," Brazil has one third of the total telephone lines in Latin America.

Background

Prior to 1962, Brazil's telecommunications infrastructure was operated by a wholly owned Canadian subsidiary of Canadian Traction Light and Power Company, Companhia Telefonica Brasileir (CTB). In 1968, the federal government took control of Companhia Telefonica Brasileir (CTB). In 1965, the military government created state-owned Embratel to operate Brazil's long distance services. Embratel's tasks were to build a network connecting all the capitals and main cities in each state and to provide international service.

Telebras was created in November 1972 to plan and operate a national telecommunications system within cities and to coordinate all long distance and international communications. Telebras created a separate telephone company in each of Brazil's 25 states. Embratel became a subsidiary of Telebras. However, investments in telecommunications infrastructure did not keep up with demand. By 1988, there were requests outstanding for 9 million telephone lines. In 1996, the average wait for a new telephone line was two years and only 2% of nonurban households had a fixed-line telephone.

With a goal of strengthening the telecommunications infrastructure, the government made a plan to privatize Telebras and Embratel and to open Brazilian telecommunications to private investments. Agencia Nacional de Telecomunicacoes (Anatel), the telecommunications regulatory agency, was created in 1997. Anatel approved the use of wireless local loop, cable television licenses and high-speed Internet access over the cable TV infrastructure.

In July 1998, the Ministry of Communications (MOC) sold off its holdings in the state-controlled provider Telebras and broke it into 12 companies: three fixed-line, eight regional cellular and Embratel, the international long distance company. World-Com, the only U.S. firm to bid, won a controlling interest in Embratel.

Following the privatization and breakup of Telebras, the government issued licenses to four companies known as "mirror" companies to compete with the former state monopolies. Three of them are wireline and the fourth provides international services to compete with Embratel. To promote construction of new infrastructure, the "mirror" companies are allowed to provide telephone service via cable TV facilities and wireless local loop technology. The mirror companies and the companies spun off by Telebras are restricted to operating only within their regions until 2002. Local number portability is mandated to start in 2005.

According to the article, "Portugal Telecom, Telfonica Unite Their Mobile-Phone Assets in Brazil," published in *WSJ.com The Wall Street Journal*, 25 January 2001, by Jonathan Karp and Keith Johnson, Brazil has five fixed-line and two long distance companies. The incumbent international long distance provider is Embratel, which owns the largest fiber optic network in Brazil. The Brazilian government gave a "mirror" concession to Intelig in 1999 to compete against Embratel.

The three fixed-line incumbents are:

- **Brasil Telecom** (formerly Tele Centro Sul) provides service in the nine central and southern states as well as the capital of Brazil, Brasilia. Brasil Telecom is owned by Telecom Italia.

- **Telesp** (Telecomunicacoes de Sao Paulo SA) is the fixed-line carrier for Brazil's wealthiest area—the state of Sao Paolo. (Sao Paolo is both a state and a city.) Telesp is owned by Telefonica.

- **Telemar** (Tele Norte Leste Participacoes SA) is the largest of the incumbent fixed-line carriers with operations in 16 states. Its territory includes Rio de Janeiro and the northeastern and northern states. In 2001, the Brazilian government took back control of Telemar on suspicion of cross ownership by three board of director members. Telemar is expected to bid for wireless licenses.

Cellular

The government increased competition to the original eight mobile providers by auctioning off eight licenses to regional cellular providers between 1997 and 1998. These licenses are for Personal Communications Service (PCS) spectrum in the 1.9-Giga-hertz (GHz) band for code division multiple access (CDMA) and time division multi-ple access (TDMA) service. MCI, Telefonica de Espana, Iberdrola, Bilbao Vizcaya Bank and Portugal Telecom won the biggest licenses. There are now 19 cellular oper-ators in Brazil. (See Chapter 9 for cellular services.)

Anatel held three auctions for nine licenses of PCS spectrum for GSM (original-ly, Groupe Speciale Mobile, but also known as Global System for Mobile Communi-cations) service in 2001. Bids were made for only four of the nine licenses. Some carriers have made plans instead to create partnerships or buy existing cellular compa-nies to avoid the cost of building new networks. For example, Telefonica SA and Por-tugal Telecom announced in September 2000 that they intended to merge their Brazilian cellular properties. If the merger is approved, the combined company will be the largest cellular provider in Brazil. It will control:

- **Tele Sudeste Celular** in the states of Rio de Janeiro and Espirito Santo
- **CRT Celular** in the southern states
- **Tele Leste Celular** in Bahia and Sergipe
- **Telesp Celular** in the state of Sao Paolo

The eight incumbent cellular carriers controlled 69% of the mobile phones as of June 2000. Telecom Italia has a controlling stake in three cellular companies: Maxitel, Tele Nordeste Celular and Tele Celular Sul. Telecom Americas, owned by Bell Cana-da International (BCI), SBC and America Movil of Mexico is the second largest cellu-lar provider in Brazil. According to Anatel, the total number of mobile phones in service between July 1998 and July 2000 grew 243%. As of January 2001, there were 22.6 million cellular phones in service.

Internet

Following privatization in 1998, companies such as Embratel and Telefonica began investing in new IP-based protocol Internet backbone networks. The backbone is the portion of the network that carries the largest amount of traffic between sites. Howev-er, access to the Internet is problematic. Embratel has stated that it intends to invest heavily in access to the Internet for business customers.

Inhibiting factors to Internet access for consumers are the cost of calls, which are still billed on a per-minute/per-pulse basis. In addition, uneven delivery and postal service inhibit e-commerce, which depends on timely delivery of goods ordered over the Internet. The Brazilian government in January 2001 announced a program to build, sell and finance new computers for consumers with the goal of promoting Internet access by consumers. An Associated Press article, "Internet Access to Expand in Brazil," published in *The New York Times on the Web*, 31 January 2001, estimated that between 8.5 and 14 million Brazilians surf the Web. The total population of Brazil is 169 million people.

Mexico

Mexico is the largest Spanish-speaking country in the world and the United State's second largest trading partner behind Canada. According to the U.S. Department of State, cellular grew from 3.6 million to 9.2 million users from 2000 to 2001. Much of this is attributed to the new policy of caller pays. Cellular users no longer pay for calls they receive. However, network capacity did not keep up with growth and service deteriorated. The regulatory agency, Federal Telecommunications Commission, Cofetel, has mandated investments in network infrastructure by incumbent cellular carriers.

While fixed-line service is growing rapidly, the number of telephones per 100 people is the lowest in Latin America. The U.S. Department of State, in its *FY2001 Country Commercial Guide*, stated that it expects 1 million new fixed wireless lines to be installed in the next few years. Fixed wireless installation is lower in cost and has shorter implementation time frames because it does not require digging up the streets and receiving permission to lay fiber optic cables.

Background

The regulatory framework for Mexico was established by The Federal Telecommunications Law of 1995. In 1997, the Mexican government authorized nine carriers to provide long distance service. However, the high interconnection rates that incumbent provider Telmex charged competitors for connecting calls to local customers inhibited profits of Telmex competitors and deterred competition. In December 2000, a four-year legal dispute was settled between Telmex and carriers in the United States. The settlement lowered local and long distance interconnection and collocation fees.

Telefonos de Mexico, SA de C.V. (Telmex) controls 75% of the Mexican long distance market. However, callers can presubscribe to the long distance provider of their choice. The interconnection settlement previously mentioned is expected to increase competitors' market share. Competition for local service was authorized to begin in 1999. However, until the preceding December 2000 agreement was reached, Telmex had refused to allow Alestra or Avantel to interconnect to the Telmex network, claiming that these companies owed them money for interconnection services.

Teléfonos de México (Telmex) is the incumbent fixed-line carrier. According to Business Monitor's Q4 2000 Quarterly Forecast Report, Telmex has 98% market share of local fixed-line service. Telmex is one of the largest, most powerful corporations in Mexico. Its owner, Carlos Slim, is the wealthiest man in Latin America. Mr. Slim bought Telmex in 1990 from the Mexican government through the holding company he controls, Carso Global Telecom, SA de C.V.

Of the following long distance competitors, both Alestra and Avantel have stated that they plan to offer fixed wireless service to business customers in Mexico City, Guadalajara and Monterrey. Mexico does not allow foreign companies to own more than 49% of any wireline company. There is no limit on ownership for cellular companies.

- Alestra
- Avantel
- Iusater
- Maxcom (formerly called Amaritel)
- Bestel
- Investcom
- MarcaTel

Competitors for local service are building out service via fixed wireless technology. Four companies acquired licenses in 2000 for spectrum for fixed wireless local service.

Cellular

Telmex's spun-off subsidiary American Movil SA (formerly TELCEL) is the largest cellular provider with a 70% market share. American Movil operates a TDMA network. The second largest cellular provider is Grupo Iusacell SA. Iusacell is licensed to operate in six out of the nine regions in Mexico. The vast majority, 87% of American Movil and Iusacell subscribers access the network via prepaid service.

Argentina

Argentina, which is second in size to Brazil, has the highest educational levels in Latin America. In 1998, its gross domestic product per capita was $8250. In the first half of the twentieth century, American company International Telephone & Telegraph Corporation (ITT) spent millions of dollars to help develop the Argentinean telecommunications infrastructure. In 1946, the government of President Juan Peron nationalized Empresa Nacional de Telecomunicaciones (Entel), the telephone company. When Entel ran telecommunications:

- Service was poor
- Rates were high
- Few investments were made in infrastructure
- People waited years for new telephone lines

In an effort to improve telecommunications services, the president of Argentina, Carlos Menem, split up Entel by geography in 1990 and sold it to two different organizations that had a duopoly. The Spanish telephone company Telefonica, through its subsidiary Telefonica de Argentina, was given a franchise for basic telephony service in southern Argentina and most of Buenos Aires. Telecom Argentina was given the franchise for service in northern Argentina.

Competition and privatization have led to improved services, more telephone lines per capita and lower prices for voice and data services. According to the U.S. Department of Commerce, in 1990 there were 3 million telephone lines installed. In December 1999 there were 9 million lines. The following is the privatization and deregulation time line:

- Entel was privatized in 1991 when it was sold to Telecom Argentina (at that time owned largely by France Telecom and Telecom Italia), which gained control of the northern parts of Argentina and Telefonica de Argentina, which gained control of the Southern part.
- The new owners immediately invested $1.9 billion into the infrastructure.
- In November 1999, Argentina opened competition to four companies for local, domestic and international calling. It also allowed the two incumbents to invade each other's territories.
- In 2000, the new president of Argentina, Fernando De la Rua, issued a presidential decree opening up the Argentinean market to competition for cellular, paging, trunked radio, data communications, cable television and value added services. The market was opened on November 8, 2000 and each license granted can be used for all markets. Separate licenses covering mobile or landline service are not required. A condition of obtaining a license for service is that carriers must invest $2 for every subscriber in their territory.

To foster competition, interconnection costs charged by incumbents for connections to their networks were decreased from 2.35¢ per minute to 1.1¢. A fund also was set up for universal service with contributions of 1% of gross sales mandated by the government. The fund is to be used to provide service in poor and rural marginal areas. In addition, 12% of the fund is earmarked for Internet access by schools.

In another effort to foster competition, local number portability is mandated. People changing carriers will be allowed to keep their phone numbers. To make it easier to change telephone companies, customers will not have to presubscribe to a particular service to use it. They will be able to access a carrier's network by dialing the prefix assigned to that carrier before making their call. In anticipation of further competition, the incumbents dropped rates by half between 1999 and the end of 2000 for long distance and international calls.

Argentina's deep recession and high unemployment are hurting competition and innovation in telecommunications. It has the highest debt of any country in the emerging world and is in danger of defaulting on its loans. Argentina's worsening financial situation is impacting other countries' economies with which it trades, particularly Brazil.

Cellular

In mid-1999, PCS licenses were auctioned off to the following companies, which started offering long distance rates that undercut those for fixed-line phones:

- Personal (the cellular arm of Telecom Argentina)
- Unifon (the cellular arm of Telefonica de Argentina)
- CTI Movil (part of Verizon)
- Movicom BellSouth

Argentina has the highest penetration of cellular phones in Latin America. Mobile phones grew from less than 200,000 in 1994 to 4.5 million in September 2000. Cellular services also are a key competitive area. In addition to the cellular providers listed above, Nextel International is expected to become active in Argentina.

Data Services

According to the September 2000 Newsletter by the Consulate of Argentina, data revenues are only 6% of sector revenues compared to 20% in Europe and the U.S. Many carriers see potential for more data services to business customers. In addition to the incumbents, CTI/AT&T and Impsat are investing heavily in the region. Impsat is building its own fiber network. In low-density sections, Impsat will utilize fixed wireless Local Multipoint Distribution Service (LMDS). Comsat Argentina SA is using a combination of satellite and fiber network to provide data transmission service. Comsat entered the Argentine data market in 1991.

Impsat and MetroRED are building fiber optic infrastructures connecting major cities in Argentina and elsewhere. They focus on high-speed connections to the Internet for business customers as well as fiber optic connections between companies.

High telephone rates have so far put a damper on the Internet service provider (ISP) market. Phone companies currently charge by the minute for dialup Internet access. This makes even free ISP service costly for consumers because of the telephone fees. However, the high education level of the Argentine population creates a possibility of higher penetration of Internet access by consumers in the future if local phone rates decrease and the economy improves.

On the residential front, cable TV competitors Multicanal and Cablevision SA sell Internet access to consumers. Cable TV facilities reach over half of the homes in Argentina.

Impact of Poverty

Income disparity between the wealthy and the rest of the population is a major issue in Latin America. This disparity is reflected in statistics on cellular and Internet access. For example, the article, "Latin America Looks to Wireless," published in the online edition of *The Standard*, 9 May 2000, stated that in Argentina, only 10% of the population has a cell phone. The article further stated that in Brazil, 32% of the wealthiest people have Internet access but only 2.1% of the middle class has it.

Table 10.2 Key Carriers in Argentina, Brazil and Mexico

Entity	Owners	Details
Alestra	AT&T 49% Mexican conglomerates 51%	Provides local and broadband service in Mexico.
Algar Telecom Leste SA (ATL)	Temporarily under control of state but 15% America Movil	Cellular in Rio de Janeiro, Brazil.
America Movil SA (previously Telcel)	Spun off from Telmex	Largest cellular provider in Mexico. One of the ten largest cellular providers worldwide.
Avantel	WorldCom 45% Grupo Financiero Banamex-Accival SA 55%	Local service in Mexico.
Argentina STET France Telecom SA	Nortel Inversora, a holding company equally controlled by France Telecom and Telecom Italia SpA holds a controlling interest	Incumbent carrier in northern Argentina.

Table 10.2 Key Carriers in Argentina, Brazil and Mexico *(continued)*

Entity	Owners	Details
AT&T Latin America	AT&T Formed from purchases of FirstCom Corporation of Miami & Netstream of Brazil	Fiber networks in four Brazilian cities plus presence in Argentina, Chile, Colombia and Peru.
BCP Telecomunicoes S.A.	BellSouth International	Cellular operator in Sao Paolo state and six states in the NE region of Brazil. 800-MHz CDMA.
Brasil Telecom	Telecom Italia Opportunity, a Brazilian investment group	Fixed-line operator for 17% of Brazil's population. Serves central and southern states and Brasilia. Formerly owned by Telefonica consortium CRT until Anatel ordered divestment due to Telefonica ownership of cellular company Telesp Celular.
Cablevision S.A.	Ownership may be split up, now Telefonica 33.28% CEI Citicorp Holdings SA 33.28%; UnitedGlobalCom 28%	Largest cable TV operator in Latin America. Holdings in Peru, Argentina and Mexico.
Comsat International	The telecommunications arm of Lockheed Martin Corporation, which has stated it will sell Comsat	Mainly data transmission via satellite and wireline, also planning national and international long distance in Argentina. Argentina, Brazil, Colombia, Venezuela, Peru, Mexico and Guatemala.
Embratel	WorldCom	Incumbent long distance provider—Brazil. Plans to enter local data market January 2002.
Global Telecom	Portugal Telecom 49% of the common shares and 100% of the preferred shares	Cellular operator in wealthy Brazilian southern states of Parana and Santa Catarina must be approved by Anatel. Will become part of the Telefonica–Portugal Telecom cellular operation when approved.

Table 10.2 Key Carriers in Argentina, Brazil and Mexico *(continued)*

Entity	Owners	Details
Grupo Iusacell, S.A. de C.V. Formerly Nuevo Grupo Iusacell, S.A. de C.V.	Verizon 37% Vodafone 34.5%	Second largest cellular carrier in Mexico. Uses CDMA. Has joint ventures in Ecuador, Chile, Colombia and Nicaragua. Expanding to data communications.
Impsat Fiber Networks, Inc.	20% British Telecom, 21% Morgan Stanley, 59% IMPSA, an Argentine holding company	Data transmission, mainly Argentina but also Columbia, Venezuela, Ecuador, Mexico and the U.S. Long distance and local service in Brazil. British Telecom ownership being offered for common stock.
Intelig	50% National Grid (a UK company) 25% France Telecom and 25% Sprint	Brazilian competitor to incumbent long distance provider Embratel.
Iusater	Grup Iusa Verizon Communications	Long distance services in Mexico.
Maxcom (formerly Amaritel)	The Aguirre family, owners of radio stations and programming that it syndicates throughout Mexico	Early competitor for local services in Mexico.
MetroRED	Fidelity Investments	Building fiber optic data networks in Argentina, Brazil and Mexico.
Movicom BellSouth	65% owned by BellSouth	Cellular provider in Argentina.
Multicanal	Grupo Clarin SA	Cable TV provider in Argentina. Grupo Clarin owns newspapers, magazines, TV and radio stations in Argentina and carrier CTI.
Tele Centro Oeste Celular Participacoes SA	BellSouth 16.5%	Cellular in capital of Brazil and Amazon region.

Table 10.2 Key Carriers in Argentina, Brazil and Mexico *(continued)*

Entity	Owners	Details
Pegaso PCS, SA de CV	20.1% Leap Wireless, also Pegaso Grupo, Sprint PCS, Citicorp Equity Capital, The Latin American Infrastructure Fund and Nissho Iwai	CDMA PCS cellular carrier in four areas of Mexico including Mexico City, northern Baja California.
Telintar	Grupo Telecom and Telefonica Argentina	Argentina international telecommunications services.
Telefonica de Argentina SA	Telefonica SA	Incumbent carrier in southern Argentina.
Telemar (Tele Norte Leste Participacoes SA)	Brazilian consortium	Largest fixed-line carrier in Brazil. Has an Internet access group.
Tele Nordeste Celular Participacoes SA	Telecom Italia Mobile Spa (TIM)	Cellular in northeast Brazil.
Telesp (Telecomunicaco es de Sao Paulo SA)	Telefonica	Fixed-line operator for state of Sao Paolo.
Telecom Americas Ltd	Bell Canada International and América Móvil 44.3% each SBC 11.4%	Second largest cellular provider in Brazil. Cellular operations also in Columbia. Broadband fixed wireless in Venezuela and Argentina; cable TV in Brazil.
Telemig Celular	Telesystem International Wireless (TIW) operates Fido brand of cellular in Canada plus operations in Asia and Europe; TIW controlled by George Siros	The fifth largest cellular provider in Brazil; operates in the central region of Minas Gerais. Operates CDMA and TDMA at 800 MHz.
Telmex	Carso Global Telecom SBC 10%	Incumbent phone company in Mexico. Owns prepaid cellular and prepaid local companies in the U.S. as well as numerous ventures throughout Latin America.

Table 10.2 Key Carriers in Argentina, Brazil and Mexico *(continued)*

Entity	Owners	Details
Telefonica Moviles—Portug al Telecom	Jointly by Spain's Telefonica SA and Portugal Telecom SA	Second largest cellular provider in Latin America if merger approved by Anatel. Holdings in Sao Paulo state and the southern states of Brazil (Telesp Celular), Rio de Janeiro state (Tele Sudeste Celular), Tele Leste Celular in Bahia and Sergipe and CRT Celular in the southern states.

ASIA

Because of their vast populations, there is a great deal of interest in telecommunications in Asia. In Japan, large sums of money are being invested in fiber directly to businesses and residences for high-speed Internet access.

China

According to the ITU, 21% of the world population lives in China. China itself is a fragmented market with sharp regional and dialect differences between its 30 regions. Seventy percent of the population lives in 30% of the land area in the eastern and coastal sections where the cities of Beijing, Shanghai and Guangzhou are located. According to the U.S. Department of Commerce, this area carries about 75% of the domestic telephone traffic. In addition to regional differences, major gulfs exist in the level of infrastructure between rural and urban areas in standards of living and very basic items such as roads and waterways. The Chinese government has a major push underway to develop the infrastructure in the western part of China over the next 10 years.

The December 2000 International Telecommunications Internet Report, *IP Telephony,* page 56, states that there were 8.7 telephones per 100 people in China on January 1, 2000. According to the February 7, 2001 online magazine *Public Network Wire,* about 10 million new subscribers are added each year. The article stated that analysts expect that by 2005, China will have the highest number of cellular and landline phones of any country in the world.

The government controls China's telecommunications carriers. The main focus since 1999 has been in building up the infrastructure for cellular, broadband data networks, Internet services and fixed-line voice telephony. While there is no official competition to government-controlled monopolies, unofficial unauthorized competition exists in the form of IP for voice phone calls. A gray market has existed in China where people make calls through IP gateways linked to the Internet. Fees are lower than those charged by traditional carriers and are seen by the government as losses in revenue worth millions of dollars.

While potential for development is large, there are stumbling blocks. According to the article, "China Hits Snag in High-Tech Plan," published in *The New York Times on the Web*, 4 February 2001, by The Associated Press, there is a shortage of skilled labor. Another major snag to development, according to the article, is that most of the companies in China are small and investments in these companies are scarce. There are concerns by foreign investors about piracy and theft of intellectual property by the Chinese.

Few foreign entities participate in the Chinese telecommunications sector. China has not entered the World Trade Organization (WTO) in which members agree to lower barriers to imports within their respective countries. However, China has indicated that it will join. If China does join the WTO, it has stated that it will then allow foreign companies to own 49% or 50% of specific types of joint ventures by the end of three years. Currently, foreign investments in joint ventures are officially banned.

While many foreign businesses have signed agreements with Chinese companies, many of them have not been fulfilled. For example, in 2000, China Unicom's parent, China United Telecommunications Corporation ended 40 contracts with foreign companies after the Chinese government stated that they were illegal. A Chinese saying illustrates some of the frustrations of doing business in China:

"When a contract is signed that means negotiations begin."

Prior to 1998, telecommunications were regulated by the Ministry of Post and Telecommunications, MPT. In 1998, the MPT and the Ministry of Electronic Industry (MEI) were merged to form the Ministry of Information Industries (MII). The MII not only controls telecommunications but it also owns China Telecom, China Mobile and China Unicom, which compete with China Mobile.

China has a mobile phone industry second in size only to the United States' 100 million subscribers. According to Pyramid Advisory Alerts, as reported in the article, "China Mobile's Wireless Data Revenue-Sharing Scheme," *Yahoo! Finance*, 11 January 2001, its 78 million subscribers at the end of 2000 represents only a 6% market penetration. Because of its low penetration, the cellular market is expected to quickly become the largest in the world.

The two mobile carriers in China are China Mobile, the largest, and China Unicom. According to Unicom's Executive Director, Shi Cuiming, Unicom had 12 million subscribers or 12% of the total subscribers by November 2000. The government has decreed that caller-pays cellular service will start at the beginning of 2002. Currently, users pay for cellular calls they receive as well as outgoing calls they make.

In 1999, the Ministry of Information Industries broke the largest fixed-wireline company, China Telecom, into four companies. The goal was to introduce competition in the telecommunications sector and encourage construction of an advanced infrastructure. There are six licensed carriers in China. All are government backed:

- **China Telecom**—Currently provides fixed-line phone and data service to 67% of the market. It owns 80% of China's fiber long haul network. Most competitors sell fixed line data networking on China Telecom's fiber infrastructure. It is backed by the MII and has been highly profitable. It is selling 30% of its shares in a public stock offering in 2001 to raise capital for expansion. It is expected to enter the cellular service market. It announced its intention in February 2001 to build a nationwide broadband network across China.

- **China Mobile**—The incumbent cellular provider has an 88% share of the cellular market. Its network is based on the European GSM standard. According to the article, "China's Coming Telecom Battle," published in *Fortune Magazine*, 27 November 2000, page 209, China Mobile is the world's most profitable carrier. It is second in size worldwide to Vodafone Group, which has a 2% stake in China Mobile. According to the *Fortune Magazine* article, "Its market is growing so fast that every three months China adds enough subscribers to equal the entire Australian mobile-phone population." They added 19.4 million new subscribers in fiscal year 2000, bringing their total number of subscribers to 45.1 million.

- **China Unicom**—Set up in 1994 for paging, it now also operates fixed-line and cellular services. It has the second largest data network in China in addition to its cellular service. Great Wall and Century Mobile Communications' assets, both previously owned by the military, were transferred to Unicom. Unicom's network is based on GSM and Great Wall's is based on CDMA. To help it gain market share and foster competition, Unicom has been given permission by the government to price its services 10% lower than China Mobile. Another advantage for Unicom is that, unlike China Mobile, it is not required to serve rural areas and is allowed to concentrate on economically well-off areas. It is expected to use the proceeds from its year 2000 public offering in a minority stake to upgrade its network for high-speed data communications for mobile users. China Unicom is upgrading to cdma2000, a third generation CDMA technology that has more capacity for voice and higher data speeds (see Chapter 9).

- **China Network Communications (China Netcom)**—China Netcom is the first carrier to build a fiber optic network across China for high-speed data. Netcom is a carrier's carrier. It sells capacity to carriers, not to end-user customers. Netcom also has a highly lucrative business in prepaid IP phone cards that customers use to make long distance calls over Netcom's

IP network. Netcom has signed an agreement with Singapore Telecom to offer Frame Relay services between major Chinese cities and international centers. Although majority-owned by the government, Netcom has equity financing from a number of foreign firms that it is using to build out its network. Its stated goal is to reach 100 cities by the end of 2002. The presence on Netcom's board of directors of Jiang Mianheng, the son of Jiang Zemin, the Chairman of China, gives it a great deal of political clout for expansion into new service areas.

- **China Railway Telecom**—Known as Railcom, is owned by China's railway authorities. It operates fixed-line telephone service including long distance, data communications and Internet services. It was formed on December 26, 2000. Service is starting in 2001. Railcom has facilities in place from the 1-million end-user private network it runs for its employees. It has the added advantage of being able to lay fiber cabling relatively cheaply along its existing railway lines. It's slated to merge with Unicom in three years and already supplies 80% of Unicom's network capacity. Railcom lacks last-mile infrastructure between its network and end users' homes and businesses.

- **Jitong Communications**—Operates an IP-based Internet and data communications backbone that connects 50 cities in China. Jitong offers collocation, ATM, Frame Relay, Internet access, virtual private networks (VPNs) and Web hosting. (See Chapter 6 for explanations of ATM and Frame Relay. See Chapter 5 for VPNs.) Its subsidiary, Jitong Network Communications Company, provides international voice and fax services.

Hong Kong

The Hong Kong telecommunications market was deregulated in 1995. In January 2000, the Hong Kong government awarded five new fixed licenses and 12 licenses for long distance services. There are six cellular carriers in Hong Kong. Hong Kong Telecom and Hutchison Whampoa are key carriers in Hong Kong.

- **PCCW-HKT (formerly Hong Kong Telecom Ltd.)**—The largest fixed line, second largest mobile phone and major Internet service provider in Hong Kong. One hundred and twenty-five-year-old Hong Kong Telecom Ltd. was purchased by ten-month-old Pacific Century CyberWorks Ltd. in 2000 from Cable & Wireless. Pacific Century CyberWorks is an Internet startup. Telstra, the incumbent telephone company in Australia has joint ventures with Pacific Century CyberWorks Ltd for an IP backbone network, data centers and a cellular network.

- **Hutchison Telephone**—Telecom operator in Hong Kong, which owns about 2% of China Unicom. It has fixed-line, mobile and paging operations and is owned by a holding company, Hutchison Whampoa Limited, controlled by Li Ka-shing, one of the world's wealthiest men. NTT DoCo-Mo owns 25% of Hutchison Telephone.

Internet Services

The Internet in China is largely controlled by the state. It has decreed that "chat rooms" only cover politically approved topics. In addition, state-run newspapers have published rules that portals can only cover news issued by government sources. While trying to prevent the use of the Internet for dissension, the government actively promotes it for e-commerce and as a way to advance its views. For example, to encourage Internet use, in December 2000 it announced 50% telephone rate cuts to access the Internet. To date, less than 1% of the Chinese population owns a personal computer or has access to the Internet. However, personal computer and Internet use is expected to grow rapidly. Two Internet portals are Chinadotcom Corporation and Netease, which is the biggest portal in China.

The Impact of Voice over IP

In countries where telecommunications services are regulated, rates for international and long distance are often high to subsidize local service. This enables carriers to set affordable rates for consumers. High international rates afford opportunities for competitors to enter these markets by offering lower priced international calling. They often do this using voice over IP before authorities give regulatory approval for competition.

China is an example of illegal IP traffic catching the attention of authorities, which then license governments' own companies to carry IP traffic at greatly reduced prices. When governments own carriers, they receive a fee for each call made through the public switched telephone network (PSTN). Therefore, when IP operators circumvented the public network, the Chinese government lost money. The February 5, 1999 *WSJ.com The Wall Street Journal* online edition carried a Dow Jones Newswires story, "Beijing to Break Up China Telecom; Seeks Control Over Internet Telephony." The following quote is from a director of its Ministry of Information Industry about illegal voice over IP gateways: "This is tantamount to information smuggling…and we will crack down very harshly on these illegal operations of IP telephony." In 1999, China licensed domestic companies for trials of IP telephony. In 2000, it issued IP licenses to China Telecom, Unicom, Jitong and Netcom.

This illustrates the point on page 61 of the December 2000 International Tele-communications Internet Report, *IP Telephony*: "The rise of IP Telephony has affect-ed the evolution of the regulatory environment as much as, if not more than, the regulatory environment has affected the evolution of IP Telephony. One of the most tangible effects, in those markets where IP Telephony has started to spread, is the ac-celeration of market liberalization."

CONNECTING CALLS TO CHINA VIA IP

U.S.-headquartered iBasis was awarded a license to trial IP connec-tions on calls carried into and out of China. iBasis received these con-tracts in a joint sales effort with Cisco, which supplies the hardware that iBasis uses to operate its service. Chinese providers carry the IP traffic within China and connect with iBasis for traffic coming into and leaving China. iBasis carries over 10% of the traffic between China and the Unit-ed States. It carries calls to 12 cities in 11 of the 12 largest states and is licensed for connections with China Mobile, China Unicom and Jitong.

iBasis opened its office in Beijing in 1997 and hired Chinese nation-als to work with and forge relationships with licensed carriers. It started trials of IP in 1999. China's first concern in the trials was making sure Chi-na received revenues on voice over IP service. Secondly, it wanted a strong infrastructure for development of new services the carriers could sell. By licensing only a few companies, it was felt that competition would not drive prices so low that profits would be eliminated.

Because carrying traffic over IP costs so much less than traditional switched services, many Asian and Middle Eastern countries are monitor-ing IP services in China with the thought of using the technology them-selves. They are interested in lowering infrastructure costs and adding new types of service such as voice messaging in conjunction with IP. Sav-ings on new infrastructure is less of an issue for established carriers in de-veloped nations where much of the infrastructure is already in place. Voice over IP savings are more crucial when replacing central switches, adding significant capacity or in the case of new carriers and emerging nations building new infrastructure.

Japan

Japan has the world's second largest economy in terms of gross domestic product (GDP). Japan's two largest cities, Osaka and Tokyo (its capital and the most populous metropolitan area in the world), are both on the island of Honshu. Japan is made up mainly of four islands of which four-fifths of the land is mountains.

Japan experienced booming economic conditions following the post–World War II U.S. occupation of Japan during which the United States invested heavily in Japanese infrastructure. The state was heavily involved in engineering the recovery after World War II. It decreed who should compete with whom and had many rules in place. Bureaucrats, many of whom had attended elite universities, were regarded as scrupulous civil servants above the fray. Economic growth continued in the 1970s and 80s.

In the 1990s, growth slowed and recessions occurred. The number of bankruptcies increased and exports and household spending decreased. Moreover, gradually corruption was revealed in terms of government deals with companies. For example, the Ministry of Finance let some companies know when it was doing an audit in return for money or company secrets. As a result, faith in government lessened. Experts asked if it made sense to have government so involved in business. They questioned whether businesses thrived because of protection, not competency.

In telecommunications, the incumbents NTT, which supplied local and long distance service, and KDD, with the franchise for international long distance, were protected against competition and had no incentive to build infrastructure or develop technological innovations. They were not burdened with the obligation to succeed or fail based on sheer market demand or conditions. While telecommunications is in the process of being deregulated, there are still numerous rules in place. These government rules and privileges from government protection that NTT enjoys include:

- Detailed rules on how and when streets can be dug up to lay new cable
- Access to connect cables to wiring interfaces within buildings is controlled by NTT
- Registration of public IP addresses is complex and takes up to three months
- ISPs own IP addresses, so when customers change Internet providers, they must change their public IP address
- High interconnection fees NTT charges competitors to complete competitors' calls (an agreement is in place to lower these fees)

These kinds of regulations where telecommunications is run in large part by government-mandated regulations make it more difficult for foreign companies to do business. They are also an important factor in the high prices Japanese customers pay for telecommunications services, the slower speed data services available to businesses and the relatively low penetration of Internet access by consumers. To promote investments in telecommunications and more availability of high-speed data and

Internet services, the Japanese government has been in the process of deregulating telecommunications.

Interestingly, cellular services are the arena in which the most technological progress has been made to date.

Regulatory Highlights

Prior to 1985, the government owned NTT and KDD. In 1985, the government privatized a majority of NTT. The goal was to make NTT more efficient prior to deregulation. At the time, NTT was perceived as bureaucratic and corrupt. It retained its monopoly on domestic service and KDD Corporation kept its monopoly on international calling. In 1990, NTT started developing a digital cellular network and in 1995 launched cellular service. The cellular arm, NTT DoCoMo, was spun off in 1992.

In 1996, the government unveiled a plan to break up NTT into separate parts for local and long distance services. NTT was broken up in 1999 into NTT East and NTT West for local service and NTT Communications for out-of-region long distance and international service. This model somewhat mirrored the breakup of AT&T in 1984 with the exceptions that NTT had not done manufacturing and that as a holding company, NTT owns all three carriers. When AT&T was broken up, it no longer owned the Regional Bell Operating Companies (RBOCs), which sold local services.

To further encourage competition and in accordance with the World Trade Organization, in February 1997 the Japanese Diet passed a law effective February 1998 that removed limitations on foreign investments in telecommunications providers. WorldCom in 1998 became the first non-Japanese company to offer facilities-based services.

Competitors have taken the most market share from NTT Communication's international and long distance services unit. New common carriers (or NCCs as competitors to NTT are called) had an increase of 43 million long distance subscribers, a growth of 11% in 1999. Carriers that sell local service in competition to NTT had only 52,000 subscribers. In 1999 the number of fixed lines in service through NTT dropped 3.9% to 57.28 million (8.6% decrease in business lines and 2% decrease in residential lines). Included in the preceding totals were 5.1 million basic rate ISDN (BRI) lines in service.

Deregulation of Local Services • Local services were deregulated in 1999 with unbundling and access to NTT's facilities mandated. However, interconnection rates to NTT's facilities are high. The U.S. Department of State *FY2001 Country Commercial Guide* for telecommunications estimates that NTT's rates are five times higher than rates in some U.S. cities and twice as high as those in the UK and France. This makes reselling services a costly proposition where competitors have to either charge high rates for service they resell over NTT's cabling or operate at a loss.

Interconnection Fees Hinder Competition and Result in High Calling Charges • Roughly 40% of competitors' revenues go to interconnection fees that NTT charges to connect other carriers' calls to customers in locations where the carriers don't have their own fiber networks. These high interconnection costs are factors in high rates for end users, higher costs for competitors and NTT's near monopoly of the local services market. In anticipation of competition, telephone rates have been dropping. However, they are still among the highest in the world. Currently, NTT East and NTT West hold over 90% of their respective markets. T-1 Internet access for business customers is often $2300 monthly, compared to $1200 in the United States. Most businesses connect to the Internet at lower than T-1's 1.54 million bits per second (bps) speeds. Instead they have lines of, for example, 128,000 or 256,000 bps.

In 2000, Japan agreed to lower interconnection fees over three years with 90% of the reductions in the first two years. The government's goal is to encourage infrastructure investment to promote Internet access and innovation.

Digging Up the Streets and Gaining Access to Buildings—Costly Propositions • Regulations surrounding laying fiber are a deterrent to new carriers' installation of fiber networks within cities. In Japan, the conditions of streets are immaculate—not a crack is seen. Streets may only be opened up to lay new fiber once every three to eight years with five the average. When they are opened, strict regulations surround the work. For example, new dirt must be added and the old dirt carried out in separate trucks than those carrying the new dirt. This rule pertains to laying new fiber as well as to opening manholes for connections from the street to building wiring interfaces.

These rules triple the cost of laying fiber compared to costs in the rest of the world. Companies have to be quite creative and some have used sewers and underground subway passages in which to string fiber. In addition, realtors control access to the cabling within buildings and sometimes make exclusive deals with certain carriers, blocking access to these buildings by other carriers. Thus, Internet service providers and competing carriers have challenges in reaching customers to sell them Internet access, high-speed data communications and alternative local calling services.

Number Portability and Dialing Parity to Promote Competition • To   further competition, number portability was mandated in regulations set forth in August 1999. The Ministry of Post and Telecommunications recommended that dialing parity (called MYLINE) be implemented on May 1, 2001. With dialing parity, users make calls using the carrier of their choice without dialing a special prefix.

Key Competitors

Competition (see Table 10.3) is alive and well in Japan. According to the Ministry of Posts and Telecommunications Japan in its White Paper 2000 Communications in Japan, as of March 1, 2000, there were 252 service providers with their own fiber networks, cable TV or fixed wireless infrastructure. 7522 providers resell service over other carriers' facilities. However, very little competition exists for local services.

In 1998, **WorldCom** was the first carrier granted a license to sell telecommunications services over its own cabling facilities. It is building fiber networks throughout Tokyo and Osaka and has plans to expand to other major cities in Japan. It has a data center in Tokyo where it will offer Internet services such as Web hosting.

Table 10.3 Key Competitors in Japan

Entity	Owners	Details
Asia Global Crossing	Global Crossing Microsoft Softbank (headquartered in Japan)	Web hosting centers and undersea cables throughout the Asia Pacific region.
Cable & Wireless IDC	Cable & Wireless PLC	Long distance and Internet services.
eAccess	Morgan Stanley Dean Witter Goldman Sachs Both U.S. financial firms	DSL provider.
Global Access Ltd. (GAL)	Vectant, a Marubeni subsidiary Asia Global Crossing	IP-based terrestrial connections for Asia Global Crossing's undersea fiber cables for carriers in Tokyo, Osaka and Nagoya at STM 1 (155 million bit per second) and STM 4 (622 million bit per second) speeds.
Japan Telecom	Vodafone Group 45% East Japan Railway 15.1%	Third largest carrier in Japan; sells fixed-line and data services. Started by three railway companies that used their rights of way to build fiber optic networks.
J-Phone Communications	Japan Telecom 54% Vodafone 45%	Third largest cellular company. Plans to offer 3G service in 2002.

Table 10.3 Key Competitors in Japan *(continued)*

Entity	Owners	Details
Jupiter Telecommunications	Liberty Media Group—entertainment and cable conglomerate Sumitono Corporation	Largest cable TV provider.
KDDI	Kyocera Corporation 15.8% Toyota Motor Corporation 13% Rest public	Second largest carrier in Japan.
KVH	Fidelity Investments	Fiber optic metropolitan networks in Tokyo and Osaka; targets financial companies. Also offers Internet data services.
NTT (Nippon Telegraph and Telephone)	Japanese government 46%	Incumbent carrier. Owns Verio Corporation; 49% of Hong Kong ISP, HKNet; 49% of Daytel IP network in Australia plus others. Largest telephone company worldwide.
NTT DoCoMo (DoCoMo means anywhere in Japanese)	NTT has a controlling interest	Largest cellular provider in Japan with 21 million customers as of March 2001; owns 19% of Hutchison Telecommunications Ltd., 15% of Dutch cellular carrier KPN and 16% of AT&T Wireless. Third largest cellular carrier worldwide after Vodafone and China Mobile.
TTNet (Tokyo Telecommunication Network)	The Tokyo Electric Power Company, Inc.	Switched and private-line telecommunications services.
WorldCom	Public company	Building fiber networks; provides Internet services to businesses.

Cable & Wireless IDC was formed in 1999 when Cable & Wireless PLC purchased a majority stake in midsize international carrier International Digital Communications, Inc. (IDC) based in Tokyo. Cable & Wireless IDC is building out its fiber optic infrastructure in Osaka and Tokyo. Unlike the rest of Cable & Wireless PLC, which focuses exclusively on data services, Cable & Wireless IDC sells voice telephony as well as data services in Japan.

KDDI offers fixed-line, cellular and long distance services. It plans to add infrastructure for fixed wireless services. KDDI was formed in October 2000 as the result of DDI's purchase of KDD and IDO.

- **KDD**, originally Kokusai Denshin Denwa, was created in 1953 by the Japanese government to carry international traffic.

- **DDI** was Japan's second largest cellular carrier at the time of the merger. It was controlled by Kyocera Corporation, a semiconductor materials and ceramics company.

- **IDO**, a cellular and long distance company, was controlled by Toyota Motor Corporation.

Utilities

Utilities have entered telecommunications because their pre-existing rights of ways eliminate much of the expense and difficulty of digging up streets, obtaining rights of ways and building infrastructure. They also envision more growth potential in telecommunications than in utilities.

Tokyo Telecommunication Network (TTNet) started private-line service in 1986 and dialup service in 1998. It sells local, long distance and international services plus private-line data services. It often leases circuits to Internet service providers for ISPs' access to their customers' buildings. Another utility that has a subsidiary in telecommunications is **Osaka Media Port**. It is owned by the electric utility in Osaka.

Cable TV Service

Cable TV penetration is low with a total of 1 million subscribers divided up among its many (mostly small) operators. There are a small number of cable modem subscribers in Japan. The largest cable TV company is **Jupiter Telecommunications**, which in 2000 combined its 600,000-subscriber cable company with the second largest cable company, Titus Group, which is 80%-owned by Microsoft. At that time, Titus Group had 150,000 subscribers.

DSL

DSL trials started in Japan in December 1999. In August 2000, the Ministry of Posts and Telecommunications (MPT) certified two new carriers for DSL service to small and medium-sized businesses as well as consumers. These are **Tokyo Metallic** and **eAccess**, both of which are in the process of building out their networks in major cities. DSL is available from other carriers, including **NTT and Japan Telecom**. KDDI is testing the service in Tokyo and two other cities.

According to Pyramid Research, a market research company headquartered in Boston, Japan had only 5000 DSL customers by year-end 2000. A factor in slow deployment of DSL is NTT's desire to recoup its large investment in integrated services digital network (ISDN), which is slower than DSL but which NTT envisioned as migrating to Fiber to the Home (FITH). Fiber to the Home would provide higher speeds than DSL, which works on copper not fiber. Sales of DSL could potentially cause ISDN lines to be replaced by DSL before NTT recoups its investment in ISDN equipment.

To foster competition in local services, NTT was required to unbundle the local loop and central office connections in 1999. DSL runs over NTT's outside cabling and uses central office connections. NTT presents a serious stumbling block to competitive DSL providers by requiring that they meet unnecessarily complex requirements for interconnection and by generally not cooperating with competitors on DSL installations. In 2000, Japan's Fair Trade Commission (FTC) investigated whether NTT was blocking competition. The investigation concluded that NTT might be in violation of antitrust laws and that it take steps to promote competition.

Another impediment to DSL implementation is that DSL hardware from the United States does not match Japanese standards. Providers such as NEC and Fujitsu are adapting their DSL equipment to Japanese standards.

The Internet

According to the article, "Bandwidth Briefs," published in *DJ Bandwidth Intelligence Alert*, 12 March 2001, page 3, about one-third of the population has Internet access. The brief further cites an Associated Press article as its source that the Japanese government plans to spend $16.7 billion to connect every house to the Internet within five years. NTT is constructing fiber optic links directly to homes and businesses in Tokyo and Osaka. The Ministry of Posts and Telecommunications (MPT) has stated that by 2001, all public schools are to be connected to the Internet. Most landline users access the Internet via analog dialup or BRI ISDN (two 64,000-bps or one 128,000-bps digital dialup link) lines. However, half of the Internet users use their cellular phones for Internet access.

Most businesses in Japan have local area networked computers with connectivity to the Internet. Unlike the United States, Japanese employees do not use the Internet for personal use at work. It is considered a serious breach of work ethics. Therefore, night usage from homes is heavy. However, the high cost of PCs in Japan has hampered the growth of Internet access by consumers.

The rarity of high-speed cable modems and low penetration of DSL service dampens Web surfing from personal computers. Another impediment is the high cost of metered calling to access the Internet. The Japanese government's committee on information technology has set an objective to surpass the United States in broadband networking. Japan is currently behind Singapore and South Korea in broadband Internet access.

Cellular Service

In Japan, cellular phones outnumber fixed phone lines. According to the U.S. Department of Commerce *Country Commercial Guide for Japan*, on June 1, 2000 there were approximately 58.6 million cellular phones in service in Japan. Japan, for the most part, uses a proprietary TDMA cellular technology not used anywhere else called Pacific Digital Cellular (PDC). (For TDMA service, see Chapter 9.)

By February 2001, large numbers of Japanese customers accessed the Internet from cellular phones:

- 19.5 million subscribers used i-mode phones as of March 2001. The *i* in i-mode (top speed 9.6 thousand bits per second) stands for Internet, interactive and independence.
- 5 million subscribers used carrier J-phone's J-sky phone to access the Internet.

According to the article, "Wireless—Bright Future, Tough Challenges," published in *Business Communications Review*, February 2001, page 90, 60% of i-mode users download cartoon characters and songs to be used for ringing patterns. Part of the popularity of i-mode service is that it is "always on." There are no delays while users dial into the network for service. Less than 1% downloads information from services such as restaurant listings. It is unclear if availability of higher speed wireless Internet access will change these usage patterns. DoCoMo has stated its intention of expanding its i-mode technology, which works on cellular standards in Europe and the United States, throughout the world.

The way teens use cell phones is changing their life style. They no longer make plans for specific times—rather they email their locations to each other and make plans on the spot.

SHORT MESSAGING SERVICE—A WAY FOR YOUNG PEOPLE TO SOCIALIZE

Teenagers throughout the world are using their cellular phones to send each other short text messages. (See Chapter 9 for short messaging service.) Short messaging services (SMSs) are good news for carriers' revenue. In Europe, data services (the bulk of which are SMS), contributed 9% and, in Asia, 12.5%, of Vodafone's total revenue.

Japanese and European teenagers have adopted a technology and lingo that is changing the way they interact with each other. They no longer need to make plans in advance to get together. They spontaneously send each other messages and meet at the spur of the moment. Moreover, they do not have to be in a face-to-face social setting to stay in touch with multiple friends serially.

Despite phones capable of displaying only eight lines of text, Japanese youngsters with i-mode phones have found a way unique to their culture to express feelings in their messages. They use symbols called *kaomoji* for happiness, embarrassment, confusion, triumph and apology. Many of these symbols reflect the Japanese culture of transmitting feelings through eyes. The following are a sample of kaomoji notations. They can be stored as symbols so that they can be sent easily without typing each character:

- (*^o^*), (^0^) and (^-^)—Different kinds of happiness with the ^, a symbol for eyebrows
- (^o^)V— Triumphant happiness with V for victory
- m(__)m—Apology as a person with face down and both hands on the ground
- (T_T)—Sadness as in a crying face
- (@@)—Bewilderment or surprise
- (^^;)—Embarrassment with the semicolon as an indication of sweat

European teenagers use shorthand expressions such as: GAL (get a life), ATB (all the best), BTDT (been there, done that), F2T (free to talk?) and QL (cool).

Reasons for the popularity of wireless services and Internet access are:

- High-quality wireless coverage—the phones work almost everywhere.
- Wireless costs are equivalent to landline costs.
- NTT DoCoMo lowered its rates between 9% and 21% in December 1999.
- All Internet service charges from NTT-sanctioned sites are billed on one NTT DoCoMo bill so customers don't have to bother with many different bills. Fees are based on the number of packets downloaded. NTT receives a 9% fee from Internet service providers for its billing services.
- It costs less to send a text message from an i-mode phone than from a PC connected to a fixed telephone line. Users pay per packet, not for the time it takes to download a message, so users are not hesitant about piling up large bills due to slow-speed services.
- High penetration of wireless phones—for some teenagers, the wireless is their only phone.
- In big cities people get around by walking and by train more than by automobile. This makes cellular service more convenient and safer than using the service while driving.
- Lower penetration of personal computers in homes—people without PCs use their phones for messaging.

In an effort to promote high-speed cellular network build-outs, the Japanese government awarded 3G spectrum without charging the high fees associated with 3G auctions in much of the rest of the world. This will have an enormous impact on the speed at which Japanese corporations recoup their investments in third generation cellular networks capable of supporting broadband data services. DoCoMo has committed to third generation (3G), 384 thousand bits per second, wireless service by October 2001 with 2 million bit per second speeds in the future. The new service is called Freedom of Mobile multimedia Access (FOMA). It is envisioned that FOMA phones with color screens and Internet access will be used for downloading videos, digital photographs and entertainment. Businesses might use the high-speed service with portable or hand-held computers to download email, spreadsheet, word processing and graphics files.

Personal Handyphone System (PHS) is another digital wireless technology in Japan. PHS has a top speed of 64 thousand bits per second for Internet access and is offered by DoCoMo, KDDI and ASTEL Group. As of December 2000, 5.6 million customers used PHS service. PHS is digital but does not operate on cellular technology and can't be used for roaming. It emulates walkie-talkie service, where users within a few hundred feet from each other can converse without incurring usage fees.

EUROPE ....

The UK, France and Germany are the three largest countries in Europe. Between them, they control 60% of the telecommunications market. As indicated in Table 10.6 (later in this chapter) there are many carriers that provide broadband fiber networks and long distance services for consumers and businesses across Europe. Competition for these as well as cellular services is strong. The following statistics published on December 7, 2000 by the Commission of the European Communities in its "Sixth Report on the Implementation of the Telecommunications Regulatory Package" illustrates the impact of deregulation on prices and numbers of competitors:

- 461 operators sell long distance service over the public network.
- 62 operators in eight EU states are licensed to supply wireless local loop (WLL) service but because of the recent granting of licenses, most of these services are not yet operational. More licenses will be awarded in 2001.
- Prices of international calls decreased 15.1% for business users and 13.5% for residential users from 1999 to 2000.
- Prices of leased lines decreased by about 30% from 1999 to 2000.

Denmark and Sweden are making the most progress toward high-speed Internet access for consumers. Denmark already has a high penetration of home computers. According to the article, "Europeans Free Phone Market for Local and Internet Service," published in *The New York Times on the Web*, 6 December 2000, by Paul Meller, 30% of European Union households have Internet access. This is higher than most of Asia and Latin America. To promote lower cost high-speed Internet access, Tele Denmark (TDC) has pledged to bring asynchronous digital subscriber line service (ADSL) capability to 95% of consumers by July 2002. (See Chapter 6 for DSL service.) Sweden has made the same commitment. However, because of the longer distances between homes and telephone central offices, Sweden is making slower-than-expected progress toward meeting its goal.

The focus of change and growth in Europe has shifted away from landlines to mobile service and high-speed data networking.

The European Union

The European Union (EU) issues telecommunications regulations, reviews mergers and sets technical standards for its 15-member European nations. Unlike the U.S., where the Federal Communications Commission (FCC) enforces as well as issues regulations, in Europe enforcement of regulations is up to national regulatory agencies in member countries. This has led to uneven implementation of European Commission deregulation directives. The European Union (EU) deregulated long distance telecommunications in most of Europe in 1998. In November 1999, the EU requested local loop unbundling by January 1, 2001. On December 5, 2000 the European Parliament, the body consisting of voting members, approved the unbundling of the local loop, the portion of the network from an end user to the telephone company's equipment. However, implementation has stalled, primarily due to political clout and noncooperation by incumbents who don't want to lose further market share. Incumbent telephone companies still have the lion's share of local landline service.

LOCAL LOOP UNBUNDLING

According to Pyramid Research, a division of the Economist Group, publisher of the *Economist* magazine, by the end of the second quarter of 2000, incumbents controlled the following percentages of their respective local loops:

- UK 85%
- Germany 97%
- France 98%
- Spain 99%
- Italy 99%

The European Union's greatest impact has been in setting technical standards, reviewing mergers and creating rules on privacy. The EU's technical standards committee is the European Telecommunications Standards Institute (ETSI), which developed the GSM standard for digital cellular service. Other standards it has approved are those for connections between local exchanges and long distance carriers, ISDN and cable TV hybrid fiber coaxial (HFC). (See Chapter 2 for HFC and Chapter 6 for ISDN.)

In the area of merger review, it blocked the WorldCom merger with Sprint by requiring WorldCom to divest itself of UUNET, its Internet backbone subsidiary, as a condition of approval of the merger. WorldCom backed out of the merger rather than divest UUNET. Other mergers it investigated and then approved are the AOL Time Warner merger and the Telenor Media and Viag Interkom joint venture. The approval of AOL Time Warner came with conditions on digital distribution of music and specified that AOL end its joint venture with Bertelsmann. It rejected the Microsoft effort to gain joint control of cable TV company Telewest. As a result of the EU, Microsoft restructured its investment of Telewest so that it does not have joint control of it. The EU set conditions in the AOL and Microsoft cases aimed at eliminating potential control of digital distribution of music, Internet access and digital television by AOL Time Warner and Microsoft.

In October 1998, the European Union issued a directive prohibiting the transfer of personal data to non-EU countries that did not meet EU standards on privacy protection. Because the United States' privacy rules were more lenient than Europe's, this made it illegal for American companies to gather information from registration or purchases over the Internet or from retail operations without asking consumers' permission. These stricter privacy regulations made it difficult for American companies to have the same Internet site in both the United States and Europe. To make it easier for companies to operate in both continents, the Department of Commerce and the EU signed a treaty called Safe Harbor, effective November 2000. In the United States, enforcement is based on self-regulating where companies that agree to Safe Harbor rules get a TRUSTe stamp for their Web sites or businesses. In Europe, privacy is enforced by various agencies in EU-member countries. There is concern that TRUSTe self-regulation service will be inadequate.

Cellular Service

The biggest growth in telecommunications services in the 1990s has been in the cellular services market. Scandinavia was way ahead of everyone else and along with Italy has a large penetration of mobile service. In parts of Europe, cellular service is so prevalent that students commonly take their cell phones to school. Schools require students to hand in phones when they take in-class exams so that they don't use Internet-enabled phones to dial into the Internet for test answers. Penetration of cellular services has been helped by the following factors:

- In 1990, all of Europe settled on the same digital standard Global System for Mobile Communications, GSM. Prior to that, Europe had incompatible analog systems throughout the continent.

- With a common GSM, network travelers can take their phones with them wherever they travel throughout Europe.

- Populations are denser in Europe, which makes it easier for cellular carriers to provide uniform coverage. In contrast, large sections of countries such as the United States and Brazil have sparse population, making it more difficult to economically justify investments in cellular infrastructure for fewer potential customers.

- Subscribers do not pay for calls they receive and therefore give out their phone numbers more readily than if they had to pay for all calls they receive.

- Charges for cellular service are on a par with fixed-line telephone charges. In contrast to the United States, people in Europe do not have unlimited local service for a fixed monthly fee.

Cellular 3G Auctions

In contrast to Japan, which made 3G spectrum available at no cost, European countries held auctions for spectrum in which carriers paid over $100 billion to governments in 2000. (See Chapter 9 for 3G service.) Table 10.4 lists auction results in France, Germany and the UK. In addition to costs for spectrum, upgrades for 3G require investing in 3G infrastructure and subsidizing new 3G-compatible handsets. These additional costs are expected to reach $80 billion. Bidding for 3G spectrum slowed in 2001 because carriers were concerned that profits would be nonexistent after paying for 3G spectrum. In an effort to save money on infrastructure, the German regulatory agency, RegTP, approved the sharing of cellular infrastructure such as power supplies and antennas for 3G networks by the cellular arms of British Telecom and Deutsche Telekom.

Table 10.4 3G Spectrum Winners as of February 2001

France	Germany	UK
Only the two largest incumbents bid for four "beauty contest" licenses priced at $4.74 billion each	Auctions netted the most money from 3G auctions, $45.85 billion	Raised £22.5bn from its auctions held in April 2000
France Telecom	Mobilecom—28.5% owned by France Telecom	Orange—owned by France Telecom
SFR (a unit of Cegetel)—26% owned by British Telecom	T-Mobile—owned by Deutsche Telekom AG	Vodafone
	Mannesmann Mobilfunk—owned by Vodafone	British Telcom Cellnet—owned by British Telecom
	Viag Interkom—controlled by British Telecom	One 2 One
	Group 3G—a consortium that includes Telefonica and Sonera, the Finnish operator	Telesystem International Wireless (TIW)—a Canadian company
	E-Plus—backed by KPN of the Netherlands	

Table 10.5 Largest Cellular Providers by Country—Year 2000

France*	Germany*	UK*
Orange	Mannesmann Mobilfunk 40.6%	Vodafone
SFR	DeTeMobilNet GmbH 39.4%	Orange
Bouygues	E-Plus Mobilfunk GmbH 14.7%	BT Cellnet
	Viag Interkom GmbH 5.3%	One 2 One

Regent Associates, Cambridge, Massachusetts

Mid-Year Report 2000, Regulatory Authority for Telecommunications and Posts (RegTP) for percentages of market share in Germany

Table 10.5 lists the largest cellular carriers in France, Germany and the UK. As noted in the table, France has only three cellular providers. The following largest cellular carriers in Europe are all pan-European in coverage:

- Vodafone
- Telecom Italia Mobile
- Orange
- T-Mobile
- BT Cellnet

Germany

According to the U.S. Department of Commerce in its *Country Commercial Guide FY 2001* report, the German economy is the third largest in the world. It has the largest telecommunications market in Europe. Because of its large number of exports, Germany is more vulnerable than the rest of Europe to fallout from economic slowdowns in the United States, Asia and Latin America.

Germany's incumbent monopoly, Deutsche Telekom, was partially privatized on January 1, 1998. (The government retained 58%. Following Deutsche Telekom's 2001 purchase of VoiceStream Wireless, that share dropped to 45%.) Deutsche Telekom's infrastructure has the most advanced local access capability in Europe. Germany's telecommunications regulatory agency, Regulatory Authority for Telecommunications and Posts (RegTP), reports in its *Mid-Year Report 2000* that 37% of its local lines are ISDN equipped. In addition, Deutsche Telekom installed DSL on 300,000 lines and has equipped 60 towns and regions with DSL capability. This is the most in any one country in Europe.

CELLULAR RESALE—MOBILE VIRTUAL NETWORK OPERATORS (MVNOS)

Not all cellular companies own the networks over which they sell cellular service. Providers that sell cellular service over other company's cellular networks are called mobile virtual network operators (MVNOs). Virtual operators buy cellular airtime in bulk at discount rates. They mark up and resell airtime and mobile services to their own customers. MVNOs bill customers and provide customer service for repair and billing issues.

Virgin Mobile, for example, sells services on Deutsche Telekom owned, One 2 One's network in the UK. Virgin Mobile has signed up half a million customers with its aggressive marketing campaign. One of its popular services is music downloads to mobile phones using MP3 technology. It uses cross marketing with its 200 companies by offering its mobile customers discounts on services such as Virgin Atlantic Airways and Virgin MegaStores. It also has resale agreements in place with the Singapore state-owned carrier SingTel, and the second largest Australian mobile carrier, C&W Optus. Virgin Mobile is co-owned by Virgin Group and by Deutsche Telekom.

Increasing competition for cellular services is causing prices to fall in many developed nations. This puts a squeeze on virtual operators' profits because it decreases the revenue per minute sold. For example, if an operator charges only 15¢ per minute to retail customers, it might charge 12¢ to virtual operators, which then can only mark up services a few pennies. Achieving profits in resale requires strong marketing skills or specialized services such as those Virgin offers. With the expense and capacity associated with 3G networks, resale may be a way for network owners to recoup some of their investments in infrastructure. They may sell unused capacity to virtual operators for high-speed data such as mobile VPNs for business customers. (See Chapter 5 for VPN service.)

The emergence of resale in cellular services is reminiscent of the resale market for landline services in the United States, where AT&T and MCI sold capacity to resellers, and also to carriers such as Qwest, to fill in holes where they did not have their own fiber. With resale, network owners often compete with companies to whom they sell service for resale. AT&T and MCI Group both sell at wholesale to Qwest and compete with them.

Deutsche Telekom has been losing market share in long distance and data networking revenues since 1998 when its telecommunications services were opened to competition. In addition to losing market share, Deutsche Telekom's margins have decreased with the drop in pricing that occurred with increased competition. Prices for domestic long distance have dropped 89% since January 1998. Moreover, Deutsche Telekom has incurred large amounts of debt from purchases of 3G licenses. It is decreasing its debt by offering a minority of shares in its cellular provider subsidiary, T-Mobile, and its ISP subsidiary, T-Online, to the public. It also sold its six cable TV firms to Liberty Media to raise cash. Liberty Media is now the largest cable TV provider in Germany.

RegTP, in its *Mid-Year Report 2000*, dated June 2000, stated:

- Three hundred five companies are licensed to offer voice telephony.
- Fifteen companies are building fiber networks throughout the country and within metropolitan areas.
- Eighteen companies have won licenses for fixed wireless infrastructure. (See Chapter 4 for fixed wireless.)
- Competitors have a 20% share of total calling volume.
- Competitors handle 40% of the combined fixed to mobile, domestic and international calls.

While it's clear from these statistics that competition exists for long distance services, Deutsche Telekom, in spite of RegTP regulations requiring them to partially unbundle the local loop in 1999, still has a monopoly in local services. As in France and England, competitors feel that Deutsche Telekom has put roadblocks in the way of access to the local loop. It has a 97% market share of local lines. In an effort to promote competition, RegTP mandated local number portability for customers who wish to keep their telephone number when they change provider and lowered interconnection fees effective June 1, 2001 for competitive carriers that connect to Deutsche Telekom facilities.

RegTP estimated in its June 2000 *Mid-Year Report 2000* that 48 million people, close to 60% of the population, would own a mobile phone by December 2000. Deutsche Telekom's cellular operations are controlled by its T-Mobile International group. T-Mobile's subsidiary, DeTeMobilNet's cellular network, is a close second in market share to Mannesmann Mobilfunk (Vodafone). E-Plus and Viag Interkom are third and fourth, respectively.

Deutsche Telekom owns a majority stake in T-Online, the country's largest ISP, which it spun off as a separate subsidiary in 2000. T-Online, second in size to AOL Time Warner with 8 million subscribers, has yet to make a profit. T-Online also owns Club Internet, a French ISP and Ya.com, a Portuguese Internet service. E-commerce in

Germany has been hampered by the German population's distrust of the Internet for commercial transactions. Telephone charges for Internet access are declining. RegTP reports that costs dropped 35% between 1999 and 2000 and flat-rate plans are available.

Deutsche Telekom was the major cable TV provider until it sold off majority ownership of most of its properties to Liberty Media, which is folding them into UPC. It sold control of its other cable TV properties to various U.S. and German investors. These steps, which will cut Deutsche Telekom's debt, were initiated by the European Union's mandate that former telecom monopolies divest themselves of their cable TV properties. Ownership by UPC and others might result in more investment in cable TV infrastructure for broadband Internet access and voice telephony as cable TV providers look for ways to increase their revenue per subscriber.

The United Kingdom

The UK was the first European country to deregulate telecommunications. By the beginning of 2000, there were 200 telecommunications firms doing business in the UK. In addition to the main incumbent, British Telecom, network service providers include:

- Energis
- Cable & Wireless Communications
- COLT—IP data networking over fiber
- WorldCom

BT spent large sums of money to purchase 3G spectrum and upgrade its cellular infrastructure. By the beginning of 2001, it had $44 billion of debt and was losing market share in the cellular, ISP and high-speed data communications markets. Although it is building a 3G wireless network mainly in the UK and Germany, many experts feel the staid British company has not kept up with its more aggressive rivals. Its strategy in reducing debt is to sell off its Yell directory business, its wireless business in a public offering and stakes in international assets elsewhere. British Telecommunications is splitting off its BT Wireless unit into a separately traded company.

In addition to competition from cellular, data networking and long distance carriers, British Telecom is facing competition from the two largest cable TV companies, NTL and Telewest, both of which offer high-speed cable modem Internet access and telephone service to consumers.

The largest cellular companies in the UK are BT Cellnet, Vodafone, Orange and One 2 One. In an attempt to increase market share and promote cellular as a replacement of landline service, One 2 One, the smallest of the four cellular carriers, was the first provider to offer unlimited calling plans to landline and One 2 One mobile phones for a fixed monthly fee within the UK.

Regulatory Background

While competition exists for cellular, long distance and international calling services as well as broadband data networking, local calling and high-speed Internet access over imbedded copper cabling is still largely handled by British Telecom. Efforts are underway for British Telecom to provide competitors access to its copper outside cabling and central office connections.

In recognition of the growing importance of the Internet and convergence of entertainment and telecommunications, regulation of telecommunications will be handled by a new agency, Ofcom. Ofcom will monitor radio, television, Internet entertainment and advertising as well as telecommunications. Ofcom officials have stated universal Internet access by 2005 is a goal.

The following steps have been taken to promote competition:

- Full number portability on mobile and landline service

- Sharing by telephone companies of telephone poles and cabling ducts was mandated in 1997

- Customers can preselect particular carriers for their calls and also send their calls via a different carrier at any time by dialing prefixes assigned to their carrier of choice

- Mobile carriers have agreed to open their networks to carry independent service providers' prepaid packages

- To promote Internet access, British Telecom has until February 2003 to offer unlimited local calling to Internet Service Providers so that consumers can access the Internet without costly per-minute fees

- Oftel, the current telecommunications regulatory agency, monitors interconnection fees mobile and landline charge competitors to complete calls on each other's networks

Cellular Deregulation • Cellular licenses were made available to the incumbent, British Telecom and its competitors starting in the 1980s. Analog cellular service was first launched in 1985 by Cellnet (British Telecom) and Vodafone. In 1993, One 2 One introduced its digital GSM service as did Vodafone. Orange entered the market with its digital GSM service in 1994. In 1999, in an effort to promote further competition in mobile services, Oftel (Office of Telecommunications) required that cellular carriers allow others to market prepaid packages that use facilities-based carriers' infrastructure.

Landline Deregulation • British Telecom was wholly owned by the government until 1984 when the government sold 51% of it to the public. In the same year, The Telecommunications Bill was enacted, liberalizing telecommunications and creating a new regulatory agency, Oftel. In 1981, telephones sold by independent suppliers were allowed to be connected to the British network. In 1984, Mercury Communications Ltd., a subsidiary of Cable & Wireless, launched its service. Mercury and British Telecom had a duopoly until the mid-1990s.

In 1994, Sprint, Telstra (the Australian incumbent carrier) and WorldCom International received licenses for international resale. In the mid-1990s, the following companies also started offering service: ACC, WorldCom, COLT, MFS (now part of WorldCom), Energis, Telewest, Videotron and Verizon Communications.

Local Service Deregulation • The British regulatory agency Oftel decreed that BT must allow competitors to use BT's cabling and central office facilities to sell services such as DSL in 2001. (See Chapter 6 for DSL service.) In response to complaints by competitive local exchange providers that BT claims there is no space for collocation of DSL equipment, Oftel in November 2000 ordered British Telecom (BT) to allow competitors to visually inspect 700 of BT's central offices to see if there was room for competitors' DSL equipment.

This illustrates the difficulty faced by competitors in the United States and the rest of Europe to access incumbents' facilities. BT has offered to form separate companies for its retail and wholesale functions. The wholesale group, which would be regulated, would treat British Telecom and competitors such as Energis, COLT and Cable & Wireless equally in terms of pricing and access to network facilities. The retail arm would be unregulated and free to compete with rivals on an equal playing field. Oftel is considering this proposal.

France

France's national telephone company, Direction Generale des Telecommunications (DGT, now France Telecom), was nationalized in 1889. Much of the telecommunications infrastructure was damaged or destroyed in World War II. France's infrastructure lagged behind other countries until the 1990s. The incumbent carrier, France Telecom, is still majority owned (54%) by the government. The major innovation that France Telecom (then called DGT) implemented prior to the 1990s was its online Minitel system in 1980. Small terminals were given to consumers initially for white and yellow page directory assistance and later other information services were added. The terminals were free but people paid for the service.

VODAFONE—THE WORLD'S LARGEST CELLULAR COMPANY

Vodafone has grown from an analog cellular company in 1985 to the world's largest cellular carrier with over 78 million customers by early 2001. It has a global presence in countries such as India and Kenya where there is often little market penetration of wireline services. Chris Gent, the Chief Executive of Vodafone, has led Vodafone Group PLC since its 1991 demerger from Racal Telecomms PLC, when it was renamed Vodafone (voice and data). Mr. Gent joined Racal Telecomms PLC, originally part of defense contractor Racal Electronics PLC, in 1985 when it began offering analog cellular service in the UK in competition with the British Telecom subsidiary Cellnet.

In 1999, Vodafone purchased AirTouch, a PCS cellular carrier in the western part of the United States and in 2000 it acquired Mannesmann of Germany. At the time, Vodafone had minority stakes in mobile companies across Europe and in many other countries. Mannesmann, however, had controlling stakes in cellular companies in Italy, Germany and the UK (Orange PLC). The merger with Mannesmann is the largest telecom merger to date and was triggered by Mannesmann's incursion into Vodafone's UK territory when it purchased cellular provider Orange in 1999. In 1999, Vodafone also acquired a 45% interest in Verizon Wireless, the largest cellular provider in the United States.

As a condition for approval of the Mannesmann merger, the European Commission required that Vodafone sell Orange. France Telecom bought it. Another condition of the merger set by the European Commission is that for three years it required Vodafone to provide the same price structure for roaming to all carriers that it provides to its own subsidiaries.

In addition to its growth through acquisitions, Vodafone's strategy of innovative marketing and pricing strategies has resulted in its becoming the largest cellular carrier in the UK.

- In 1992 Vodafone and Telecom Finland signed the world's first international GSM roaming agreement.
- Also in 1992, Vodafone introduced discount calling tariffs for consumers.
- In 1993, it opened its first retail centers and announced retail distribution agreements with a UK retailer.

Vodafone—The World's Largest Cellular Company (continued)

- In 1996, it was the first carrier in the UK to launch prepaid cellular service. In that same year it introduced per-second billing on its digital network, bundled minute packages and off-peak calling to fixed-line phones.
- In January 2001 it started a single flat fee service across Europe.

In 2000, Vodafone launched Vizzavi, a multinetwork-access Internet portal in Europe. Vizzavi is a 50/50 joint venture with VivendiNet. It won costly third generation wireless licenses in Germany and the UK. It has postponed its plans to roll out general packet radio service (GPRS) in March 2001 in the UK due to a shortage of compatible handsets. GPRS is a form of faster data communications for GSM cellular service. It is believed that the cash from the sales of Mannesmann properties such as Orange, Infostrada and others will help the company weather the credit squeeze facing many telephone companies.

Vodafone has interests in wireless companies in 25 countries on five continents. (See Figure 10.1.) In contrast to the BellSouth International branding strategy in Latin America, Vodafone's name is not associated with all of its properties. Its global presence will allow it to avoid paying steep fees to other carriers common for roaming. Although it owns 45% of Verizon Wireless, to date there is no phone that works on both Verizon's CDMA network and the Vodafone GSM network. (See Chapter 9 for GSM and CDMA technology.) It has stated its intention to roll out a common brand in 2002.

In 1997, the French government started the process of privatizing France Telecom by selling 20% of it to the public. In response to pending competition it started bringing prices in line with competitors by lowering long distance and international calling fees. France has lagged behind the UK and Germany in deregulating telecommunications.

Use of Minitel terminals for information gathering has predisposed French consumers and business people to readily adapt to the Internet. Business-to-business and business-to-consumer e-commerce sales increased 270% from 1999 to 2000. However, the credit crunch of 2001 is hurting Internet startups. According to an IDC survey reported in the article "Two-Thirds of French Net Firm Are Unprofitable, Survey Shows," published in *WSJ.com The Wall Street Journal*, 2 February 2001, by Jeanette Brozo, difficulty in getting financing as well as being unprofitable is hurting prospects. More than half of those surveyed expect to turn a profit in 2001.

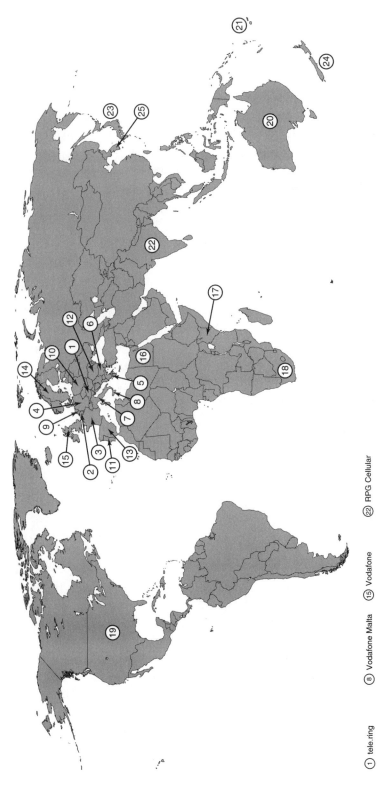

1. tele.ring
2. Proximus
3. SFR
4. D2
5. Panafon
6. Vodafone
7. Omnitel
8. Vodafone Malta
9. Libertel-Vodafone
10. Plus GSM
11. Telecel
12. Connex GSM
13. Airtel
14. Europolitan
15. Vodafone
16. Click GSM
17. Safaricom
18. Vodacom
19. Verizon Wireless
20. Vodafone
21. Vodafone
22. RPG Cellular
23. J-Phone
24. Vodafone New Zealand
25. Shinsegi

Figure 10.1
Vodafone worldwide presence.

By January 1999, 405 of the top 1500 companies had Web sites and by September 2000 over 20% of households had PCs. To spur residential Internet access, the French regulatory agency ART is considering approving flat-rated Internet access plans by France Telecom for ISPs. The goal is to lower the cost of dialup Internet access by eliminating per-minute fees.

While France Telecom still retains its hold on fixed-line local services, competitors have made headway in sales of long distance, international and data networking services. Its fixed-line revenues dropped in both 1999 and 2000 from the previous years. Competitors include 9Telecom, Cable & Wireless, Siris, COLT and WorldCom.

France Telecom owns Orange Europe and stakes in cellular companies in Belgium, Denmark, Italy, the Netherlands, Portugal and some East European countries. It has no holdings in Spain or Germany other than its minority ownership in MobilCom. It also has holdings in various electronics companies some of which it plans to sell to reduce debt incurred when it purchased 3G licenses. It also is selling its 9.9% share in American carrier Sprint for that reason.

The only three cellular providers are: France Telecom, through its subsidiary Orange, Cegetel and its SFR unit and Bouygues. No other cellular carrier has a major presence in France at this time.

Table 10.6 European Competitors

Entity	Ownership	Details
Arcor AG	Mannesmann AG, which is owned by Vodafone. Railway firm Deutsche Bahn and Deutsche Bank AG also own Arcor.	Competitive local telephone company in Germany.
Bouygues Telecom	Telecom Italia 55%	Third largest French mobile carrier.
BT Wireless	British Telecommunications PLC	Cellular provider in the UK. British Telecommunications is spinning off BT Wireless to shareholders in 2001.
Cable & Wireless PLC	Publicly traded company headquartered in the UK	Backbone Internet carrier and one of the world's largest data carriers with fiber linking Asia, North America and Europe. Sold many of its fixed-line telephone companies including Cable & Wireless HKT and Mercury in the UK. Still owns some incumbents including eight in the Caribbean.

Table 10.6 European Competitors *(continued)*

Entity	Ownership	Details
CANAL+	Vivendi Universal	Pay TV company in France with operations in 10 European countries.
Cegetel (SFR)	Vivendi Universal 59% British Telecom 26% SBC 15%	Its unit SFR, Societe Francaise du Radiotelephone, is the second largest cellular provider in France. Cegetel is the second largest fixed-line provider in France.
COLT	Fidelity Investments 51% Remaining publicly owned	Internet access and data networks via its fiber optic network in large cities throughout Europe. Fiber networks connect cities in which it has fiber.
Concert	AT&T 50% British Telecom 50%	Sells data and voice service to companies with global presence. Sells to carriers as well as end users. British Telecom has announced its intention to sell its stake in Concert.
Energis	The National Grid Group 36% (a utility)	A UK broadband provider with fiber backbone to 10 European countries. Web hosting through subsidiaries including Energis Squared and ISION; also owns ISP Freeserve.
Debitel AG	Swisscom AG, incumbent telco in Switzerland	Mobile services provider, billing solutions for IP calling and prepaid service; headquartered in Germany with offices in France, Belgium, Denmark Netherlands and Slovenia.
Deutsche Telekom AG	German government 45%	Largest telecom company in Europe. Its T-Mobile unit is the second largest cellular company worldwide. It owns French fixed line carrier SIRIS.
E-Plus	BellSouth Corporation 50% KPN Mobile 50%	Third largest mobile operator in Germany.

Table 10.6 European Competitors *(continued)*

Entity	Ownership	Details
Equant	France Telecom 54%	Dutch data networking company originally providing services to the airline industry. France Telecom combined it with its Global One unit in 2001. Has points of presence in 220 countries.
Flag Telecom	Verizon Communications 19% Dallah Al Barakah Group (Saudi Arabia) 16% plus shareholders	Undersea fiber optic cables between the U.S. and Europe and between Europe and Asia. Flag will help develop the terrestrial fiber network across Europe that Verizon is building.
Global Crossing	Publicly held, headquartered in Bermuda	Pan European broadband network provider. Its purchase of Racal Telecom gave it an extensive fiber network throughout the UK.
Interoute	Privately held; largest shareholder is Sandoz family	Building a fiber optic network across Europe. Also offers Web hosting, wholesale and retail voice and collocation services. Headquartered in London.
Kingston Communications	Kingston upon Hull City Council 44% Remaining shares publicly owned	Incumbent Kingston upon Hull carrier in the UK. Subsidiary Torch Telecom sells data networking services in the UK. Broadband network in UK.
KPN Mobile N.V.	Royal KPN 85% NTT DoCoMo 15%	Cellular provider in Germany, Belgium and the Netherlands. Developing 3G services with DoCoMo and Hutchison Whampoa throughout Europe.
KPNQwest	Royal KPN N.V. Qwest Communications	Fiber network throughout Europe. Its owner, Royal KPN, is the incumbent Dutch telco.

Table 10.6 European Competitors *(continued)*

Entity	Ownership	Details
Level 3 Communications, Inc.	Publicly traded company headquartered in the U.S.	IP fiber networks to carriers in U.S., Asia and Europe. Also collocation services to carriers, ISPs and large corporate customers. Owns 33% of RCN.
Mannesmann Mobilfunk	Vodafone Group PLC	Largest cellular provider in Germany, Mannesmann AG (part of Vodafone) owns second largest cellular company in Italy, Omnitel.
Mannesmann Arco	Vodafone Group PLC	Second largest fixed-line voice and data provider in Germany. Has a fiber backbone across Germany.
MobilCom	France Telecom 28.5%	Fifth largest cellular provider in Germany; also sells Internet and fixed-line services.
9Telecom	Telecom Italia	French ISP and voice telephony provider. Plans to offer Internet access via ADSL and television to its subscribers.
NTL Inc.	France Telecom 25% Publicly traded company	Largest cable TV provider in Britain; offers Internet access and phone service over its cable facilities. Also sells cable TV service in Ireland, France, Germany, Sweden and Switzerland. Headquartered in New York City.
One 2 One	Deutsche Telekom AG	UK's smallest cellular operator. Started as a joint venture of Cable & Wireless and U S West.
Orange	France Telecom	Largest cellular provider in France. Combination of France Telecom mobile subscribers and Orange. Second largest wireless company in Europe. Second largest cellular carrier in the UK

Table 10.6 European Competitors *(continued)*

Entity	Ownership	Details
QS Communications AG (QSC)	Publicly traded company	Largest provider of DSL infrastructure and Internet services in Germany with equipment in 850 exchanges that reach 25% of the population. Has agreements to furnish DSL infrastructure with Cable & Wireless and WorldCom.
Telecom Italia Mobile	Publicly traded company	Largest cellular company in Italy. Spun off from Telecom Italia in 1995. Has cellular holdings in Asia, Europe, the Middle East and South America.
T-Mobile	T-Mobile International, which is owned by Deutsche Telekom	Largest cellular company in Germany. T-Mobile International controls parent company Deutsche Telekom's mobile assets.
Teleglobe Inc.	BCE Canadian incumbent telephone company	International broadband provider in 110 countries. Operates undersea cables as well as fiber networks. New initiative called GlobeSystem, an IP network with Internet services.
Telewest Communications PLC	Microsoft 24% Liberty Media 25% to be sold to United Pan-Europe Communications (UPC)	Britain's second largest cable company; operations in Scotland also. Sells Internet access, data services to business as well as cable TV service.
United Pan-Europe Communications N.V. (UPC)	UnitedGlobalCom 61%—a cable TV giant in 23 countries. 45% of UnitedGlobalCom is owned by Liberty Media, which is the largest cable TV operator in Germany.	Largest private cable TV operator in Europe (in 18 countries). Provides cable modem and voice telephony over its facilities. Buying fixed wireless licenses in Europe. Its broadcasting unit is UPC Media and its programming unit is UPCtv. Bought German cable company Primacom AG, creating third largest cable company in Germany.
Viag Interkom	British Telecom 90%	German mobile carrier. Purchased by BT from utility E.on and Norwegian telco Sonera pending approval of the EU.

Table 10.6 European Competitors *(continued)*

Entity	Ownership	Details
Vizzavi Internet Portal	Vivendi Universal Vodafone Group PLC	Internet portal throughout Europe. Vivendi, headquartered in France, is an entertainment conglomerate that also owns Universal Studios.
Vodafone	Publicly traded company headquartered in London	Largest cellular provider in the world.
WorldCom	Publicly traded company	Fiber optic network throughout Europe. Sells voice and data to multinational corporations and carriers. Offers service in 65 countries worldwide.

AFRICA AND THE MIDDLE EAST— EMERGING MARKETS...

There is an evolution toward liberalizing telecommunications regulations in emerging markets. This evolution is driven by the desire to attract private money. The government is the main driver of the economies in Africa and Middle East. It owns the incumbent telephone companies that have monopolies in their respective countries. African businesses that apply to the World Bank or the International Monetary Fund (IMF) for funds are required to meet conditions liberalizing and privatizing enterprises. Another factor in most of the countries is their desire to be part of the World Trade Organization, WTO to gain trading partners. Countries that join the WTO have to meet treaty liberalization clauses to open markets. They can then buy and sell goods with member countries.

A technological pressure eroding monopolies is the presence of cyber cafés and ISPs selling low-cost voice over IP illegally in Africa and the Middle East. This technology plus call-back is undercutting profits governments receive from fees for international and domestic long distance.

In both Africa and the Middle East, the key technology for new services is wireless—mainly in the form of cellular services. The appeal of cellular in building up poor countries' infrastructure is its relatively low cost compared to fixed-line service. In the article, "Cell Phone Surge Among World's Poor," published in *The New York Times on the Web*, 19 December 2000, by Simon Romero, Ken Lupberger, Manager of Communications Investments at the International Finance Corporation, the investment banking arm of the World Bank, cited the cost of adding a new line as less than

$600. It cost $1500 five years ago. Another benefit with cellular is that there generally are no regulations prohibiting competition in the cellular arena.

Most countries are adopting cellular services relatively quickly. In many African countries there are more cellular than fixed lines in service. As is the case in Europe, there are no fees for incoming calls to inhibit user acceptance. According to Guy Zibi, Manager, Africa and the Middle East for Pyramid Research, at least 80% of the cellular service in Africa and the Middle East is prepaid. All of these cellular networks are based on GSM or TDMA except Israel's, which uses CDMA. (See Chapter 9 for wireless technologies.)

Africa

Poverty and lack of infrastructure are enormous hurdles to telecommunications growth in Africa. The Internet is still in its nascent stages. PC penetration is improving, driven by the desire for Internet access. However, the initial base is so low from almost 0%, 50,000 to 100,000 PCs for populations of 25 to 30 million people. Personal computers are too expensive for consumers but business usage is growing. Governments are taking measures to increase PC purchases. Currently, 25% to 50% of their cost is made up of customs charges.

Fixed wireless also is starting to be introduced mainly for business rather than for residential customers. It is being deployed for Internet access more than cable and DSL. However, there are problems to solve with fixed wireless. Although it is less costly than laying cabling, installation of fixed wireless is still expensive. For example, the monthly price in Nigeria for fixed wireless is $1000. Even getting local electricity for the service can be problematic. Moreover, there is a lack of local expertise to install and manage the service. It is not unusual for the spectrum to be mismanaged and for operators to be given duplicate spectrum already in use by another carrier.

An exception to the lack of infrastructure and a middle class is South Africa. It's on par to some extent with Brazil, Argentina and Chile and has an emerging black middle class. There are some imbalances within the white population, but it is well off by western standards. South Africa has a larger base of businesses than the rest of Africa. Other countries with more advanced infrastructures than the rest of Africa are Botswana, Namibia and Morocco. Ghana, Nigeria and Uganda are the furthest ahead in deregulation of telecommunications. Of these countries with more advanced infrastructure, only Nigeria has deregulated its local service. Nigeria is the largest country in Africa and is considered to have the most potential growth in telecommunications.

The Middle East

Like Africa, Middle Eastern telecommunications markets are not open to competition and states still own the PTTs. However, the state telephone companies are wealthier

than those in Africa. Thus, they have developed their network infrastructures but customers have limited options and high costs for specialized services. The most highly developed infrastructures are in the Gulf region countries of the United Arab Emirates, Qatar and Oman. Leased lines for voice and data communications are extremely costly. However, telephone lines to homes and business are not costly. Costs for ISPs to connect to international backbones via PTTs are high and ISPs pass these costs to subscribers. This results in $30 to $40 monthly charges for dialup Internet accounts.

The number of cellular users is growing faster than in Europe, Latin America and Asia because penetration rates are lower. According to Guy Zibi, in the Middle East, 5% to 10% of the population has cellular service compared to below 2% in Africa. Middle Eastern governments started to allow competition in cellular services in 2000.

According to Pyramid Research, LAN and PC penetration in the Middle East are low by western standards. Saudi Arabia, as of late 2000, had 1.2 million PCs, penetration less than 6%. In Kuwait and the UAR PC penetration was closer to 10% in the same period.

CONCLUSION ....

In most of the twentieth century, governments subsidized telecommunications monopolies and guaranteed their rate of return on investments in exchange for monopolies building and maintaining national networks. At that time, network construction was so capital and labor intensive that it was felt that only large monopolies had the necessary resources to build secure networks. However, as new technologies such as microwave, fiber optics and computer-controlled switches were developed, private companies became capable of supporting backbone networks to reliably carry enormous amounts of traffic. Carriers today are building wireline and wireless networks and adding innovative new Internet, data and messaging services.

However, no single competitive carrier has emerged with the financial strength to provide high-speed service to all of the subscribers in metropolitan, suburban and rural areas. As has happened in the United States and recently in parts of Europe, fiber connects large financial institutions, hospitals, high-rise apartments and multistory office buildings in developed nations and in parts of Latin America to high speed services. These sites have numerous options for data, Internet access and low-priced voice service. Consumers and small and medium-sized businesses in rural and suburban areas do not.

Cable TV so far offers the most promising means of reaching the largest number of consumers in Europe and Latin America. Fixed wireless might emerge as a better option in emerging markets and possibly rural areas. NTL and United Pan-Europe Communications (UPC), the largest cable TV companies in Europe, are burdened with heavy debt. NTL reported a $3.1 billion loss in 2000. At any rate, it requires enormous investments to install either type of infrastructure and, in the case of cable

TV, to upgrade it for cable modem service. Even in places where cable TV is available, it is for the most part sold only to residential customers so small and medium-sized businesses are left out of the loop.

A major problem for telecommunications providers is the large capital investment required to build new networks. Private companies and shareholders do not have the patience to wait years for returns on their investments. The recent economic downturn combined with massive debt levels are an enormous problem. Another problem is the vast amount of investment lost when large numbers of telecommunications and Internet companies went out of business.

It is clear that new models need to be explored so that telecommunications companies retain their innovative edge but basic telecommunications as well as affordable high-speed Internet access are made available to consumers and small businesses as well as large enterprises. Some interesting proposals and undertakings are already being looked at. In the UK, British Telecom has suggested that it be broken up into two entities: one that supplies local loop infrastructure to carriers at wholesale prices and one that sells service to end users. This has the possibility of improving cooperation between new carriers such as DSL providers and the British Telecom wholesale company. They will no longer have an incentive to delay service to providers they view as competitors. Another interesting approach is the Japanese government's pledge to invest in high-speed Internet infrastructure for consumers. The Japanese government also is subsidizing the deployment of 3G service by not charging for new spectrum capable of supporting 3G devices.

Others in the industry are looking at cooperation between carriers in building out 3G networks and upgrading cable TV. NTL is in talks with United Pan-Europe Communications about sharing resources to upgrade its facilities. Cellular providers in Europe are in negotiations to share costs of building parts of their third generation networks. Some of the challenges facing the world telecommunications markets are:

- Building high-speed infrastructure to serve consumers where revenues might not be high enough for carriers to earn back their investments in the short term

- Making high-speed infrastructure in cities and local rural areas available to many carriers for innovative service without building duplicate, wasteful local facilities

- Finding the resources to build 3G networks

- Providing adequate capacity for voice on fast growing cellular networks

- Finding the means to supply affordable, basic service to consumers (many of whom have no phone service) and commercial entities in emerging markets

Solutions to these problems are critical to the deployment of next-generation Internet and wireless services.

Glossary

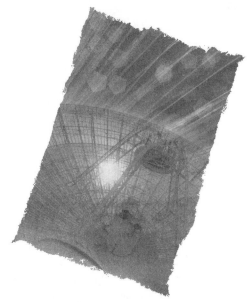

5ESS

A digital central office manufactured by Lucent Technologies, formerly part of AT&T.

10base-T

An IEEE specification for unshielded twisted pair cabling for Ethernet local area networks which transmit at 10 million bits per second. The distance limitation on 10 base-T networks is 100 meters.

100base-T

An IEEE standard, compatible with 10base-T for transmitting at 100 megabits over twisted pair cabling on local area networks.

ANI (automatic number identification)

The business or residential customer's billing number. Customers such as call centers pay for callers' ANI to be sent to them simultaneously with incoming 800 and 888 calls.

Applet

A small Java program that can be executed on any Java capable browser regardless of PC model. Animation in Internet ads use applets. Document sharing programs work by sending Java applets to the participants in the document sharing session.

ATM (Asynchronous Transfer Mode)

A high-speed switching technique that uses fixed size cells to transmit voice, data and video. A cell is analogous to envelopes that each carry the same number of bits.

Backbone

A segment of a network used to connect smaller segments of networks together. Backbones carry high concentrations of traffic between on and off ramps of networks.

Bandwidth

The measure of the capacity of a communications channel. Analog telephone lines measure capacity in hertz, the difference in the highest and lowest frequency of the channel. Digital channels measure bandwidth in bits per second.

Bit error rate

The percentage of bits received in error in a transmission.

BOC (Bell Operating Company)

One of the 22 local Bell telephone companies owned by AT&T before 1984. Examples of Bell operating companies are Michigan Bell, Illinois Bell and Pac Bell.

Bps (bits per second)
The number of bits sent in a second.

BRI (Basic Rate Interface)
The ISDN (integrated services digital network) interface made up of two B channels at 64 kilobits each and a signaling channel with a speed of 16 kilobits.

Bridge
A device that connects local or remote networks together. Bridges are used to connect small numbers of networks. Bridges do not have routing intelligence. Organizations that wish to connect more than four or five networks use routers.

Broadband
A data transmission scheme where multiple transmissions share a communications path. Cable television uses broadband transmission techniques.

Broadcast
A message from one person or device forwarded to multiple destinations. Voice messaging and e-mail services have broadcast features whereby a user can send the same message to multiple recipients.

CAP (competitive access provider)
Originally provided large- and medium-sized organizations with connections to long distance providers that bypassed local telephone companies. CAPs are now often referred to as competitive local exchange carriers (CLECs). They sell local and long distance telephone and Internet service.

CCIS (common channel interoffice signaling)
A signaling technique used in public networks. Signals such as those for dial tone

and ringing are carried on a separate path from the actual telephone call. CCIS allows for telephone company database query used in features such as Caller ID, call forwarding and network-based voice mail. CCIS channels are also used for billing and diagnosing public network services.

CDMA (code division multiple access)
CDMA is one way that carriers transmit digital cellular signals between handheld devices and cellular carriers' networks. CDMA assigns a unique code to every voice and data transmission using a channel of a particular carrier's airwaves. CDMA is a spread spectrum technology.

Central Office
The site with the local telephone company's equipment that routes calls to and from customers. It also connects customers to Internet Service Providers and long distance services.

Centrex (central exchange)
Centrex, like private branch exchanges, routes and switches calls for commercial and non-profit organizations. However, local telephone companies manage Centrex service. The computerized Centrex equipment is most often located at a telephone company's central office rather than at a customer premise.

Channels
A path for analog or digital transmission signals. With services such as ISDN, T-1 and T-3, multiple channels share the same one or two pairs of wires or fiber.

CIC code (carrier identification code)
The four-digit code (previously three digits) assigned to each carrier for billing and call routing purposes. AT&T's CIC code is 0288. If someone at a pay telephone dials

1010288 and then the telephone number they are calling, their call is routed over the AT&T network.

CIR (committed information rate)

A term used in frame relay networks to indicate the speed of the transmission guaranteed between each customer's site and the frame relay network.

Circuit switching

The establishment, by dialing, of a temporary physical circuit (path) between points. The path (circuit) is terminated when either end of the connection sends a disconnect signal by hanging up.

CLEC (competitive local exchange carrier)

A competitor to local telephone companies that has been granted permission by the state regulatory commission to offer local telephone service. CLECs compete with the incumbent telephone company. CLECs are also simply called local telephone companies.

CO (central office)

The location that houses the telephone company switch that routes telephone calls. End offices are central offices that connect end-users to the public network.

Compression

Reducing the size of the data, image, voice or video file sent over a telephone line. This decreases the capacity of the telecommunications line needed to transmit the file.

Concatenation

The linking of channels in optical networks together so that voice or video is transmitted as one stream. This is done to ensure that there are no breaks in the transmission.

Connectionless Service

The Internet protocol is connectionless. Each packet travels through the network separately. If there is congestion, packets are dropped. Packets are re-assembled at their destination.

CPE (customer premise equipment)

Telephone systems, modems and terminals installed at customer sites.

CSU/DSU (channel service unit/data service unit)

A digital interface device that connects customer computers, video equipment, multiplexers and terminals to digital telephone lines.

Dark fiber

Fiber optic cables without any of the electronics, that is, multiplexers and amplifiers. Carriers can quickly lay dark fiber and add SONET, Gigabit Ethernet and wavelength division multiplexers later.

DCE (data circuit-terminating equipment)

A communications device that connects user equipment to telephone lines. Examples are modems for analog lines and CSUs (channel service units) for digital lines.

Dedicated line

A telephone line between two or more sites of a private network. Dedicated lines are always available for the exclusive use of the private network at a fixed monthly fee.

Dense wavelength-division multiplexing (DWDM)

A way of increasing the capacity of fiber optic networks. DWDM carries multiple colors of light, or multiple wavelengths on a single strand of fiber. Also known as WDM or wavelength-division multiplexing. Some people use the term dense wave division multiplexing.

DID (direct inward dialing)

A feature of local telephone service whereby each person in an organization has his or her own ten-digit telephone number. Calls to DID telephone numbers do not have to be answered by on-site operators. They go directly to the person assigned to the ten-digit DID telephone number.

DMS 100

A digital central office switch manufactured by Nortel, formerly Northern Telecom.

DNIS (dialed number identification)

The service used to identify and route toll free and 900 numbers to particular agents or devices within a customer site. For example, if a customer has multiple 800 numbers, the network provider routes each toll free number to a different four digit extension number at the customer's telephone system. The onsite PBX, key system or Centrex system then routes the call to a particular group of agents, voice response system or department.

Domain name

Everything after the @ sign in an e-mail address. It includes the host computer, the organization's name and the type of organization (e.g., com for commercial and edu for educational site). Dot com and .edu are top-level domain names. The domain name can also designate the country such as .bo for Bolivia. A domain name is part of the TCP/IP addressing convention.

DS-0 (digital signal level 0)

The digital signal level 0 is 64 thousand bits per second. It refers to one channel of a T-1, E-1, E-3, T-3, fractional T-1 or fractional T-3 circuit.

DS-1 (digital signal level 1)

The T-1 transmission rate of 1.54 million bits per second. There are 24 channels associated with DS-1 or T-1.

DS-3 (digital signal level 3)

The T-3 transmission rate of 44 million bits per second with 672 channels. (T-3 is equivalent to 28 T-1s.)

DTE (data terminal equipment)

Devices that communicate over telephone lines. Examples are multiplexers, PBXs, key systems and personal computers.

E-1

The European standard for T-1. E-1 has a speed of 2.048 megabits with 30 channels for voice, data or video, plus one channel for signaling and one for diagnostics.

E-3

The European standard for T-3. E-3 has a speed of 34.368 megabits, with 480 channels. It is equivalent to 16 E-1 circuits.

Ethernet

A local area network protocol defined by the IEEE. It defines how data is transmitted on and retrieved from local area computer networks.

FDDI (fiber distributed data interface)

An ANSI-defined protocol whereby computers communicate at 100 million bits per second over fiber-optic cabling. FDDI may be used on backbones that connect local area network segments together. It is not widely used.

Fiber-optic cable

A type of cable made from glass rather than copper. The key advantage of fiber-optic cabling is that it is non-electric. Thus it is immune from electrical interference and interference from other cables within the same conduit. Fiber optic cabling can be used for higher-speed transmissions than twisted pair copper cabling.

Firewall
A firewall is software and hardware that prevents unauthorized access to an organization's network files. The intention is to protect files from computer viruses and electronic snooping.

Fractional T-1
Fractional T-1 lines are cheaper and have a fraction of the 24 channel capacity of T-1 lines. The most common capacities are 2 channels = 128 kilobits, 4 channels = 256 kilobits and 6 channels = 384 kilobits.

Fractional T-3
Fractional T-3 lines have a fraction of the 672 channel capacity of T-3 lines. For example, they might have the capacity of six T-1s or 144 channels. Fractional T-3s are cheaper than a full T-3 line.

Frame relay networks
Public data networks commonly used for local area network to local area network communications. Customers connect to frame relay services over telephone lines from each of their locations to the frame relay network. Frame relay services require less maintenance, hardware and upkeep than traditional private line data communications services for customers with more than about four locations.

FTP (file transfer protocol)
A part of the TCP/IP suite of Internet protocols. It is software that lets users download files from a remote computer to their computer's hard drive.

Gateway
A gateway device allows equipment with different protocols to communicate with each other. For example, gateways are used when incompatible video systems hold a videoconference.

Gigabits
Billions of bits per second. Fiber optic cables carry signals at Gigabit or billions of bits per second. Gbps is short for Gigabits per second.

GPRS (General Packet Radio Services)
A cellular data packet network service. Upgrades to digital cellular networks are required to provision the service. This is an "always on" data service that users do not have to dial into to access.

H.320
The standard for enabling videoconference equipment from multiple vendors to communicate with each other using ISDN service.

H.323
An ITU-based standard for sending voice via the IP, Internet Protocol. H.323 was originally developed for videoconferencing.

H.324
An ITU (International Telecommunications Union) standard for sending video, voice and data between devices over a single analog, dial-up telephone line using a 28,800 bit per second modem. Compression is used on the voice, video and data.

Home page
A home page is the default first page of a World Wide Web site that users see when they visit an organization's Web site. A home page is analogous to the first page and table of contents of a book.

Hub

Each device such as computers and printers on a local area network is wired to the hub, generally located in the wiring closet. Hubs enable local area networks to use twisted pair cabling rather than more expensive, harder to install and move coaxial cabling. Hubs are sometimes referred to as concentrators.

ILEC (incumbent local exchange carrier)

ILECs refer to the Bell and independent telephone companies that sell local telephone service. This term differentiates telephone companies that were the providers of telephone service prior to the Telecommunications Act of 1996 and new competitors such as Allegiance, WorldCom and AT&T. The Telecommunications Act of 1996 decreed that local Bell telephone companies may sell interstate telephone service when they meet FCC guidelines for connecting competitors to their networks.

Independent telephone company

An incumbent local telephone company other than a Regional Bell Operating Company. Examples of independent telephone companies are Alltel Corporation and Cincinnati Bell, Inc.

Internet

The Internet, with a capital I, is composed of multiple worldwide networks tied together by a common protocol, TCP/IP.

Intranet

An intranet is the use of World Wide Web technologies for internal operations. Intranets are used by organizations as a way to make corporate information readily accessible by employees. An example is a corporate telephone directory accessed by a browser.

Inverse Multiplexer

Instead of combining individual channels into one "fat" pipe, which is what a multiplexer does, an inverse multiplexer separates out channels into smaller "chunks." Inverse multiplexers are used for video conferencing where the 24 channels may be transmitted in groups of 6 channels at a speed of 386 thousand bits per second.

IP (Internet Protocol)

The part of TCP/IP that performs the addressing functions for networks. Each device on an Internet network is assigned a 32-bit IP address. The Internet is running out of addresses, and standards bodies are reviewing ways to upgrade the address schemes so that more addresses will be available.

ISDN (integrated services digital network)

ISDN is a digital network standard that lets users send voice, data and video over one telephone line from a common network interface.

ISP (Internet service provider)

An Internet service provider connects end-users to the Internet via telephone lines. The ISP has banks of modems and devices such as ISDN interfaces for its own customers to dial into which are connected to telephone company central offices. The ISP rents telephone lines to the Internet from its own location. Some Internet service providers such as UUNET also own Internet backbone networks. ISPs supply services such as voice mail, hosting and domain name registration.

IXC (interexchange carrier)

Interexchange carriers are the long distance companies that sell toll free 800, international, data networking and outgoing telephone service on an interstate basis. They now also sell local telecommunications services.

Java

A programming language created by Sun Microsystems. Multiple types of computers can read Java programs. They increase the power of the Internet because programs written in Java can be downloaded temporarily by client computers. They do not take up permanent space on the client hard disc. Interactive games can use Java programs.

Key system

Key systems are on-site telephone systems geared to organizations with under 100 telephones. Like PBXs, they switch calls to and from the public network and within users' premises.

LAN (local area network)

A local area network is located on an individual organization's premise. It enables computer devices such as personal computers, printers, alarm systems and scanners to communicate with each other. Moreover, LANs allow multiple devices to share and have access to expensive peripherals such as printers, fax servers, modem servers and centralized databases.

LATA (local access transport area)

At divestiture in 1984, LATAs were set up as the areas in which Bell telephone companies were allowed to sell local telephone services. LATAs cover metropolitan statistical areas based on population sizes. For example, Massachusetts has two LATAs and Wisconsin has four LATAs, but Wyoming, which has a small population, has one LATA. The rules of divestiture decreed that long distance telephone companies such as AT&T, Sprint and WorldCom were allowed

to carry calls between LATAs but that Bell telephone companies such as Illinois Bell could carry calls only within a LATA.

Layer 4

Layer 4 devices can route and prioritize packets based on the source of the packet, the destination port number, the protocol type and the application. For example, layer 4 devices can prioritize voice and video so that networks using the Internet Protocol for voice and data can handle voice without the delays and lost packets associated with lower level protocols.

LDAP (lightweight directory access protocol)

A standard for storing information in a common format. Examples of LDAP directories are the address books in Netscape Communicator 4 and Microsoft Outlook Express browsers. LDAP enables companies to use one central directory to update multiple corporate directories.

Leased line

A leased line is analogous to two tin cans and a string between two or more sites. Organizations that rent leased lines pay a fixed monthly fee for the leased lines that are available exclusively to the organization that leases them. Leased lines can be used to transmit voice, data or video. They are also called private or dedicated lines.

LEC (local exchange carrier)

Any company authorized by the state public utility commission to sell local telephone service.

LMDS (local multipoint distribution service)

A high-speed fixed wireless service used to provision local telephone service without laying fiber to individual customer sites. Some competitive local exchange carriers employ LMDS as a way to provision local telephone, high-speed Internet access and video service.

Local loop

The local loop is the telephone line that runs from the local telephone company to the end user's premise. The local loop can be made up of fiber, copper or wireless media.

MAN (metropolitan area network)

A metropolitan area network is a network that covers a metropolitan area such as a portion of a city. Hospitals, universities, municipalities and large corporations often have telephone lines running between sites within a city or suburban area.

Mbps (million bits per second)

A transmission speed at the rate of millions of bits in one second. Digital telephone lines measure their capacity or bandwidth in bits per second.

Millimeter wireless services

Millimeter wireless services operate at microwave and above very fast frequencies. They include LMDS (local multipoint distribution service) and MMDS (multipoint multichannel distribution service). Millimeter refers to the very short wavelengths of high-frequency services. The wavelength is the distance from the highest or lowest point of one wave to the highest or lowest point of the next wave.

MMDS (multipoint multichannel distribution service)

MMDS is a fixed wireless technology for high-speed data, video and voice. It is a way to provide high-speed Internet access without laying fiber or cable to each customer. It was originally conceived of as a way to supply cable TV services. WorldCom is investing in companies that supply MMDS gear. MMDS uses a lower frequency than LMDS and has less capacity than LMDS. MMDS has a larger range than LMDS; the dishes can be up to 35 miles apart.

Multiplexing (mux)

Multiplexing is a technique whereby multiple devices can share a telephone line. With multiplexing, users do not have to lease individual telephones for each computer that communicates. T-1 multiplexers enable many devices to share one telephone line.

NEBS (Network Equipment Building Standards)

Requirements published in a Bellcore (now Telcordia) technical reference for products placed in a central office environment. Bellcore is the former Bell Telephone central research organization. There are eight standards referring to issues such as environmental, electrical and cabling requirements as well as resistance to natural disasters such as earthquakes.

Network

A network is an arrangement of devices that can communicate with each other. An example of a network is the public switched telephone network over which residential and commercial telephones and modems communicate with each other.

NT1 (network termination type 1)

The NT1 device sits between an ISDN line and an ISDN terminal adapter. The NT1 plugs into the ISDN jack. It provides a point where the network provider can test the ISDN line. The NT1 also converts the ISDN line from the telephone company's two-wire to four-wire cabling. The four wires are the portions of the cabling inside the customer's premise.

Number pooling

Allows local carriers to share a "pool" of telephone numbers within the same exchange. Number pooling is a way to allocate scarce telephone numbers more efficiently. Without pooling, a single local telephone company has rights to the entire 10,000 block of telephone numbers but they may only use a portion of the block.

Packet switching

A network technique that routes data in units called packets. Each packet contains addressing and error checking bits as well as transmitted user data. Packets from a transmission can be routed individually through a network such as an X.25 or frame relay network and be assembled at the end destination.

PBX (private branch exchange)

PBXs are computerized on-site telephone systems located at commercial and non-profit organizations' premises. They route calls both within an organization and from the outside world to people within the organization.

PCMCIA (portable computer memory card industry association)

An industry group that has developed a standard for peripheral cards for portable computers. PCMCIA cards are used for functions such as modems and for additional memory.

Photonics

All of the elements of optical communications. This includes fiber, lasers and optical switches and all elements involved in transmitting light over fiber.

Ping (packet internetwork groper)

A software protocol used to test communications between devices. "To Ping" means to send a packet to another device or host to see if the device sends back a response. The Ping also tests round-trip delay, the time it takes to send a message to another device.

POP (point of presence)

A POP refers to a long distance company's equipment that is connected to the local telephone company's central office. The POP is the point at which telephone and data calls are handed off between local telephone companies and long distance telephone companies.

POTS (plain old telephone service)

Telephone lines connected to most residential and small business users. POTS lines are analog from the end user to the nearest local telephone company equipment. People using POTS service for data communications with modems are limited in the speed at which they can transmit data.

PRI (primary rate interface)

PRI is a form of ISDN (integrated services digital network) with 23 paths for voice, video and data and one channel for signals. Each of the 24 channels transmits at 64 kilobits per second.

QSIG

A standard for networking PBXs from different vendors together over ISDN PRI trunks. The signaling channel of the ISDN circuit carries signals such as those allowing users connected to different PBXs to dial each other using only their three or four digit extension number. Signals can also be used to turn voice mail message lights on and off so different sites can share the same voice mail system.

RBOC (Regional Bell Operating Company)

At divestiture, in 1984, the Justice Department organized the previous 22 Bell telephone companies into seven Regional Bell Operating Companies. Examples of RBOCs are Qwest and BellSouth. Since divestiture, Pacific Telesis and Ameritech merged with SBC, and NYNEX merged with Bell Atlantic. SBC has announced a merger with Ameritech. There are now four RBOCs. Before divestiture, all of the Bell telephone companies were owned by AT&T.

Router

A device with routing intelligence that connects local and remote networks together. Routers are also used in the Internet.

SDH (Synchronous Digital Hierarchy)

A world standard of synchronous optical speeds. The basic SDH speed starts at 155 megabits, also called STM-1 (synchronous transport mode-1) in Europe. SONET (synchronous optical network) is a subset of SDH.

Server

A server is a specialized shared computer on the local area network with corporate files such as electronic mail. It can also be used to handle sharing of printers, fax machines and groups of modems.

SLA (service level agreements)

SLAs are often provided to customers by frame relay, virtual private network and ATM carriers. The SLA defines service parameters such as up-time and response time.

SMS (Short Message Service)

Short, 160 character (including header address information) text messages that can be transmitted between digital cellular telephones.

SMTP (simple mail transfer protocol)

The electronic mail protocol portion of the TCP/IP protocol used on the Internet. Having an electronic mail standard that users adhere to enables people on diverse local area networks to send each other e-mail.

SONET (synchronous optical network)

A standard for multiplexing high-speed digital bits onto fiber optic cabling. SONET converts electronic impulses to light impulses and vice versa. Telephone companies use SONET to transmit data from multiple customers over the same fiber cables.

Streaming video and audio

A means of starting to play a message while the rest of it is being copied. Streaming uses compression to make the voice, video and data smaller so that it can be transmitted in less time. Streaming video and audio are used in broadcasting video and audio over the Internet.

Switched 56

A digital "dial-up" data communications service. It was used more commonly when ISDN was less widely available. If ISDN is not available, switched 56 services can be used for video conferencing.

T.120

The ITU defined standard for document sharing and white boarding. People using T.120 adherent software can participate in document sharing conferences with each other over the Internet. For example, vendors can demonstrate their products to potential customers via computers connected to the Internet at dispersed sites.

T-1

A North American and Japanese standard for communicating at 1.54 million bits per second. A T-1 line has the capacity for 24 voice or data channels.

T-3

A North American standard for communicating at speeds of 44 million bits per second. T-3 lines have 672 channels for voice and/or data. Fiber optic cabling or digital microwave is required for T-3 transmissions.

TA (terminal adapter)

Used with BRI_ISDN service. The terminal adapter allows multiple voice and/or data devices to share a digital ISDN line. The terminal adapter sits between the data communicating device or the telephone and the ISDN line.

TCP (transmission control protocol)

Includes sequence numbers for each packet so that the packets can be reassembled at their destination. The sequence numbers ensure that all of the packets arrive and are assembled in the proper order. If some packets are discarded because of congestion, the network retransmits them. The numbering and tracking of packets make TCP a connection oriented protocol. Router based LAN internetworking uses TCP.

TCP/IP (transmission control protocol/Internet protocol)

The suite of protocols used in the Internet and also by organizations for communications between multiple networks.

TDMA (time division multiple access)

TDMA is one way that carriers transmit digital cellular signals between handheld devices and cellular carriers' networks. It assigns a time slot to every voice or data transmission.

Tier 1 Provider

A loosely defined term for Internet service providers that own Internet backbone fiber optic facilities in addition to ISP services such as hosting and e-mail. Examples include Cable & Wireless, Sprint, WorldCom, UUNET (which is part of MCI WorldCom) and AT&T.

Tunneling

Tunneling is a method of securely transferring data between sites connected by networks such as a virtual private network, the Internet, an intranet or an extranet. Tunneling puts a new header in front of the data so unauthorized users can't read it.

UDP (user data protocol)

Part of the TCP/IP suite of protocols. UDP protocols have less overhead because they do not have bits with packet numbers and acknowledgments. UDP is considered a connectionless protocol because packets arrive at their destination independently from various routes without sequence numbers. There is no assurance that all of the packets for a particular message arrive. The header is smaller with UDP than TCP because UDP headers do not have sequencing and acknowledgment bits. UDP is suited for applications such as database lookups and short messages.

UNE (Unbundled Network Element)

Unbundled Network Elements are parts of the incumbent local telephone company infrastructure that they are required to lease out to other local exchange carriers. Examples of unbundled network elements are the copper lines to customers' premises and ports on central office switches.

URL (Universal Resource Locator)

An address on the World Wide Web. The address is made up of strings of data that identify the server, folder location and other information indicating the location of information on the Internet.

UTP (unshielded twisted pair)

Most inside telephones and computers are connected together via unshielded twisted pair copper cabling. The twists in the copper cables cut down on the electrical interference of signals carried on pairs of wire near each other and near electrical equipment.

VPIM (Voice Profile for Internet Mail)

VPIM is an IP-based digital networking standard for sending voice mail and fax messages as attachments to e-mail messages.

VPNs (virtual private networks)

VPNs provide the functions and features of a private network without the need for dedicated private lines between corporate sites. Each site connects to the network provider's network rather than directly to another corporate location.

WAN (wide area network)

Wide area networks connect computers that are located in different cities, states and countries.

WAP (wireless application protocol)

A protocol that defines how Internet sites can be written to fit on cellular devices' screens and how devices access and view these sites.

WDM (Wavelength division multiplexing)

Also known as dense wavelength division multiplexing; enables multiple colors or frequencies of light to be carried on a single strand of fiber. WDM greatly increases the capacity of network providers' fiber optic networks.

WWW (World Wide Web)

The World Wide Web has multimedia capabilities. It links users from one network to another when they "click" on highlighted text. It was developed in 1989 to make information on the Internet more accessible. A browser is required to navigate and access the World Wide Web.

X.25

An ITU-defined packet switching protocol for communications between end-users and public data networks. X.25 is slower and older than frame relay service.

XML (extensible markup language)

A software language for e-commerce and Web searching. XML is like a data dictionary in that uniform "tags" are attached to elements so those diverse programs can read them. For example, tags can be used to identify elements such as prices, model numbers, product identities or quantities ordered.

Bibliography

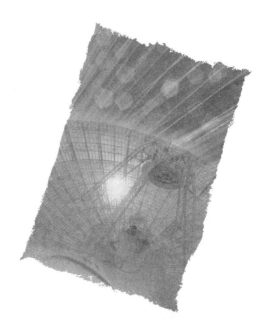

Dornan, Andy, *The Essential Guide to Wireless Applications*, New Jersey: Prentice Hall PTR, 2001.

Marckini, Fredrick, *Search Engine Positioning*, Texas: Wordware Publishing, Inc., 2001.

Muller, Nathan J., *Desktop Encyclopedia of Telecommunications*, New York: McGraw-Hill, 1998.

Muller, Nathan J., *Mobile Telecommunications Factbook*, New York: McGraw-Hill, 1998.

Newton, Harry, with Ray Horak, *Newton's Telecom Dictionary*, 17th edition, New York: CMP Books, 2001.

O'Driscoll, Gerard, *The Essential Guide to Digital Set-Top Boxes and Interactive TV*, New Jersey: Prentice Hall PTR, 2000.

Stallings, William, with a contribution by Richard Van Slyke, *Business Data Communications*, 4th edition, New Jersey: Prentice Hall, 2001.

Weisman, Carl J., *The Essential Guide to RF and Wireless*, New Jersey: Prentice Hall PTR, 2000.

Index

About the Author

Annabel Z. Dodd, adjunct professor at Northeastern University's state-of-the-art program, teaches courses in Telecommunications and Data Communications for the Non-Technical. She was an adjunct professor in the Master of Science in Technology Management program at the State University of New York at Stony Brook in 2000, where she taught in a joint program with The Institute of Industrial Policy Studies, Seoul, South Korea. Formerly in marketing at New England Telephone and Telecommunications and Manager at Dennison Manufacturing Company, now Avery Dennison, she consults with major corporations and institutions and gives seminars to organizations worldwide. The Massachusetts Telecommunications Council honored her as the Professor of the year 2000. Annabel Dodd can be visited on the Web at www.doddontheline.com.

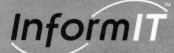